D1430385

To Sell Is Not To Sell

Stop Selling and Start Making Money!

Greta Schulz

iUniverse, Inc.
New York   Bloomington

To Sell is Not to Sell

Stop Selling and Start Making Money!

iUniverse books may be ordered through booksellers or by contacting:

iUniverse
1663 Liberty Drive
Bloomington, IN 47403
www.iuniverse.com
1-800-Authors (1-800-288-4677)

Because of the dynamic nature of the Internet, any Web addresses or links contained in this book may have changed since publication and may no longer be valid. The views expressed in this work are solely those of the author and do not necessarily reflect the views of the publisher, and the publisher hereby disclaims any responsibility for them.

ISBN: 978-1-4401-0748-1 (pbk)
ISBN: 978-1-4401-0750-4 (cloth)
ISBN: 978-1-4401-0749-8 (ebk)

Printed in the United States of America

iUniverse rev. date: 11/20/2008

Edited By:

Mary Jessica Schulz

Dedication

I dedicate this book to the wonderful people who helped me with all of the other "stuff" so I could work for many hours...

My amazingly wonderful husband Peter, our kids Jessie, Clayton and J.P. and my sister and brother who inspire me everyday!

Forward

Professional selling is a vital vocation for high achievers seeking rewards associated with dedicated and focused effort. Salespeople are critical to moving our world forward. With millions of inventors, artists, writers, professional services, companies, and manufacturers, someone has to get the product distributed to the end user. And this is the job of our salespeople.

This book offers powerful insight into why the traditional sales paradigms are changing and why selling in today's market is now more about partnerships between buyers and sellers. Growing relationships with buyers has become imperative to the selling scenario regardless of the sales arena. The straightforward, highly effective strategies outlined in *To Sell is Not to Sell* show salespeople everywhere how to establish a quality relationship with consumers in order to facilitate the first sale and encourage repeat business.

One of the many valuable points emphasized throughout this book is that in sales, you must *really* listen to the client's needs, interests, and wants. The average person loves to buy but hates to be sold to, and people really dislike the typical salesperson. Selling is an interactive human endeavor and, as you will learn in these pages, one of the secrets to selling is treating each person in the way she or he wishes to be treated. By finding out what you can do to help a buyer succeed, you are adding mutual value to a buyer-seller relationship and you are moving from good selling to great selling.

These chapters will enable you to offer real value to your buyers, therefore creating a solid foundation on which to build a prosperous sales career. You will discover how to focus on truly helping the buyer, how to treat him or her as an equal partner in the sales transaction, and how to ask good questions in order to foster and maintain two-way quality communication (not just relentlessly talk up your product or service and push the sale until the buyer is exhausted into defeat). In short, you will learn how to grow a fiercely-loyal customer base and ensure that your buyers keep coming back.

A true leader and innovator in the sales field, Greta has built a long and very successful career out of using these communication tactics and strategies. The years of experience she brings to the table coupled with her invariably effective sales advice make *To Sell is Not to Sell* the handbook that will empower an entire generation of salespeople to become leaders in their profession. And guess what? ... *People like to buy from leaders!*

Ivan R. Misner, Ph.D.
Ivan Misner is founder and CEO of Business Network International, the largest business networking organization in the world, and author of seven books, including three best sellers: *World's Best Known Marketing Secret, Masters of Networking* and *Masters of Success.*

Table of Contents

Management vs. Leadership, It is not the same.

Management vs. Leadership—Not the Same	4
A CEO Dilemma	6
War Games	9
Are You Salespeople Hunting The Right Prospects?	12
It Takes Reinforcement	15
Hiring Sales Superstars	17
The Ideal Candidate	20
Training a "Killer" Sales Staff	22
Hire People to Do Their Jobs—Sales Will Follow	25

Tightening Your Belt. Doing the right thing in and out of a soft economy.

Recession-Proof Your Business	30
Economic Uncertainty	35
Top Ten Sales Tips to Help in a Bad Economy	37
Money or Excuses, You Can Not Have Both	40
Do Not Use an Economic Downturn as an Excuse	43
Our Patriotic Duty	45
Going Green, Will Make You Green	47

The Experience Economy. Real over-the-top customer service.

For the Love of Pants	53
Follow the Banker, Not the Bank	57
Always Give First	60
Let Customers Know What Is Important	62
Just Say "No"	64

Pitch Is For Baseball. Old sale belief that kill sales today.

Pitch Is for Baseball	68
What to Put on a Business Card	70
I Will Give It a Try	72
My Famous Car Story	74

VITO and Seymour   77
Top Ten Most Common Sales Mistakes   79

Dating and Sales. The 80/20 Rule.

Dating and Sales…More Similar than You Think   84
Ask, Don't Tell   87
Listen, Listen, and Listen   89
Do Not Show Up and Throw Up   92
Stop "Filling in the Blanks"   94
Telling Is Not Selling   97

Sell Naked. Only you will make the sale.

Sell Naked   102
Take Notes, Not Brochures   104
Pre-Qualify Every Meeting   106
Practice Makes…Well, Less Frustration   108
Product or Service?   110

Through Our Own Rose-Colored Glasses.

Our Own Rose-Colored Glasses   115
When Perception Becomes Reality   118
Do Not Let Beliefs Block Your Thinking   121
Awareness   124
Passion   127
Get Out of Your Comfort Zone   130
Buying and Selling Is an Even Trade   133

Pay It Forward. Prospecting the right way.

Prospecting Confidence   138
It Is Not Net-Sit, It Is Not Net Eat…   141
Six Degrees of Separation   144
What Have You Done for Me Lately?   148
The "New" Elevator Speech   150
Cold Call Dilemma   153
Cold Call Legislation   155

Setting and Reaching Goals. Creating maps for your business growth navigation.

Everyone Needs a Plan 159
Little Steps to Long-Term Goals 161
Stop the Excuse Insanity 163
Get Your Head in the Game 166
Your Most Successful Year 168

Opposites Attract. Creating the unexpected.

"I Have Heard That Line Before" 175
Silence Is Golden 178
When the Prospect Fights You on Price 180
Take It Away! 182
The Holiday Brush-Off 185
Sit in the Power Seat 187
So What's Next... 190

Introduction

I have been in sales basically all of my life. Even as an eighth grader, we had to sell magazines to pay for a trip to Washington D.C. and I won the contest for selling the most subscriptions.

In college, I majored in Business Management but took so many classes in psychology and sociology that my guidance counselor said with one or two more classes I would have a minor. That was not my reasoning for taking those classes, I just found it so interesting to discover what made people really tick. Little did I know, years later, those classes would be more beneficial then any business class I took.

I remember when I was graduating from college, one of my best friends, Renae asked me what I was interviewing for, (Renae was interviewing for a position in international finance with one of the country's largest corporations) and I told her a job in sales. "Sales? Really? Greta you are smarter then that!" I still remember all of these years later how I felt about that comment. I never saw it that way...I wondered if others did?

Well I did get a job in sales and with one of the largest sales organizations in the world, and one of the most respected. I felt better about that but truly people were only impressed with the company, the word "sales" was still somewhat looked down upon. Now let's remember I was about twenty one years old and was still worried about what others thought.

Though, through the years, I really began to love every aspect of the job and hey, I was making a heck of a lot more money than most of my friends who had "professional careers". I began to quickly get over the stigma. I have always wondered why people have that pre-conceived notion about sales and I have come to the conclusion that in many cases, they were right. Not about the career choice, it does not get any better than this: your own hours, no earnings cap, and control of your own destiny. But they were right, because so many of the morons going into sales were just that!

Why did this industry, that became my professional career, attract so many people that were at the very least disrespected and often just complete idiots! Well I was determined to find out. I kept a very close watch on what people were doing to sell and looked at success and failure. Generally, the pushier you were, the faster a quick sale was gotten. I said a "quick" sale because I had observed the "one time sale and walk away" was the one that was most often sold, and years ago, that was good enough. Basically the industry hired pushy, fast talkers to shove a product on someone before they even knew what happened to them. Nice. I do believe back then, they were taught to get an appointment, give "features and benefits," and try to sell at every opportunity.

Today this is frowned upon because to have a career in this business, you need to be seen as a professional, help the client, and have a good reputation in order to go back and sell additional products and services as well as ask for referrals.

To sell today, you need to be smart, thoughtful, a good listener, and able to treat sales like a career which means, hard work, no quick success, and the development of a process which includes being different than any of the "old-school" stuff out there.

The stories I have included will give you some ideas of how this should work. This is not a how-to book but I do have a program to follow-up this book that will help you in some more detail, if you dare...

Management
vs. Leadership

Introduction by Courtney Lynch,
LeadStar Leadership by Angie and Courtney and Author of
Leading From The Front.

There are many misconceptions about leadership in our society. Many believe that leadership has something to do with power, prestige, and notoriety. Others equate leadership with position – they value a fancy job title or management role at the top of an organizational chart. Some even believe their job title alone makes them a leader. These notions of leadership could not be further from the truth.

The best leaders focus on the responsibility to serve others, not on the privilege of a position. They view leadership as an opportunity to influence outcomes and inspire others – two qualities also critical for a sales professionals' success. As a sales leader, your clients respect your insight and value your contributions when you channel your efforts into being an effective leader.

Leaders are not just born with an extra dose of charisma or a special "leadership gene." Leadership skills are behavioral skills, which allow everyone the opportunity to become a stronger leader. In fact, the foundation of your leadership is something you can control everyday: leadership begins with your daily performance. How good are you? What can you do better? How can you raise the bar on your past success? Your performance is demonstrated on your consistent ability of meeting standards and then taking the opportunity to exceed standards.

True leaders also know they are responsible for making progress and they have the courage to challenge routine and take risks when necessary. Leaders are proactive with their decisions in order to create opportunities. The most effective sales leaders are those who make the decision to take initiative.

In addition to personal performance and being decisive, leaders are also accountability seekers. When problems arise or challenges are present, leaders do not waste time placing blame, instead, they identify their role in the situation and work towards owning the problem and resolving it efficiently. This ability to be accountable allows a leader to be trustworthy, confidence inspiring, and approachable.

Leaders are also those who solve problems – they bring calm to chaos. In challenging and stressful times, leaders are the ones who can be predictable and consistent with their emotions. Leaders don't lose their cool, they don't scream, they resist gossip and they maintain a presence that invites the truth, even when the news you need to convey to them is bad.

As a sales professional, your organization expects you to focus on the numbers. As a leader, choose to exceed that expectation by leading those who make the numbers possible: your sales team and your clients, customers, and prospects. Leaders constantly challenge themselves by asking: Who needs my leadership – what can I do to make a positive difference in the lives of these individuals? Sales teams fail when they are managed by individuals who have limited leadership ability. Sales teams excel when every member of the team is committed to improving their leadership skills.

Ultimately, leadership is not about being complex, it is about being effective. Your ability to influence outcomes and inspire others grows when you demonstrate leadership behaviors daily in simple, but profound ways. When you take the time to be a leader, you are able to enjoy the results your leadership brings.

Management vs. Leadership—Not the Same

Leadership and management are often misunderstood as one and the same...but they are not. Certainly, a good leader should be able to manage and vice versa. But it is important to understand the difference because both are important to the success of an organization.

The key difference between the two is that management is about processes and leadership is about people. You manage your accounts payable, but you lead your accounts payable administrator. Understanding this is the key to motivating, coaching, and growing your people to the very best of their ability.

This misunderstanding occurs in an organization for several reasons. Most often, it is because we promote the wrong people and promote for the wrong reasons. Possible reasons for promotion include, length of service (the next manager is the one who has worked there the longest) and demonstrated ability for the task at hand. Neither foretells an ability to lead and lead well.

Unfortunately, we learn management skills, as opposed to leadership skills, very early. Our parents tell us what to do, as opposed to teaching us to think of answers to our own questions. This is one of several reasons why management, as opposed to leadership, becomes the common way to run an organization.

Management is about effecting positive change in the organization by recognizing process problems, correcting those process problems, and teaching others how to implement the new processes. Management is a necessary skill. But it is not leadership.

The four most important aspects of leadership are:

- **Recruiting.** The ability to attract and retain the best is imperative to the success of an organization.

- **Coaching.** Coaching is always teaching, rarely telling. Teaching is helping subordinates self-realize the answer on their own, rather than you blurting out the answer for them.

- **Accountability.** Creating a clear and detailed written plan that involves thirty- sixty and ninety-day written goals—not only revenue goals but behavior goals as well.

- **Motivating.** Understanding what motivates individuals is what elevates them to the next level. Motivation is different for each individual, and a true leader knows how to unlock the potential of each person he is responsible for by using the form of motivation that best works with that person.

Are you leading your people or simply managing them?

A CEO Dilemma

"Are my salespeople the best they can be? Are they doing all they can do?" These are questions I often hear from CEOs and other executives in the business world. When I ask them how they are doing, they refer to their revenue. "Beautiful"…but how do you know you have long-term, A-team players? Are they executing the correct behaviors to grow your business in the long run, or are they just collecting "low-hanging fruit" for today?

Complete this simple exercise, and calculate how much profit improvement potential exists within your sales force. Ask yourself these four sets of questions:

1. a) On average, how many new-prospect contacts does my average salesperson make per month?

   b) How many would the ideal "A-team player" salesperson make?

2. a) On average, what is the closing ratio (percentage) of my average seller?

   b) What would it be for an "A-team player"?

3. a) On average, what's the dollar value of an average sale for my average seller?

  b) What would it be for an "A-team player?"

4. a) What is the total number of people in my sales force?

  b) How many "A-team players" do I have now in my sales force?

Now complete the following simple math to examine your existing sales force:

1. Subtract the answer to 4b from the answer to 4a. This represents your "talent-gap."

2. Multiply the answer to 1a by the answer to 2a by the answer to 3a. This represents the "old you."

3. Multiply the answer to 1b by the answer to 2b by the answer to 3b by the answer to 4b, and multiply that number by 12 (months). This is how much incremental revenue you could book in the year ahead, simply by raising your expectations. Staggering, is it not?

By now, you should be asking yourself how you get these results. The answer? Raise your performance expectations, which demands improvement from your sales team in three areas, and from you, in one.

Here is what to look for from your team:

1. Your sellers must become more effective at prospecting. That means creating a prospecting plan...and holding themselves to it. That means "calling high" in your prospects' organizations. That means creating and delivering a compelling message about the problems you can solve for your prospects. That means pre-qualifying before agreeing to an appointment instead of just sending literature or going on an appointment because they are "willing to see you."

Your sales force must also understand the process and skill of true networking. I do not mean going through the motions of showing up at an event, with drink in hand, while speaking only to friends and colleagues who they already know. Networking means having a plan and a goal before walking in, and not leaving without its completion.

2. Your sellers must improve their closing ratios. That means learning how to listen to a prospect's real problems. That means getting your prospects to discover your company is worth a premium. That means getting prospects to make and keep commitments. That means delivering powerful, moving presentations that hit your prospects' real needs, every time. That also means your sellers stop wasting time with people who are not going to do business with them.

3. Your sellers must raise the amount of money they ask for. That means calling on larger prospects. That means giving your price, at your terms, and having your customers agree to that level of value.

And the commitment that you, as CEO, must make? Simply, it is this: You must do whatever it takes to eliminate the status quo in your sales force. If you don't have the best, develop those who are not, or replace them with those who are.

War Games

In his book *Victory Secrets of Attila the Hun,* Wess Roberts credits the battle-savvy leader with having said, "Chieftains should never intentionally place [soldiers] in a situation where the price of losing outweighs the rewards of winning." How often can you honestly say that you, as a sales manager, apply this rule to your salespeople? And what systems do your salespeople have to ensure victory, even before they go into battle?

You have two challenges when your sales force prepares for battle:

Challenge 1 – As with any kind of warfare, you have a distinct advantage when you can tap good and reliable intelligence. Here is the problem: Your salespeople don't get enough accurate intelligence about their prospects. As a result, their pipelines are filled with flaky opportunities. And you, as a sales manager, may lack enough guts to call them on it.

Here is the litmus test: When your salespeople submit their forecasts, do you "adjust" them down for realism? It is typically easier for salespeople and their managers to discuss why they did not win business instead of asking themselves the right questions *before* going to battle.

Here are the right questions:

1 – "Can we win, and should we pursue this opportunity?" If yes, then

2 – "Which strategy should we adopt to ensure that we win?"

To begin, ask your salespeople: "How much does it cost to win a new account?" Calculate the actual costs associated with generating a lead, a contact, an appointment, a proposal, and a sale. Now add in the opportunity cost of missed business they could have won if they were not wasting time on business that will not close quickly.

If yours is like most selling organizations, the cost can be several thousand dollars. Multiply that by the number of opportunities you chased and didn't close in the last twelve months. Staggering, is it not?

Before your salespeople charge off to fight the next battle, ask them, "If this were your money, would you spend it on perusing this account?"

Challenge 2 – Your salespeople do not do enough planning work before going to battle.

Before they go into battle again, make sure your salespeople can answer these questions (honestly):

- **What are you trying to sell?** Sounds simple enough until you actually try to quantify it.

- **Is the project funded?** What if there is not enough? Who has discretionary use of the funds? Who can get more?

- **What is the sale worth?** Does the ROI justify the investment of time, money, and effort?

- **Have we sold this prospect anything in the past?** Who? What? Where? When? How? Why?

- **How many contacts have you already had with this prospect?** How many phone calls, face-to-face meetings, and so on? Do you have a clear next step?

- **Do you have an organizational chart?** Do you have an inside coach?

- **What has been (or will be) your sales strategy?**

- **Where are you in the selling process?** Here is a checklist:

  1. Did you pre-qualify before the appointment?
  2. What were the prospect's reasons for seeing you?
  3. What were the challenges, problems, and frustrations that you identified in the interview?
  4. How important is it to the prospect to fix those problems?
  5. How committed is the prospect to fixing those problems? (Time, effort, money,)
  6. What happens next if you make a recommendation they like and agree with?
  7. Did you send a follow-up email outlining all of the above before your proposal?

Make sure your sales force is "armed" with all the necessary intelligence, and make sure the cost of this campaign is justified by a reasonable assessment of their chances. Then…and only then…send them off to do battle.

Are You Salespeople
Hunting The Right Prospects?

A smart sales consultant I respect shared this analogy with me years ago, and I never forgot it.

Elephants, deer, and rabbits—is your sales force, hunting the right game at the right time…or are they questing after the wrong animals?

Twenty million years ago, our caveman ancestors lived or died based upon their ability to hunt the right kinds of opportunities. Today, can you say the same thing about your sales force?

Here is the test: List your six best customers. First identify the *measurable* criteria that are common to those six: (e.g.: size, profitability, distance, how well your product fits their needs). Now list the common criteria you *can not* measure (the things you value about them, and they value about you—e.g.: they place value on your contributions, they want to partner with you, they do not beat you down on price, they pay for performance).

Next, rank the top five criteria on each list, and score each of your customers on a 0-10 point scale. Two lists with five items each yield

12

a possible score of 100 points. Grade each customer, and study the results. Finally, apply the 80/80 test: If 80% of your customers don't score 80+, your sales force is hunting in the wrong place, hunting the wrong way, or both.

As a CEO of a growing company, your ability to sleep at night is directly related to the quality and quantity of new business that your sales team drags in. So, how do you decide what is good or not so good? How do you aim them in the right direction?

Step 1: Have your sales team identify your accounts by category. Rabbits are the plentiful opportunities you need a lot of to feed the family. Deer are less plentiful, require more work, but feed the family for several weeks. Elephants are the large ones you have to hunt with great care and effort, but they will feed the entire village for six months.

Step 2: Have each salesperson establish his or her personal goals list, and then get him/her to discover how many elephant, deer, or rabbit accounts they will need to close, in order to meet their goals.

Step 3: Build the plan. This step invokes discussion about where your people should spend their time hunting and for which type of account. If your sales team does this correctly, you will hear things such as, "When I see how much time I waste chasing rabbits, no wonder you tell me I can close better and more qualified business!" Blend a balance. At least 60% should be deer accounts. Be careful you *do not* build a business based on elephants. If elephants leave you, it can be a big blow to your business.

Step 4: Monitor your salespeople's plans. Make sure your sales team reports to you (weekly is best, monthly at least) as to how many cold calls or referrals they are getting, based on their personal activity plans.

Step 5: Reward/punish. Make sure your rewards program rewards the activities you want. Some progressive CEOs actually pay higher commissions for the right type of accounts. And if your sales people are not working their agreed-upon prospecting plans, set and enforce the consequences.

Step 6: Prune the tree. Over Time, Cut out the C accounts, those customers who do not fit your profile. Cut out the weak, dying limbs and focus your efforts on turning B accounts into As. Then super-serve the A accounts. Let them refer you to more A accounts.

When 100% of your customers are 90+ on the score list, you will find the safaris yield lots of game…and *big* game. Or, to change metaphors for a moment, you will find you have built a bicycle that pedals itself.

It Takes Reinforcement

I am writing this at the Kansas City airport, on my way back from meeting with one of my clients. Last month, we offered a training program in selling skills for her staff. She reported that they saw an immediate increase in sales after the program. She listened in on the sales staff's calls to see what had changed.

To her pleasure, they were asking good, open-ended questions. They were taking time to listen to the client's responses and using their comments to match them with the right products. They were even closing right at the correct time. She was excited.

Unfortunately, not all the reps kept it up. Within weeks, some of the reps' sales had slipped back to their original levels. Another listening survey showed the cause.

Each of the reps whose sales were down had slipped back into his or her old ways. It was as if they were on a high during training, and now it was business as usual. Surprised? I am not. For years, these reps had been trained to operate in "telling mode." They gave the same pitch to every caller. Now, we were asking them to change, and change takes time.

So what do you do? Forget training? No, but you may want to think about the reinforcement that it takes to make a training program stick.

Whether you are offering training for your team or simply taking a training program yourself, recognize that old habits are hard to break. There must be a reinforcement regimen to turn that training into practice and the practice into habit.

Just like growing a garden, you need to plant the seeds, water them, fertilize them, and water them again and again. Then you will start seeing the benefits. Eventually, the flowers will all begin to grow, but you need to work hard, have faith, and not give up. Then you will see the results.

Like anything in life, learning a new skill takes time and change. Change doesn't happen quickly and, if it does, it typically goes away just as fast. There is no liquid diet out there that really works forever. Do not expect that with your people, either. If we were training five-year-olds who did not have bad habits already, our trainees could make the new information stick a lot quicker. That is why our children can learn a new language or even two much faster then we can.

Unfortunately, five-year-olds do not have the rest of the pieces to the business pie. Too bad – because I would love to train for a few hours and then have everyone lie down for a little nap.

Hiring Sales Superstars

A smart hiring expert said the secret to hiring a sales superstar is to radically change your hiring process, which concludes with a powerful twenty-minute interview. Ready?

Step 1. Define the ideal candidate. Describe your selling environment as it identifies the perfect salesperson. For example: "Our ideal candidate has successfully cold-called CEOs, presidents, and owners of medium-size companies and can close sales for conceptual service prospects. Our ideal candidate is successful at finding budgets when there are none and can close $50,000 worth of long-term contracts in two calls or less. The candidate must have had prior earnings of at least $80,000 per year." Be very specific, not about what you sell—that is secondary—but about the environment you sell in.

Step 2. Search. Write compelling, advertising copy that describes the ideal candidate so, when it is read, he or she says, "That is me," and understands how your organization is different from any other. Look outside your industry, so you do not get stuck with industry re-treads with below-average selling skills. If someone is leaving an organization, there is usually a reason. Plus, someone from the outside, once hired, can objectively ask the question, "Why can we *not* do that?" while someone inside the industry might have a stagnating preconceived notion.

Step 3. Qualify: In a five minute telephone screen, read your pre-determined key criteria and ask the candidate to prove he or she can meet them.

Step 4. Test: Use a proven test to separate those who *will* sell from those who merely *can* sell.

Step 5. Conduct the interview. *Do not* describe your company and why it is a desirable place to work. Make your candidate *sell you* on why you should make this hire.

To separate the "real candidate" from the "interview face," you must run the interview dramatically different from most employment interviews. In twenty minutes, you must unveil how the candidate would act in a tough selling situation.

How? Act like the toughest prospect the person will ever encounter. Yes, you need to be tough—like the toughest experience you have ever had in front of a prospect.

Begin the interview without the normal pleasantries. You are not there to make the candidate comfortable; you are there to test abilities. Start with, "Are you my two o'clock? Go in the conference room. I will be there in ten minutes." Make your candidate wait. Do not smile. Do not be nice. After ten minutes, walk in and say, "We have got only twenty minutes for this interview to cover an hour of information. Ready?"

This is the first test. You want someone who will push back to get control. At the very least, you want someone who will try to break the ice and bond with you. If the candidate rolls over and acts like a compliant puppy dog (by answering, "Yes" or "Sure"), you know he or she will wimp out in front of tough prospects.

Ask "prove-it-to-me" kinds of questions. "We are looking for strong closers who can handle themselves well in front of presidents and CEOs. Prove to me that is you."

Keep the pressure on. Look for signs of discomfort or emotional involvement, such as rapid eye movement, giggling, staring at the ceiling or out the window, movement in the chair, and changes in voice pitch or volume.

Here is a strong move to determine if your candidate really *will* make cold calls: "If we get beyond this interview to the next step [remember to keep the pressure on!], you will be required to find $250,000 in new business. Once you have identified whom to call, how would you get appointments?"

The answer you are looking for is some form of cold calling *and* referrals. In a new position such as this, cold calling will be a necessity. If your candidate says it is the only way to start in a new position, you know the cold calling will actually happen. If your candidate starts talking about research, letter campaigns, and marketing, you know you do not have a hunter in front of you.

You expect your salespeople to qualify their prospects; *you* need to qualify your candidates, to weed out the wannabes and hire only the superstars.

The Ideal Candidate

It is a well-known fact, that building a successful organization can not happen without success in sales. So how do you build a successful sales department? Start by recruiting the right people. Here are some steps involved in recruiting the salesperson of your dreams:

- Identify the ideal candidate. If a job candidate says she is good, or if the candidate says he has experience, that does not matter. You need to identify the qualities that will make a candidate successful for your company, not for just any organization. Have the candidates sold high-priced products like yours? What level of a decision-maker do they need to be in front of to be successful?

- Search for the ideal candidate. A good way to start this step is by asking yourself, "If I found someone better than my best person, would I find a place for that individual in my organization?" If the answer is a resounding yes, then why are you looking only when you need someone? Searching for a candidate is something that should go on every single day. Whenever you meet with colleagues, friends, or clients, ask them, "What salespeople do you meet with that you believe add value every time they come? I want to meet that person."

- Pre-qualify the candidate. That should be done on the phone and should take no more then ten minutes. You should have questions ready to ask the candidate, and they should be asked quickly and succinctly so as to not allow the candidate too much time to think. You will have a gut feeling whether the candidate is pre-qualified to go to the next stage.
- Assess the candidate. Be sure to keep within the EEOC Guidelines for Hiring, which give a few pertinent specifications when it comes to your company's hiring process.

Use a pre-employment test to assure objectivity. The test must be reliable and consistent in its findings, while showing no adverse impact on protected minorities. The same test must be administered to all applicants.

Assess the candidate using some sort of benchmark. The assessment should be able to uncover weaknesses that are not normally picked up in the regular interview process.

Some examples of a candidate's weaknesses are an inability to discuss money, an overwhelming need to be liked, and the inability to say what really needs to be said.

- Interview the candidate in person. Concentrate on things such as eye contact, handshake, personality, and the ability to ask questions.

You should also have a battery of questions to ask, depending on the outcome of the assessment. Ask about the weaknesses that were exposed in the assessment to see how you feel about the candidate's problems with those issues.

When you have a crew of sales superstars, the sky is the limit. So go out there and build that sales department of your dreams. It is not as hard as you think.

Training a "Killer" Sales Staff

When the US military recruited young men for service in Vietnam, they faced a serious challenge: How do we train someone to kill? Their approach provides a fascinating clue to the sales training dilemma of many businesses: Why do we spend so much time and money on training that fails to deliver?

Imagine a radically new selling system (strategies and tactics) so powerful that, when implemented, it would allow each of your salespeople to double or triple their income. The secret would be training your sales force to use this new system.

Why do so many businesses fail to implement new sales strategies and tactics? There are two reasons:

1. Lack of executive commitment to change. Few executives are strong enough to break the paradigms of tradition. They become handcuffed to the ways of the past simply because they are afraid to try the un-proven.

Are you a pioneer or a settler? Settlers want the security of knowing "This way is safe." Pioneers are those who take the risks, charting the path into the unknown. Pioneers reap the spoils…they're always first to earn the big payoff because they take it all and leave nothing for the settlers.

2. **Poor implementation.** How many times have your sales managers tried to implement new sales techniques, only to have salespeople resist? How many times have you heard a salesperson counter her manager's suggestion with, "I tried that and it did not work because…(fill in the excuse)"?

So how do you implement new sales approaches in your group so you can insure success? Adopt the principles the military used to insure their new recruits would pull the trigger when faced with a battle situation. Here's how:

First, it is imperative that every soldier understand leadership's unfaltering commitment to the strategies and tactics.

Second, implement the right type of training. Here is where you can learn from military training.

The challenge in selling is the same as in military combat. How do you train people to be brave? How do you get people to perform when they are fearful, or if they do not agree in principle with what you want them to do? Answer: Conditioning.

Sales training and combat training have the same objective: Condition recruits to act without thinking. In sales, that means conditioning them so they act without thinking. Salespeople get into trouble on sales calls when they begin thinking about what to do next. They need to be working off of the prospects responses.

Strategizing on the fly is a symptom of being emotional during the sales process…a big problem. The salesperson who is emotionally involved starts talking to herself: "What do I say now? If I say that, he will say this, then what do I do?" As a result, the salesperson stops listening to the prospect, and she drifts off, failing to stay "in the moment." In a combat situation, this would get you killed. In a selling situation, you simply fail to close.

What is the answer? Conditioned responses, the ability to respond off of the prospect's questions. Implement the training using hours of practice every week. Then debrief every selling situation. Start with the outcome of the call and work backward. Why did your seller get the outcome she got? Where did she screw up the call?

Military recruits spend hundreds of hours and tens of thousands of rounds of ammunition conditioning themselves to pull the trigger when a silhouette appears in the field of fire, until it falls. You can apply this same concept in training your salespeople. Condition them to respond to the situations they hate the most, and drill them hours every week.

Then watch them go out there and "Make a killing."

Hire People to Do Their Jobs— Sales Will Follow

You can make excuses or you can make money, but you cannot do both. Which do *you* want to do?

Lack of accountability is the enemy in most sales organizations, and it is killing your business. If excuse-making is a symptom, you have got the disease. Warning signs to look out for include:

"The customer said he was happy."

"They do not have a budget."

"The owner will not see me."

"We do not have any good leads."

"We are too expensive."

"The economy is down."

"Our prices are too high."

"My commission program is unfair."

"They can not buy now."

Blah, blah, blah...*excuses.*

How do you cure your company of this cancer? You must create a culture that does not allow excuses by holding everyone accountable.

How? Stop accepting them. Yep! It starts with you. If you allow these kinds of excuses to be used and allow them to justify a job not getting done, then *you* are the cancer-causing agent.

In setting up goals for your sales organization, you must set up ones that are based not on dollar volume alone. Why? Because goals need to be controllable for the salesperson.

Revenue that comes in is not controllable; therefore, it cannot be a goal. Revenue is merely the *result* of accomplishing your goal. The actual goals are the activities that your salespeople set to achieve financial results. If the goal is to meet sixteen new contacts a week, for example, your salespeople cannot control how many of the contacts actually buy, but they can certainly control the number of appointments they set. If they do not meet this number, it is their problem…no one else's.

Often I get the question, "But what if none of them buys?" There are three things—and three things only—that will determine success:

1. The activities that you commit to (such as meetings and sales calls).

2. The sales approach that you use to uncover a need when in front of a prospect.

3. Your attitudes and beliefs about yourself, your business, and your product.

If these three things are being done, and being done every day, every week, and every month consistently, then you will be a success.

I am going to tell you a story about Michelle, age twenty-five, who works with me and truly "gets it" more than most professionals who have been in business for twenty-five years!

When Michelle first started working with me, she telephoned me one day. "Greta, this is not working," she said. "For the last six weeks, I have been meeting with all of these people [fourteen a week at that time], and I have not closed anything!"

I thought a minute and said, "Michelle, did you commit to meeting with fourteen people a week to see how you could help them?"

"Ye-es," she said with hesitation.

"Have you done that?" I asked, knowing full well that she had.

"Yes," she replied.

"Did you ask them good questions to identify if they had a need?"

"Yes," she replied again.

"Michelle, I did not hire you just to close business," I told her. "I hired you to meet your goals, and those goals were to meet with the number of people you could commit to...which was fourteen, right? You are doing exactly what I hired you to do. Do not forget, it is about the steps, not the sale. Follow the process, and the sales will come."

And sure enough, by the next month she was fifty percent ahead of the revenue plan, and the month after that, almost seventy-five percent ahead. Those were the results of the goals that we had set. They were the payoff.

These activities are controllable, and therefore no excuses can be made for not meeting with people to try to help them by learning about their business. Make sure your salespeople have controllables as goals. Then excuses are not even an issue.

Tightening Your Belt

Introduction by John Rojas, Wachovia Investments

Why do people stop doing the things that made them successful? Hello my name is John Rojas. I am a financial advisor for Wachovia Securities in West Palm Beach, FL. As I read this chapter on *Tightening Your Belt*, I found myself reflecting on how all the points mentioned in this chapter have helped me grow my business by twenty percent or more since 2003. This chapter shares great strategies you can use in your business daily. The caveat is you must implement some of them to get results.

It takes a committed focused effort to concentrate on the activities that work and ignore the negativity you face daily. As I write this, the Olympics are taking place. Michael Phelps has now become a household name. He is the best the world has ever seen. How long and how hard of a price has he paid for that glory? How long and how hard of a price will you pay for your glory? To me that is what this book is all about. I have a purpose greater than myself. By applying the steps in this chapter daily, I bring myself closer to that purpose. I know from personal experience that reading ideas in a book and wanting to implement them when they seem new to you is sometimes difficult to imagine, you can get lost in the steps it would take to implement this new skill. There are three strategies in this chapter that are habits within me. I apply them daily and never lose focus of them. Since they have served me well I would like to share at least one of them with you.

I stick to the basics of my business. There are a couple of tasks that I need to do consistently to ensure that I am constantly growing my practice. I must talk to people, I must ask for business, I must ask for referrals, I must close the business, and I must follow up and follow through. These are the basics of my business. Everyday I have a piece of paper on my desk with my top three goals on it. My goals are as follows:

1. Ask for 2 referrals daily

2. Ask for 3 orders daily

3. Set 3 appointments daily (one from network, one from client base, one from prospect base)

That is it. I know if I continue to focus on these three items daily, it will not matter what the economy is doing, or even what the stock market is doing.

I had a friend call me the other day and he asked me "How is business? This environment is really tough. My revenue is down thirty percent for the year. How are you doing?" I replied, "How many people have you talked to this week? How many introductions have you asked for this week? How many contacts have you made this month? What is your next seminar topic going to be on?" My friend sighed and replied "Not much is going on. I have not prospected in over a month. I do not have a seminar scheduled. I can not remember when I last asked for an introduction." So here is a person who I once had high regard for and he has forgotten the basics of how he achieved the level of success he was accustomed to.

This chapter does a great job on helping the reader understand the need to get back to the basics. It points out the need for us to do our best so we can support our economy. I hope as you read the chapter you do your part to make this world a more profitable and greener world to live in.

Recession-Proof Your Business

Boom or bust? Regardless of what phase of the cycle our economy is in as you read these words, the one sure thing is that good times will be around again…and so will bad times. The economy is cyclical. That is a fact. The question is: Are you prepared for the bad times as well as the good?

Long-term successful businesses sit and strategize in both good and not-so-good times. It is funny, but whenever there is a threat to our economy, that is when businesses tighten their belts. They cut back on lavish expenses, keep only the best and most profitable employees, and concentrate on only the most profitable products or services they offer. Gosh, is there any reason we are not doing this *all* the time? Companies that have the most successful profit growth are the ones that act as if they *always* have to tighten their corporate belts.

By focusing on the good of the customer/client base, we naturally focus on the good of our individual businesses.

In order to become a recession-proof business, careful, strategic planning, human asset investment, and more effective systems and procedures must be put into play in order to *thrive*, not just survive.

Below is a guideline of eight areas to focus on and invest your business in, so that you may come out on the other end of any downturn riding the wave of success.

1. Marketing:

Is the money you are spending resulting in dollars in your company's pocket? Take a serious look at your current marketing campaign and make sure you are focused on consistent advertising. Then find the right publications out there, for example, your local Business Journal is a smart move for a B2B seller.

2. Marketing, word of mouth:

Develop a strong word-of-mouth marketing campaign so you may increase business through referrals. This will help dramatically increase sales without costing you any "hard dollars." The "soft dollar" cost will be your time networking. If you are not a member of the chamber of commerce, join it. If you are a member, get more active in committees and events. It is these local business professionals who will support and help you. If you are not a member of a BNI chapter in your area, join one. These chapters are made up of business professionals in your area who have the same mindset of growing their business through referrals by helping others do the same.

3. Sales:

What you did to close sales during boom times may not work in a down cycle. Invest in a sales development course for you and your people. This short-term investment will bring both short- and long-term results for your business. Increasing your sales performance, especially during trying times, is like an athlete trying to increase his or her physical performance. He does not keep trying the same thing over and over. He focuses on increasing his knowledge, skills and attitude, so he may break their current barriers and perform at that next level. You and your salespeople must do the same. Your sales department must be the top-performing department in your company.

Your sales department is the place to "trim the fat." Keep only top performers and allow *no excuses*! ("The economy is tough." "We need to lower prices.") These excuses are unacceptable. Your salespeople need to have a "whatever it takes" attitude. You know the saying,"When the going gets tough…" During downswings in the business marketplace, nothing is more important than sales for your business. Without these, no money is made and companies do not survive.

4. Service:

Customer service is of the utmost importance during slow cycles in business. Studies have shown that it takes seven times as much effort and money to gain one new client as to receive repeat business from current clients/customers. You must bring your customer service to the next level. Sit down with your people and discuss how to make your clients happier. If you work alone or with only a couple of people, besides speaking with them, put together a short survey to find out from your current clients how you could improve your service or what other services or products they would like to see you offer. In turn, they become your research and development department as well as your marketing advisors.

5. Management:

Do you or your people have the skills necessary to bring the business where it needs to go? The key to any business is its people. You must be able to focus them, motivate them, and keep them on track. This is a delicate balance of helping set performance criteria, having good communication skills, and giving consistent encouragement. To get your organization to perform at the next level, especially during difficult times, is not easy. Like the athletes we discussed earlier, as a manager you must now focus on increasing your knowledge, skills, and attitudes to get your people to perform at the next level. Do not hesitate to invest in a consultant or a quality management development course.

6. Solidify the Team

If you are a business owner or a leader of people, it is essential that you create a strong team atmosphere, even more in bad times than in good ones. As people start to hear the media talk about a recession, they get nervous and fearful about their jobs. If they see the business slow, mild paranoia will set in, and they may start to look for something new as opposed to helping keep the business where it needs to be.

Get together with your people regularly. Have an initial meeting that discusses your vision and plan for the next one to three years. This gives them a vision of a future and the confidence that you have a definite plan of how to grow the business. Everyone wants to be connected to a winner, and it is your job, as the leader, to make sure they know that your company is well positioned and can handle what the future has to bring.

Without your team, you will not be able to succeed, and without your instilling confidence in them, they will not be willing to put in the work it takes to bring the company to where it needs to be. Share the vision, recognize them at meetings in front of others, and show them that you care about them as individuals and as valuable assets to the company. Remember, "people do not care how much you know, until they know how much you care."

7. Strategic Planning:

Do you have a strategic plan in place for your business for the next one to three years? This is so essential, I cannot emphasize it enough. The process of developing the plan is even more important than the final plan that you produce. The formality of developing this plan with other professionals forces you to think about all the aspects of your business—in detail. It makes you go through all the "what-if" scenarios so you are aware of all the worst-case scenarios and already have a plan of action for if and when they occur. When a business is doing well, the plan is important, but companies that have not developed it will still survive...not as profitably, but they will survive. However, during a recessionary time, those businesses that do not have it, may not make it through to the upswing of the economy. Find a strategic planning program or a professional who can help you strategically plan your success.

The keys to helping your business not just survive but also thrive during an economic downswing are planning and skill development. When you sit down and plan your businesses success over the next three years, you need to focus on the four main aspects of your business: marketing, sales, service, and management. Planning takes the guesswork out of business and allows you to make logical, strategic decisions when unexpected circumstances arise. The best way to handle crisis situations is to have thought them out ahead of time.

Developing the business growth skills of your people and yourself allows your business to operate with a new level of expertise. There is nothing more valuable to a business than its "human capital." Develop your team of people, and create a company with an infrastructure that can survive even the toughest of times. As Americans, we have the persistence, discipline, and creative mindset to accomplish anything.

Whether we are in an economic downturn as you read this, or riding high in good times again, it is time *now* to invest in your company's future, not just sit and watch your profits dwindle away. Please plan and invest in your people so we may all benefit from your products and services.

Economic Uncertainty

When I first wrote this particular story, we were in the middle of an economic downturn. And now, as I assemble it into a book, we are in the middle of another. Business and the economy are cyclical. Even if, as you are reading this, we are in good times again, wait! Bad times will be back sooner or later…plan on it.

But you know what else? The information below is good advice in *any* economic times, good or bad.

In light of the current national financial situation, I am hearing much concern about the business economy. This is not time for tightening the belt—it is time to acknowledge that the easy times have passed. Everything is about to change, and adjustments must be made to your sales force and the way you approach sales, before your competitors do the same.

Most of your salespeople were probably hired during the economic "comfortable high," and as such have not really been put to the test. Few would argue that during the good times, most salespeople who received an audience with a prospect would generate business because it was there for the taking. But what about now? With the buying frenzy ending and concerns about a recession looming, what can we expect from this presenter, order-taker breed of salespeople? As economic conditions worsen…well, not much.

If ever there was an Achilles heel in a company, it is the sales force, and if ever there is a time when that Achilles heel is exposed, it is during lean times. As companies begin to spend less, look for lower pricing, and make decisions more slowly, they will quickly become frustrated with their salespeople's inability to sell. As well, salespeople will become discouraged with their sudden inability to get deals done, oblivious to the fact that they were not really *selling* before but merely showing up and getting the orders.

Some companies will wait—until it is too late—and then start the cost-cutting and layoffs that we have seen in the past. *Smart* companies will take action *now* by evaluating their sales forces to learn who, among their current team, *does* have the potential to sell effectively in down times. An evaluation will also suggest what kind of development help these people will need in order to become more effective. Who lacks the elements necessary for this type of selling, and can they be trained, or will you have to replace them? If they need to be replaced, who should you replace them *with*?

We will not realize at first that the diminished sales are a result of their skills (or lack of them)…oh, no. We will believe them when they say, "People are spending less," "they need to cut back," "it's a result of the economy," or of some other factor. Excuses, excuses! We will believe them because they have done well in the past, so they must be right. But now ask yourself, d*id they really* sell *in the past, or was it luck from being a good order-taker?*

Not sure? Assess their skills. Go out with them and see how it is done in the real world. Give them an assessment that really shows the skills they have…or do not. Those hidden weaknesses do not always show themselves in a healthy environment.

By the way, excuse-making is one of them.

Top Ten Sales Tips to Help in a Bad Economy

The economic climate, as we know by now, is cyclical—good times and bad, boom and bust, riding high and struggling mightily. You may be reading this in bad times or in good, but whichever is the case, one thing you can be sure of: Even if the economy is thriving at present, bad times will be around again.

How can you prosper during lean times? How can you best offset the effects of a bad economy and prosper even when your friends and neighbors are struggling? Here is how:

1. **Prospect.** But do not *just* prospect...out-prospect your competitors! How? Make sure your sales force is making more calls, getting more referrals, and networking more than anyone else. If they are good closers (and if they are not, why are they still working for you?!), you will close more deals than your competitors and not just survive but *thrive*.

2. **Over-qualify when you prospect.** To be sure of closing deals, be sure projects are critical to prospects. If your clients or prospects have problems whose consequences are severe, they will

prioritize and fund the solutions to those problems. Non-prioritized situations will get delayed by budgetary holdups, but crucial situations *will* be dealt with. Do not chase deals unless you know the project is crucial to the prospect.

3. **Take a good look at your sales force.** Who among them is underperforming? If a rep is not satisfactorily effective but has the desire and commitment to improve, insist that he or she invest in a good sales coaching program. If the rep is weak and has limited growth potential, it is time to replace him.

4. **Do not take a look at your sales reps just once.** Monitor each rep's prospecting performance on an ongoing basis. If you do not keep on top of things, you can not keep a handle on the situation…and you will not know when it is time to clear out "dead wood."

5. **Besides monitoring your sales staff's prospecting performance, track each rep's closing ratios.** What is the correlation of proposals to deals won? If the rate of closing is below sixty percent, a rep is under-qualifying, and/or she cannot differentiate, and/or he cannot get commitments. Again, now you will know when it is time to get rid of "dead wood."

6. **Leads are like beautiful flowers.** They are no good once they get old. Do not let leads sit around longer than a day. Qualify (or *dis*qualify) all leads immediately.

7. **Be like William Tell and aim high.** Call high in organizations—to C-level executives. Deal with the people who have the authority to thaw frozen budgets. *This is the key in lean economic times.*

8. **Seek openings for partnership opportunities with new prospects.** More likely than not, the recession is hitting their businesses too. How can you mutually help each other increase revenues?

9. **Use the Strategic Alliance route.** There is no better time then now. Meet with the "movers and shakers" in your community and see how you can help them; in turn, ask them to introduce you to some of your potential decision makers.

10. **Remember that *you* can have a share in ending the recession.** If we all go out and sell-sell-sell, we can get the economy booming again!

Money or Excuses,
You Can Not Have Both

Excuses or money—which do you want to make? Because, let's face it, you can not make both, and since excuses do not pay the bills, then making money should be the obvious choice. But if it is so apparent that money is the proverbial "goal," then why are we allowing lack of accountability and excuses to slaughter our sales?

Most successful business professionals understand the importance of holding themselves and others responsible for their actions. But if it is so important, then why do not most people *do* it?! Simple— because they are allowing excuses to take over their business. If excuse-making is the symptom, then they have the disease.

How often do you hear your salespeople dancing around the task at hand? "The economy is in a slump," "Our price was too high," "Our competitor advertised better." All excuses! Excuses are the toxins that are polluting your business.

Let's be honest. If your business was reaching its full potential with non-stop phone traffic for your product, all sales goals being met, and impeccable operations, then you would not need your salespeople! But since we do not live in a perfect world, we need our salespeople to help our imperfect companies stay in business.

So in our imperfect sales world, how can we keep excuses out of the mouths of our salespeople, who keep our boats afloat?

We, as business owners, CEOs, and sales managers must create a world in which excuses are not tolerated and everyone is held personally accountable for their actions. Easier said than done, you say? Think again! Here is a step-by-step accountability process that begins and ends with you, the executive:

Step One: Individual Goal-Setting

Have all your salespeople set individual goals that are in *their* best interest, not just the company's best interest. It is human nature for us to be selfish. If your sales team is not motivated to work hard for reasons other than "the common good," then it will be much easier for them to give excuses when it comes down to producing.

Step Two: Analyze Those Goals

Is the ten-million-in-two-weeks revenue goal that Jim set realistic? Can Sally really meet with ten prospects a day? If the goals your salespeople set are impractical, then they need to be addressed and adjusted before there is disappointment on both your end and theirs when those goals are not met.

Step Three: Address Commitment

The definition of commitment is: "Willingness to do whatever it takes to get the job done, even if you are afraid or uncomfortable with the task at hand." How committed are your salespeople to carrying out the activity required to meet their goals?

Step Four: Make Your Expectations *Clear*

If your sales team doesn't know what is expected of them, how can they be sure they are completing the task at hand the proper way? They can not. Be very upfront with exactly what you require for the job to be done to your standards.

Step Five: Track Goal Progress

Track and review activity goals weekly. This way, if a salesperson is getting off track, the problem can be addressed and corrected (see step six) before the waters get too deep.

Step Six: Corrective Actions

• Review the salesperson's individual goals. Has he/she lost his or her importance?

• Review the required activities. Can they be adjusted, or are they still a necessity?

• Review the salesperson's commitment. Do changes need to be made to keep that fire in his or her belly?

• Review the expectations. Are they still fresh in everyone's mind?

When the excuses begin to flow (and they will!), ask, "What else could you have done if you could not use that excuse?" or "If you could not use that excuse, what else could you have done to be successful?"

Step Seven: One-Two-Three Strikes, You are out!

After a new and improved commitment has been made, you must warn your salesperson that if he/she continues to miss his activity goals, there will have to be consequences. Remember they are uncontrollable, therefore no excuses. Strike one should be like a bee sting: enough to make you gasp but not enough to make you cry. For example, stop reimbursing her travel expenses. Strike two should be stronger, such as taking him off an account. Strike three—you are out. Employment terminated.

Remember, removing the excuse-makers sends a message to A-players. Starting today, accept no excuses.

Do Not Use an Economic Down-turn as an Excuse

As I have already said, the economy is, inevitably, cyclical. Like the rest of us, it has its ups and downs. Yet, when we are in a down cycle, do you get nervous about the economy? And do other factors external to your industry, including world events such as wars, cause you to tighten your belt?

Downturns in the economic cycle and other times of national or world uncertainty are not a time for anxiety but a time to be realistic and acknowledge that tough times lie ahead. Your sales team needs to be able to respond. If it does not, the competition's sales team surely will.

During the last economic high, I am sure your sales team grew. But if your salespeople are accustomed to having sales fall in their laps, they have yet to be put to the test. With the buying frenzy coming to a close and a possible recession peering from the wings, what should we expect from our order-taking breed of salespeople?

Probably not a lot.

Right now, your sales team could be the weakest part of your company. Businesses become aggravated very quickly when their salespeople are not selling.

Salespeople also get discouraged when they do not close sales. And many fail to recognize that their sales in the good times simply came to them, with little or no work involved.

A lot of companies wait until they are desperate. Then the layoffs and cost-cutting begin. But smart companies do not wait. They know that, if we are at the apparent beginning of a down cycle, they should evaluate their sales force *now*, finding out who has effective selling skills to utilize in the slump that may lie ahead.

When assessing your team, ask yourself the following questions:

• What are the necessary elements for selling in this economy?

• Which salespeople have those elements?

• Who does not have the necessary skills, and should we replace them?

• Whom should we replace them with?

Do not fall victim to a salesperson's belief that "people are spending less" or "these are uncertain times." Excuses, excuses, excuses. If salespeople are not strong enough to make it through tough times, they probably do not belong on your team. Evaluate their skills. Go on a sales call with each salesperson and see how he/she performs in the real world. Another option is to have them each take an assessment that shows the skills they truly have—and the ones they do not.

Hold your ground and act as though the economy were flourishing. Keep in mind that the economy is cyclical. When things are bad, nothing should change. That way, you are not falling into a slump but simply continuing to work hard until things come back around—which they always do.

Now is when the real sales professionals can shine.

Our Patriotic Duty

It is your patriotic duty to be the best salesperson you can...for the good of your country.

You think that is a lot of hoo-ha? Ha! The article that follows was written just after 9/11...but I am including it in the book because it is still true today...

• • •

I got up Friday morning and got ready for work, and I thought about going to the awards luncheon I was scheduled to attend. My thoughts were, "How do we go and do this? It seems so unimportant, compared to all of the things going on in the world. What do our jobs matter, compared to the firefighters, putting their lives on the line to find every last victim, working tirelessly and without sleep or a break. The military, saying goodbye to their families on this day to go fight for us, even though they may never return..."

Then I had a light bulb moment: "We are expecting them to do their jobs, to rescue as only they know how, to fight as only they have been trained to do." And it hit me: *Our job as businesspeople is to keep the economy going* for them! *We are the ones who can boost the economy; we are the ones who can make transactions happen.*

We owe that to them. Their job is to protect and save us. Our job is to keep the economy healthy. We cannot accept from our colleagues answers like, "It is harder to sell now," "We can not meet our goals," and any other excuses that we, as businesspeople, might make. We do not hear the firefighters of New York saying, "Oh, it is so much harder than usual," "We can not do this—it is too hot—I am tired."

We are expecting them to do their job. Let's do ours...let's do whatever it takes! For the first responders, and for the military, who need the economy to rise above this, do it for them. Sell something today. Just go out, do your job and sell something!! Though the American political situation is ever-shifting, one thing remains true: We, the businesspeople of America, can best help our nation by keeping our country's economy firm and strong. While the military does what they do best and the first responders do what they do best (and while we appreciate what each of these groups do for us), we can do what we do best: Keep the economy strong.

Get out there and make money. It is, in a sense, your patriotic duty.

Going Green, Will Make You Green

Several days ago, I headed to a coffee shop to pass some time between appointments. When my order was ready, the woman at the counter asked if I would like a hot sleeve for my coffee - or if I would like to help save the planet by burning my fingers.

As much as I love the Earth, I went for the hot sleeve. I grabbed my drink hastily and made my way to the only available table in the shop.

When I sat down, I could not help but reflect on what had just happened.

To the unsuspecting eye, I had merely ordered a cup of coffee. But as I added up the gross revenue this shop was bringing in, it hit me: Concerns about global warming, greenhouse gases and rising oil prices have trickled all the way down to my local coffee shop.

The entire world, it seems, is obsessed with going green.

Research shows that within the next eight years, the market for green energy will more than quadruple. That means we business owners will need to support the green market.

The trend can teach us a much better way to sell, such as using more face-to-face contact with customers and relying less on printed promotional materials.

When you do not have reams of collateral material, you are forced to really have a conversation. That is how sales are done.

Your brochures can be saved for someone you have already spoken to and believe would be a good fit.

Change will be necessary for you to jump on the green bandwagon. But sacrifice will not. Here is why: Going green can help you get more green (as in the folding stuff in your wallet).

Consider the following steps you can take to help save the planet:

- Stop passing out stuff: The next time a prospect asks you for information on your products or services, do not just blindly hand over a brochure and business card.

Ask a few questions to identify what the prospect is looking for.

Once you identify which of your products or services will be a good fit, then -and only then - should you provide promotional materials to help make a sale. And you should e-mail that information instead of mailing it in printed form.

- Quit preparing lengthy written proposals: Gone are the days when we needed to present our prospects with 100 pages of material outlining a proposal.

If you are in an industry where a proposal is required, make sure to keep it short and sweet by identifying the products or services the prospective customer needs. Once that is done, only those items should be identified in your proposal. If your prospect doesn't need it, why propose it?

- E-mail, e-mail, e-mail: After an appointment, type up a quick e-mail message, citing the important points from your conversation.

That will serve multiple purposes. You can thank prospects for the meeting, remind them why your product or service is needed, and remind them of the next steps you both agreed upon.

More than twenty five billion cups are thrown away every year, with less than twenty percent of those cups being recycled. Shocked? You should not be.

As Kermit the Frog says, "It is not easy being green."

But make the effort. You and your clients will be glad you did.

The Experience Economy

Introduction by Chris Huffman, Braman Motor Cars

When I was asked to write an introduction for the "Experience Economy" chapter of this book, I started to think about what means the most to the customer in a business relationship. I found that many of the key points in this chapter reflect those that are most important to me and to Braman Motorcars/BMW in delivering the best luxury automotive experience anywhere, anytime.

The first things that came to my mind were trust, confidence, and personal attention.

I then read this chapter and found those exact same words.

Creating trust in a relationship does not happen in an instant, however trust can be earned by doing so many little things right. How to earn trust?

- Be honest with a customer, do not tell them what you think they want to hear, always be honest and tell your customer what reality is and what you believe to be in their best interest.

- Mean what you say and deliver results. Setting the correct expectation and meeting or exceeding that expectation reinforces that you are honest and the customer can "trust" your actions and what you say.

- Trust builds by continually reinforcing the purchase decision through outstanding repetitive performance.

When you have earned trust you build confidence. The customer trusts that you will do what you say and has confidence that you will "care for them and have their best interests in mind". When a customer has confidence in you, and what you do for them, they will be very loyal to you and tell others how they can depend upon you to help them meet their needs. Customer satisfaction is worthless, customer loyalty is priceless!

Personal attention is the critical component in the "experience economy". By giving personal attention to every detail, you demonstrate the "caring" you have for your customer. Behave with your customer as if the product or service you are delivering is for yourself. How do you want to be treated? How do you express sincerity? What do you do or say that demonstrates to anyone that you personally care for them and their well being? Not something you do for show, but what you do for someone you really care about? Would you say hello to a customer if you saw them outside the work environment? Show your customer that you really care about them, their well being, and their success. Their success is your success!

If you do not pay personal attention to the details, the message you are sending is "they do not really care about me, I must be just another customer". If they do not care about me I cannot trust them. If I cannot trust them I do not have confidence in them to take care of my needs. Why would I ever do business with someone I cannot trust and have no confidence in? Am I not important enough for them to give me the personal attention I need as a customer?

Delivering an experience that earns trust, builds confidence, and pays close personal attention to details is what it is all about in the "experience economy". Approaching every customer with the intention of building a lifelong relationship that makes every transaction seamless creates added value to your customers, your company, and makes you a true professional. To be the best, give the best!

Trust + Confidence

_____ = Experience Economy at its best!

Personal Attention

For the Love of Pants

Last week, after two full days of training, I met a few friends in the female shopping wonderland called Chicago. Boy, that Magnificent Mile sure is named appropriately!

After sharing my "wealth" with lots of different retail stores, I found a neat little boutique.

I tried on several pairs of pants (because God knows I need more) and found a fabulous pair that fit me like a glove. After I bought them, my friends and I quickly realized that we had overextended our stay and needed to hightail it to the airport – or we would be staying yet another day in "the wonderland." Neither my pocketbook – nor, for that matter, my marriage – could sustain another day of that. We made it, and the rest, as they say, is history. I woke up the next day and put on my new fabulous pants, only to discover that the security tag was still attached to one of the pant legs. To say I was angry was an understatement!

I immediately called the salesperson who sold me the pants and expressed my unhappiness. Her reply was: "I am sorry. Send them back and we will take care of it." I am in Florida and she is in Chicago. There is no better way to make me happy? She could not think of one, so I told her I would send them back for a refund. But still I thought about the pants and how nicely they fit. When you are over forty, things like this are important.

My next call was to the Nordstrom department store here in South Florida. I asked the saleswoman if they had the pants in stock and explained the situation. She checked and said yes, they did, but she made another suggestion that floored me. "Why not bring the pants in and we will take the security tag off for you? Then, you will not have to send them back at all and you can wear them right away!" "No, no, no – I did not get these at the Nordstrom in Chicago; it was at a small boutique," I quickly explained. "Yes, I understand that. But would it not be easier to just bring them in here?" Not quite sure of all this but with a sense of fascination, I took the pants with me and after work, I went to the store.

"Is Judy here?" I asked, because she told me to ask for her. "Actually, she is not, but (looking at the bag in my hand) are you Greta?" Like a deer in headlights I answered, "Y-y-yes?" "Oh, Judy explained the situation. My name is Phyllis and I can help." I gave her the pants and she called their loss prevention department. Someone came down and whisked my pants away. While I was waiting, Phyllis showed me the pants (that made me look so good) in other colors, and asked if I wanted to look at any. Why not? I was standing there anyway.

Loss prevention came back and said my pants had a different type of security tag than the one they use, so it would not come off. Disappointed but appreciative, I said thank you and was on my way when Phyllis said: "Let me make a call." She took my pants and said she would be right back. "Where are you going?" I said with confusion. "Oh, I think Saks has this type of tag, so I am going to see if they can take it off." "What? Wait a minute. You remember I did not get these here?" "You still need it off though, right? So let me take it and I will be right back."

And she did! Holy customer service! Do you think I will continue shopping there? Do you think I will question pricing? Do you think I will tell others? I am telling you, right?

Gee, I wonder if this helps them sell.

It Is About the Experience, Not the Coffee

I admire Starbucks. The company gets it. I go to its coffee shops and meet business associates there…even though I do not care for their coffee. It is way too strong for me. But I still go there and encourage others to as well. Company Chairman Howard Schultz (no relation to me, unfortunately) has figured it out. He has created an experience like no other.

So why do I go there if I do not care for the coffee? Is that not what Starbucks is about? No! The coffee is only one part of the experience. There are also the comfy couches. How many customers would rather sit on a hard stool as opposed to a cozy sofa? Then there is the soft music that plays ever so lightly in the background, and the Wi-Fi. Some other coffee shops now offer similar touches, but I believe Starbucks was the first. The walls of its shops are dark and feature nice artwork. It makes me feel like I am in my living room and not a coffee shop. (And if, like me, you do not care for their coffee, try the caramel apple cider.)

So how do we accomplish that kind of experience in our own businesses?

First, it is not about having the best product. "Best" is merely subjective anyway. Have you ever told someone your company was ranked number one in the industry? If that were so important, everyone would switch to you, and there would be no number two—or any other competitor.

So what experience are you leaving your customers with? What feeling are they getting when working with you? Is it different? Is it unique? Can they not achieve that experience anywhere else?

Are they getting a good feeling from working with you, or are they feeling that you do a good job?

A good job is intellectual: "I got what I paid for." A good feeling is an emotion. And emotion is the extra something, the wow factor that is beyond the expectation.

It is similar to Starbucks' comfy, cozy couches.

What are some things you do to create the wow factor? What is the something extra customers experience in working with you that makes you different from your competitors?

If you want to create more of that experience, you should brainstorm. Meet with a few people you admire and shoot around some ideas.

Maybe you can do that at your local Starbucks.

Follow the Banker,
Not the Bank

My husband, Peter, is a great sport when it comes to making appearances with me at networking functions. Being a business owner himself, he really does "get" the importance of networking to build a profitable business. Recently, he and I attended a dinner at our local chamber of commerce.

We entered the room and began to make our rounds, greeting all the people we knew and introducing ourselves to the people we did not. While I was catching up with a former client, I happened to overhear Peter introducing himself to Sam, a business development officer from a local bank.

After they exchanged the usual name, position, and company information, Sam proceeded to ask the question every banker seems to ask: "So, Peter, who do you bank with?"

Peter, without hesitation, answered, "Patti Dent."

"No, no—your bank," Sam said, looking confused.

"Patti Dent," Peter said again.

"That is not a bank," Sam said, chuckling under his breath.

"I know," Peter replied, "but I bank with Patti Dent. She is who I deal with, she is who I trust and, regardless of what the sign on the building says, she is the person I have confidence in to make sure my finances are taken care of. Do you think the person, not just the building that person is in makes the difference?"

"Well...yes," Sam said, coyly.

Peter's response makes perfect sense. We have all seen the banks out there, pushing their features and benefits, advertising point five percent under prime, and giving away a free blender when you open a new checking account. Get serious. If a free blender is why you decided to move your millions from Bank A to Bank B, then you need to get your head examined.

Client relationships

The same person who opened your account ten years ago is still managing your account today. She is the one to greet you by name every time you walk through the bank doors, congratulate you on your marriage, and help you get a loan to start your new business.

Regardless of how many times the sign on the building has changed, she has stayed the same. We are not married to the brick and mortar. We are married to the person or people we do business with.

How strong are *your* client relationships? Are your customers getting the impeccable customer service they deserve...or will they switch to your competitor if the price is right?

Best ways

Here are five tips to ensure your connections with your clients are top-notch:

1. Communicate

Communication is not raving about your latest discounts; it is listening to what your client needs and making sure you can accommodate him. If you can not give your client what he needs, tell him. He will appreciate your honesty, and trust that you will be honest with him when times get tough.

2. Exceed their expectations

Do your best to go above and beyond the call of duty. If your customers ask for a specialty item or last-minute favor, try to accommodate them, if at all possible.

3. Ask for constructive criticism

When it comes to understanding what your clients need, it is imperative that you see things from their eyes. Ask what you are doing well and how things can be improved. If you know your current customers are happy, you can be certain they would feel comfortable recommending your products and services to their friends and family.

4. Follow through

Nothing is worse than asking for feedback, then not making any changes and ignoring your findings. Next time you look through your comments box or hear a complaint from a client, do what you can to fix the problem at hand. If your customers see that speaking up gets things accomplished, you will keep the line of communication open and keep everyone happy.

5. Make things personal

Do your best to put a human face on your business. Staying in front of your clients is a great way of saying, "Thanks for your business." If nothing else, try to learn about your regular customers. Call them by name, instead of "ma'am" or "sir." Make sure they know you are there to help.

An interesting statistic: It is five to six times more expensive to attract a new customer than to keep an existing customer. I am guessing that is from all the blenders you are giving away.

Though free appliances may be enticing, it is not what is going to keep you faithful to the same bank, year after year, acquisition after acquisition. Like any business, it is all about building client relationships.

Always Give First

Last week, I sat down with Jacob, a friend who is a sales rep at an ink and toner supply store. We were exchanging the usual "So, how is the family...how is business?" when Jacob started to look troubled. "You know, Greta, I thought business was going great," he said. "My sales have been through the roof, and I have more clients than I know what to do with. There is just one thing that has been bothering me the past few weeks."

"What is that?" I asked.

"Well, I was reviewing my order totals for the quarter when I saw that my biggest client, ABC Graphics, had ordered only half as much toner in June as it did in May. I was not too surprised. Many of our clients have a slow month here or there. I figured things would pick up. Well, lo and behold, at the end of the next month, not only had ABC Graphics not increased back to its regular toner order, it had barely ordered anything."

I asked, "So tell me something, Jacob. When you recently visited your contact at ABC Graphics, how did it go?"

"Well, to be honest, the last time I followed up with them was at the end of last year," Jacob replied. "I told you we have been crazy—I mean busy—and besides I didn't have anything new for him, they just want to order and not have us bother them." Bother *them!*

So why was Jacob rapidly losing ground on his biggest account? Because he did not stay in front of his client, and someone else moved in on his account. And if Jacob's client perceives a visit as a "bother" then he needs to analyze what he says and does while he's there.

One common characteristic we as salespeople have, is the belief that "once a customer, always a customer." Of course, as time goes on and good customer service does not, another salesperson sees your client as his prospect. So how can Jacob—or you—make it right?

Sit down with your client list the first week of every month and think about each client individually. Then jot down something you can do for each person or company on the list. Take off your salesperson hat and really consider the well-being of your client. Think referrals, introductions, invitations to network with you…anything to make your client say, "Wow, he really does care about me."

Not only will you be helping out your clients, but you will also be keeping the line of communication open regarding your product or service. Then you can resolve their issue instead of your competition doing it…while getting their business.

Rather than worrying about the other guy moving in on your clients, take some preventive measures to ensure you are keeping your clients happy. Remember the "givers gain" philosophy: The more you give, the more you get in return. If you are always giving, you will never lose.

Let Customers Know
What Is Important

A basic rule of Selling 101 is to ask potential clients questions before trying to make a sale.

That is not rocket science. It is widely known that in selling anything, you first need to find out what your prospect or client wants and needs.

Apparently, not everyone follows that rule.

I am writing a book. I have spoken with publishers, literary agents, and book-publishing representatives, and almost none of them has asked me what the book is about.

Can you believe it? Maybe it is because they do not think they are in sales, or maybe they believe that if they tell me enough about how they do things, I will buy their services.

At first, I was flabbergasted. But then I thought: Why should they be any different from any other people who believe "if I tell you enough about what I do, you will buy from me?"

So, let's go back to the basics.

People want to tell their story. Even if you, as the salesperson, believe you have heard them all, it does not matter. You need to ask prospects and clients about their interests and their concerns.

Whatever it is you are there to discuss, let them tell you. They want to. They need to. And, most of all, you need them to.

Do not tell them why your product or service is better than what your competitors offer. Customers do not care – at least not yet. You need to match what they say is important with what you have. No more and no less.

Find out from them what they are looking for in addition to your particular product or service. You may be able to introduce them to someone else who can help them in a different way, or make a suggestion that will fill a need they have.

Keep first things first. Customers will tell you what is important to them.

These are the things that create value and make customers sit up and listen to what you have to offer.

Until you understand that, the "features and benefits" of your product are completely irrelevant.

Remember: There is a reason you have two ears, but only one mouth.

Just Say "No"

Just say "No." When Nancy Reagan gave us that advice, she was talking about drugs. I have something else in mind: personal issues that adversely affect your work and work issues that adversely affect your personal life.

A certain PepsiCo executive was offered a promotion some years ago that would have involved a lot of traveling and would also have meant a move. At the time he was a young father of four, and he felt that both the move and the traveling would not be a good thing for his family, or his relationship with them.

He said no.

A less brave or less self-respecting individual might have agreed out of fear that he would be fired for saying no (which was not the outcome in this case). For example, what if the job required working evenings or weekends, or if it in some way impeded your ability to work out regularly, spend quality time with your family, or to eat healthy?

By the same token, what if something in your personal life got in the way of you performing your job properly? Obviously you can not and do not want to sacrifice your spouse or kids! But what if you have a hobby that keeps you up late at nights, robbing you of the chance to get an adequate night's sleep? That would certainly affect your job performance. Or what if some other facet of your personal life is having a negative effect on your job performance?

Obviously you are facing a conflict, and you have to work it out. Would you take a stand at work and refuse to do that which is harmful to your family life or your health? Would you have the self-discipline at home (or elsewhere in your personal life) to stop whatever activity is getting in the way of your job performance?

Be true to yourself...and to both aspects of your life.

Pitch is for Baseball

Introduction by Ellen Sherberg, Publisher,
St. Louis Business Journal

All I ever wanted to be when I grew up was a newspaper reporter. When I worked on the junior high newspaper, I loved getting out of class early to interview the school principal. Being a reporter seemed so easy. All you had to do was ask questions. Other people were the ones who had to have the answers.

As much as technology has changed the media industry, a reporter's responsibility is still pretty much the same: We ask questions to find out what is happening. We have more research tools now, especially through the internet, but the ability to ask pertinent questions and listen carefully to the answers remains the key to reporting.

I was stunned to learn the same set of skills is critical to the sales process. When I was named publisher of the St. Louis Business Journal, I became responsible for the advertising and circulation efforts, as well as, the editorial product that was my purview when I was editor. I had never sold an ad or a subscription. In my whole life, the only time I sold anything other than Girl Scout cookies was the summer after my freshman year in college when I worked in the women's department of a local department store.

I was petrified to go on a sales call because I did not want to be seen as the lady on the infomercial pitching cookware or makeup. Yet I wanted to grow revenues so sales calls were a necessity. I never expected to enjoy them but now I truly do. That is because I am doing the same thing that brought me to reporting: Asking questions. Other people still have the answers.

Learning what sales is – and what it is not – will help you understand what it takes to succeed. Just be ready to ask a lot of questions!

Pitch Is for Baseball

In my recent search for additional sales consultants, I have discovered something interesting: People are afraid of working in what they perceive as "sales."

OK, so I did not just discover that; I obviously have known it for a long time. I would tell prospective consultants that I heard a hesitation in their voices when interviewing them, and I asked why. "What do you think will be involved?"

I heard several different things, but mostly just, "Well, lots of cold calling and pitching your product." Yuck! I would be hesitant, too, if that was what my business called for.

But the truth is, most of the sales jobs out there are just that: cold calling and pitching. No wonder so many salespeople are unsuccessful and burnt out.

First things first, I tell them. You are not there to "pitch" anything. Your job in sales is to find enough people to ask questions to, and determine if you have what they need. That may or may not involve cold calling—and people who have read my column know I am not a fan of cold calling—but it most certainly does not involve "pitching."

Our son is a pitcher for his high school baseball team—and a darn good one, I might add. When a batter comes to the plate, he knows it is his turn. The batter is expecting a pitch, and he has a plan of what he will do when the ball arrives. I have a feeling that if our son were walking down the hall on a regular school day and decided to "pitch" a ball to someone, even one of the batters from his team, he would get in some trouble (at the least) and could very well wind up with a black eye from the guy he threw the ball at.

But this, people, is what we do all the time. Yep, we cold-call people, on the phone or in person, and "pitch" them our product without them being ready or qualified to receive it. Most of the time we get a polite (and sometimes not-so-polite) "No, thank you," but the result is the same. The old adage "Throw enough stuff against the wall and something is bound to stick" is the most ridiculous load of garbage I have ever heard.

Let's go back to baseball for a second. Suppose Randy Johnson had been taught that if he threw enough balls, he would become a great pitcher…do you think he actually would be? No! It is not only the quantity you throw; it is the quality and who you are throwing to. Is the person you are throwing to a lefty, a righty, or a switch-hitter? Nervous? Ultra-aggressive? Preparation and analysis of the batter is key.

Sales works the same. Stop pitching to everyone you see. Take some time to learn what the prospect wants and what he needs, and then prepare the correct solution. Who knows—you might actually be successful.

What to Put on a Business Card

When I go anywhere—lunch, a networking event, a fundraiser—people always give me business cards...sometimes even before "hello." We put so much emphasis on these two by three cards, and for what? Do you think the card is going to sell for you? Have you experienced the people who hand out so many cards that you want to know where they get them printed, so you can buy stock?

We also get this question from many of our clients: "What title should we put on our salesperson's business cards? I mean, if we want them to be consultants, should we should say 'consultant', or how about 'account manager'?" I shake my head. They do not get it. Who cares! It is how you act, not what you say on your card that makes you a salesperson or a consultant.

While we are on the subject, let's address business cards in general. I do not think the format has changed in a hundred years. Ask yourself, when you look for a business card, what are you looking for 90% of the time?

Let's start from the top: You should have a logo or name of your company on the card. Top left corner or across the top is fine. No need to scream across the card what your company name is. Do not worry. We can see it.

Next, your name. Let's make that one legible and large enough to read. If you want the people you meet to spell your name correctly, it needs to be clear on the card, though this does not guarantee accuracy on their part. My name gets spelled incorrectly all the time!

Third, the phone number. Why we put the most important thing on the card in six point type that I still can not see even with my granny glasses (no snickering!) is beyond me. *Make it easy to see!*

Next, the fax number. When was the last time you pulled out a business card to fax something? You did not. You spoke to them on the phone, and they asked you to fax something, at which point you asked for their fax number. So that information—if you include it at all—can be in small type.

Email address? Pretty important these days. Be sure to include it.

Now, how about the business you are in? If the company name is Acme Widgets, it is pretty clear what product you are dealing in. But if your company's name is XYZ Unlimited or Excelsior Partners, you had better have an explanatory line underneath the name, or somewhere prominent on the card. Otherwise your prospect is not going to remember that you are the Nike manufacturer's representative he met at the chamber event last month.

What about fancy business cards—unusual colors, patterns, typeface, or designs? Let me put it to you this way: Do you really think they help to sell your product, or *you,* to your prospect? Your card is a necessity, so people will know who you are, what company you are with, and where to find you if they want to get in touch. But it is not *your card* that you want to be memorable. It is *you* and the product (or service) you represent.

So put your effort into making a good impression, and a memorable one, on the people you meet, and as for the cards…well, in the immortal words of Sgt. Joe Friday (Jack Webb's character on the classic *Dragnet* series): "Just the facts, ma'am."

I Will Give It a Try

Have you ever *tried* to pick up a pencil? Have you ever *tried* to take a drink of water? No, you have not. You just *do* it. Lack of commitment is the failure of most salespeople, and even of their clients. "I tried" is the lamest excuse I have ever heard. I would like to share an example from the world of advertising that illustrates this point.

There are approximately one hundred and twenty thousand salespeople selling some form of advertising in America. Each of these salespeople will make "prospecting calls" to an average of three business owners per day. One business owner out of twelve will say, "Well, maybe it does make sense for my business. I will go ahead and buy a small schedule and *give it a try.*" What they may add aloud, and if not, they are at least thinking it, is, "And if it works, I will use your station/publication (fill in the blank) on a regular basis."

Sounds pretty good, right?

This is perhaps the dumbest thing I have ever heard. Let me share a similar example with you to prove my point. Let's say you are in Vegas, standing at the roulette table, and you think, "I am going to place a small bet on black, and if I win, I will start betting on black on a regular basis." Sounds a little ridiculous, don't you think?

There are thousands of business owners who will be making a decision to "*give it a try*" today. Most of them will experience poor results. Will they be disappointed? Yes. Surprised? No. They will not be surprised because they have "*given it a try*" before, with very limited success.

Why would business owners do what they have done before and expect different results? Because bad salespeople have taught them to do this. Not every product or service works this way. But if you have ever heard the old adage "over-promise and under-deliver," it gives the same result.

"I will give it a try" or "Let me test the waters" is the signature of an uncommitted customer. I think we would be hard pressed to find these customers experiencing a high degree of reward from their efforts…because there is none. With risk comes reward. Show me a committed and focused client, and I will show you success in the making.

My Famous Car Story

I often try to illustrate how professional sales really work. Simply, it works by helping your prospect *self-realize* that he needs (or in some cases does not need) your product or service. One of the best examples is the story I tell about buying a Jeep.

Several years ago, I got engaged to a man who had two children. I had one child of my own, and between the two of us and our kids, we needed a more "Brady-esque" car. We decided after much research that a Jeep Cherokee would do the trick. At the time, leasing a Jeep Cherokee Laredo, the base model, would cost two hundred and ninety nine dollars per month for three years, with one thousand dollars down. This was a good deal by all accounts.

Since I know how car dealers work (or so I thought), I felt strongly about staying emotionally detached and just purchasing the car for the price I wanted. I called the Jeep dealership in Stuart, Florida and asked for the sales manager. Richard (who I believe is still there) answered the phone.

I explained to Richard that I wanted a Jeep Cherokee Laredo, dark green in color, and that I would be willing to buy it today if he could match the price I wanted: two hundred and ninety nine dollars for thirty-six months and one thousand dollars down. I was strong in my demand, making sure he knew I was in charge. Richard said he could match the price, but he had the vehicle only in army green, not dark green. Even though I was disappointed, since the dark green was so much more "me," I decided this was the route to go.

Upon arrival at the dealership, the kids and my then-fiancé piled out of our car. "Wait here," I commanded. "I will handle this!"

I entered the showroom, and a man came out to greet me. "You must be Greta," he said, smiling and seeming sincere.

"Yes, I am," I said cautiously.

"Well, let's go drive the car."

"Oh no," I exclaimed. "I want to talk money first."

Richard responded, "Okay, but you said two hundred and ninety nine dollars for three years with one thousand dollars down? Well, that is what we agreed to, so that is what it is, right?"

With a half smile on my face, I proudly proclaimed, "Right."

As we walked through the lot to the army green (a bit more of a pea green, if you asked me) Jeep, Richard asked, "So, which car is yours?" I pointed to a blue BMW in the customer parking lot. As we got into the Jeep, Richard pointed out, "This car does not have a leather interior, it has cloth…but that is not a problem. I am sure your kids do not spill things at their age."

"No, no that is okay," I quickly replied. As I pulled out of the dealership in the car for the test drive, Richard played with the radio stations. He asked, "What type of music do you like?"

"Oh gosh, jazz, top forty, lots of different things."

"Really? Do you have a lot of CDs?" he continued.

"Oh, yes," I proudly proclaimed.

"Hmm, you know, this car does not have a CD player, but I am sure you still have cassettes."

"Or I can just play the radio," I said with some reservation.

"Of course you can," he said confidently.

As we pulled back into the dealership lot, Richard asked, "So what do you think?"

"Pretty nice," I replied with hesitation. "It drives more like a truck, but, hey, it is not a BMW, and you have to give up something, right?" Silent, I walked into the showroom to sign the papers.

"Hey Greta, that emerald green down there on that car…was that the color you originally asked me for?"

Excitement filled my face. "Yes, but I thought you did not have one."

"Oh no, that is a Grand Cherokee. It has all the bells and whistles, you know—CD player, leather seats, and a smoother drive train, but you didn't want that," Richard said.

"Ummm…how much more is that one?" I could not resist.

Guess which one I drove away in and paid seventy dollars more a month for? You got it! And guess what I said to my fiancé when we were walking toward our new Grand? "Honey, it is more expensive, but I am in sales. My car is like my office. I have to be comfortable…"

So, what happened? Well, Richard did a really good job of finding out what was important to me. But he never told me those things were important. Instead, he asked me the right questions to get me to self-realize that I wanted them.

And what did I do? I made an emotional decision and justified it intellectually to my family. Remember, people love to buy—they just hate to be sold. So help them buy, and stop selling them. It even worked on me…and I saw it coming.

VITO and Seymour

I would like to share a story with you about Lisa, a representative for a professional firm, who just was not hitting her numbers. Her industry was growing rapidly, demand for her services was clearly there, and the firm was a leader in its market. Lisa made lots of calls, and her prospects generally welcomed her visits. She even brought small gifts with her when she called on them, to set herself apart from her competitors. But still the business failed to materialize.

Frustrated, Lisa asked, "What am I doing wrong?"

On examination, it turned out that Lisa had fallen into a pattern that eventually causes many young and often inexperienced salespeople to fail. She was not getting to the real decision maker (VITO, the Very Important Top Officer*). An important rule in Sales 101 says you must get in front of the decision maker.

As it turns out, Lisa had several classic problems. When she started selling, she knew the importance of being in front of VITO. But getting an appointment with VITO was not so easy. Frequently, VITO asked her to see his assistant, "Seymour" (the data gatherer, who just wants to "see more" information). Often, Seymour even claims to be the decision maker, though he is not.

After this had happened a few times, Lisa saw a pattern, believed it was the norm, and decided to simply skip a step and go straight to Seymour. "I mean, why should I see VITO when Seymour will see me, listen to me, and says he recommends to the president anyway."

Since Seymours are easier to get appointments with, Lisa got more appointments. This was starting to make sense after all. Take the easy road and, if you see enough Seymours, you will be on the road to success. To top it off, Lisa's company, like so many others, rated her on the number of proposals she made, thinking this was the key indicator of sales effectiveness. So Lisa got lots of appointments and kept very busy doing proposals, but her sales did not improve.

The solution? Lisa, Lisa, Lisa, nobody said selling was easy. If it were, everyone would be successful, but they are not. Seymour will only pump you for information, turn you into an "unpaid consultant," and lead you down the road to failure.

Half the problems that sales reps bring to us are caused by their failure to get in front of VITO. I hear stuff like "He will not see me," "It is hard to get to him," and (my favorite) "I do not want to upset Seymour." *What?!* Do not accept mediocrity and do not let your prospects be in charge of your process. If you decide that Daniel Jones from ABC Mega Company is the VITO you would like to get in front of, then figure out a way to get it done! Just go do it! Sales is a no-whining activity!

***

*Thanks to Tony Parinello for the VITO/Seymour concept. His book, *Selling to Vito,* is a good reference for anyone who sells.

Top Ten Most Common
Sales Mistakes

If your sales results have been disappointing, I hope you're learning something valuable from reading this. Or maybe you're a dynamo whose efforts are amply rewarded with sales-and commissions-but you still wouldn't mind a little improvement (more is better, right? Well, most of the time) in your sales figures.

In either case, stop and ask yourself if you're guilty of any of these Top Ten Sales Mistakes. As you read through the list, do you see yourself looking back at yourself from the mirror? If so, you know where you need to start making improvements.

10) Not pre-qualifying a potential appointment before you commit to going. I still hear people sway, "I go for the appointment, if I can get in front of them I have a better chance of selling it". You also have a better chance of wasting lots of time on nothing but an opportunity that has a high chance of going nowhere.

9) Not allowing the power of silence. Silence is an important tool in negotiation. It is powerful because most people are so uncomfortable with it that they will speak again before they allow the prospect to answer. When you ask a question, allow the prospect to have time to think about the answer. If you do not, you have lost control of the conversation and more importantly, some people need time to think before answering. For those people, you have interrupted their train of thought. Stop talking!

8) Not uncovering the next steps clearly enough. Some of us are sharp enough to know that we should ask what the next step is when on a sales appointment, but there is more to it than that. For example if you asked the question, "If I come back with a proposal you like, what will happen next?" (Good question by the way) and they say, "We will move forward" you would probably assume that means sign the deal...are you sure?? Move forward could mean lots of things so make sure you understand what it is specifically. Do not assume it means sign the deal without asking, because you know what happens when you assume.

7) Putting a proposal together before understanding all that should be included. I am floored how many people still do the show up, ask a few questions, and ask for the "privilege" to come back with a proposal. What exactly are you proposing? Do not get caught up in the "if I can show them all the great things we do they will buy" syndrome. They will buy what is relevant to them and only then!

6) Not utilizing relationships they have in the community. These help to form alliances and get them introduced to a potential prospect at a higher level than they could have done alone or by cold calling.

5) Defending your product or service. If someone asks why you did something or why your organization made a particular decision, do not defend the decision, ask why they are asking? Do not assume you know why. You can get yourself in deep trouble that way.

4) Not asking for a referral because you are uncomfortable. This is an unbelievable reality to me. The number one complaint I hear from salespeople is they hate cold calling. Then get yourself out of the cold call business and start asking for referrals. The two reasons why we do not get more referrals are: 1) we do not ask and 2) we do not ask properly! You must be specific about who and what you are looking for. No one knows better then you what a good referral looks like.

3) Not setting an agenda for a meeting. If you are calling on someone and you go in with the attitude that you will "wing it" you are in trouble. No one respects your time if you do not respect theirs. Set an agenda, discuss it with them at the beginning of the meeting and get their agreement. They will also be on the same page with you instead of an adversary.

2) Do not give the "features and benefits" of your product until you know they are relevant to the potential client. Do not assume they are because you know his/her industry. Assuming this, is a mistake in many ways. The most damaging, is not letting them tell you the issues they are having before you make your recommendations. Even if they end up being the same ones. People need to be heard.

1) Not shutting up.

Dating and Sales

Introduction by Sandy Donovan, Executive Director, BNI

When a relationship works - really clicks – it is palpable. The energy is there, both parties share the same enthusiasm, and everything seems effortless. When it does not, everything seems to require more effort. There seems to be a slow leak that drains your energy over time. Same goes for your client list. There are your good clients - you know the ones who take your advice, get great results, and sing your praises to others. They never cause you headaches and stay with you for the long term. Then there are the clients that make you want to recommend your competitor…after all – if someone has to suffer, who better than your competitor, right?

So what similarities do we find that create this comparison between dating and sales? Well, my friends, I hate to bring up the dreaded "C" word, but you know that is where I am going. Yes… Communication. More specifically…*listening*.

Have you ever gone out on a date with someone who, after ordering their drink, launches into a monologue that would rival that of a candidate running for President? They are so busy telling you about all their successes, accomplishments, and achievements that they forget this was meant to be a dialogue. Meaning they need to find out about you before they can hope to see if they would be, in fact, a good match for you. Same goes for your clients.

So the uncovering of information must begin with simple questions. Only then, can you determine if what you have to offer would benefit your client. If they are looking for a product or service like yours, you will only find out if you ask the right questions. Or if neither of you knows if they could use your product or service, the only way to find out is if you get them to tell you what they need help with. Then…and here is the hard part…*listen* to their responses.

When someone feels as though another is asking questions and actively listening to the responses, they open up. Only when they open up, does their guard come down and allow you to see how you might meet their needs. Not unlike dating. It is a lot of give and take. Sharing of information and gradually opening up to another. When you are comfortable, the red flags are lowered, and there is the ability to move to the next level.

So the next time you are in front of a prospect, do not forget that the most important thing you can do is listen. Once they feel they have been heard, they will never feel like they have been "sold". That is the first step toward building trust. And when you have that, you have the foundation of any great relationship!

Dating and Sales...
More Similar than You Think

Remember when you were dating, and you went out with someone for the first time? For the sake of this discussion, let's say you are female (though the same principle applies to males). You really felt when you first met this particular gentleman that he was charming, romantic, he seemed to love kids...you know, he was different from other guys.

Then you went out on that first date. He took you to a nice dinner at a beautiful restaurant. After you ordered the meal, he started the conversation, which sounded something like this:

"You know, I am really glad we had an opportunity to get together. I am so busy with my career that I do not really date a lot. It is a shame because I am really a romantic person and would love to share that side of me more often. I can not wait until the day when I can settle down and have a family. I would love to have kids and spend all my time with them. I really want to be a great dad..."

At this point in the date, if you had half a brain in your head, you were ready to bail. Why? These are all the things you wanted in someone, right? Right. But this guy was probably none of them. Yes, he did tell you he was all these things and more…but you did not believe it, did you? Why not?

Because when someone tells you how wonderful he is, especially right up front, you do not believe it, do you? (Of course not!) Besides, if these things *were* true, he would not *say* them. He would *demonstrate* them. And a wonderful way to do that is to ask about you. He should have found out what you like, got you to talk, and stopped telling you about himself.

Selling works the same way. Until we start selling to robots, we are dealing with humans. Human nature is the same, whether it is personal or business. People often make decisions and assumptions from the things we *do not* say, rather than from the things we do.

Am I suggesting you just sit there without talking? Actually, yes…at least at the beginning, when you need to ask and not tell. No one believes how wonderful and terrific you and your product are until they trust you and your word. You have to build credibility. And credibility is not something you establish by telling someone how great you are or how great your company is.

Most of you are saying right now, "But, Greta, I do not do that." Really? Let me demonstrate.

"So John, why should we go with your product when we have been using ABC's product for so long and it has worked fine?"

"Well, Mr. Jones, one of the reasons we stand out is the blah blah blah, and we also have superior customer service and blah blah blah…" Sound familiar? So many of you do this. This is exactly what I am talking about. But that is not how you gain credibility. You gain credibility by *listening*. So shut up and listen! Ask some good, solid questions and listen to the answers. Listen for some things that you may be able to help with; then, when it is your turn, use the answers your prospect gave after your questions to persuade him that your company's product or service is the best answer to his situation.

Let's go back to our dating example. What if you went out with this same guy we were using in our example but, after dinner, he asked you a few questions:

"So, you said you are an attorney. Do you enjoy practicing law? How long have you lived here? Do you have family here? Yes, mine is up north, too. I love it here, but I do miss them sometimes. How about you? I hope to have my own family some day."

You say, "Really? Do you think you will be a good dad?"

"I do not know, but I hope so."

Sound better? Yes, of course. Did you learn something? Sure did. Do you want to learn more? Ask and listen; do not tell. This is true both on a date and in a sales call. Remember, it is just about people. Relax, learn, ask...and stop selling!

Ask, Don't Tell

"I have to tell you, I hate dealing with salespeople," said the prospect we called on.

"Wow, someone must have really gotten you upset for you to say that! What in the world happened?" was my response.

"Oh, you know…the usual: coming into my office and telling me why I should buy what they have without even understanding what I need."

"So they do not know what you need…. How do you know?" I asked.

"Well, they proceeded to tell me that other companies like ours have used their product, and it has really helped them. I do not even know another company like ours."

I hear more of these types of stories, and it really gives salespeople a bad name. So here is what a salesperson's mantra should be, "Ask. Do not tell." Ask the prospect about his needs, his situation. Do not tell him what he needs if you do not really know.

No matter how much experience you have in sales and/or the industry you are in, if you tell a prospect that you know your product or service will help him, *before* asking him what his issues are, you are in deep trouble. You may think all your prospects/clients are alike but if you hint at that idea, he will tell you otherwise. "My daddy started this company, and we pride ourselves on… (fill in the blank)."

If you *try* to tell them that you know their issues without asking, you are dead, dead in the water, and rightfully so. How dare we believe that we know the issues of an organization just because we work with others *like* them—in the same business, in the same geographic area, of the same size, or otherwise similar? And even if we really have succeeded in intuiting, or ferreting out, their situation, no one appreciates that kind of arrogance.

So what do we do? Ask! Ask about their issues, their problems. Ask about what is important to them, and ask how they have tried to solve this in the past. This will give you all of the information you need to solve their issue.

Their issue! It is no one else's, and if you assume that it is the same as someone else's, you have formed no customization at all. So stop it. Stop the assuming (because you know what happens when you assume), and stop telling them you know better. Remember this: No one cares what you know, only what you know about *him and his issues*. You must ask about these and then find the appropriate solution…for this particular client or prospect. That is what he wants.

So always ask first. Ask about this client's issues, this customer's situation, this prospect's needs, this company's wants. Ask first. And, only then, after he's answered your questions, you can finally tell. Tell him of the solution you have for him with your company's products or services. Because now, finally, he will be receptively listening.

Listen, Listen, and Listen

It is amazing how many people have absolutely no idea how to listen.

Hearing is totally different from *listening* because lots of things can be heard without really paying attention. News flash: *Listening to* and *understanding* what people really mean are not the same as just hearing the words they say.

Let me say that again because it is really important. *Hearing* is simply taking notice of the words they say. *Listening* is uncovering what people mean. Words are not what you should be paying attention to, because the meaning behind them is much more important.

We all know what that means. When your spouse asks, "What is wrong?" and you say, "Nothing," you know that is not true. You are saying words that really have a hidden meaning.

When someone makes a statement or asks you a question, you need to understand what the person really means before you answer. Here is an example:

You are in the document-recovery business, and a prospect asks, "Do you work with ABC Documents?"

ABC is number one in the business. So you proudly answer, "Well, yes, we do. We have been successfully doing business with them for several years and have helped them tremendously in a couple of areas."

The answer from the prospect is, "Oh. Umm, ok." The prospect's real issue could be that he is afraid inside information could mistakenly be shared, and he would never consider working with anyone involved with ABC.

Of course, you will never know that from his words. You did not find out why the prospect asked the question. You just answered it, assuming he would be impressed with the answer.

The cost of not listening is huge. Contrary to popular belief, sales is all about listening—not talking.

I wish I could get people to understand how important it is to listen at the deepest level. Listening is how you get prospects to self-realize that they need what you have. The idea of asking them good questions and not *telling* them to buy is a difficult concept to get across.

Listening skills are the most valuable ones we have when it comes to learning what the market wants, what our people want, and what it takes to solve virtually any problem. The challenge is that we actually think we are listening when we are really only "surface listening."

Why do we do that? We want to make a great first impression, show how smart we are, list our attributes and successes, and tell 'em what we can do for them.

Not!

When we slow down to listen to what is really meant by the questions prospects ask and the statements they make, and truly connect with the thought, feeling, and person, then we learn what is really going on inside the client or business. And "inside" is where the decisions are really made.

So, how do we listen? Listening is a participatory sport. So we need to follow these rules:

- First rule of listening: Shut up.

That may sound extreme, but I need to get your attention. People want to be heard and valued. You can not hear them when you are speaking.

Do not let the pressures of time close your ears and stimulate your tongue. You do not have to prove anything. You know what you know. But you do not know what your prospect knows. That is the voice you want to hear.

- Second rule of listening: Listen. Okay, so that sounds obvious. But do you actually do it?

Typically, we listen for a clue or "buying signal" (whatever that is), and then we start to tell. For example, someone says, "Well, we have had trouble getting copies fast enough."

You instantly reply, "Oh, we can help with that. Our machine is fast and—blah, blah, blah."

Stop talking. You have a great opportunity to really understand what is going on with the prospect. Dig deeper. That is where the real issue is. You will miss it if you do not really listen and ask the prospect to elaborate.

- Third rule of listening: It is all about them.

Here is a challenge for you: Observe conversations you are participating in or that others are having. Notice how many are "me" conversations. People tell you something—for instance, about their vacation or their child. Many of us respond with something about our vacation or our child. Now, who is listening?

You know what you have to offer. So, the more airtime you give to "them"—your family, your staff, your clients—the more beneficial it will be to you. Rather than jump in with a response, just listen. It is not about you. It is all about them.

Listen. It is amazing what you will learn.

Do Not Show Up
and Throw Up

Sherry was just hired as an account executive for "Glossy Magazine, Inc." She was alone in the sales area, waiting for her manager to begin her training, when the phone rang at the desk where she was sitting. She answered it.

"Glossy Magazine…can I help you?"

"Yes. I would like to speak to you about advertising."

Sherry asked the woman's name and then politely asked if she would hold a moment. She looked around the sales bullpen, but there was no one to be found. Her manager was on the phone behind closed doors, and Sherry did not know what to do. She got back on the phone to let the woman know someone would call her back, to which the woman replied that she only had a few questions.

Before Sherry could respond, out came the questions. Sherry, in fear, asked a few questions as well but really had no idea about anything she was talking about. "What is your product?" "What are you looking to achieve?" "Is this a new product?" "What have you been doing to advertise?" and "How did that work?" She kept the woman on the phone as long as possible with this series of questions.

Finally Sherry said, "I feel like I have a pretty good idea of what you are looking for. Let me put together some thoughts and call you later this afternoon. Will you be available around four o'clock? We can take thirty minutes or so to discuss some ideas my manager and I might have for you, once I give her this information. How does that sound?" The woman agreed, and Sherry was off the phone…and off the hook!

When Sherry's manager got off the phone, Sherry told her what happened. She mentioned that the prospect was a residential decorator, but before Sherry could tell her manager the rest, the manager told Sherry to call back immediately. The prospect needed to be informed, per the manager's request, that *Glossy Magazine* has been in business for seventeen years, and was the number-one decorating and design magazine in town, specializing in residential and upscale homes.

The manager wanted to make sure the prospect knew that the magazine was more than qualified to help with any of her needs. "Here is the media kit we market with. Tell her you will send it right out," the manager said. "Better yet, tell her you and I will go out there and present it to her."

Gee, if I were the prospect, I would just be jumping up and down, waiting for that visit! Wouldn't you?

Of course not.

Sherry was good enough to ask the right questions, even if she did not know what she was doing. But her manager was about to ruin it by doing the old "show up and throw up" routine.

No one wants to be *sold to*. Now, do not misunderstand that to mean no one wants to *buy*. Oh no…we *love* to buy! We just hate someone *selling* to us. We want it to feel like it was *our* decision.

Remember, when in doubt, ask a question. It will allow your prospect to talk, give you additional information, and give you some time to think. It will help you formulate a strategy for how to most effectively persuade the prospect to say yes. And it will give your prospect a chance to sell herself on signing with you.

Telling is not selling; *asking* is.

Stop "Filling in the Blanks"

The prospect looked off into the distance and said to Steve, "I am just trying to think about the different ways I could use your product." She continued to stare into the distance, and the uncomfortable silence seemed to carry on for hours.

Steve hastily offered some ideas: "The majority of our clients use our product to reduce their operating costs." As Steve waited to see if that hint hit a nerve, he noticed the prospect appeared quite confused, so he quickly added, "I would love to give you some customer references so you have some insight on the product, if you would like."

"Well, I guess that would be nice," the prospect said.

"Fantastic," Steve said. "Any other questions?"

"Not that I can think of."

"Hey," Steve said, "as soon as I get back, I will send them, and you can call and see how much they like our product. Thanks for the opportunity."

Do not "help" the client with answers

Steve left. The prospect did not care whether Steve faxed over the client references. Actually, she knew from experience that salespeople rarely follow through.

So, what went wrong? Steve tried to "help" his prospect instead of having the self-control to allow the prospect to make her own decisions about why she needed the product.

In sales, that uncomfortable silence places the responsibility where it is needed: right on the prospect. Silence is golden—and filling the silence is the wrong thing to do. After you ask a question, be quiet and let the prospect answer. If the prospect is silent, she is probably thinking. Do not interrupt. Let her think. Silence is a good sign.

Most people in the sales industry have been taught their entire lives to answer questions. So when a prospect has difficulty finishing a statement, it is human nature to help her complete the thought. If we allowed the prospect to help herself, sales would roll in without effort.

Ask, do not answer

But why do we have the innate desire to help?

For the most part, it is because salespeople are unable to let a prospect struggle, thinking the sale will be lost. The salesperson believes that if he helps the prospect, he keeps the sale heading in the right direction. But in fact, this is a big, fat misconception.

We also feel like the prospect will be grateful for our help, and as a result, will trust us more.

So, how do you make it right? Next time you are with a prospect, ask her how she would use your product. Your job then is to wait. It will seem like forever, but nine times out of ten, the prospect will answer in ten seconds or less.

In fact, your prospect probably will be more uncomfortable than you because she is not anticipating the silence. After she answers, you can then dig a little deeper into the "how and why" using your product or service is best.

Prospects might sell themselves

Do not resort to saving each other. If the process is gone through properly, the prospect will sell herself.

Here is how Steve should have responded after his prospect said she was trying to think about how she could use the product: "Well, what are some of the thoughts that come to mind when you think about the product?"

The moral of the story: Your prospect does not need your help. She will help herself. When she comes to her own conclusions, she will feel better about them because they are hers. Remember, you are a salesperson, not a lifeguard...so act like what you are.

Telling Is Not Selling

Jim arrived early at the office of Bob Simmons, president of the Hilo Tool & Dye Co., so he could sit in the parking lot and review what he wanted to say. Jim practiced each step of his presentation in his head—exactly what he wanted to say and how he wanted to say it. He knew his Power Point slides were perfectly in order and were just what he needed to land this account. He knew what this company needed because of his experience with others like this one. Taking a deep breath, Jim walked into the building. "I have got this one down," he thought, and proceeded in the door.

Once the pleasantries were over, Jim got right down to business. "Mr. Simmons, I have been with my company for the past three years, and our company has been in business for over fifty years. We are the leader in our industry and have worked with many companies that have had the same needs as yours."

"Well, that is why I agreed to meet with you, Jim," stated Mr. Simmons. "We do have a need for a product like yours, and this might be a good fit."

"I am glad," Jim said proudly. "Our product line has the best reputation for fewest failures on the job, the result of which is that downtime is at the lowest in the industry, which will keep you up and running more efficiently."

"Great, Jim, but our service department is not sure if they can retrofit your model into our existing equipment," Mr. Simmons said.

"Oh, I would not worry about that. We do it all the time, and with companies that have bigger problems than yours. As a matter of fact, I have brought a Power Point presentation that I believe will help you understand why we are number one in the industry."

After the presentation, Mr. Simmons said, "Thanks for the presentation, Jim, but I am still a little concerned about our existing equipment and the retrofit we will need to do. We ca not afford any downtime with the change, or production could be compromised."

"Mr. Simmons, I understand the concern, but we do this all the time. Do not worry, we can handle it," Jim said.

Fifteen minutes later, Jim said goodbye to Mr. Simmons and promised him a proposal in a few days. After Jim left, Mr. Simmons buzzed his assistant and said, "When that proposal comes in, just 'round file' it."

What happened?

Jim ignored the real issue that Mr. Simmons wanted addressed and kept telling him what *he* felt was important. Guess what? No one cares what you think is important, only as it applies to them. Jim missed lots of opportunities to really deeply understand what his prospect's issues were and assure him that he could not only solve the problem, but help Mr. Simmons understand how.

The result? Jim may very well have the best product for Mr. Simmons, but Mr. Simmons did not see it that way. When a prospect gives you a hint of a need, address that need by asking really good, pointed questions. For example:

• Tell me more about the retrofit concern.

• Have you had that issue in the past in looking to change products?

• What did you do to address it at that time?

- How did it affect production and at what cost?

These types of questions would not only have given Jim a real insight to the issue, it would have also given Mr. Simmons confidence that Jim knew and could address *his* issue.

Sell Naked

Introduction by Steve Gordon, President, Globalmind

I am not a sales person. I hate sales. I will do anything else to avoid sales.

I have got a technical background and built a successful career on solving big, complicated technical problems for my clients. But I always hated the "sales process."

By traditional standards, we did a good job with our sales efforts. We had beautiful brochures and case studies printed. We carried them into our client presentations. We dutifully presented them to the clients.

But, the clients did not care. You see, those "things" did not care about them. So the clients felt no obligation to care in return. But I wanted my clients to care about me; to care about doing business with me so much that the competition was irrelevant.

I still hated sales...until I learned to "get naked."

Getting naked--stripping away all of the brochures and case studies and "we are great because" pitches--has freed me to turn sales into the thing I love to do, the thing I am best at--consult.

I no longer "pitch" my company to prospects. With pen and pad in hand, I ask questions and listen. In fact I will not answer a question now, until I have probed to discover the real want or worry that created the question.

I care enough to probe and listen and understand the person sitting across from me. My sales "stuff" could not do that. It could not listen. It could not understand. It just got in the way.

Selling naked is about discovering your client's true need--the one they themselves may not yet understand. When you find it using these techniques, it is magic. The human being sitting across from you is understood and knows it.

You become a trusted partner in search of a solution to your client's problem. You are not selling! You are solving...and that has real value. That is the magic.

Selling naked is a human approach to selling. Not a one-size, one-sales-pitch, fits all approach. It has helped us focus on the client as a human being and in the process it has transformed our sales effectiveness.

When you think about it, these techniques are not new. They are as old as mankind. At some point, I think we, as business people, forgot that we are selling to other people.

Learn the "Sell Naked" approach and you will sell more. You will sell more easily and you will feel good about it.

If I can do it...I know you can.

Sell Naked

You know who they are; you can see them a mile away. They walk into your office with a big smile and an even bigger briefcase, overflowing with brochures, color charts, samples, and price lists. And they sound like this: "Mr./Ms. Jones (Smith, Brown, White, Green, Schnickelfritz), I am Jim from the Convenient Copier Company, and since your equipment lease has almost expired on your copier, I have come to demonstrate our latest and greatest new Zippy Fast Copier. Based on your copier usage, the latest model Zippy is going to be perfect for you." (Out comes the fancy brochure.) "It slices and dices as well as copies…blah, blah, blah."

You tell him that you do not make as many copies now because of emailing.

"You don't? Then this Zippy Junior is great for you. It has six hundred and seventy five jigawatts of power, and see right here… the little button on the side? That will help the paper re-adjust if it goes offline. If you look, you can see the holding tray is larger, even though the copier is smaller…"

"Does it have a warranty?"

"Yes!" (Said very enthusiastically.) "Here is a copy of it."

Now you are buried in junk…but what did he really tell you? Nothing.

For all the salespeople out there who do this (and yes, that includes you too, even if you think you don't), take my advice: Sell naked!! That is right, sell *naked*!

What does that mean, "naked"? "Naked," in this case, means stripped of everything—no brochures, no samples, no demos, no pricing sheets, and no testimonials. *But why??* You ask. Good question…and I have an awfully good answer: Because selling does not happen by *showing*; it happens by *asking*. Asking the right questions. And more than that when someone asks you, as a salesperson, if you have this type of doohickey or if it does this type of thing, if you go in with nothing, it forces you to find out why they are asking. This helps you discover what issue they are *really* trying to solve, instead of showing them something *you* think they want.

"But Greta," you ask, "why can I not just bring these things in with me and not pull them out?" Great plan, but it does not work. You are so excited to show them what you have, you will reach in there too fast. If you have nothing with you, you must ask the good questions and really learn what they need and why. *That* is selling.

Can you keep it in your car? Absolutely…and only when you have gathered all the information you need, and you are confident, and you understand why and how much they are willing to spend, *then* and *only then* can you go get it.

Getting to the real issue is the point here, and getting commitments after you demonstrate the benefits of the product, is what you need to achieve to close the sale and not just get a think-it-over. So if you are getting put-offs now, doing it the way you are doing it, just try this. Make sure you go in prepared with good questions, to really help you discover what is best for them and why.

You may not like this radical approach, but if you are getting stalls and put-offs now, I ask you the question I am well known for asking: How is that workin' for ya?

Take Notes, Not Brochures

You know the feeling: You are firing on all cylinders. Mr. Big has called you for an appointment, and you are sitting in the parking lot ten minutes early, reviewing your Power Point presentation one last time. You are confident and prepared.

You stride into his office with your computer in your briefcase and your brochures tucked under your arm. Introducing yourself, you tell him you are ready to make your presentation. Mr. Big listens attentively—at least, at first. You finish quickly, look him straight in the eye, and ask if he has any questions.

Yes, he says—he is concerned your product is not strong enough to handle the volume of work in his office and will break down.

No problem, you say, brushing off his concerns. You have worked with much larger companies than his and never had a breakdown. OK, maybe once or twice—but the service department is great and responds in a timely manner. As a matter of fact, here is a letter of satisfaction from a happy client.

He asks one more question about the product warranty, and you quickly whip out the brochure that explains it in detail. Mr. Big seems to accept your explanation and says you can send him a proposal.

You are nearly whistling as you leave his office, sure of your next sale. You do not even hear him tell his assistant that he will not need to see your proposal. He will not be buying from you.

What went wrong? You were so well-prepared.

Honestly, you would have been better off selling naked.

Keep your shirt on (literally). But on your first sales call, all you should bring is your keen interest in your potential client. No brochures. No Power Point. Taking notes is about all you should do.

Why? Because what you really want is to establish rapport and have an interesting conversation to learn about the prospect. Learning is listening, not showing.

For those of us who are used to having props, selling naked can be a scary experience. It seems so much easier to show our fancy brochures and well-prepared paraphernalia. But think about how you like to buy, and from whom. The person who can look you in the eye, listen, and carry on a conversation, demonstrating an understanding of what you need is the one who will get your business.

But that will come with the next call. Or maybe even the next. However, when you, the prospect, leave the office, you will know where you stand, because your last question will be: "What is our next step?"

Pre-Qualify Every Meeting

Ben was twenty-five minutes into a scheduled one-hour meeting with Janice, and he could not wait to leave.

He had been polite during the meeting, allowing her to vent about being overworked and underpaid. But the last thing he remembered contributing to the conversation was saying, "Nice to see you, Janice," twenty-five minutes earlier. Ben could not help but let his mind wander as Janice delivered her monologue.

When they had been introduced to each other at a board dinner the previous week, Ben thought Janice fit his perfect client model. From what he understood from their brief conversation at the dinner, she made all the office-supply decisions for Mr. Printing, a company that had been on his top ten list for months. But when Ben's questions at their meeting were met with a confused stare, he knew he had assumed wrong. He thought about the torture he could have avoided if only he had asked a few questions over the phone before setting the appointment.

Ben's dilemma is common in the great wide world of sales. We are taught to go for the appointment. I hear salespeople tell me their managers measure them on the number of appointments they make, not on the quality of those appointments. But what is it we really should strive for...quantity or quality?

That is where the pre-qualification call comes into play. The pre-qualify phone call is made to prospects to determine whether they truly are potential customers before setting an appointment.

It is such a significant step in the sales process, but it often gets overlooked. Before you say, "I do not need to pre-qualify my prospects," and "I can sell them if I can just get in front of them," take a look at the benefits of the pre-qualify phone call:

• You waste less time.

• You have fewer cancellations.

• You are able to come prepared.

Here are some important factors in the pre-qualify phone call:

1. Set some ground rules for the appointment. It is important to make sure you and the prospect are on the same page and understand how the appointment will be a good use of time for both of you.

2. Ask a few specific questions, such as "What are you doing to address this issue now?" or "What are you finding is the biggest challenge when it comes to ...?"

3. If it seems the person is truly a potential customer, then mention that you think the two of you should meet. Set a time and date. And follow up with an e-mail summarizing your pre-qualify conversation and the purpose of the in-person meeting.

If it does not appear the prospect is a good candidate for you, do not force it. If you do, you will waste your time with little fish when the catch of the day could be right around the corner.

Practice Makes...
Well, Less Frustration

Well, this weekend was it. All the fear, all the years of anticipation, all the extra cost we will now incur...and the bumps and bruises, as well. It is here—my teenage son has begun driving!

He proudly walked into our bedroom on Saturday night with the torn paperwork he had pulled out of the printer, with the word "passed" on the top of the page. It was his permit. I wanted to show him how proud I was, though all the while I was sweating from anxiety. Sunday morning, my short trip to the grocery store was driven with white knuckles...mine...as a passenger in my own car.

If you talked to my son, he would tell you that he knew how to drive already. He had read the permit book in less than two hours and passed with flying colors. "Mom, I have seen you drive a million times. Anyone can do it. No problem!"

I asked him to park waaaaay down at the end of the parking lot and pull into a parking space (or in the middle of two). I told him to slow down, since there was really no need to even touch the gas. "Just touch the brake and ease into the space," I said. Just then we sped up and over the little cement stop that is meant, of course, to stop the car from going too far. *Boom*, we were up and over the cement stop, on top of the grass, and into a metal shopping cart.

Why do I tell you this story? To have you feel sorry for me, maybe; to have you pray for me, definitely; but the real reason is to understand that learning a skill is not done by watching others or reading a "how-to" book. Learning something new is all about practice.

Most people in sales, or in any aspect of business, have reluctantly come to the realization that doing the same thing again and expecting different results is insanity. Somewhere along the way, we have made the decision that doing it differently is probably the best course of action. Now, that being said, it does not mean it is the *easiest* course of action, especially for us folks who have been out there doing it the same way for, say, more than a couple of years. (It is not like you do not have an idea of how old I am—I just admitted to having a sixteen-year-old son.).

Learning a new skill, or changing an old habit, is not easy for most folks. It is human nature to want it quick and fast. "Tell me what to do and I will do it." You say. Ahhh, but you won't. Or at least, you will not do it well. Not at first, anyway. Set yourself small goals with timelines attached. Learn the new steps of your approach, one piece at a time. Do not move to the next until you feel completely comfortable with the one you are presently learning. Always pat yourself on the back when achieving each step along the way.

Have patience when learning a new skill, and if you are a manager, have patience *teaching* a new skill as well. Remember, if you get frustrated, at least *your* end result will not be to "crash and burn"…I hope!

Product or Service?

Is it easier to sell a product or a service?

"It is easier to sell a product because you have something you can actually show the prospect."

"Oh no, it is much easier to sell a service because you can really sell them on the features and benefits!"

Guess what—you are both wrong! You are never selling a product *or* a service—you are selling what the product or service *can do for your prospect.* The solution your customer perceives is the answer to the problem he is experiencing—that is the only one that matters. What your product or service does is irrelevant, until the prospect tells you what actually is relevant.

We have a friend named Rich. Rich and I had a discussion one night at dinner on this very subject. Rich told me he could "never" (and I love that word) sell a service because a product is so much easier.

"Why is that?" I asked.

"It is just easier to compare when you have something in your hands. You can show your products' 'features and benefits', [another of my favorite terms] and really compare apples to apples against your competitor," Rich stated proudly.

"Rich, how do you know what 'apples' they want in the first place? What if they want oranges?"

"Oh, I ask them upfront what their needs are, and then I show the differences."

"I am confused…why can you not do that with a service?"

"Well, Greta, I guess you can, but it is easier with a product."

"OK, Rich, I got it," I said, even though I did not, but at this point my husband was kicking me under the table to leave it alone.

In sales, you are a matchmaker of sorts. Your job is to uncover as much as you can about the prospect's issues as they see them and the effect these issues are having on them and their company. Once you have a good understanding of all this, you will recommend the proper solution, irrespective of whether you are dealing with a product or service.

Often salespeople misunderstand the word "benefits" for solutions. Features-and-benefits selling is typically a pre-set dissertation of what the prospect *should* see as a benefit, not what *they* decide is a benefit. For example, suppose you say, "The feature of this copy machine is the speed of the copies, and the benefit is that you can get them faster and have your copies ready earlier." Well, if your prospect does not have an issue with time, and her issue is something completely different like ease of use, will she really care about your so-called benefit?

If you are selling properly, it should not matter whether it is a product or a service because what you are really selling is what the client is ultimately looking for, not how you get there.

Anyone can demo a product or talk "features and benefits," but a real pro gives solutions only to the issues the prospect is having, no more and no less.

Through Our Own Rose-Colored Glasses

Introduction by Jeannine Rizzo, President, The Inside Edge

We have often heard that our experiences in life are dictated by our thought process ... more commonly referred to as our perception. And you know what, that statement is absolutely correct. Everyday in addition to the conversations we have with other people, we engage in high levels of inner dialog or inner chatter with ourselves. I am referring to the times when we are not focused on one particular activity and our mind starts to wander. Where our mind is wandering is important for us to pay attention to. Are we thinking about what is wrong or are we thinking about what is possible? Here lies the factor which will determine our outcomes. Let me caution you though, I have come to realize that there are many people in the world that "think" they are positive and they are actually very negative. How do you know which one you are? Simple. Pay attention to two things ... the inner chatter taking place when your mind wanders and the external conversations you engage in.

Inner Chatter

Are you thinking about what happened yesterday? What might happen tomorrow or the next day? What you did wrong? What did you not do? What you should be doing? What someone else did or did not do? When this happens, it is critical that we take note of who is actually speaking ... our "inner coach" or our "inner critic"? Our inner critic is very harsh. That is the voice that is continually passing judgments on our behavior or the behavior of others. Conversely, our inner coach is supportive and encouraging. Both voices influence our perspective. When our inner coach is speaking we are thinking about innovative and creative ways to achieve our outcomes. Regardless of what is happening or what we are told by others, our inner coach helps us to maintain focus on our outcome like a guided missile and works tirelessly to provide solutions to get there. Our inner critic does just the opposite. Driven by fear our inner critic paints the picture of the horrifying scenarios that "might" take place, virtually paralyzing us from taking action. In essence it becomes a wall separating us from everything that we want and what we are capable of.

External Conversations

Are you complaining about a problem or talking about a solution? Are you talking in terms of what you need to do, what you should do, what is not happening, what you did wrong or what someone else is not doing? If so, I am sorry to inform you, you are not as positive as you think you are. In fact, if this is the process of your thoughts on a regular basis, you are operating from a negative mindset rather than a positive mindset. Let me give you an example. Let's say you are a team leader and one of your team members is always late. Are you addressing the issue with your team member? If the answer is yes and you are having a conversation and talking in terms of "lateness", in other words you are telling your team member they cannot be late, that lateness is a problem, then you are in a negative mindset. You may think you are being positive because you are addressing the problem and holding someone accountable, but you are not. You are actually reinforcing a behavior you prefer to move away from. Instead try this, change your perspective and your focus from what is wrong to what is right and talk in terms of "being on time". Now you are being positive because you are talking in terms of a desired outcome.

Analyzing every thought we have can be a grueling process because the average person has over sixty thousand thoughts each day. An easier way to determine whether or not we're actually thinking positive instead of negative is to pay attention to how we are feeling. What are we feeling as a result of the thoughts we are thinking? The instant we recognize that we are feeling negative; we have got to change our perspective. You see, our emotions are like a GPS system in a car. They tell us two things ... one, the direction we are moving (positive thoughts mean we're moving forward and negative thoughts mean we are moving away from our intended outcome) and two, the speed at which we are moving. It is important to note here that speed has two variations ... intensity and frequency. Intensity refers to high/intense levels of emotional engagement such as passion, energy, enthusiasm – all positive emotions which mean we are moving quickly toward our intended outcome; all negative emotions, including worry, fear, frustration, and insecurity mean we are moving quickly away from our intended outcome). Frequency is somewhat different; those are the repetitive thoughts that have a tendency to weigh on our mind. They do not necessarily have the same intensity but the fact they are recurring indicates that we are moving quickly in the direction that we are thinking. For example, if we are worried about an upcoming appointment and we are afraid that we will not close the deal because we are inexperienced or the person holds a high level position, causing us to feel inferior to them, and we continue to think these thoughts over and over again, we are almost insuring the outcome we fear the most ... a lost deal.

Do yourself a favor, pay attention to the thoughts and emotions you are experiencing because they are our compass. They are always pointing us in the direction we are moving. Keep them focused on the outcomes you desire and write your ticket because you will be on track to achieve all your outcomes.

Our Own
Rose-Colored Glasses

There is a glass sitting on a table, and it has water in it that reaches halfway up the glass. Is the glass half full or half empty?

Actually, both are accurate, it depends on your view. And talk about "views"…the old saying that "Some see the glass as half full, and some see it as half empty" is a terrific illustration of seeing things through your own filter. Most views of life are merely subjective. Suppose you are a sales manager, and you hear one of your salespeople say, "I had a great meeting, and this guy is very interested. I feel like it is ninety five percent closed." You analyze the account yourself and realize it really was not qualified properly, your sales rep did not discuss the dollars it would take to get the job done, and most importantly, the fellow he spoke with is not the ultimate decision-maker. You would put a fifty/fifty chance on this at best.

How did you and your salesperson come to two such different conclusions about the meeting?

Well, the salesperson bonded with the prospect. They talked baseball for twenty-five minutes of the meeting, and laughed about their toddlers' curiosity in the team. This convinced your salesperson that he won the prospect over, and he would buy.

On the other hand, you feel that, since the proper questions were not asked and the proper presentation was not done, the proposal is bound for either failure or luck—and it would be strictly luck—but has a fifty/fifty chance of either.

Which of you is right? Which of you is wrong? No one really knows, which makes forecasting pretty difficult and illustrates the point that we see things through our own "filters." These filters, just like ones on sunglasses, can make the world appear darker, rosier, or bluer. Most often, two people will not see the same occurrence at all.

Why do you and your salesperson see this sales call so differently? It is mostly because of those filtering glasses. The sales guy sees the bonding as a huge buying sign, because that is what he looks for when he buys. You, the sales manager, see the technique of the call, which was flawed, and without the proper steps. You feel it can not work unless luck steps in and lends a hand. And since you do not believe in luck, only in fact and process, you have a very skeptical view of the outlook for this particular prospect signing a contract. You believe that all of the "T"s need to be crossed and the "I"s dotted before the prospect will buy.

So who is correct? While time alone will tell whether this particular prospect will sign or not, the larger truth is that there is not always a right or wrong answer to how you view situations. Everyone sees things very differently. How important is that to know? Well, let's take this from a few angles. First, that of a sales manager. Do you see how an enthusiastic salesperson can paint a picture so rosy that they have it practically booked and it is not even close?

Or take it from the point of view of a salesperson. A sales rep may call on a quiet, thoughtful prospect and conclude that this prospect does not like her because he does not become gregarious and friendly during the pitch. In reality, it is simply that she is calling on a reserved, studious, deep-thinker type. He was merely going through the questions he felt were important, sticking to business, and mentally reviewing her answers instead of reacting to them verbally. Actually he had all intentions of buying the product, but the filter she sees through is, "He did not talk to me…that means he does not like me," which to her, means no sale.

Sometimes we see through other people's filters. As salespersons, we do this most often in the presentation stage. Rather than giving all of the "features and benefits" of the product as we see them, we give them as someone in corporate decided we *should* see them. We are not even being true to our own vision.

This reminds me of a car sales encounter I had years ago. I was looking for an SUV. After looking at several vehicles of the "This car reminds me of something that totes a small village" type, I looked at a smaller version. I began telling this salesman a little about my situation. He obviously had some training because he did ask me a few questions. "Is anyone in your family tall?" was one of them.

"No, no one is tall" I answered with curiosity while walking toward the car. I got in the car to drive, and he proudly started telling me about the twelve extra inches of headroom that this car had as opposed to the other I had been looking at. He had asked me the question but did not truly listen to the answer because someone in Marketing obviously felt this was an important feature. My response to his question made it plain that, to me, this feature would not be particularly important at all.

It is best if we can see a situation as clearly as possible…with a minimum of filtering, whether rosy, gloomy, or simply distorted. But note that I said "as clearly as possible." I recognize that seeing things completely unfiltered is a near-impossibility. Still, for the most accurate assessment of your chances with a prospect, your most accurate assessment of what the prospect you are facing wants (in the case of my SUV, headroom was clearly not one of my issues and there was no need for it to have been mentioned), and your most accurate assessment of the best tack to take in any sales situation, try to remove the filters as much as possible and see the situation as clearly, as plainly, as true-to-just-the-facts as you possibly can.

It will help you to react more appropriately to what is going on, deal more appropriately with the client, and assess the encounter more accurately after the fact.

Is the glass half full or half empty? Both. It is all in your viewpoint. Try to make *your* viewpoint as unfiltered as possible.

When Perception Becomes Reality

Value—everybody wants it. As a consumer, you want value for your money. And your prospects as well as existing clients want value, too, when they are making decisions about whether to purchase, what to purchase, and whom to purchase from.

To be clear, let's take a minute to define "value." *Webster's New World Dictionary* gives these definitions: 1) A fair or proper equivalent in money, commodities, etc. for something sold or exchanged; fair price. 2) The worth of a thing in money or goods at a certain time; market price. 3) Estimated or appraised worth or price; valuation. 4) That quality of a thing according to which it is thought of as being more or less desirable, useful, estimable, important, etc.; worth or the degree of worth.

Surely we all understand these meanings. But how you utilize the concept of value when talking to a client or prospect may make or break your presentation. Her perception of your product's value may be as important as (or more so than!) its actual value.

Take the word "fair" in definition 1. What does a fair price, a fair equivalent, mean to you…and to your prospect? (Strong hint here: It may well not mean the same thing to both.) The price (fair or otherwise) is, in most cases, set by the seller. (Even when there is dickering or bargaining, the starting point is normally a price established by the seller.)

Much of the buyer's perception of fairness may rest with his or her need to buy the product or service you are representing. The buyer with a great need for your product will be, on the average, a lot quicker to agree that your price (if it is not totally outrageous) is fair. The buyer with a minimal need is, on the other hand, less likely to agree your price is fair. She may well try to bargain you down or simply say, "No."

This puts pressure on you, the salesperson. If you are feeling pressured by the fear of failure, by the stress of trying to find the right prospect for your product, or by the need to meet a sales quota, you are not going to do well at all. Pressure is not conducive to making sales. Working under gotta-do-it pressure is a near-guaranteed path to failure. Not only will you not be at your best performance level, but the prospect will see, or sense, that you are working under duress and will feel that you are pushing too hard.

You need to convey that you are interested in your prospect's needs, not your own. This helps instill the feeling of value in the prospect. If she feels that you are just there to make a sale or make quota, rather than to solve her needs, she will not feel that she is likely to get fair value for her money…even if the true value of your product is high indeed.

Worth—another word from the Webster's definition—is related to value and is another concept that is subject to perception. What is silk worth to a manufacturer of fine dresses? What is it worth to a manufacturer of children's toys? The same product has a different worth according to the circumstances—the customer and his or her needs. The cost of the silk and the quality of the silk does not change…but the worth of it does, according to the customer's need.

It is up to you, the salesperson, to uncover the prospect's needs and priorities before trying to sell her your product. If you know what her needs are, you will know how badly she needs your product—

how much it is worth to her—*and why*. Then you can decide how to approach the sale…or whether to pass her by and focus on a different prospect instead.

If she has little or no need for your product, you are wasting your time. And if she *does* need your product, make sure you know *why* she needs it, so you know what approach to take when you are meeting with her.

Quality is another word that pops up in Webster's definition. And it is a word that many salespeople stress. They hammer hard on the quality of their product or service, or the quality of the company or its reputation, or the quality of the service department that stands behind the product.

But be careful: By stressing that yours is the quality company, you are implying that the company your prospect may have dealt with previously is lacking. And now you are insulting your prospect as, once again, perception comes into play: the perception that the prospect is not smart enough to have dealt with the right people before.

What is the fair value of your product or service? What is its worth? How good is its quality? There is the reality…and then there is the perception. Sometimes selling the perception is just as important as selling the reality. Make sure your sales approach is one that lends the perception of quality…of fair value…of worth.

There is a great deal of value to perception!

Do Not Let Beliefs Block Your Thinking

I have a client company that has raised its prices every year it has been in business. Nothing so unusual about that. Most of the sales associates are relatively new—they have been on the job a year or so at the most—so for them, it is what it is.

But there is an associate working there, named Maureen, who has been there since day one. Maureen has seen increases year after year and always sweats it when the company announces the percent of increase for that year.

One recent year, when the CFO put out the figures—an astonishing seventeen percent increase, the highest the team had ever seen—the other associates took it in stride, but not Maureen. "There is no way anyone is going to pay that amount. When I started, we were charging less than half of that. Enough is enough. We need to be able to sell this, and no one will buy at this price!" Maureen declaimed.

The newer associates did not see it the same way Maureen did. It was just business to them. They discussed her concerns in the meeting, and the sales director seemed to get most of them comfortable with the new pricing…but not Maureen. He was not giving in to her, so she did a little internal politicking.

It was not intentional, but she vented her fears around the office sufficiently that the others were now doubting their comfort with the higher pricing. "What if she is right? The market *is* a little soft, and what if we can not sell enough to make quota?" one associate timidly questioned over lunch.

"And how much flexibility do we have to negotiate, if need be?" asked another.

A mountain had now been created out of a molehill. And why? Because someone decided her perception was reality. What is worse, she not only created her own reality, she created others' as well. So, let's see what happens when a prospect one of them is meeting with says, "Well, how much is it?" and they tell him.

If the prospect as much as hesitates, the sales rep will feel as though he is uncomfortable with the high cost and will probably open her mouth and say something like, "We have a little flexibility there, of course," when all that may have been really going on was that the prospect was thinking about where he was going to move money from to pay for it!

So why does this happen? Because we let our own beliefs infiltrate reality, and we see things through our own reality, not the prospect's. Let's put some of this into perspective.

For my female readers: I want you to think about the conversation you have had with your husband, boyfriend, significant other…you fill in the blank. You come home with a pair of Stuart Weitzmans (I know you women know what these are), and you tell your partner you bought them for one hundred and twenty five dollars! You are jumping for joy, knowing that is half of their usual price, and looking for a little high-five action from him.

But he says, "What, are you crazy? Why would you spend that on shoes?!" And you look at him like he has three heads. Does he not realize how great this deal is? Does he even know how much money you just saved him?

For my male readers: Do you remember the day your buddy called you with the news that he got a hold of two Super Bowl tickets on the fifty-yard line, and they were only six hundred dollars apiece? Your wife said, "Are you kidding? We could pay a car payment with that and have enough left over to have a party here for Super Bowl!"

Perception is merely that. Do not let yours get in the way of closing a sale.

Awareness

From talking to my friend and colleague Jeannine Rizzo, of "The Inside Edge," I have learned a lot about what is important in the world. I hope you can learn from this too. It will help you both in your career and in the rest of your life as well.

Every day we should be striving to be the very best we can be in all aspects of our lives: career, family, relationships, health/fitness, finances, community, education, and leisure. How often do you evaluate your progress in each of these areas? Which areas are most important to you? Why are they important? How far are you from being exactly where you want to be in the areas that are important to you? What needs to change in those areas for you to move closer to what you desire?

Throughout my career I have had the opportunity to work with many people, and I have found that most people have at least one area they thrive in, but typically it is at the expense of some or all of the other areas...or, at the very least, that is the excuse

For example, many people are successful in their career components, but their families suffer, their health suffers, their relationships suffer, and when questioned about it, all the "excuses"

come to the surface: not enough time, can not afford it, too tired...
You know what I am talking about. Even if you have not used these
excuses yourself, you have certainly heard them from other people.

I like to refer to this as "limited thinking." Many people buy into
the idea that for one area in their life to thrive, sacrifices must be
made in other areas. Think about it: Is that not what we have heard
throughout our lives, especially when we were kids? Pick one...do
you want "a" or do you want "b"? You can have only one.

Well, guess what—we can have it all...assuming you want it all,
that is. Not only is everything possible, but we are in complete control
of the process. So if this is true, why do you not have everything you
want? The truth is, it has to do with your thinking.

Developing an awareness of who you are, what makes you tick,
and what you are really striving for, as well as acknowledging that
you are responsible for your results, is a great place to start. The truth
is this: If you want to be at the top of your game in all aspects of
your life, you must understand that you are in control of it. You must
acknowledge this truth: All the results we experience in our lives are
a result of our own thinking...our results are a reflection of what we
believe.

Try this: Identify something you want in your life, and then
ask yourself why that is so important to you. What is your internal
motivation for achieving that result? Keep asking yourself "why?"
until you get to the core of who you are. This is so important! When
we think about this, we realize there is an internal desire driving us,
a "feeling" we are seeking that is so much more important than the
actual "thing" we originally thought we wanted.

Use your current results as your benchmark. What is on target;
what is not? What are you basing your interpretation on...what other
people say, or what is important to you? Is it an outside result or an
internal feeling? Assess yourself honestly and identify how you are
contributing to the situation. Instead of playing the "blame game,"
play the "ownership game."

Remember, you can not control what others think or do, but you
can control what *you* think and do. Identify your internal motivation,
and start doing what you need to do to move toward it. The key here
is knowing *why* you want something. Remember, the *thing* alone

will motivate you for only so long...it is the *feeling* you associate with, the end result you must focus on, when the going gets tough.

Wayne Dyer said, "When you change the things you look at, the things you look at change." Expand your level of awareness when it comes to yourself, and watch your results change.

Passion

"He plays with a lot of heart." "She is so enthusiastic about what she does." "Even when he is just talking about his hobby, you can hear the joy in his voice."

We have all heard or said something like one of the statements above. And what is it that makes the people we are talking about play sports, do their work, or pursue their hobbies with such zest? Passion. Passion is the highest form of human motivation. When you are passionate about what you are doing—whether it is work, recreation, or cooking dinner—you really throw yourself into the task at hand.

Passion brings focus and commitment. Passionate people are inspired and undistracted. They have *chosen* to do one thing well as opposed to doing several things with average capability and interest level. Having a passion for your work is a great guarantee of a higher rate of success in your endeavor. (Yes, there are other factors that can impact the outcome; but even then, if you have a burning passion for what you are doing, you are going to work harder to overcome those obstacles or impediments.)

The average person has trouble saying no. We would rather do something we are not passionate about, something not in our focus or our goals, than say no. So we take on a job we do not like, or agree to represent a product or service we do not feel passionately about… or, as a sales manager, we take on a new sales rep whom we do not feel has the requisite passion for the job or the product. We hire them only because we are short-handed and this gal or fellow has the right credentials.

Wrong! In the absence of passion, we are likely to do a half-hearted job or "phone it in," or at best do a merely adequate, competent job. But an adequate, competent job is not an inspired one and is never going to win awards, set records, or bring in notable sales for the company or commissions for us.

What, then, are we to do?

Let's begin at the beginning. Ideally, you are passionate about sales. You are someone who enjoys the thrill of the chase, the joy of identifying and tracking your quarry, the process of the hunt itself, and the flush of victory when you have brought down a big one (or even a small one). If this does not describe you, then to be blunt, you likely do not belong in sales at all.

Second, you should be passionate about the product or service you are representing. Notice that I did not say "the company." You might not love Top Management. You might even think your sales manager is unbearable and insufferable. You might feel the commission structure is thoroughly unfair. But, that said, hopefully you are still passionate about the product/service itself. If you truly believe in what you are selling, you will do a hell of a better job selling it. Your passion for what you are doing will elevate your sales ability, carry you through times when prospects turn you down one after the other and throw impossible objections in your face, and manifest itself in a palpable zeal for what you are selling.

And if you are a sales manager, you should be passionate about both the product/service *and* your sales staff.

Many of us have had the experience of representing a product/service we were not one hundred percent committed to. Pretty rough, was it not? We took the position out of necessity, most likely. We had mortgage payments to make, and that dream position just was not available. Or it was our first job, and without a glowing resume, we had to settle for what was out there.

But hopefully by now you are in a better position. You can pick and choose the company you represent (and, presumably, you are also in sales by choice, not by default or necessity), and you have chosen one whose product/service you are passionate about. When you get out there to call on prospects, you give it your all because you really care about what you are representing. You are passionate about your work, and that passion sets you aflame with a fire you communicate to your prospects.

Passion. It is the difference between doing a half-hearted or barely adequate job and one that is afire with zeal and enthusiasm that brings in great results.

It is also the difference between slogging through your job and loving it.

Are you passionate both about sales and about the product or service you are representing?

If not, you are either in the wrong line of work or working for the wrong company…and you know what you have to do.

Get Out of Your Comfort Zone

A story I recently heard explains why some salespeople—and, for that matter, businesspeople in general—fail while others are successful.

A mountain resort in the Swiss Alps caters to businesses that encourage their employees to hike up the mountain trails together. The goal is to build camaraderie and teach teamwork. It is about an eight-hour trek to the summit, but anyone with normal walking ability can reach the top.

Each morning, hikers gather at the base of the mountain for a pep talk before starting the climb. Usually, participants are so excited they can hardly wait to head up the slopes to celebrate their victory. They hike for hours before taking a break.

Comfort sometimes hinders progress

About halfway up the mountain is a quaint restaurant. About noon, weary hikers trudge into the restaurant, peel off their hiking gear, and plop down by the fireplace to have coffee or hot chocolate and eat their lunch. With the mountain as their backdrop, the hikers savor the warm, cozy, picturesque setting.

After they are full and comfortable, fewer than half the hikers choose to continue climbing to the top of the mountain. It is not because they are not able, and it is not because the climb is too difficult. They choose not to continue because they are satisfied with where they are. They lose their drive to excel, to explore new horizons, to experience vistas they would never previously imagined possible. They have tasted a bit of success and think, "This is good enough."

Progress not equal to success

We each have goals we want to reach—perhaps losing some weight or paying off our credit cards. At first, we are excited and we are fired up. But, over time, we get lazy and complacent. Maybe we see a little improvement, but then we get comfortable where we land. Where we are may not be a bad place, but we know it is not where we are supposed to be. We are not stretching ourselves. We are not pursuing the excellence that we have inside us.

Listen to two people who were enrolled in a self-improvement program:

"I am doing pretty well with my goal," one man said. "I used to smoke two packs of cigarettes a day, and now I smoke only one."

Another person said, "I used to be fifty pounds overweight, but I have lost ten pounds recently."

That is a good start, and it took some real effort to get where they are. But do not get comfortable. Do not be satisfied with a little improvement. Press on to do your best.

Do not be satisfied with improved sales

In sales, similar things happen. Maybe you have experienced a bit of success. Lately, however, you have been thinking that perhaps you have reached your limit. You are not stretching yourself. You do not believe you can reach the next level. You are satisfied with where you are.

You need to step out of your comfort zone. You have so much more in you. Keep pursuing and keep believing.

It does not take any more effort to believe and stay filled with drive than it takes to develop a negative and defeated attitude. I am amazed what people can achieve if they want to. So, go ahead—*want to*.

Satisfaction is the death of sales and business. Never be satisfied. Once you are, it's over.

Buying and Selling
Is an Even Trade

"Your product or service and their money are an even trade."

I have made this statement many times, but I am still not sure anyone really gets it.

Nick told me a story about getting lucky enough to finally land an appointment with the president of a food distribution firm. "Greta, I have been trying to get in front of this guy for months," he excitedly spat. I asked how it happened. Nick began, "Well, after months of trying to reach him, I called late one evening, and he answered the phone himself. We talked for a few minutes, and I asked for an appointment, and he said he guessed that would be okay. Amazing, huh?"

"Boy, you really got lucky all right, but Nick, don't forget how lucky *he'll* get in having an opportunity to see how your tools can help his distribution center make more money."

We are so excited when we get the possibility of a new prospect, we forget that, though we really want the money, what we are giving the prospect in exchange is just as valuable as the green stuff. Money is merely the currency a person is willing to give in exchange for your goods. Money, and goods (or a service) being exchanged….neither is of any more value than the other.

Why do we attach such high value in our minds to the green stuff? It is nothing but the tool we established years ago to make it easier to barter for the things we need and want. Yet, if you really truly believed that, would you stop acting like there is more value in what *they are* giving than what *you are* giving? *Your product or service is worth just as much as the client's money!*

The job of the professional salesperson is to understand the true needs of the prospect and then fit the need into the goods/services that best help solve their issues. The "not taking no for an answer" attitude does not seem to fit here, and neither does "the customer is always right." If we could truly "get" this, how much better would we be at the sales process?!

We would ask the right questions, tell the truth if the prospect wanted something that was not right for him or her, and since the prospect would be feeling like he was making his own decisions rather than you telling him your product/service is so great, he might be able to convince himself of his need for it.

Do not give the prospect more power than he should have. Remember, his money and your product/service is an even trade. If you do not believe this, you should not be there.

When you act like the green has more value than what you have to offer, it is blatantly obvious. And who wants to pay more money for something that even you, the salesperson, seems to perceive is less valuable than its price?

Pay It Forward

Introduction by Bob Burg. Author of *Endless Referrals* among others

It is safe to say that Networking is a term used by many, yet understood by far too few.

In its most basic sense - and in the context of business - networking may be defined as:

The cultivating of mutually beneficial, **give-and-take,** *win-win relationships.*

Notice the emphasis on the *give* part. When practiced correctly, with the needs, wants, and desires of the *other* person in mind, you will dramatically increase the number of qualified prospects and referral sources with whom you will have the opportunity to work.

Perhaps one of the most unnerving, if not scariest times in the life of a business person or sales professional is when they realize they have a lack of new, qualified prospects to call on. What can be worse than going into a presentation desperate for the sale because you have "no one else to talk to?" Let's face it; most people do not want to do business with people who *need* them too much. And, when they have that sense of desperation . . . it typically comes across as such!

If you are not consistently cultivating new, qualified prospects and referral sources, you will soon be effectively "out of business", denying many otherwise willing and even desirous people from utilizing your expertise and realizing the outstanding value they could have received from your exceptional product or service.

Networking correctly, on the other hand, will dramatically fill your sales and prospect funnel, and keep it continually filled and overflowing with new, A-list, highly-qualified prospects and referral sources. This makes your business a lot more fun, a lot less stressful and, certainly, a lot more profitable.

The basic premise - or what I call, The Golden Rule - of Networking, is that "All things being equal, people will do business with, and refer business to, those people they know, like and trust." Your goal is to develop these types of relationships on an ongoing, everyday basis, and in such a way that is both non-intimidating (to you as well as them) and effective.

Think about this: It is now commonly accepted wisdom that the typical person knows about two hundred and fifty people. Which means that every time you meet just one new person and cultivate a relationship where he or she "know, like, and trust" you, where they want to see you succeed and find new business, you have just increased your personal sphere of influence by a potential two hundred and fifty people every . . . single . . . time!

Networking correctly will allow you to cultivate relationships with the new people you meet; the result is that you will eventually present to and/or obtain referrals from those who are appropriate. And, some of those people will eventually be your *Personal Walking Ambassadors*, promoting you and your business to the world. Or, at least to *their* world. Wow, what a terrific way to leverage your time and energy.

Of course, in order to cultivate the relationship, first you must meet them. Fortunately, opportunities constantly arise to meet new people. At local business events, Church, Synagogue, Mosque, charity functions, social functions, your child's ballgame, PTA meetings, and a myriad of other places. And, whether or not these new people will ever personally become customers or clients, the chances are good they know other people who very well could. And, remember, each of them knows about two hundred and fifty other people.

Yes, you have "diamonds in your acres." It is up to you to "mine" them. But if what you have been calling "Networking" is not working for you - if you just are not getting the results you want – it is time for a new approach. And that is what you will learn in this chapter.

Prospecting Confidence

You know the guy—he walks into the room with a big smile, and everyone knows who he is. Before he goes for food or drink, he walks around, talking and listening. He attends several networking functions, knows everyone by name, and knows what is happening in everyone's life. He is the great "mover and shaker" of your business community.

We are all jealous of him. You can not deny it. But as we are running to the bar at the back of the room, reaching for a cup of courage, he is out building his business into an empire.

At the last networking function you attended, where were you? Were you in the middle of the room, working to create a name for yourself? Or were you going to one of the three B's: the buffet, the bar, or the bathroom?

If you are like many business professionals, you struggle with confidence—and that is really what this is all about. Mr. Webster defines confidence as "a feeling or consciousness of one's powers or of reliance on one's circumstances." In layman's terms, confidence is projecting a feeling of adequacy in public.

Confidence is key when it comes to approaching people we would like to meet and asking for things we deserve. Even though confidence may seem like something your older sister was born with—and that is why she got all the guys—it can be obtained with a little assistance. Here are a few very easy tactics to help you feel more confident in public.

Make the first move

When you are the one to approach other people, you have taken the pressure off them to find someone to talk to. If you are uneasy about what to say, just concentrate on walking up and introducing yourself. You need to act as if this is a party and you are the host. Please do not misunderstand me: It *is* a business function, but at one of our parties, are we not trying to make people more comfortable?

Use a "memory hook"

As you approach people and introduce yourself, follow up with a clever catchphrase to describe your business and what you do, a tactic adopted from BNI (Business Network International) that I have also suggested elsewhere in this book. For example, a web designer might say, "Hi, I am John Jones. I help you expose yourself," instead of saying "I design websites." If you say something that sticks out in the minds of your colleagues, you will be more likely to receive business from them. It also helps bring in the human factor, the thing we sometimes stuff underneath our three-piece suits.

Concentrate on the other guy

After you have introduced yourself and given a quick explanation of what you do—the operative word here is "quick"—ask a few questions to get the other person talking. Here are some I use:

- What do you do?
- How long have you been doing it?
- What do you like most about it?
- What is a good referral for you?

Take notes on the back of his or her business card to help you remember.

Do not forget to follow up

After the event, follow up with a short note. Handwritten is best. Make sure you do not send any sales material. This is not about selling the people you met; it is about building relationships. The business will come.

It is a self-fulfilling prophecy. When you appear confident, you have no professional boundaries. If you are confident, others will come to you because they are hoping that somehow it will rub off on them. Build strong relationships and listen to others. Believe me: Confidence will come...and so will business.

It Is Not Net-Sit,
It Is Not Net Eat...

Steve was a "good chamber member" by all accounts. He came to all the functions, socialized with people he knew, and always met the new members. He had been a member of the chamber for a number of years, so when the other members heard that he was not going to rejoin, they were baffled. "Steve, I hear you are not rejoining. What is up?"

"Well, I have met some good friends and gotten some referrals, but I feel like I should be getting more. I mean, I come to everything, I meet people, and I *always* tell them *all about what I do.*"

Does this sound familiar? Often when we join organizations, we think just being a member is enough. In Steve's case, he knew that he had to do more, and he did, which should have worked...right? Wrong!

The reason Steve focused on the referrals he was *getting* is that he did not understand this reality: Building business through referrals is about *giving* referrals, not *getting* them. Networking is a skill, and a skill is something we learn. You have to *learn* how to network well.

There is truly a system for getting more referrals, and poor Steve was just "winging it." Building relationships is the key to networking. The philosophy is "givers gain." When we learn how to give to others, we sell more business.

There certainly are some keys that will help you with this process. I have outlined a few.

1. How are you introducing yourself?

When you are at a networking function, you are competing with everyone else in the room to be remembered. How do you introduce yourself—"Hi, I am John, and I am a financial consultant"? The typical response will be, "Oh that is nice." (Interpretation: *I have no earthly idea of what that exactly means.*) It is important to help someone understand what you do *in relation to him or her*. Try "Hi, I am John. I teach people what to do to insure early retirement," or "I help people play more golf and travel more often." Sound different? Well, is that not the point?!

2. What questions are you asking *them*?

Though others seem interested in what we do, really they are most interested in how it relates to them. I can explain this best with a story.

About eight years ago, my mom was telling me about her new friend Nancy. "Oh Greta, you have to meet Nancy—she is terrific, she is wonderful…" That Christmas Eve, we went to my mom's house for a party. Walking in, I saw a woman I did not know. She had a big smile on her face and was coming toward me. I said, "You must be Nancy," and she replied, "And you must be Greta. I have heard so much about you. Your son is so well mannered. Do tell me how you have done so well!" she continued, "And your new home—I hear it is beautiful. Tell me about your decorating plans…"

After a lengthy discussion about my favorite subject (me), I walked into the kitchen and said," Oh, Mom, you are right. I met Nancy, and she is terrific!" It was much later that I realized I knew nothing about her, yet she had impressed me. Why? Hmmm, because she was talking about me, perhaps!?

3. Create a picture.

People see in pictures. Create a scenario in which they can see themselves. A chiropractor might say, "The next time you are playing golf, and the ball goes one way while your back goes another, that is when you call me."

4. Ask the big question.

The big question is one that will differentiate you for sure. Here it is: *"What would be a good referral for you?"* Simple. Yet it is all about them. It is the reason they have come. They will then ask about you and your business.

These are a few of the skills that will help you become a better networker. Remember, It is not net *eat*, it is not net *sit*, it is net*work*.

Six Degrees of Separation

(Or Using Your Chamber of Commerce Effectively)

You have heard the expression "six degrees of separation." It refers to knowing someone who knows someone who knows someone who knows someone. The point is, everyone is within six steps of knowing any other person.

I do not know about you, but I would bet dollars to doughnuts (another often-used expression, this one meaning that I am so sure of myself that I will bet dollars and you have to put up only donuts for your bet) that in many communities, there are only perhaps two degrees of separation. It seems that everyone knows everyone. Once you meet someone, you can bet someone else you know already knows that person.

With this knowledge, I am always amazed when I am in a seminar and I ask for challenges. Why? Because someone inevitably says, "My challenge is that I can not get by the gatekeeper." And before I even get to address this issue, someone else always has an answer such as, "Tell them you want to talk to John, and if they ask what it is in reference to, tell them you are a personal friend."

Are you kidding me?! Deceit certainly is not my idea of the way to go. I do not think tricking someone to get on the phone with you is a long-term plan to help your prospecting.

Then what is? Using your networking sources…that is what. Networking is a very successful way to do business. Now, I am not saying that you should not cold call. There are certain industries in which it is inevitable, and certainly at the beginning of most careers it is necessary to build a database of potential customers. What I *am* saying is that you should work yourself out of the cold call business over time.

How do you do that? Through a process of networking. Networking is something most businesspeople do, yet few do well. This is what typically happens: You get a notice from your chamber of commerce that there is going to be an after-hours networking event. You call the chamber and RSVP; Thursday evening comes. You leave work, get in your car, and head to the event.

Your car desperately wants to head home, but no, you are committed to going to the event. You pull up to the front, park your car, and take a deep breath. You reach the front door, put on your name tag, and walk into a room with a sea of faces. Now you feel like you are standing in a room with your pants down around your ankles. So you quickly look around for someone you know. (Not necessarily someone you *like*…just someone you *know*.) If you can not find anyone, you go to one of the "three Bs": the bar, the buffet, or the bathroom. Now that you have gotten a "cup of courage," you walk around the room giving out business cards as well as collecting them.

You leave with a handful of cards, not exactly sure what you will do with them. And you go through the same thing the next month, and then the next. After a few of these, you ask yourself, "Why am I doing this? I get nothing out of it!" and you stop.

Big mistake. The even bigger mistake, though, is doing it the way you have been.

How do you make networking successful? Do it using a process. Winging anything is a big chance, and these types of chances in growing your business involve more risk than I am willing to take.

There are a few steps that will make networking successful:

145

1. Pick a few organizations that you feel would be the right ones for you. Do not go to every networking event. How do you know which to attend and when? Good question. Start of course with your local chamber of commerce. Also, try googling "networking meetings" + "(your area)" and see what you come up with. Check the business section of your local newspaper too, or ask your chamber of commerce.

2. Set a goal. When you go to an event, do not just walk around picking up business cards. Decide how many strategic alliances you will try to set meetings with outside of the event, and do not leave until you reach that number.

What is a strategic alliance? A strategic alliance is a connection with someone you can share referrals with. It is a person who is out and about in the community, who can introduce you to the people you are trying to meet, in return for you introducing this person to people you know, who might help them. This is who I recommend looking to meet at a networking function, as opposed to simply trying to meet prospects.

3. Introduce yourself in a way that will make you remembered. You are in competition with everyone in that room—even if they are not your competitors in business. What do I mean by that? Typically we remember only ten to fifteen percent of what we hear. This means the attendees at the networking function are going to remember only ten to fifteen percent of the names and other introductory information they hear. You do want to be one of the small percent they remember, don't you? One way to accomplish this is to be clever and/or funny in your introduction. For example, if you are a travel agent, when introducing yourself to someone who asks you what you do, try answering, "I am the only person who can tell you where to go." An office products salesperson might say, "I get into your drawers." Does this seem silly to you? Just remember, bringing the human factor into the conversation will break the ice and at the same time help people remember you.

4. Follow-up is very important in networking. You are trying to be remembered and to form relationships. One of the ways to do this is to send a hand-written note to each person you met at one of these events within a day or two. This is not a sales opportunity, so do not try to sell. Just touch base to reinforce the impression you made and keep yourself alive in the memory of each of the people you met…and you should follow up with *all* the people you met, not just the strategic alliances you set up. Send each person a little note.

5. Make Swiss cheese out of your newspaper. Do you ever look in the newspaper and see either a picture of, or an article about, someone you know? How about an article that you think someone you met might find interesting? Cut it out and send it to them. This is something lots of people think about, yet few actually do.

Networking can be done very effectively, if you use a process to do it right. Or you can always cold call! The choice is yours.

What Have You Done for Me Lately?

"Why do I not get more referrals from my clients!" asks a new client of ours. "I ask every time I see them, and only once in a great while will I get one."

Remember the saying, "What have you done for me lately?" This is actually a pretty relevant question. If you *want* more business, you need to *give* more business. If you *want* more referrals, you need to *give* more referrals. Additionally, when you ask, you need to ask specifically.

Now, to address the above question.... First, congratulations on asking at all! Most of us do not even do that. Asking for referrals successfully is a skill, but have no fear—it is a learned skill.

Here are a few tips that may help.

1. Be specific.

There are two reasons why we do not get more referrals: Either we do not ask, or we do not ask *properly*. What I mean by "did not ask properly" is saying something like, "Do you know anyone else who you think might need my widgets?" So basically in this scenario you are asking people to identify who a good prospect would be for you. It is *your* job to be specific about what a good prospect is, because even though you assume they know, they really do not. For example, rather than saying, "If you know anyone else who might be looking for a good CPA..." you could say, "The next time you have lunch with a friend or colleague, and she says, 'I have a very large tax bill to pay. I did not anticipate it!' Obviously her accountant was not working closely enough with her, and that is a good referral for me."

2. Give and you shall receive.

The philosophy is one I borrowed from BNI: Givers Gain. If you want more referrals, *give* more referrals. Find out what *exactly* is a good prospect for the person you are speaking to, and help build business for them. If you are always looking to help others build their business, yours will always grow.

3. Make swiss cheese out of your newspaper.

Follow-up with the people you meet and stay on top of the mind of each of them. One way you can do this, which I have mentioned previously, is to "make Swiss cheese out of your newspaper." As you look through your local paper, I am sure you read or see things that make you think of different people. When that happens, stop, grab a pair of scissors, and cut away. Put this in a card and send it to that person. "Thought you would enjoy this," "Did we not talk about this?" "This seems relevant to your situation." It is always good to cut out and send a copy of someone's promotion announcement, but going one step beyond that is what differentiates you from everyone else.

Remember, referrals are increased by asking more specifically for what you want and by looking for referrals for others.

The "New" Elevator Speech

Linda knows no strangers. About two weeks ago, Linda excitedly exclaimed that she had an appointment with a new prospect. Trying to match her excitement, I said, "Great—tell me about it."

"Well, we were both in the elevator going to the fourteenth floor. I said, 'Hello, I am Linda, and you are...?' He introduced himself as Rolando. I said, 'What do you do, Rolando?' 'I have a roofing company,' he told me. 'Commercial or residential?' 'Both,' and he laughed a little. Then I said, 'Rolando, what is a good referral for you? I mean, if I were to meet someone who would be good for you to meet, who might that be?'

"'Rolando shook his head and laughed louder.' 'I know this sounds crazy,' I went on, 'but I am actually on my way to a networking meeting, and I am sure there are people there who would like to meet you, Rolando. Would you like to join me?'"

"'I can not, Linda. I am on my way to a meeting myself, but I would love to talk to you further about business. What did you say you do, anyway?' 'Actually, Rolando, I help people build their businesses.'"

"'I will be back in my office after three o'clock. Can you call me?'"

"You know," Linda said, "I was so surprised that he wanted me to call him. I mean, he does not even know what I do."

"Well, I am not," I told her. "You took a genuine interest in him right away. Additionally, everyone wants to engage, to say hello, but very few people know how to begin that conversation. You just jumped in and made him feel important. That is what it is really all about."

So what did Linda do? She took an interest in someone else... that is all. Now, I am not saying you should accost people on an elevator, but...if you want to be successful, take on the job of making others feel comfortable. I heard someone say once that everyone is walking around with an invisible sign on their chest saying, "Make me feel important." I believe that is true.

What are some of the things we should do when we meet someone? Here are a few ideas:

1. **Smile and look the person right in the eye.** Sounds easy but is truly important. Make him or her feel that you are truly interested. They will never forget it.

2. Ask **only a few questions and make them about the other person**. For example: *What do you do? Do you enjoy it? How long have you been doing it? What is a good referral for you?*

3. **Try to introduce him to someone else**. Even if you do not know the person you are attempting to introduce him to, you are probably helping both of them. Imagine how they will feel when thinking of you!

4. **Be the host of the party, even if it is not yours.** If you had groups of people at your home, including some co-workers you did not know, that your spouse invited, would you walk over and introduce yourself? Well, someone has to play that role at a business event as well. Might as well be you.

The idea is, "Fake it till you make it." Once you get out of your comfort zone and make others feel comfortable, they will go out of their way to make you feel the same. Asking for referral help from them? Piece of cake.

We all feel insecure at one time or another. Push yourself to help someone else feel good. Not only will it make him feel better, but imagine how that confidence will help you.

Cold Call Dilemma

"When I am cold calling, what should I leave on a voice mail message to get a call back"? I get this question about once a week and yes, it is the one hundred thousand dollar question. First of all there is no miracle answer to this question, if there were, and I could share it, I would be living on the beach in Hawaii drinking pina coladas with my toes in the sand. I will tell you, when cold calling and getting a message machine, I believe, when in doubt, do not leave one.

Here are some reasons why you should not leave a voice mail message.

1. **The prospect will hear your name and the name of your company, and, not recognizing either.** Then will delete your message without listening to the rest of what you have said.

2. **The prospect will hear your "pitch" and delete it.** They will because unless he has been thinking about what you have to offer at that particular time, he is too busy to act on it.

3. **The prospect will hear your one-way communication and be frustrated,** because there is no opportunity to ask any ques-

tions. Then, he will hit "delete," and click to the next message without thinking about it again.

4. **You may say something in your message that you assume is important to the prospect.** And we all know what happens when you assume…

5. Most importantly, **the more times you leave a message, the more your name and your company's name is burned into his memory, negatively.**

So what is the answer? I will tell you again there is no perfect answer to the voice mail message question. But there are a few things that have worked for some.

I truly do believe less is more. The more information you leave, the more opportunity for the prospect to decide that he is not interested in what you have, even if he does not fully understand what that is.

If you are going to call someone, have a legitimate reason for the call. For example, look on their web site to see if there may be a connection to something that you do. Read about them in the paper or on-line and use what you have read to call with some educated reasons to connect, and some good thought out questions to ask them to see if there is a match.

Unfortunately the lost art of cold calling is just that. You need to be much more creative in reaching prospects and see if they are a fit for you. Do not forget the statistics, for every one hundred calls you are lucky to actually speak to five people and that does not mean they are the decision maker. So with all of this non-supporting information on cold-calling, what is your plan B?

Cold Call Legislation

The following legislation has been in place a few years. The message is still relevant.

Lately, people have asked me lots of questions about the new bill that passed on the subject of phone solicitations, which we affectionately call "cold calls."

"So, Greta, you do think it is unfair they do not allow people to do their job? Thousands of people are employed by these 'marketing' companies, and they will be out of work."

First, let's understand the legislation. It does not say that you cannot solicit on the telephone; it allows people to put their name on a national list so they will not be called.

I have not seen the percentage of potential prospects that actually have made that request, but do you really think it will decrease your business?

Second, stop whining. Our country was built on entrepreneurs creating businesses based on opportunities. The telephone, and the wide usage of it, led to the brilliant idea of using it to solicit business. Times change, however, and so do ways of doing business.

Third – and most of all (some of you are not going to like this) – stop cold-calling. Okay, maybe in some cases, at least in the beginning, you need to do some cold-calling. But are you developing a system for referrals and networking? Are you asking for referrals as a part of your business plan, or is your plan haphazard?

You do want to conduct business in the most effective, efficient, and pleasant way, which is through networking and referrals, right?

How many of us would rather do business with someone we were referred to? The meeting is more pleasant, more interactive, and, if someone referred a customer to you, someone probably has already sung your praises. (Which is so much better that you doing it, right?)

Here are some tips:

1. **Create a system to generate more referrals**. That means actually setting goals for how many referral meetings you will hold in a particular week or month. Then talk to as many clients, friends, colleagues, etc., until you meet your goal.

2. **When you have those meetings, remember, they are not about you**. The philosophy is "givers gain" – That means ask about the people attending, their businesses, and how you can help *them*. Help them grow their business, and they will help you grow yours.

3. **Create a picture for them**. I have a great example I heard from Wendy Widmann, an office-products sales consultant who said, "A good referral for me would be if you see one of those big red office products trucks parked in front of an office building, give me a call." I bet when you see one today, you will remember this example.

4. **Make a top ten list**. When someone asks if they can help you, be very specific and help them picture your ideal customer. Show them your list of the top ten you would like to be introduced to. You never know whom they know.

So do not worry about rules and changes. After all, change makes us better. It forces us to think in other ways. This is growth. Have at it.

Setting and Reaching Goals

Introduction by Frank DeRaffele, National Radio Host of
The Entrepreneur Hour

Why is it so important to set goals?

I mean, what is the difference between a vision and a goal?

And...why does everyone keep telling me that you have to WRITE DOWN your goals?

What if I am just not that type of person? In fact, when I have goals all set and defined I feel restricted, almost held captive by them.

I have been an entrepreneur my whole life. I have worked with entrepreneurs, helping them create the success they wanted in their life. How did we achieve the desired success? By not only setting goals but by understanding that a goal is merely a way of stating what result you want to achieve.

So for now, forget about goals. Let's talk about the results you want.

Here is reality, if you are a sales professional or an entrepreneur and you are looking to achieve greater results in revenue production you need a clear plan to make that happen. Why? Because entrepreneurship and sales are creative endeavors. Being successful at either means having the ability to tap into your creative problem solving skills.

The way you stay sharp with your creativity, your ability to negotiate and have meaningful conversations and resolving issues for your prospects and clients, is by having your mind able to focus on the topic matter at hand. If your mind is filled with stuff that doesn't need to be there, than you are not using your intelligence, experience, and creativity to the best of your ability.

One of the ways to be at your best is by having very clear and defined goals and a systematic and strategic plan of achievement. Once you have that then you no longer have to worry about thinking of what to do but just doing. You can focus your energy on achieving results. Those that can't do that get caught up on what to do next… and find it hard to leave that cycle of being stuck in the place of no results and failure.

When your mind is able to focus on the doing, not the planning or wondering, then it is clear to resolve problems and issues when they arise. You become "solutions focused", results focused and customer focused. This is where effortless success will be seen.

Do not shrug off the importance of setting goals and achieving them. In fact, embrace the process. Dive in and put more work into the setting and achievement plan so you are crystal clear of what you have to do step by step to end up where you want to be.

If you do this, you will now be able to use your creativity, intelligence and experience to truly enjoy the work you have in front of you. You will now achieve with less effort and greater joy. Guaranteed.

Everyone Needs a Plan

Businesses are failing daily—not because business owners did not start a viable business, or had a bad product, or because of a weak economy, but due to a lack of planning. That is right—*planning*. I am talking about the kind of planning that it takes to generate sales.

Many business owners have started out with talent and an idea for bringing a product or service to the marketplace. Along with the skill he or she needs to provide the product or service, there is the initial plan to finance (usually under-finance) advertising, marketing, and public relations, along with a projection of sales for growing the business. Then there is the task of either hiring a sales force or having the owner(s) wear the sales hat. Either one can be the formula for short-term death without a working sales plan.

A great explanation of this is from the book *The E Myth* (which refers to the entrepreneurial myth), by Michael E. Gerber: Here is what happens—someone says, "I really love to cook, and I am going to open a catering company." Then that person has what Gerber calls "an entrepreneurial seizure" and thinks that, because Uncle Joe always compliments her pies, and all her friends ask for her recipes, she has got the makings of a business.

Wrong! Remember, your product or service is merely the venue you use to make money in your business. Working *on* your business is the most important thing you can do, not working *in* it.

What does that mean? Stop cooking and start marketing and planning how the pies are going to get sold!

Here are some basics that you need to be able to answer before you open those doors.

Profile. What should your customers look like? If you already have an existing business, then what are the character traits that make up your current customers? Are they the ones you really want? To identify your customer base, you want to recognize things like type of business, industry, size of business, potential buying power, number of employees, and geography.

Categorize. Breaking your customer base into somewhere between two and four categories can help to eliminate putting all your eggs in one basket. These categories can be based upon such delineators as size of business, amount of business conducted with your company, type of business, etc. Then develop a plan for each category of business. The message here is to build a strong foundation of customers, so that no single customer keeps you in business nor puts you out of business.

Strategize. How are you going to successfully reach each of these different types of prospects and sell to each? What products or services will you sell to each? What will the profit margins be for each? Making some key decisions before moving forward is invaluable.

So, you do not have a plan? How long do you think you will have a profitable business?

Little Steps to Long-Term Goals

This last New Years, I put weight loss on my resolution list. Actually, I set a goal to get healthier. I have committed to eating properly and exercising—and to stop using my travel schedule as an excuse.

On the recommendation of a friend, I am trying Weight Watchers. It has not been very long, but I already see a difference—a small difference, but a difference. Would it be nice to have dropped lots of pounds already? Of course. But just as in business and in sales, taking little steps at a time is smarter and has a much better chance for success.

Setting Sales Goals

Many of my contacts tell me they have resolved to set higher sales goals in the year, quarter, or other period ahead. A resolution and a goal are two different things. Let's talk about how you should set goals for yourself.

Begin with your revenue goals—not necessarily your company's goals but your own. What do you need to get what you want? When do you want to be able to retire? How much will you need? If you do not have answers to those questions, you should meet with a financial consultant and figure it out.

Once you understand what you need, add at least five percent because I am sure you have underestimated.

Next, move to your daily and weekly activities. Start detailing what you need to do every day, week, and month to reach your revenue goals. You need to estimate what your daily, weekly, and monthly activity should be.

Track goals every day

After you guesstimate those numbers, you need to track them every day. You should do that for at least ninety days to begin to have an idea of what it will really take to meet your goals.

As long as you meet your daily goals, you will be successful day by day. That is important. Most people look at the whole revenue goal and do not break it down into small pieces. It feels overwhelming unless you break it down into small hurdles that can be jumped.

Find ways to pat yourself on the back every day—then every week, then every month. That way, you can meet your goal one step at a time.

So I am not striving to lose twenty pounds. Rather, I am eating twenty-three points a day. And that I can handle.

Stop the Excuse Insanity

Have you stopped recently to evaluate how you are doing? How are your sales and other yardsticks of success measuring up to the plan you had going into the new year? Boy, it is great when you start out with a clear and concise plan, right?

What is that? You do not have a plan? You mean every goal you set last year was met purely by chance? Oh—you did not meet all your goals for last year? Say it is not so!

Why is it that we start out with the best intentions on January 1, and a month later, we are back to our old routine? The routine of procrastination, excuse-making, and acceptance of mediocrity.

There are several reasons for this. Here are three:

1) We are lazy. Yep, it is often as simple as that. It is easier to justify all the reasons we can not do it instead of finding reasons we can! Some people are happy with mediocrity. It is OKAY to admit it.

2) "I am too busy!" That is one of my favorites. Who is not "too busy"? Typically, when you hear "I am too busy," you can replace it with "I have no real idea how to prioritize." So instead, we fill our schedules with things that are not activities directly related to identifying business. It is always stuff that is easier to do (there is a reason why they call it *busy*work!)

3) **We set monetary goals instead of activity goals**. When we set goals by a dollar amount to achieve instead of daily, weekly, and monthly activities, we set ourselves up for failure. Why? Because we can not control who buys. What we can control is what activities we are involved in, and that is how success starts to happen.

Let's talk a bit more about the third reason. The other two often get caught up in the misinterpretation of dollars (or sales) that are being set as goals. They are not. Instead, they are the result of your goal. When we set dollar-volume goals only, we do not often reach them, and then give up too quickly. So how can you set a goal of something you can not control? You can not! That is not a goal. It is a wish. Wishes are wonderful for your kids at Christmas, but they are no way to run a business.

I am not telling you to ignore dollar amounts for yourself and your salespeople. Not at all. All I am saying is that *they are not goals*. They are merely the *result* you should expect from the goals you do set.

This is a good place to begin.

Let's say that you want your results to be $120,000 this year. First, you have got to identify what this breaks down to per month. In this case, it is around $10,000.

Second, what is an average sale for you? If it is $2,500, then you need four sales a month.

Third, how many prospects do you need to meet with to close one deal? This may take some review of your past closing ratio. Remember, a prospect is someone with whom you have identified a need and pre-qualified them as such. So let's say you have got to meet with three prospects to get one deal. Then, to meet your goal, you will have to meet with twelve prospects per month.

Fourth—and this will take some estimating—how many suspects do you need to meet with to get a single, qualified prospect? A suspect is someone you could be meeting with for a variety of reasons: you may be exchanging referrals, or the person may be a past client, a strategic partner, someone interested in your business, etc. Let's say it is five. Then your monthly goal is to meet with sixty suspects.

Now you have a goal! To meet with sixty suspects a month, you need to see approximately fifteen appointments per week.

The most important thing is to track your numbers for thirty-sixty-ninety-day cycles. This tells you not only whether the numbers are correct but where most of your business referrals are coming from.

Too complicated? Fine—go back to the old theory: If you get in front of enough people, eventually some will close. It is exactly how you fall into the "I am too busy" category.

And how is that workin' for ya?

Get Your Head in the Game

Every year, or quarter, or however else you delineate your sales seasons, the clock runs out, and a brand new season starts. All your business requirements for that year/quarter/season were met...or not. But either way, that time period is gone. It is time to start over at a place where all our numbers go back to zero. Will your next year/quarter/season be more productive than the last one? To make that happen, you are going to have to get your head in the game.

January 1ˢᵗ is the most obvious, though not the only, delineator of old/new, of what was/what will be. The name "January" derives from the Roman god Janus, the patron of beginnings and endings. Janus is depicted as having two faces—one looking forward and the other looking back. It is OKAY to reflect. But there is no looking back in order to get your head in the game. You have to make a decision to look ahead and not dwell on the past.

I am convinced the battlefield for most people rests between their own two ears. Let's face it: We have all fallen victim to the January blues. That is the condition in which salespeople think, "Wow! I did great last year! But how will I repeat it? Where will my business come from? It is a tougher market."

Make a choice today to shake off that kind of thinking. In my house, we call it clicker control. Change the channel to something positive, and use the gifts that are in you.

The good news: Anybody can be transformed by a renewing of his or her mind. But you have to exercise the mind, and that requires lots of work. It is not like going to a drive-through pharmacy and picking up a prescription for success. Rather, your mind has to be reprogrammed to focus on the positive. You can do that first by feeding it with proper nutrition.

Can you imagine what it would be like if our minds started to ache every time we put something bad into them? Sadly, most salespeople do not realize how serious an effect dwelling on the negative can have on performance.

As you head out for the workday, start visualizing all the good things you are positively thinking about. It really is true: If you picture something, are specific about it, and keep it at the top of your mind, it will happen.

Always follow that up with thinking about something good—be it business-related or personal—that is coming up.

Make an immediate choice to shake off the negative stuff. Get your head in the game.

-Written with Ira Martin of Martin Touch Consulting

Your Most Successful Year

Was the past calendar year, or were the past twelve months (regardless of where in the year we are as you read this) as successful as you would have hoped? Perhaps you have achieved all of your personal and professional goals.

Or perhaps not.

If you did, congratulate yourself and plan to make these next twelve months or four quarters even better. But if not, do not give up. It is never too late to resolve that the next twelve months, or four quarters, will be your most successful ever. No, I do not have any secret formula for winning the lottery, but I do know what steps you can take to insure your success.

Various studies over the years have related important information about the distribution of wealth. These numbers have remained constant for the past thirty years: 3% of the population is independently wealthy, 10% live comfortably, 60% live paycheck to paycheck, and the remaining 27% need some kind of support to live.

The primary factor explaining this distribution is the degree to which people set and follow specific goals and plans. The 3% of the population who are independently wealthy have specific written goals, written plans to achieve those goals, and have tracking systems in place. The 10% group has specific goals. The remainder rarely, if ever, set any goals at all. What happens to inherited wealth and lottery winnings? The statistics show us that they are quickly spent because the recipients have no goals to do otherwise.

The reality is that you will ultimately earn what you believe you are worth—not a dollar more, not a dollar less (Emerson's Law of Compensation). This also applies to every single facet of your life—mental, physical, and spiritual. You are in charge.

I suggest that you answer the following nine questions so that you will have more control of your destiny.

1. Do you have a passion?

Why are you in business? Is it just a way to make a living, or is there something else driving you? What makes you get out of bed every day? Start with a dream and turn your dream into a goal. Commit to your goal in writing and put it some place that you can see it everyday. This will remind you of why you go through the rigors of selling and managing every day.

2. Do you have focus?

Focus on where you want to be at the end of the year, and then commit to getting there. Do not keep hedging your bets: "I do not know if I should be selling, or managing, or not…. Maybe I will try for another week." Jump in with both feet and go for it. As Stephen Covey says, "Begin with the end in mind."

3. Have you put together your business plan with a map?

Hoping to achieve your goals without a business plan is like driving from Vancouver, WA to Fort Lauderdale, FL without a road map. If you get there, it will be by accident. You must work out the details step by step.

Do not let the words "business plan" scare you. You do not need to do the lengthy business plan a bank might require. Really, what you need is a marketing plan.

4. Do you have four major goals for the year?

Pick four goals that are important to you—personal and professional. Prioritize those goals. As tools, use sight, hearing, and feeling (not the sense of touch, but emotional feeling). Visualize them so they are really clear: see yourself accomplishing your goals, hear the sounds that come with success, and imagine how you will feel at the end of the year when you accomplish your goals.

5. Can you master the discipline to manage your activities?

Take it one day at a time. Once you have established your plan, can you take the action necessary to work it day by day? Too many people in sales have a conditional commitment to their plans. They will make ten face-to-face calls every day...unless.... Unless it is raining...they do not feel too good...it is sunny...traffic is slow...or they have paperwork to take care of. The list goes on. I call that a serious case of *"call reluctance."* You must have an unconditional commitment to your plan and do it regardless of the obstacles or distractions.

6. How do you make it your plan and not everyone else's?

What is the amount of money that you need to survive month by month as you pursue your goals? What are your expenses, and how much money do you need to cover them? Undue financial pressure will greatly affect your attitude. The desperation will show in your eyes, and in your tone, and in your body language; and worst of all, it will be very obvious to your prospects. Budget your expenses. Create a savings plan, and put money aside for emergencies. Then you are free to pursue your goals.

7. Will you start over again each day, or do you have a system for working smart?

Amateur salespeople make cold call after cold call, day after day. They work their lists A through Z. Cold calling is predictable: on average you will do business with about 1%. It is hard work but... it will yield results. Professionals know that the best source for their next sale is a referral from a present client. They know how to professionally target referrals so that the outcomes are win, win, win—a win for them, a win for the person who refers them, and a win for the prospect. Make your clients a part of your sales force.

8. Do you keep track?

Do you keep track of what worked and what did not? Do you debrief each sales call so that you can learn and grow stronger? Successful people are always learning..."What did I do well?"..."What could I have done better?" A simple tracking system will help you stick to your plan and fine-tune your skills. Remember, you can not manage anything you can not measure, and 94% of all *written* realistic goals are achieved.

Finally, remember a goal without a plan is merely a dream.

The book *The Secret* talks about the law of attraction. I believe this works if you picture exactly what success is to you and see it clearly everyday. It will come to you...because you have pictured it!

If you are serious about making the next twelve months or four quarters your most successful year ever, you will set goals, develop a plan and a system to track your progress, and......"Just do it"!

Opposites Attract

Introduction by Jay Berkowitz, President and author of
10 Golden Rules of Internet Marketing Workbook

Thinking outside the box is a term that refers to the approach of applying new strategies or approaches to deal with existing issues, tasks, or job functions. It often involves brainstorming and business planning, or this creative approach can apply to solving personal issues and applying new ways of thinking for an individual.

1. **Stay current** – Knowing the latest strategies and tactics in your field will help you apply innovative thinking in your work. Use multi-media to stay current on leading trends in your industry. Subscribe to blogs from the thought leaders in your space. Audio books and podcasts are an excellent way to gain more time to learn and stay current. To find leading podcasts search the main phrase that describes your industry in the iTunes Store and listen to the most popular podcasts on this list. These audio shows can be downloaded to an iPod or copied to a CD and you can listen while commuting, exercising, or waiting for a plane. A new media source called Twitter is also an excellent way to follow the leading experts,

simply search the name of a top knowledge leader in your space and Twitter on Google or another search engine to see if they have a Twitter account. You can 'follow' anyone on Twitter and you will see their one hundred and forty character 'tweets'.

2. **Keep a great ideas file**. Whenever you receive an email with an interesting headline - print it for your ideas file. If you receive a smart direct mail piece, add it to your collection. Notice an innovative ad in a magazine, tear it out. When you need to come up with out of the box ideas, your idea file is a great place to start.

3. **Apply thinking from other business areas**. If you are in the textile business, you have likely analyzed your company and competitors extensively. Rarely will you find completely new ideas by looking within your industry. Pick up a jewelry industry trade magazine; go to a hi-tech trade show, read a leading transportation blog, what promotions are on the back of the cereal boxes in the grocery store? Adapt innovative ideas that are leading the way in these industries to apply to your business or problems.

4. **Be contrarian**. One way to develop creative problem solving and ideation is to think about the issues in a contrary manner. Challenge the current way of doing things and take the mindset that the current strategy is completely wrong, how would you do things if the current way was not working or was ruled unavailable? What is the completely opposite policy or approach?

5. **Brainstorm**. You can brainstorm yourself, but you will be better working in small groups of two or three. Lennon and McCartney. Elton John and Bernie Taupin, Bill Gates and the other Harvard dropouts he started Microsoft with. Great creativity often comes from pairs of two. If you have a large group, break into pairs or small groupings. Assign everyone a specific task to brainstorm and then ask each small group to bring the best two to three ideas back to the larger group. Vote on the best ideas and then break into small groups again to brainstorm on how to improve and implement those ideas.

6. **Set high standards for your ideas**. 'New' or 'different' is not a high enough standard for great thinking. An out of the box strategy that is going to make a demonstrable difference for your job or your business is going to be something that adds value for your customers and is so appropriate and relevant for their needs that they would

tell others about it or they would recommend you or your company because of this new out of the box approach.

7. Get twenty magazines from different subject areas. Flipping through magazines can spur innovative out of the box thinking. Work quickly, write down every idea that comes to mind and then revisit the list and build on great ideas. Look for threads or themes in your notes. Are there great ideas in the mix?

8. Just do it. An easy way to think outside the box is to spend time doing it. Schedule time with your associates or yourself, to think about new approaches to your current job. Use brainstorming, and build on ideas to develop new approaches and new solutions.

9. The rules of threes. I have a personal rule of threes, this means that the first time I hear about something I do not jump right in to try it. When I hear about something two to three times and one of them is a trusted source such as a good friend, a leading blogger, or a keynote speaker, then I know that I need to understand how this new tool or technology works or what is so interesting at a new store or restaurant. Take the time to understand why new products, companies or websites become 'hot'. What drives the consumer's behavior? Understanding the core motivation behind trends and consumer preferences will serve as the catalyst for a future out of the box solution.

10. What would _____ do? Who is the most innovative problem solver you know? Who was calm under pressure and made great decisions? When faced with a problem or challenge, put yourself in the frame of mind of this creative individual, how would he or she approach it? How would Thomas Edison approach the problem? What would Donald Trump do? How about Sherlock Holmes?

Applying out of the box thinking can move you and your business to a higher level. Defining new categories for your business, developing approaches to selling, or ideas for new products and services can deliver incremental personal and professional growth.

Good luck getting outside the box!

"I Have Heard
That Line Before"

At 4:45 pm on the last Friday of the month, Robert was still struggling to seal the deal with Sam, the prospect he had been sitting with
for nearly two hours. If he could only close this sale, he would meet
his quarterly goal and earn that bonus he had been gunning for.

"Sam, I know I probably should not mention this..." Robert said,
"But I like you, so I will. Monday starts a new month, and I have
been informed that a seven percent price increase is going to take
effect. But if you sign up now, I can guarantee you the reduced price
that we discussed."

After hearing Robert's "moves," Sam could not help but let out
a chuckle. With Robert looking at him a little confused, he felt he
should explain. "Robert, I was in sales. Your 'impending event' close
is not going to work with me. Let me get this straight: If I walk out
of here right now and come back Monday morning with a check
written for today's price, you are going to turn it away?"

"Ummm...well...." Robert nervously hedged, knowing he had
been caught.

"Robert, do not try to trick me into buying because it will not work. Every salesman in the country has worked that line into the ground."

"Well, really, if you look at the positive and negative aspects...." Robert said, trying to redeem himself.

"That is the Ben Franklin close—and it is just as old and dead as Ben Franklin," Sam said. "You know what...why do you not just give me a call sometime next week."

Not everyone knows the names to the "ol' reliable" closing methods used in sales, but nearly everyone has been worked over by those techniques at one time or another. Now, I know what you are thinking: "But if these lines still work, why should I stop using them?!"

The answer is simple: They *do not* work! Certainly, they do not if you want anyone's respect...including your own.

Think about it. The last time you went to buy a car, did you *buy* or were you *sold*? If your experience was par for most car dealerships, you were sold. And let's face it—no one likes to be sold. Yet using the standard closing lines prints the word "SALESMAN" in big, bold letters on your forehead. This reminds the prospect that you are in it for *your* well-being, not *his*, prompting him to raise objections to the sale. Not only that, these "lines" are becoming so old that they are often easily recognizable to prospects like Sam, who love to give the automatic "No, thank you" at the first hint of a closing line.

So it is time to learn a new strategy. Start by making a list of all the "closing lines" that you currently use. The next time you are in a meeting and you are at the "insert closing line here" section of the meeting, simply ask your prospect what he thinks the next step should be. Because this is not a yes-or-no question, the prospect will be forced into replying with a statement. Unless the reply is something along the lines of "nothing," turn his statement into a question.

Here is an example:

Salesperson: "To review, so far we have discussed some of your issues being ____ [summary]. Have I covered everything?"

Prospect: "Yes that seems right."

Salesperson: "OK, what would you like to do now?"

Prospect: "Well, I need some referrals to speak to."

Salesperson: "OK, and then…?"

Prospect: "That is it."

Salesperson: "So, if I give you some referrals, and they answer your questions to your liking, then what?"

Make sure to wait until you get a response, no matter how long it takes. This way, the prospect is responsible for closing the sale, not you and your tired lines.

Does it sound just like this? Maybe, maybe not, but here are a few points to note: The conversation was pulled, not pushed. It was not a line or move—it was a conversation. It was real.

Be real. Do not use a line—use an outline, a process…one that incorporates your own words and style.

So the next time you catch yourself thinking about using "Ben Franklin" in a meeting, think about the one hundred dollar bill in your pocket and use it to pay the tab!

Silence Is Golden

One weekend last holiday season, I was doing some shopping with my husband. As we worked our way through one of my very favorite department stores, we just happened to wander into the shoe department. (I can not imagine how that happened!) There I saw a beautiful pair of black shoes, and God knows a woman can not have enough black shoes!

Anyway, I loved the shoes but showed the saleswoman that the pair I was trying on had a small mark on the side of the heel. She went to look for another pair but returned to announce that there was no other pair in stock in my size. As we stood there quietly, I looked at the mark, trying to decide if I could get it out at home with a little elbow grease. Suddenly the salesperson blurted out, "If you want that pair, I can give you ten percent off."

I had not asked for ten percent off, or *anything* off, nor was I going to turn the shoes down at full price. I had been thinking about asking her, if I went home and could not get the mark out, if they would take the shoes back, but I never got that far.

I looked at my husband with *that* look...you know the one: "Hmmm, something is happening here...." This is his cue to walk away because he is uncomfortable with any negotiation, even if he is not the one doing it. So I stood there in silence for another few seconds because now I was going to have fun.

"Hmmmm," I mumbled, saying nothing, and in no more than three seconds, the sales associate said, "Okay, I can give you fifteen percent off, but no more. I am not authorized to go higher without a manager's approval, and they rarely give any more than that."

Interesting...who was she negotiating with? Not me—I had not said a word. She was negotiating with herself! So I waited a bit longer, but that was the best she did, so I bit and got my shoes at fifteen percent off.

Silence is uncomfortable for so many of us, so our nature is to jump in and end that uncomfortable silence. Yet if you just hang in there and do not fill the silence, you will probably win because the other person will typically break if you wait long enough.

"Win"? Did I say "win"? When you are in control of your negotiating ability, it is really a fun game. So shut up and have at it!

When the Prospect Fights You on Price

As a consultant, seller, or even CEO, how many times in your career have you heard prospects fight you on rate or price? "I like your proposal, but your price is too high," or "I can get other companies at a lower cost," or "What can you do about your rates?" or "I will do the deal, but you have got to knock 20% off...take it or leave it."

Here is a story, told by a banking rep named Jennifer. Jennifer had finished a presentation to a prospect after qualifying the prospect on need and investment, and she had all the decision-makers in the room. She had gotten each of them to agree to make a decision at the end of the presentation. Her presentation was textbook. She had each person involved; she addressed each of their requirements. Her presentation points covered each of the prospect's issues in their priority...and she addressed only issues that were relevant to the sale.

At the end, one of the prospects made a simple statement: "Jennifer, this is great, and we love the job you did for us. We would love to begin, except we want you to give us a discount. What can you do for us about your price?"

Jennifer was confused. In fact, Jennifer listened to all the kudos and responded, "I could raise it." She actually thought the prospect was kidding.

The prospect laughed and said, "Jennifer, I know you have got more leeway on your interest rate."

Jennifer calmly said, "I am sorry. I guess I did not help you see the advantage of doing business with us, even being priced slightly higher."

The prospect responded, "What do you mean?"

Jennifer said, "Simple. My price is too high, and I understand that." She held out her hand to thank him for his time when…

"Wait, Jennifer. Your rates are high, but your ideas are better than any we have seen."

"I appreciate that," responded Jennifer, "but you are not going to go with us, and I wanted to thank you for the opportunity."

"Do not be too hasty to leave," the client said, stopping her. "Actually, Jennifer, we *are* going to do this.

Remember when you were a child, and your parents told you that you could not have something you really wanted? You actually wanted it even more. Not that your prospects are children and you are parental, but the concept still applies.

This can work when the prospect gives you some objection when it is time to close. But for this tactic to work, the prospect must have stated how your solution will solve their concerns and clearly understand your differences. When you go forward, proceed with conviction. When you make the statement, you must convey to the prospect that you believe the sale is *never* going to happen.

And when the prospect tells you that it is not really over, offer your help by saying, "Oh. I got the wrong impression. What would you like me to do now?"

Then wait…forever, if necessary…for a response.

Take It Away!

"Sue, I am really not sure that what I have seen does anything for me," said Phil, the prospect. "Actually, your color choices are nowhere near as extensive as your competitor's. In fact, he was just in here, showing me some new additions this morning."

Sue detested this type of prospect. And, unfortunately, this was the only type she had for the past six months. Sue knew this would be another one of those meetings at which the prospect objects a thousand times, and she would have to come up with a way to beat all the objections down.

"There has got to be a better way to make a living," she thought. Then aloud, she said to Phil, "I did not know you had met with ABC Competition."

"Well, I really feel obligated to shop around. And, to be perfectly honest with you, their prices are looking pretty good. I doubt you will be able to beat them."

All right, let's get started fighting the objections, Sue thought.

Dealing with the Objections

"Let's talk about colors. Our colors are by far the...." Sue droned. An hour and a half later, she all but crawled out of the office, exhausted and feeling beaten...but she walked out with an order.

Sue's sales manager greeted her with a "Good work!" and a pat on the back. But after a glance at the dollar amount sold, he asked, "Why is Phil ordering less than he did last time?"

"ABC Competition had a proposal on the table. You would not believe what I went through just to get that much." Feeling second rate, she added, "I am going back there next week to see if I can get the rest back."

Sue was so afraid she was going to lose Phil as a client that she was prepared to do just about anything to keep his business. In fact, she had the guts to spend another hour and a half confronting Phil's objections, but not enough guts to ask the questions to find out if the objections were real or a test on his part.

It Is Not for Those with Weak Knees

Taking a sale away—or taking yourself out of the running and then waiting for a response from the prospect—takes some serious guts. This approach is not for those with weak knees.

No one can hold Sue responsible for her commitment to ask. In fact, most salespeople and sales managers would agree that, in the situation above, the best thing to do is simply "gut it out."

But something else could have been done.

Before Sue began answering every objection Phil had, she could have simply said, "You know, you mentioned that ABC Competition has more colors and a better price, and they were already here this morning. So I am confused. Why did you not order from them? I mean, we can not do all of that."

For the take-away to work, you must honestly be prepared to lose the sale and walk out the door without looking back. If you are not able to do this, it could backfire right in your face. But if you are one hundred percent committed to making it work, then this is incredibly compelling when it comes to eliminating objections. Your task is simply to mirror back what your prospect is saying to you.

For example, when the prospect tells you how great and wonderful your competitor is, reply with: "So you ordered from them." Do not speak until you get a response. If he did already order, it probably really is over for you. But if not, then you deserve to know the reasons. And while your prospect is telling you why, you are learning what you need to do to get his business.

The prospect's famous last line is often "The other guy can do it better for less." Well, guess what? Let him!

Then and only then will you find out the real truth.

The Holiday Brush-Off

It is December, and Jessica is making her calls to potential clients to fill her calendar with appointments. She has spoken to lots of people and, when one shows a strong interest in her company's product, she asks for an appointment. She gets this response: "Well, Jessica, I think it might make sense for us to talk further. Call me after the holidays, and we can get together then."

Jessica is excited about all the interest, but she is frustrated with the procrastination. She speaks to her manager and others on her team, and they say, "Oh, yeah. That is par for the course, this time of year. That is just the way it is."

What? I do not know about you, but in the typical December, I am already getting booked up for January and beyond. If I were to wait until after the first of the year to book appointments, I would not be working very efficiently. I bet that if you happen to be reading this in December, you also have at least a half-dozen appointments already set for well into the next year—dentist, doctor, CPA, etc. So why can we not set business appointments in advance similarly?

Here is why: If you are selling a product or service, and someone asks you to call after the first of the year, it is a bush-off. They do not feel it is important enough to set it now. Why? Because *you* have not gotten them to see it that way. Do you accept that brush-off?

Here is how you need to handle the situation:

You get to the point in the conversation where you ask for an appointment, and the prospect says, "You know, that sounds good. Call me after the holidays and we will set something up."

I would say, "I appreciate that, Bob. But it will be so crazy after the first of the year, with all our calendars filling up. Let's go ahead and schedule something now, so we can have it already done."

At that point, if Bob still asks to have you call later, say, "I have got to tell you, Bob, when someone tries to make an appointment with me and I am really not interested in meeting, I find a reason to put it off. And the holidays are what I use this time of the year as a believable excuse.

"If you do not think we have some things to talk about that could really be worth our while, let's just say that now and not set anything. I am a big girl, Bob. I can take it. But if we do want to talk further, let's go ahead and set a time. Either way is fine with me. So, Bob, what do you think?"

Some of you may not feel good about that response because you believe you would then lose your opportunity with the prospect. Guess what? You really did not have one anyway.

Once you get real with prospects and they understand where you are coming from, either they will schedule the appointment or they will respect you for being honest about it.

Wouldn't you?

Sit in the Power Seat

After only a brief conversation with Ben at the chamber dinner last week, Janet, an attorney, saw that he fit the criteria of her "ideal client." He was unhappy with his current attorney, and he was willing to spend a little more to get the job done right the first time.

"After all," Ben said, "it is worth a little more to ensure proper legal advice." Janet was thrilled. Finally, someone got it.

She barely prepared for their meeting because she had a feeling that Ben would be an easy sell. After all, she did not even have to explain why her small, local firm was different from other, larger law firms, or justify her somewhat higher prices. That night at the chamber function, he had practically sold himself. Just thinking of what an account of this magnitude was going to do for her firm, Janet could not help but speed all the way to Ben's office. When she arrived, she jumped out of her car and pranced through the front door of the building.

When she walked into the office, she was reminded of the inside of a honeybee's nest that she had seen on the Discovery Channel. People were hurrying all over the office, shuffling through documents and talking loudly on cell phones. Before Janet had a chance to introduce herself to the secretary as Ben's 3:00 p.m. appointment, Ben walked right in front of her, almost stepping on her toes, not seeming to notice she even existed.

"Hi, Ben Nice to see you again," Janet interjected, hoping to get his attention.

"Janet. Hi. Listen, I really only have ten minutes or so. Is that enough time for you to show me some numbers? I will go get Johnson Company's. last proposal."

Janet managed to get out an "Uh…well….yeah, sure" before Ben began to wander off down the hall.

This has happened to most of us before. You meet someone who seems to be interested in your product, then will shy away from deciding on anything definite. When you discuss numbers, he seems okay, yet when the proposal comes out, he acts surprised.

He is open and excited about having a need and a budget for your product/service but then may be vague or perhaps even negative when it comes time to close or make a decision. So, how do we understand and sell effectively in this situation?

Simple. Be in the "power seat" at all times. The bottom line is this: If the prospect is giving you the "yes today, no tomorrow" schpiel, he is taking power; do not allow him to have more power than you. If you want to close this sale, stay in control. Address openly what this person is avoiding. Do not allow the prospect to dangle a carrot in front of your nose, enticing you to do what he says in order to close the deal. I do not even like carrots, and you should not either in this situation!

Here is what Janet should have done to handle her prospect:

Ben: "Janet. Hi. Listen. I really only have ten minutes or so. Is that enough time for you to show me some numbers? I will go get Johnson Company's. last proposal."

Janet: "Actually, Ben, let me save you a trip. Before you do that, let's go back to our conversation at the dinner last week. You mentioned how important it was to get things right, even if it costs a little more. So I am confused. Help me understand what has changed?"

From this point, you need to understand what is important to this prospect and open the conversation up before you even get to proposals. The reality is, do what you are supposed to do right all the time, and do not assume that, just because someone shows a hint of interest, the deal is sold or even close. Do the work upfront. It will pay off in the end.

###

So What's Next...

THE OFFICIAL B2B SALES PLAYBOOK

The intention of this book was to give you some tips and ideas on how to sell more professionally and more consultatively while keeping your pride in tact.

If you would like more of an instructional how-to book, I have developed *The Official B2B Sales Playbook*. A Play by Play instruction manual that works through the process of story telling of common situations that happen every day and what you should and shouldn't do in these situations to be successful.

In addition to the actual playbook and monthly new instructional stories you will receive by mail, there is a members-only web-site that has instructions, blogs, message boards, pod casts, newsletters and conference calls available so you can *really* get the results you want.

I have developed the playbook based on a football theme.

Your instructional stories are assembled with the following;

THE PLAY

The set up of what the salesperson did in the actual sales situation the salesperson was in, scenarios so many of us go through every day.

THE FUMBLE

The fumble will highlight the issues with the sales scenario that were not done properly. It will identify where the actual sale started to go south.

THE TOUCHDOWN

This will repeat the sales situation but this time executed correctly using the actual sales process.

Monday Morning Quarterback

I will then give my overall assessment of the situation and the rules to stick by for you so you don't make these same mistakes! I will coach through the situation to assure success in the lessons you should have learned.

Because I believe that adults learn little bits at a time and need a sounding board for questions and clarifications along the way, THE OFFICIAL B2B SALES PLAYBOOK is a binder that will hold all of the teaching stories. You will be sent the entire package and then you will be sent new stories every month. Again I believe it is important to take baby steps because adults change their behavior by learning new information, trying it, reviewing it and then trying it again.

What you get with a one year membership:

Binder with subject dividers for all of the sales subjects

Collection of *Sales Playbook* instructional page inserts mailed to you monthly

Password to an exclusive web site for members of the Playbook team

Blogs by me, Greta Schulz, on a website exclusively for team members

Message board for team members to ask questions, post successes and challenges

Monthly pod casts

Monthly call-in conference calls

Monthly audio conferences on file

Quarterly newsletter

And more!
Check it out and sign up!
Go to our Website at:
www.B2BSalesPlaybook.com

Acknowledgments

Berkowitz, Jay

Jay Berkowitz is the author of *The Ten Golden Rules of Online Marketing Workbook*, the Founder and CEO of www.TenGoldenRules.com, a strategic online marketing consulting business based in Boca Raton, Florida, and the host of the Ten Golden Rules of Internet Marketing Podcast.

Mr. Berkowitz has over twenty years of marketing experience; he has managed marketing departments for Fortune 500 brands: Coca-Cola, Sprint, and McDonald's Restaurants, and leading health and fitness website eDiets.com.

Mr. Berkowitz is a popular presenter at conferences and events such as The Inc 500 Conference, Ad-Tech, Affiliate Summit, Webmaster World, The Direct Marketing Association, The American Marketing Association, and The CEO Executive Forum. He is the Research Co-Chairman for SEMPO, the Search Engine Marketing Professionals Organization, a Founding Board Member of The South Florida Interactive Marketing Association, and Past President of the South Florida Chapter of The American Marketing Association. He is a Gold Medal winner at the Association of

Women in Communications PR Olympics and the recipient of two SOFIE Award nominations.

Burg, Bob

Bob Burg is a sought-after speaker on the topic of Business Networking.

He is perhaps best-known for his book *Endless Referrals: Network Your Everyday Contacts into Sales* (over 175,000 sold!).

His newest book, *The Go-Giver* (co-authored with John David Mann) is a business parable that both touches hearts and builds bigger bank accounts. It shot to number six on the Wall Street Journal Business Bestsellers list just three weeks after its release.

Bob is a staunch advocate, supporter, and defender of the Free Enterprise system, believing that the amount of money one makes is directly proportional to how many people they serve. He currently serves on the Board of Directors for Safe Harbor, the Humane Society.

DeRaffele, Frank

Frank is the executive producer and host of the nationally syndicated Entrepreneurial Excellence radio show. He incorporated his first business at the age of eighteen while attending college at Syracuse University and since that time has been an entrepreneur. He calls himself "unemployable" and has started, grown, run, and sold several companies over the last twenty seven years. His ability to understand his mistakes, learn from them, and implement his corrections has been a key to his success. This, along with his inspirational communication style is what allowed him to found his Consulting and Training firm and become one of the most sought after speakers in the USA, Europe, and Asia.

Frank is the co-author of *Successful Business Networking* (Chandler House Press 1998) and a contributing author along with Stephen Covey, Jack Canfield, Jay Conrad Levinson, Dr. Ivan Misner, Zig Ziglar, and Ken Blanchard to the Wall Street Journal & New York Times Best Seller *The Masters of Networking* (Bard Press 2000). In 2007 he was contracted for additional books titled: *Business, Networking and Sex: Not what you think!*, *Black Belt Business,*

Entrepreneurial Excellence Less Effort – Greater Profitability. He has written his own business development column for the Westchester and Fairfield County Business Journals. He is an internationally acclaimed motivational speaker, trainer, and CEO performance coach.

Donovan, Sandy

Sandy Donovan is the Executive Director of BNI in South Florida, which has been an award-winning region since she opened her first chapter in January, 1997. She is a contributing author to two New York Times Best Sellers, *"Masters of Networking"* and *"Masters of Sales"*.

Donovan spent the early part of her career in sales and promotions, first for Pepsi, and later in radio, at top Palm Beach County stations WRMF 97.9 FM and WIRK 107.9 FM, respectively. She now runs BNI with a team of Assistant Directors and conducts training and coaching for BNI members, helping them propel their businesses to the next level and surpass their competitors.

Gordon, Steve

Steve Gordon is the President and CEO of GlobalMind. GlobalMind helps land developers stop spending money during the critical phases of site selection, due diligence and entitlement.

In 2004 he was elected President of the Florida Surveying and Mapping Society, an industry advocacy group. In 2004 and again in 2005 he was named the Florida Surveyor of the Year.

In October, 2007 Steve created Tycoon Ventures, Inc. and launched the first Internet land search tool for land developers and investors--beaTycoon.com [pronounced Be a Tycoon dot com]. The site maintains a database of 8.5 million properties in Florida and plans to expand nationally in 2009. He currently serves as president and CEO and manages an international team of technologists.

Huffman, Chris

Chris Huffman is the Director of Service for Braman Motorcars in West Palm Beach Florida, the leading luxury automotive group ranked second in Ward's Automotive for Service and Parts Sales in the country. Braman Motorcars sells and services BMW, Mini Cooper, Porsche, Audi, Rolls-Royce, and Bentley out of separate facilities in Palm Beach. Chris is responsible for the "customer experience" for all service customers at all franchises.

Chris' career includes stints as Vice President of Rolls-Royce and Bentley Motorcars of North America, Executive Vice President of Operations for Cunard Cruise Lines. He has over twenty-five years of experience in delivering "the luxury customer experience" in the automotive and hospitality field. His passion is to make other people happy.

Lynch, Courtney

Courtney has found success by living her life as a leader. Notable achievements include her nine years of service as a Marine Corps officer, managing a top-notch sales team for Rational Software, earning her law degree at William & Mary, practicing at one of the nation's leading law firms, and creating Lead Star.

Beyond Courtney's government and private sector accomplishments, she is an entrepreneur, business owner, and best-selling author of *Leading from the Front*. Her success has been recognized throughout her professional career, but most recently she was awarded the 2006 National Stevie Award for Best Female Entrepreneur and *BusinessWeek* profiled her achievements as a leadership expert. A frequent guest on CNBC, FOX News, and CNN, her efforts with Lead Star have also been noted in publications ranging from *Fast Company* and *Inc.* to *The New York Times*.

Rizzo, Jeannine

Jeannine is a Transformational Speaker and trainer. She has years of experience with some of the top organizations in the world before going out on her own. She customizes and designs leadership development programs for Corporations to ignite and transform team performance Jeannine speaks and trains all over the world.

Rojas, John

John received his business degree from LBU. He has eleven years experience as an investment professional and is currently working towards obtaining the CFP designation. John has lived in the community for more than twenty five years and is active with The Rotary Club, Business Networking International, and Leadership Palm Beach County. He also established a private donor scholarship at Northwood University in West Palm Beach. John believes in practicing what he teaches. He has a written plan outlined for his short-term and long-term personal and financial goals. John believes in the importance of educating his clients, so the client can have an active role in the decisions affecting their money. He is an avid surfer and golfer.

Sherberg, Ellen

Ellen Sherberg has been a publisher of the St. Louis Business Journal since 1990. She joined the local business newspaper in 1980 and has served as a reporter, managing editor and editor.

Under Ellen's leadership, the Business Journal has received the award for Best Weekly Newspaper in the state of Missouri, the American City Eagle Award for best performing newspaper in the company, American City Business Journal Inc. and numerous other journalism awards.

Ellen's extensive community involvement includes serving on the executive boards of the United Way of greater St. Louis as well as on the board of directors of the Teach for America, the Regional Business Council, the St. Louis Sports Commission, the Regional Commerce and Growth Association, the March of Dimes and many, many more.

Before joining the St. Louis Business Journal, Ellen worked as a reporter for KMOX (CBS) Radio and for the St. Louis Globe-Democrat. As a freelance writer, she has had articles published in Time, Newsweek, The National Observer, Parents Magazine, Seventeen and Working Woman Magazine.

Ellen is a native St. Louisan. She attended Vassar College and Columbia University Graduate School of Journalism in New York City. She received an honorary doctorate from the University of Missouri-St. Louis.

CPSIA information can be obtained at www.ICGtesting.com
Printed in the USA
LVOW101750240112

265337LV00002B/2/P

Antología de la poesía española
(1939-1975)

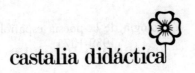

castalia didáctica

Director:
Pedro Álvarez de Miranda

Antología
de la poesía española
(1939-1975)

*Con cuadros cronológicos,
introducción, texto seleccionado,
notas y llamadas de atención,
documentos y orientaciones
para el estudio
a cargo de*

José Enrique Martínez

EDITORIAL CASTALIA

*Queda prohibida la reproducción total o parcial de este libro, su
inclusión en un sistema informativo, su transmisión en cualquier forma
o por cualquier medio, ya sea electrónico, mecánico, por fotocopia,
registro u otros métodos, sin el permiso previo y por escrito de los
titulares del Copyright.*

© Editorial Castalia, 1989
Zurbano, 39 - 28010 Madrid - Tel. 319 58 57
Cubierta de Víctor Sanz
Impreso en España - Printed in Spain
Talleres Gráficos Peñalara, S. A.
Fuenlabrada (Madrid)
I.S.B.N.: 84-7039-542-4
Depósito Legal: M. 28.065-1991

SUMARIO

1939-1975: La poesía y su tiempo   8

Introducción   19
    1. *1939: fin de la guerra civil. La poesía del destierro* . .   21
    2. *La posguerra inmediata: años 40*   23
    3. *La consolidación de la poesía social: años 50*   32
    4. *La promoción del 60*   35
    5. *La renovación poética: la aparición de los «novísimos»* .   39
    6. *1975: el fin de una época*   46

Bibliografía   49

Documentación gráfica   51

Nota previa   57

Antología de la poesía española (1939-1975)   59

    Luis Rosales   61
    Luis Felipe Vivanco   70
    Leopoldo Panero   75
    Dionisio Ridruejo   80
    José García Nieto   83
    Victoriano Crémer   88
    Gabriel Celaya   94
    Blas de Otero   100
    José Hierro   109
    Eugenio de Nora   119
    Rafael Morales   126
    Vicente Gaos   129

José Luis Hidalgo 133
Carlos Bousoño 136
José María Valverde 142
Carlos Edmundo de Ory 148
Miguel Labordeta 152
Ricardo Molina 157
Pablo García Baena 163
Ángel González 169
José Manuel Caballero Bonald 178
Carlos Barral 183
José Agustín Goytisolo 189
Jaime Gil de Biedma 195
José Ángel Valente 203
Francisco Brines 210
Claudio Rodríguez 215
Carlos Sahagún 220
Antonio Gamoneda 225
Félix Grande 233
Antonio Martínez Sarrión 240
Pere Gimferrer 245
Antonio Colinas 251
Guillermo Carnero 256
Leopoldo María Panero 261
Luis Alberto de Cuenca 266
Jaime Siles 273
Luis Antonio de Villena 278

Documentos y juicios críticos 283

Orientaciones para el estudio de la *Poesía española (1939-1975)* 299

Índice de poemas 323

1939-1975: LA POESÍA Y SU TIEMPO

Año	Acontecimientos históricos	Vida cultural y artística
1939	Termina la guerra civil española. Comienza la Segunda Guerra Mundial.	Exilio de intelectuales, artistas y escritores. Muere en Collioure (Francia), A. Machado. C. Vallejo, *Poemas humanos*. M. Hernández, *El hombre acecha*.
1940	España, neutral en la Guerra Mundial. Ley de Unidad Sindical. Muere Manuel Azaña en Francia.	P. Laín Entralgo y D. Ridruejo fundan *Escorial*. C. Vallejo: *España, aparta de mí este cáliz*. L. Cernuda: *Las nubes*. F. García Lorca: *Poeta en Nueva York* y *Diván del Tamarit* (póstumos).
1941	Japón entra en guerra con los Estados Unidos. La División Azul combate en Rusia. Muere Alfonso XIII. Creación del Instituto Nacional de Industria.	Azorín, *El escritor*. G. Diego, *Alondra de verdad*. R. Alberti, *Entre el clavel y la espada*.
1942	Ley de Constitución de las Cortes.	Muere en la cárcel M. Hernández. C. J. Cela, *La familia de Pascual Duarte*. L. Cernuda, *Ocnos*.
1943	Ley de Ordenación Universitaria. Regreso de la División Azul.	T. S. Eliot, *Cuatro cuartetos*.
1944	Desembarco de los aliados en Normandía. En España, aparecen los «maquis».	D. Alonso, *Oscura noticia* e *Hijos de la ira*. V. Aleixandre, *Sombra del paraíso*. Aparece *La Estafeta Literaria*.
1945	Bombardeo atómico de Hiroshima y Nagasaki. Termina la Segunda Guerra Mundial.	J. Guillén, *Cántico* (3.ª ed.). C. Laforet, *Nada*. G. Mistral, Premio Nobel.
1946	Cierre de la frontera francesa con España y bloqueo económico y diplomático de nuestro país.	Fundación de la revista *Ínsula*. P. Salinas, *El contemplado*. E. Prados, *Jardín cerrado*. J. R. Jiménez, *La estación total*. Fundación de la UNESCO.

Vida y obra de los poetas

Primer libro de amor, de Dionisio Ridruejo (Burgo de Osma, Soria, 1912). *La mejor Reina de España* (drama histórico), de L. Rosales (Granada, 1910) y Luis Felipe Vivanco (El Escorial, 1907).

Víspera hacia ti, de José García Nieto (Oviedo, 1914). L. F. Vivanco, *Tiempo de dolor*. D. Ridruejo, *Poesía en armas*. L. Rosales y L. F. Vivanco, *Poesía heroica del Imperio*.

Dionisio Ridruejo se alista en la División Azul.

D. Ridruejo es detenido y confinado en Ronda primero y después en un pueblo catalán. *Sonetos de la bahía*, de José Luis Cano (Algeciras, 1912). *Cántico espiritual*, de Blas de Otero (Bilbao, 1916). Nace la revista *Corcel* en Valencia (1942-49).

Nace la colección y el premio Adonais, concedido por vez primera a los *Poemas del toro*, de Rafael Morales (Talavera de la Reina, Toledo, 1919). D. Ridruejo, *Sonetos a la piedra*. Aparece en Madrid la revista *Garcilaso* (1943-46).

Creación en León de *Espadaña* (1944-51) y en Santander de *Proel* (1944-50). *La estancia vacía*, de Leopoldo Panero (Astorga, 1909). *Tacto sonoro*, de Victoriano Crémer (Burgos, 1907). *Arcángel de mi noche*, de Vicente Gaos (Valencia, 1919). D. Ridruejo, *En la soledad del tiempo*.

Poemas del dolor antiguo, de Ildefonso Manuel Gil (Zaragoza, 1912). *Ansia de la gracia*, de Carmen Conde (Cartagena, 1907). *Subida al amor*, de Carlos Bousoño (Boal, Asturias, 1923). *Hombre de Dios*, de José María Valverde (Valencia de Alcántara, Cáceres, 1926). Un único número de la revista *Postismo*.

Alba del hijo, de Leopoldo de Luis (Córdoba, 1918). J. García Nieto, *Del campo y soledad*. R. Morales, *El corazón y la tierra*. C. Bousoño, *Primavera de la muerte*. *Pueblo cautivo*, libro anónimo y clandestino de Eugenio de Nora (Zacos, León, 1923). *Poema de la condenación de Castilla*, de Gabino Alejandro Carriedo (Palencia, 1923).

Año	Acontecimientos históricos	Vida cultural y artística
1947	Plan Marshall de ayuda económica a Europa. Ley de Sucesión en la Jefatura del Estado.	L. Cernuda, *Como quien espera el alba*.
1948	Comienza la «guerra fría». Gandhi, asesinado. Se crea el Estado de Israel. Acuerdos comerciales con Francia y Reino Unido.	R. Alberti, *A la pintura*. Nace *Cuadernos Hispanoamericanos*.
1949	Se crea la OTAN.	Creación del Premio Nacional de Literatura y del «Boscán» de poesía. J. R. Jiménez, *Animal de fondo*. P. Salinas, *Todo más claro*. A. Buero Vallejo, *Historia de una escalera*.
1950	Comienza la guerra de Corea. Regreso de embajadores a Madrid.	P. Neruda, *Canto general*. M. Delibes, *El camino*.
1951	España ingresa en la OMS. Primeras huelgas importantes en Barcelona y País Vasco. Ruiz Jiménez, ministro de Educación.	P. Salinas muere en Boston. C. J. Cela, *La colmena*. A. Barea, *La forja de un rebelde*.
1952	Eisenhower, Presidente de Estados Unidos. Supresión de las cartillas de racionamiento. Congreso Eucarístico de Barcelona.	R. Alberti, *Retornos de lo vivo lejano*. D. Alonso, *Poetas españoles contemporáneos*. Estreno de *Tres sombreros de copa*.
1953	Muere Stalin. Acuerdos con Estados Unidos. Concordato con la Santa Sede. España ingresa en la UNESCO.	R. Alberti, *Ora marítima*. A. Sastre estrena *Escuadra hacia la muerte*.
1954	Kruschev, en Rusia.	V. Aleixandre, *Historia del corazón*. J. Fernández Santos, *Los bravos*. A. Castro, *La realidad histórica de España*.
1955	Ingreso de España en la ONU.	Muere J. Moreno Villa. P. Salinas, *Confianza* (póstumo). D. Alonso, *Hombre y Dios*. Muere Ortega y Gasset.

Vida y obra de los poetas
José Luis Hidalgo (Santander, 1919) muere días antes de la publicación de *Los muertos*. *Movimientos elementales* y *Tranquilamente hablando*, de Gabriel Celaya (Hernani, Guipúzcoa, 1911). *Tierra sin nosotros* y *Alegría*, de José Hierro (Madrid, 1922). V. Crémer, *Caminos de mi sangre*. R. Morales, *Los desterrados*. Nace en Córdoba *Cántico* (1947-49 y 1954-57).
Elegías de Sandua, de Ricardo Molina (Puente Genil, Córdoba, 1917). *Mientras cantan los pájaros*, de Pablo García Baena (Córdoba, 1923). *Sumido 25*, de Miguel Labordeta (Zaragoza, 1921). *Mujer de barro*, de Ángela Figuera (Bilbao, 1902). E. de Nora, *Contemplación del tiempo*. L. de Luis, *Huésped de un tiempo sombrío*.
L. F. Vivanco, *Continuación de la vida*. L. Panero, *Escrito a cada instante*. L. Rosales, *La casa encendida*. G. Celaya, *Las cosas como son*. J. M.ª Valverde, *La espera*. R. Molina, *Corimbo*.
Blas de Otero, *Ángel fieramente humano*. J. Hierro, *Con las piedras, con el viento*.
L. Rosales, *Rimas*. Blas de Otero, *Redoble de conciencia*. G. Celaya, *Las cartas boca arriba*.
V. Crémer, *Nuevos cantos de vida y esperanza*. G. Celaya, *Lo demás es silencio*. J. Hierro, *Quinta del 42*. *Las adivinaciones*, de José Manuel Caballero Bonald (Jerez de la Frontera, Cádiz, 1928). *Antología consultada de la joven poesía española*, de F. Ribes. C. Bousoño, *Teoría de la expresión poética*.
L. Panero, *Canto personal*. Claudio Rodríguez (Zamora, 1934), *Don de la ebriedad*.
Gloria Fuertes (Madrid, 1918), *Aconsejo beber hilo*. R. Morales, *Canción sobre el asfalto*. E. de Nora, *España, pasión de vida*. J. M. Caballero Bonald, *Memorias de poco tiempo*.
G. Celaya, *Cantos iberos*. Blas de Otero, *Pido la paz y la palabra*. José Agustín Goytisolo (Barcelona, 1928), *El retorno*. José Ángel Valente (Orense, 1929), *A modo de esperanza*.

Año	Acontecimientos históricos	Vida cultural y artística
1956	Rusia interviene en Hungría. Independencia de Marruecos. Graves agitaciones estudiantiles en Madrid.	Muere Pío Baroja. J. R. Jiménez, Premio Nobel. Nace *Papeles de Son Armadans*. Sánchez Albornoz, *España, un enigma histórico*. R. Sánchez Ferlosio, *El Jarama*.
1957	Creación de la Comunidad Económica Europea. Primer sputnik ruso al espacio. Miembros significativos del Opus Dei en el Gobierno.	J. Guillén, *Maremagnum*.
1958	Juan XXIII, papa. Promulgación de los Principios del Movimiento Nacional. Huelgas en Asturias. Ingreso en la OCDE.	J. R. Jiménez muere en Puerto Rico. M. Hernández, *Cancionero y romancero de ausencias* (póstumo). Pensiones March de Literatura.
1959	Fidel Castro triunfa en Cuba. Eisenhower visista España. Emigración hacia Europa.	Muere M. Altolaguirre. J. García Hortelano, *Nuevas amistades*.
1960	Kennedy, presidente de Estados Unidos. Se inicia la corriente turística hacia España.	Muere J. J. Domenchina. S. Espriu, *La pell de brau*.
1961	Encíclica «Mater et Magistra». Primer astronauta soviético en el espacio. Protestas laborales y estudiantiles.	J. M.ª Gironella, *Un millón de muertos*.
1962	Concilio Vaticano II. Independencia de Argelia. Aumentan los ministros del Opus. «Contubernio de Munich».	Muere E. Prados. V. Aleixandre, *En un vasto dominio*. L. Cernuda, *Desolación de la Quimera*. L. Martín Santos, *Tiempo de silencio*. L. Olmo, *La camisa*.
1963	Asesinato de Kennedy. Pablo VI, papa. Protestas en Europa por la ejecución de J. Grimau.	Muere en México L. Cernuda y en Buenos Aires, Gómez de la Serna.
1964	En Rusia cae Kruschev. «Veinticinco años de paz» en España. I Plan de Desarrollo Económico.	L. Cernuda, *La realidad y el deseo* (póstumo). *Cuadernos para el diálogo*.

Vida y obra de los poetas
V. Crémer, *Furia y paloma*. José Luis Prado Nogueira (El Ferrol, 1919), *Oratorio del Guadarrama*. Ángel González (Oviedo, 1925), *Áspero mundo*.
L. F. Vivanco, *El descampado*. J. Hierro, *Cuanto sé de mí*. C. Bousoño, *Noche del sentido*. R. Molina, *Elegía de Medina Azahara*. Carlos Barral (Barcelona, 1928), *Metropolitano*.
A. Figuera, *Belleza cruel*. Blas de Otero, *Ancia*. J. A. Goytisolo, *Salmos al viento*. C. Rodríguez, *Conjuros*. Carlos Sahagún (Alicante, 1938), *Profecías del agua*.
G. Celaya, *Cantata en Aleixandre*. Ángel Crespo (Ciudad Real, 1926), *Junio feliz*. Jaime Gil de Biedma (Barcelona, 1929), *Compañeros de viaje*.
Blas de Otero, *En castellano*. J. L. Prado Nogueira, *Miserere en la tumba de R. N.* Francisco Brines (Oliva, Valencia, 1932), *Las brasas*. J. A. Goytisolo, *Claridad*. J. A. Valente, *Poemas a Lázaro*. J. M.ª Castellet, *Veinte años de poesía española (1939-1959)*.
V. Gaos, *Concierto en mí y en vosotros*. A. González, *Sin esperanza, con convencimiento*. C. Barral, *Diecinueve figuras de mi historia civil*. C. Sahagún, *Como si hubiera muerto un niño*.
Muere Leopoldo Panero. D. Ridruejo participa en el «Contubernio de Munich». V. Crémer, *Tiempo de soledad*. G. Celaya, *Episodios nacionales*. C. Bousoño, *Invasión de la realidad*. A. González, *Grado elemental*. J. M. Caballero Bonald, *Dos días de setiembre* (novela).
Eladio Cabañero (Tomelloso, Ciudad Real, 1930), *Marisa Sabia y otros poemas*. J. M. Caballero Bonald, *Pliegos de cordel*. Félix Grande (Mérida, Badajoz, 1937), *Las piedras*. F. Ribes, *Poesía última* (Antología). En León, *Claraboya* (1963-68).
Blas de Otero, *Que trata de España*. J. Hierro, *Libro de las alucinaciones*.

Año	Acontecimientos históricos	Vida cultural y artística
1965	Termina el Vaticano II. Crisis estudiantil universitaria.	A. Serrano Plaja, *La mano de Dios pasa por este perro*.
1966	Ley Orgánica del Estado. Ley Fraga de Prensa e imprenta.	J. Goytisolo, *Señas de identidad*. M. Delibes, *Cinco horas con Mario*.
1967	Guerra árabe-israelí. Muere «Che» Guevara. Ley de Libertad Religiosa.	J. Benet, *Volverás a Región*. G. García Márquez. *Cien años de soledad*. M. A. Asturias, Premio Nobel.
1968	Rusia interviene en Checoslovaquia. «Mayo francés». Independencia de Guinea. II Plan de Desarrollo. Graves disturbios en Universidades de Madrid y Barcelona.	Muere León Felipe en México. En Málaga renace *Litoral*. V. Aleixandre, *Poemas de la consumación*.
1969	El hombre llega a la Luna. Ifni pasa a Marruecos. Franco designa sucesor a Juan Carlos, a título de Rey. Escándalo Matesa. Estado de excepción.	C. J. Cela, *San Camilo, 1936*.
1970	Allende, presidente de Chile. Acuerdo preferencial con la CEE. Ley General de Educación.	J. Benet, *Una meditación*. J. Goytisolo, *Reivindicación del conde don Julián*. Grupo Tábano, *Castañuela, 70*.
1971	China Popular ingresa en la ONU.	Neruda, Premio Nobel.
1972	Grave incremento del problema del orden público en el País Vasco.	Desaparece por orden gubernativa el diario *Madrid*. Muere Max Aub. G. Torrente Ballester *La saga/fuga de J. B.*
1973	Asesinato de Carrero Blanco, Presidente del Gobierno. Arias Navarro, nuevo Presidente.	Muere en Francia Picasso. En Chile muere Neruda. C. J. Cela, *Oficio de tinieblas, 5*.

Vida y obra de los poetas

D. Ridruejo, *Cuaderno catalán*. Alfonso Canales (Málaga, 1923), *Aminadab*. C. Rodríguez, *Alianza y condena*. L. de Luis, *Poesía social* (antología).

J. García Nieto, *Memorias y compromisos*. G. Fuertes, *Ni tiro, ni veneno, ni navaja*. J. Gil de Biedma, *Moralidades*. F. Brines, *Palabras a la oscuridad*. J. A. Valente, *La memoria y los signos*. F. Grande, *Música amenazada*. Pere Gimferrer (Barcelona, 1945), *Arde el mar*.

C. Bousoño, *Oda en la ceniza*. A. González, *Tratado de urbanismo*. F. Grande, *Blanco Spirituals*. Manuel Vázquez Montalbán (Barcelona, 1939), *Una educación sentimental*. Antonio Martínez Sarrión (Albacete, 1939), *Teatro de operaciones*. G. Carnero (Valencia, 1947), *Dibujo de la muerte*.

Muere Ricardo Molina. G. Celaya, *Canto en lo mío*. G. Fuertes, *Poeta de guardia*. J. A. Goytisolo, *Algo sucede*. J. Gil de Biedma, *Poemas póstumos*. P. Gimferrer, *La muerte en Beverly Hills*. Félix de Azúa (Barcelona, 1944), *Cepo para nutria*.

Muere Miguel Labordeta. Antonio Colinas (La Bañeza, León, 1946), *Preludios a una noche total*. Jaime Siles (Valencia, 1951), *Génesis de la luz*.

Blas de Otero, *Historias fingidas y verdaderas*. Carlos Edmundo de Ory (Cádiz, 1923), *Poesía 1945-1969*. José Miguel Ullán (Villarino de los Aires, Salamanca, 1944), *Antología salvaje*. Agustín Delgado (León, 1941), *Cancionero civil*. A. Martínez Sarrión, *Pautas para conjurados*. Leopoldo María Panero (Madrid, 1948), *Así se fundó Carnaby Street*. J. M.ª Castellet, *Nueve novísimos poetas españoles*.

J. M.ª Valverde, *Enseñanzas de la edad*. F. Brines, *Aún no*. G. Carnero, *El sueño de Escipión*. J. Siles, *Biografía sola*. Luis Alberto de Cuenca (Madrid, 1950), *Los retratos*. Luis Antonio de Villena (Madrid, 1951), *Sublime solarium*.

L. Rosales, *Segundo abril*. A. Colinas, *Truenos y flautas en un templo*. L. A. de Cuenca, *Elsinore*.

Muere Juan Eduardo Cirlot. G. Celaya, *Función de uno, equis, ene*. C. Bousoño, *Las monedas contra la losa*. J. A. Goytisolo, *Bajo tolerancia*. C. Barral, *Usuras y figuraciones*. C. Sahagún, *Estar contigo*. Antonio Carvajal (Albolote, Granada, 1943), *Serenata y navaja*. L. M.ª Panero, *Teoría*. J. Siles, *Canon*.

Año	Acontecimientos históricos	Vida cultural y artística
1974	Crisis económica internacional a causa del petróleo. Ejecución de Puig Antich, anarquista catalán. Atentado de la calle del Correo en Madrid.	V. Aleixandre, *Diálogos del conocimiento*.
1975	Terrorismo en varios frentes. Ejecución de cinco terroristas y violentas reacciones en Europa. Muere Franco. Juan Carlos I, rey de España.	Juan Goytisolo, *Juan sin tierra*.

Vida y obra de los poetas

Muere el poeta Alfonso Costafreda. L. F. Vivanco, *Los caminos.* José María Álvarez (Cartagena, 1942), *Museo de cera.* J. Gil de Biedma, *Diario del artista seriamente enfermo.* J. M. Caballero Bonald, *Ágata ojo de gato* (novela).

Mueren D. Ridruejo y L. F. Vivanco. J. Gil de Biedma, *Las personas del verbo.* Juan Luis Panero (Madrid, 1942), *Los trucos de la muerte.* A. Martínez Sarrión, *Una tromba mortal para los balleneros.* A. Colinas, *Sepulcro en Tarquinia.* G. Carnero, *El azar objetivo.* L. A. de Cuenca, *Scholia.* F. Millán y J. García Sánchez, *La escritura en libertad (Antología de la poesía experimental).*

Introducción

En julio de 1936 la sublevación de una parte del ejército español contra el Gobierno de la República dio lugar a una guerra civil que duró tres años. En los anteriores al estallido de la contienda la literatura española había llegado a tales niveles que algunos no han dudado en hablar de un segundo Siglo de Oro. Dentro del campo de la poesía, a los grandes maestros —Unamuno, Machado y Juan Ramón Jiménez— se unía la calidad técnica de los poetas del 27 —Guillén, Salinas, García Lorca, Alberti, Aleixandre, Cernuda, Gerardo Diego— y el brote de una nueva promoción de jóvenes poetas que iban a publicar sus primeras obras en torno a 1935 ó 1936, destacando entre ellos la figura de Miguel Hernández, además de Luis Rosales, Luis Felipe Vivanco, Juan y Leopoldo Panero y Germán Bleiberg.

La poesía se encaminaba en los años treinta por nuevas sendas. La «poesía pura» estaba en retroceso y, frente al concepto orteguiano de «deshumanización», se iba extendiendo un proceso contrario de «rehumanización» o vuelta al hombre, en el que confluían varias líneas poéticas: por un lado, una nueva orientación romántica —«neorromanticismo»— que se tradujo en la vuelta a Bécquer (patente en las obras del momento de Cernuda, Salinas y Alberti) y a Garcilaso de la Vega, leído como poeta romántico vitalista;

por otro lado, el conocimiento y la práctica de las técnicas surrealistas por parte de poetas como Aleixandre, García Lorca, Alberti y Cernuda; se iniciaba, además, el cultivo de la poesía social y revolucionaria, que contó con la presencia y el ejemplo de Neruda en el Madrid de 1934, y que escribieron poetas como Alberti y Emilio Prados; por fin, una serie de jóvenes empezaban el camino de la «poesía trascendente», que tuvo su órgano de difusión en la revista *Cruz y Raya* de J. Bergamín y que contó con la obra primera de un grupo de poetas amigos: Luis Rosales, Leopoldo Panero y Luis Felipe Vivanco, que quisieron conjugar la calidad artística de los poetas del 27 con los planteamientos éticos de Unamuno y Machado.

La guerra civil rompió este estado de cosas y dividió a la sociedad en dos bandos, lo cual tuvo su reflejo en la poesía: Antonio Machado, la mayor parte de los poetas del 27 y Miguel Hernández siguieron fieles a la República; la España nacional contó con poetas como Manuel Machado, José María Pemán y jóvenes como Rosales o Ridruejo. En uno y otro bando la poesía se cultivó intensamente, porque sirvió como arma de propaganda y de combate; sin embargo, en cantidad y calidad la producción fue mayor en el bando republicano; en cantidad porque la presencia en él de buena parte de los poetas consagrados sirvió de estímulo a muchos otros; en calidad porque, frente al pensamiento obligadamente monocorde del bando nacional, el republicano permitía enfoques de mayor riqueza ideológica. En su conjunto, la poesía de guerra fue circunstancial, contó con miles de poetas ocasionales que a través de ella liberaron sus odios o afirmaron sus creencias; no es, por ello, una obra de calidad, pero sí un testimonio histórico que tuvo en periódicos y revistas su principal medio de difusión. A pesar de las diferencias ideológicas, muchas características de la poesía de los dos bandos en lucha son comunes, basadas en una visión maniquea del mundo que temáticamente se expresa en los ataques al bando contrario, a los símbolos y a los héroes enemigos, y en la exaltación de los héroes y los símbolos propios, y retóricamente, por medio de antítesis del tipo *luz-sombra, valentía-cobardía, libertad-opresión, leones-liebres, alegría-tristeza,* etc.

1. 1939: fin de la guerra civil. La poesía del destierro

La guerra civil cortó bruscamente las líneas poéticas que a la altura de 1936 se mostraban en toda su variedad y riqueza y, tal como se ha visto, cambió el signo de la poesía. A partir de 1939 había que reconstruir no sólo un país en ruinas, sino, en cierta manera, también la poesía. Algunas orientaciones pudieron tener continuación en la posguerra, pero otras quedaron interrumpidas. Tras de la guerra civil, la situación era totalmente distinta: Unamuno había muerto a fines de 1936, García Lorca había sido asesinado en los primeros meses de la lucha, Antonio Machado moriría en el destierro en 1939, Miguel Hernández era una voz encarcelada y la mayor parte de los poetas e intelectuales de renombre optaron por el exilio. Este último hecho prolongó en el tiempo la división ocasionada por la guerra: por un lado, la España del interior, a su vez dividida en vencidos y vencedores, y éstos interesados en crear una cultura oficial que respondiera a los ideales y directrices del nuevo régimen político; por otro lado, la «España peregrina», quebrantada y dispersa. Conviene inicialmente referirse a la poesía creada por esta España, la llamada poesía trasterrada, del exilio o del destierro.

Entre los poetas que, fieles a la República, optaron voluntaria o violentamente por el exilio hay que nombrar a Juan Ramón Jiménez, a León Felipe y a la mayor parte de los poetas del 27: Salinas, Guillén, Cernuda, Alberti, Prados, Altolaguirre; cabría añadir otra serie de nombres que, más jóvenes, compusieron toda su obra prácticamente en el exilio, pero cuya importancia innegable aún necesita ser valorada en su conjunto.

No se puede estudiar la poesía trasterrada como un bloque monolítico, puesto que su característica más llamativa es la diversidad. Era inevitable que así sucediese. Republicanos como eran, había, sin embargo, entre ellos diferencias ideológicas, pero el exilio, además, causó la dispersión geográfica de los poetas y el desarrollo de un destino individualizado, por más que México y Argentina agruparan núcleos importantes de exiliados españoles que contribuyeron a enriquecer el panorama intelectual y editorial de cada país; a su lado, Londres, Estados Unidos o Puerto Rico contaron también con la presencia de otros poetas españoles. A las diferencias ideológicas y a la dispersión geográfica hay que unir otro problema de orden diferente: el conocimiento fragmentario y tardío que en España se tuvo de la obra de los poetas exiliados, limitación que les llevaba a preguntarse para qué y para quién seguían escribiendo.

Pese a lo dicho, puede intentarse sintetizar los rasgos comunes a la poesía trasterrada. España como patria perdida fue el tema clave y ante él se adoptaron dos actitudes diferenciadas que, en parte, corresponden a dos momentos temporales: en el primero predomina un tono apasionado, desgarrado y violento que acogía la negación de la patria abandonada e imprecaciones contra los vencedores, tal como se ve en poemas de Alberti y, sobre todo, en el León Felipe de *Español del éxodo y del llanto* (1939). Más adelante, la distancia geográfica y temporal transforma la exasperación en nostalgia de la patria perdida, al tiempo que se recuerda a los amigos muertos y a las tierras lejanas, dando lugar a libros de serena añoranza, como *Retornos de lo vivo lejano* (1952), de Rafael Alberti. Esta nueva actitud propicia una poesía más honda y reflexiva, la aparición de nuevos temas y la recuperación del «espacio interior», es decir, del mundo personal del poeta, que aparece en libros verdaderamente trascendentales, entre los que cabe citar *El contemplado* (1946), de Pedro Salinas y el gran poema «Espacio», de Juan Ramón Jiménez, parte central de *En el otro costado*. Por este camino entroncan, sin duda, con el proceso de «rehumanización» que se seguía en la España del interior.

2. La posguerra inmediata: años 40

No hará falta insistir en el vacío poético dejado por los poetas muertos y exiliados; tras de la guerra civil sólo tres poetas del 27, que iban a disfrutar de un extenso y profundo magisterio, permanecieron en la Península: Dámaso Alonso, Gerardo Diego y Vicente Aleixandre. A ellos hay que añadir el caso de un poeta más joven, Miguel Hernández, que hacia 1936 se hallaba ya en plena madurez poética, pero que, encarcelado al término de la contienda, compuso un magistral *Cancionero y romancero de ausencias* y unos *Ultimos poemas* que sólo fueron conocidos en su totalidad a partir de 1963, por lo que la importantísima obra del poeta de Orihuela, muerto en 1942 de una tuberculosis contraída en la prisión, quedó al margen del proceso evolutivo de la lírica de posguerra, sobre la que, sin embargo, la influencia de *El rayo que no cesa* (1936) fue temprana y capital.

2.1. Comienzo de la poesía de posguerra. La llamada «Generación del 36»

Apenas terminada la guerra, la poesía parece encaminarse por vías aparentemente diversas, pero convergentes. De acuerdo con la idea imperial de España difundida por los vencedores, se intenta crear una poesía artificiosamente heroica siguiendo el modelo que L. Rosales y L. F. Vivanco proponen en su *Poesía heroica del Imperio* (1940), que fue una amplísima antología de los poetas españoles del Siglo de Oro. Dentro de esta veta heroica, el fruto del momento fueron los *Sonetos a la piedra* (1943) de Ridruejo, cuyo título es fiel reflejo de la línea formalista y clasicista que predominó en los años iniciales de la posguerra. Es la misma que observamos en los otros dos temas frecuentados por la poesía del momento: el amoroso y el religioso. Este último constituyó un buen refugio personal ante las ruinas, y ya en 1940 publicó Valbuena Prat una *Antología de poesía sacra,* correspondiente también a la época áurea, en cuya senda hay que inscribir el *Retablo sacro del nacimiento del Señor* (1940), de Rosales, con los tradicionales motivos navideños vertidos en décimas y sonetos de gran maestría formal. Por lo que se refiere al tema amoroso, Dionisio Ridruejo ofreció en 1939 un *Primer libro de amor,* escrito años antes, pero inevitablemente también en sonetos, de forma que puede considerarse como punto de enlace entre la corriente formalista de preguerra, representada por *Abril* (1935), de Luis Rosales, y *Sonetos amorosos,* (1936) de Germán Bleiberg, y el neogarcilasismo de posguerra que analizaré más adelante.

Como puede verse, la lírica de posguerra la inician dentro de la Península poetas que habían surgido inmediatamente antes de la contienda. Se trata de un grupo unido por la amistad y la poesía y formado fundamentalmente por Luis Rosales, Luis Felipe Vivanco, Leopoldo Panero y Dionisio Ridruejo. El grupo ha recibido el nombre de «Generación del 36». Tal denominación cuenta a su favor con una fecha histórica que marcó sus vidas, pero tiene la desventaja de haberse utilizado para nombrar a un conjunto muy restringido de poetas, olvidándose de los que se fueron al exilio y empequeñeciendo la rica variedad de la poesía en los años cuarenta. De ahí que muchos prefieran abandonar el nombre de «generación» y adopten otros más precisos como «El grupo Escorial».

Escorial fue una revista de Falange que nació en 1940, pero que, dirigida en su primera etapa por Ridruejo, se apartó de la simple función propagandística para adquirir un cierto aire liberal. No fue una revista prioritariamente de poesía, pero acogió en sus páginas la teoría y la práctica poéticas del grupo de poetas anteriormente citados y propició unos modos líricos que tendrían su continuación inmediata en la revista *Garcilaso*.

Entre las características más llamativas del «grupo Escorial» suelen citarse:

a) Vuelta al intimismo, a la intimidad cotidiana, que incluye una poesía «arraigada» en el terruño natal, en la familia y en Dios.

b) Un formalismo clasicista en sus comienzos que parte de la métrica tradicional —el soneto— y de las fórmulas poéticas del Siglo de Oro.

c) Lenguaje deliberadamente sencillo, pretendidamente cotidiano.

Tales características han motivado el apelativo dado al grupo por García de la Concha de «poética de la intrahistoria». De cara a la poesía posterior hay que valorar la recuperación de Unamuno y Machado, y la revalorización de la poesía de César Vallejo, los matices existenciales de su poesía y, sobre todo, algunos de los poemarios más notables de la lírica posterior al 39, como *La casa encendida* (1949) de Luis Rosales, *Escrito a cada instante* (1949) de L. Panero y *El descampado* (1957) de Vivanco.

2.2. *Garcilasismo y garcilasistas*

La revista de poesía *Garcilaso* nace en 1943 con apoyo oficial y fundada por un grupo de poetas que se autoapellidaban «juventud creadora»: Jesús Juan Garcés, Jesús Revuelta, Pedro de Lorenzo y José García Nieto, que fue el director de la revista y el poeta sobresaliente del grupo.

El título de la revista pretendía trazar un paralelismo histórico con el poeta·del siglo XVI, llevando consigo —como ha escrito un crítico— una visión «castrense, imperial, caballeresca y amorosa» de la vida, al tiempo que la poesía tomaba aires neoclásicos con el cultivo del endecasílabo y del soneto. Se trataba de crear una poesía oficial de acuerdo con los intereses políticos del régimen, pero con García Nieto triunfó más bien otra línea cercana al «arte por el arte», que es a la que se alude cuando se habla de «garcilasismo» y que, siguiendo a García de la Concha, presenta una serie de caracteres que me permito resumir:

a) Reviviscencia del Cancionero del siglo XVI y del neopopularismo de Alberti y García Lorca. Hay, al mismo tiempo, preferencia por los poetas clásicos (Garcilaso, Lope, Quevedo) y neoclásicos (Meléndez Valdés).

b) Temáticamente hallamos poesía sacra y religiosa excesivamente retórica; tópicos amorosos en torno a la ausencia, pérdida o desdén de la amada; paisaje castellano contemplado como expresión de espiritualidad y melancólicos motivos otoñales.

c) Formalmente, dominio de la técnica, con agudezas y burlas de tono neobarroco en ocasiones.

d) Visión positiva del mundo que calla la penosa realidad del momento.

Como puede verse, el buen gusto, la belleza formal y la evasión primaron en los poetas de *Garcilaso*, revista que, sin embargo, acogió en sus páginas a poetas de otras tendencias.

Hasta 1944 hemos encontrado:

— Los poetas del «Grupo Escorial».
— Los poetas neoclasicistas de *Garcilaso* o «garcilasistas».

— Hay que añadir, además, una tendencia neorromántica que asoma en algunas páginas de *Garcilaso* y que se plasmará en los primeros títulos de la colección Adonais, como *Poemas del toro* (1943) de Rafael Morales y *Arcángel de mi noche* (1944) de Vicente Gaos.

2.3. La «*revolución de 1944*»: Hijos de la ira, Sombra del Paraíso *y* Espadaña

1944 es un año clave, considerado por algunos como el verdadero comienzo de la poesía española de posguerra. La reacción contra el garcilasismo la encarnó una revista de provincias, *Espadaña*. Pero son dos poetas del 27 los que decididamente impulsaron la renovación poética: Dámaso Alonso y Vicente Aleixandre. El otro miembro del 27 que había permanecido en España tras la guerra civil, Gerardo Diego, se había inclinado al clasicismo con *Ángeles de Compostela* (1940) y *Alondra de verdad* (1941), y había encontrado eco principalmente en la «juventud creadora».

Hijos de la ira fue, según algunos, el gran libro del decenio. El cambio de signo poético estaba en el ambiente, pero Dámaso Alonso logró dar cauce a las nuevas inquietudes con un libro que tuvo el significado de un revulsivo sobre las conciencias lectoras.

Hijos de la ira fue un grito de protesta en sentido amplio: lejos de la serenidad o de la evasión, vertía su angustia en una poesía «desarraigada»; fue también una protesta literaria que oponía un hondo contenido humano a la problemática meramente intimista o esteticista, un léxico inusual —con entrada de términos convencionalmente antipoéticos, como *pus, hipopótamo, ciempiés*, etc.— al estilo remilgado de la época, el versículo frente al verso tradicional, el poema largo y libérrimo frente a la sonetería garcilasista.

Si ante un tiempo sombrío Dámaso Alonso reaccionó con

un grito apasionado de protesta, Aleixandre, en cambio, reconstruyó en *Sombra del Paraíso* el mito del Paraíso perdido o no alcanzado: un mundo resplandeciente para el que el poeta —el hombre— se siente nacido, pero del que se ve dolorosamente desterrado, consciente de su transitoriedad temporal. Frente a los convencionalismos garcilasistas, Aleixandre desarrollaba una obra personal y diferenciada, con rasgos neorrománticos y surrealistas, que representaban el puente de unión con la poética de preguerra, y con una palabra repristinada que devolvía a la poesía su fuerza original. A pesar de lo que algunos han escrito, la influencia de *Sombra del Paraíso* fue intensa y extensa, a lo que hay que unir al propio poeta, mentor y guía de buen número de poetas jóvenes.

No puede desconocerse la importancia que adquirieron en los años 40 numerosos focos provincianos que tuvieron su manifestación en revistas como *Corcel* (1942) en Valencia o *Proel* (1944) en Santander. Ninguna, sin embargo, nació con tanto afán de polémica como la leonesa *Espadaña* (1944), que, dirigida por Antonio González de Lama, Victoriano Crémer y Eugenio de Nora, encarnó de hecho la reacción contra *Garcilaso* y los garcilasistas. *Espadaña* alargó su existencia durante cuarenta y ocho números, entre 1945 y comienzos de 1951. Su importancia reside en los siguientes puntos:

a) Fue un enlace consciente con la generación del 27 y con la poesía de Neruda y Vallejo. El homenaje explícito que a éste se tributó en el número 39 de la revista ha sido valorado como excepcional para su momento.

b) En conexión con el humanismo vallejiano, *Espadaña* contribuyó poderosamente al proceso «rehumanizador» de la lírica de posguerra a través de una poesía comprometida con la problemática existencial e histórica del hombre contemporáneo, que desembarcó en la «poesía social». Esta temática, tratada con tono violento y expresión desmesurada en poemas de Crémer y algún otro recibió el nombre de «tremendismo».

c) En su dilatada existencia estuvo abierta a las distintas corrientes de la lírica del momento, pero, fundamentalmente, sirvió de vehículo expresivo a la primera promoción de posguerra (Celaya, Otero, Bousoño, etc.).

2.4. *Las nuevas voces de la poesía existencial*

A lo largo de los años 40 se dan a conocer o se reafirman voces que ofrecieron en las revistas sus primeras muestras. Entonces y ahora se ha querido dividir el campo poético en dos bandos: *Espadaña* frente a *Garcilaso,* «rehumanizadores» frente a «formalistas», compromiso frente a evasión, tremendistas frente a neoclasicistas, etc. Los dos polos de la poesía recibirían más tarde aportación teórica de Dámaso Alonso: «El panorama poético español actual nos ofrece unas cuantas imágenes del mundo, muy armónicas o bien centradas, o vinculadas a un ancla, a un fijo amarre: todo lo llamaré poesía arraigada [...]. Para otros, el mundo nos es un caos y una angustia, y la poesía una frenética búsqueda de ordenación y de ancla. Sí, otros estamos muy lejos de toda armonía y toda serenidad [...]. El contraste con toda poesía arraigada es violentísimo.» El grupo de Rosales y los garcilasistas estarían entre los arraigados; *Hijos de la ira* y los espadañistas entre los desarraigados. Nuevos poetas vendrían a incrementar ambas corrientes, que podemos caracterizar así:

a) Poetas de tendencia realista que adoptan una actitud ética de compromiso existencial e histórico, al tiempo que rehúyen el esteticismo formal. Se trata de poetas cuya evolución, en cierto modo coincidente, va del yo al nosotros, del hombre existencialmente considerado al hombre social.

Destacan los siguientes poetas y libros: Gabriel Celaya, con *Tranquilamente hablando* (1947); Blas de Otero, con *Ángel fieramente humano* (1950) y *Redoble de conciencia* (1951); Victoriano Crémer, con *Tacto sonoro* (1944) y *Caminos de mi sangre* (1947); José Hierro, con *Tierra sin nosotros* (1947) y *Alegría* (1947); Eugenio de Nora, con *Pueblo cautivo* (1946) —publicado de forma anónima y clandestina— y *Contemplación del tiempo* (1948).

b) Poetas de tendencia metafísica que, sin despreciar la realidad ni desentenderse de la condición temporal del hombre, intentan bucear en lo «esencial» humano. Formalmente son más respetuosos con la tradición. Destacaron: Rafael Morales, con *Poemas del toro* (1943) y *Los desterrados* (1947); Vicente Gaos, con *Arcángel de mi noche* (1944) y *Sobre la tierra* (1945); José Luis Hidalgo, con *Los muertos* (1947); Carlos Bousoño, con *Subida al amor* (1945) y *Primavera de la muerte* (1946); José María Valverde, con *Hombre de Dios* (1945).

Las dos corrientes pueden unificarse bajo el marbete de «poesía existencial». De hecho, la división en dos polos es más didáctica que real y no da cuenta de la complejidad del fenómeno poético, en el que hubo, además, voces disidentes.

2.5. *Las voces disidentes*

Al margen de aquellas líneas dominantes, la lírica ofreció en la primera década de posguerra algunas otras manifestaciones que sólo en los años setenta fueron revalorizadas. Se trata, fundamentalmente, de tres tendencias:

A) *El postismo*

Como indica su nombre, es un movimiento heredero de los demás ismos. Se dio a conocer en 1945 a través de sendos números únicos de las revistas *Postismo* y *La cerbatana*. Sus promotores eran Eduardo Chicharro, Silvano Sernesi y Carlos Edmundo de Ory. Es la obra poética de este último la que ha conocido una revalorización acorde con sus méritos. Poetas como Gloria Fuertes, Ángel Crespo y Félix Grande o dramaturgos como Arrabal y Nieva recibirían tardíamente del postismo beneficiosas influencias.

Entre los rasgos más llamativos del postismo anotamos: su carácter experimental, que se manifiesta en la ruptura formal con la poesía de la época y en la exploración de nuevos ritmos y metros, su defensa de la imaginación y del humor y su conexión con el vanguardismo de preguerra, principalmente con el surrealismo y con el dadaísmo, a través del aprovechamiento del subconsciente.

B) *La corriente surrealista*

Cada vez se ve con mayor claridad que el movimiento surrealista recorrió subterráneamente la poesía española de posguerra, hasta el punto de querer verse su presencia en libros como *Hijos de la ira* y *Sombra del Paraíso*. Hubo, sin embargo, poetas voluntariamente adscritos al surrealismo que, quizá por lo que el movimiento tenía de subversivo, fueron relegados o silenciados. Sólo en años recientes se ha recuperado la obra de estos poetas, entre los que cabe destacar a Juan Eduardo Cirlot, Gabino Alejandro Carriedo y, sobre todo, Miguel Labordeta. Este llevó a cabo en su Zaragoza natal una obra singular en la que vierte su angustia existencial, al tiempo que se constituye en testimonio desgarrado de la sociedad contemporánea; por la ruptura formal e ideológica con la de su tiempo su poesía ha podido llamarse «revolucionaria». *Sumido 25* (1948) y *Transeúnte central* (1950) son dos de sus títulos en ese momento.

C)   *El grupo «Cántico»*

La revista cordobesa *Cántico* vivió dos épocas: 1947-49 y 1954-57, bajo la dirección de Ricardo Molina, Pablo García Baena y Juan Bernier. Frente a las dos tendencias dominantes, la poesía de *Cántico* era una tercera vía que, marginada por la crítica, cobró en los años setenta una inusitada revalorización, gracias en gran parte a un poeta «novísimo», Guillermo Carnero, a quien sigo a la hora de perfilar las características del grupo: presencia abrumadora de un intimismo de contenido culturalista, heredado del Modernismo y de los poetas del 27; refinamiento formal y búsqueda de la palabra rica y justa; tratamiento vitalista del tema amoroso, en contraste con el impersonalismo garcilasista o el agonismo existencial y religioso; presencia de la poesía de tipo religioso.

Dentro del grupo merecen ser destacados Ricardo Molina, con *Elegías de Sandua* (1948) y *Corimbo* (1949) y Pablo García Baena, con *Mientras cantan los pájaros* (1948) y *Antiguo muchacho* (1950).

3. La consolidación de la poesía social: años 50

En 1952 el editor Francisco Ribes publica la *Antología consultada de la joven poesía española*, texto ya histórico que venía a confirmar las dos tendencias básicas de los poetas de posguerra vistas páginas atrás. Una de ellas, la realista, desembocó en la «poesía social», tendencia predominante de la literatura española durante la década del 50.

Del marbete de «poesía social» se ha abusado para loar o atacar a un tipo de poesía que ha recibido también los nombres de comprometida, testimonial y hasta política. Entendemos, con Sanz Villanueva, que la poesía social es «un arte de urgencia que se ve motivado por la situación

sociopolítica del país, a cuya transformación quiere contri-
buir mediante la denuncia de la opresión y la injusticia».

Si bien pueden hallarse poemas sociales antes de 1950, es
ahora cuando esta poesía cobra un auge y una vigencia que
se mantienen hasta bien entrados los sesenta. A efectos
prácticos, sus límites cronológicos pueden establecerse entre
la citada antología de Ribes (1952) y *Poesía última* (1963),
antología del propio Ribes en la que los poetas de una nueva
promoción comienzan a cuestionar parcialmente los fundamentos de la poesía social.

Entre los múltiples antecedentes de la poesía social cobran
relieve las actitudes de compromiso anteriores a la guerra
civil: Neruda, Vallejo, García Lorca, Alberti... *Espadaña* e
Hijos de la ira serían jalones importantes en el camino hacia
la poesía social. La aparición ,en 1948 del libro de J. P.
Sartre, ¿*Qué es la literatura?*, con su formulación de la teoría
del compromiso literario, supuso también un apoyo decisi-
vo. Pero en su origen obran también causas socio-políticas: a
la trágica experiencia de la guerra civil hay que unir la
división del cuerpo social en vencedores y vencidos. Cuando
el poeta toma conciencia de la realidad histórico-social, la
poesía se convierte en testimonio y denuncia e incluso
—según conocida aseveración de Celaya— en «un instrumento para transformar el mundo». Tal es, al menos, el
deseo del poeta.

No fue la poesía social la única existente en la década del
50, pero sí la predominante. Un numerosísimo grupo de
poetas la cultivaron primordialmente. Al lado de Crémer,
Celaya, Otero, Hierro y Nora pueden colocarse Ángela
Figuera, Ramón de Garciasol, Leopoldo de Luis, etc.

Y llegó el cansancio. Y las deserciones. La agonía de la
poesía social se debió tanto a una sobredosis literaria como
al cambio socio-político. España había comenzado a indus-
trializarse, era aceptada cada vez más en los foros interna-
cionales, el nivel de vida se elevaba y los poetas comprometi-

dos empezaron a perder la esperanza en la poesía como «arma cargada de futuro». No tardarían en llegar los reproches: se acusó a la poesía social de prosaísmo, de convertir a la poesía en un medio y no en un fin, de no llegar al pueblo, que era su destinatario, de falta de imaginación y humor, de inadecuación entre una técnica conformista y un mensaje revolucionario, etc.

Entre los caracteres de la poesía social destacan:

a) Parte de una concepción realista de la literatura, que implica una visión histórica de la sociedad, referida a un aquí y un ahora.

b) Sus fines son: constituirse en testimonio crítico de su época, redimir a los humildes y transformar la sociedad en otra más justa.

c) La poesía se define como comunicación y se dirige a la inmensa mayoría.

d) Tono narrativo y estilo sencillo, coloquial y directo que, en los casos extremos, puede caer en el prosaísmo. Por otra parte, las dificultades con la censura pueden dar lugar a refinamientos elusivos de no fácil comprensión.

e) El tema es el eje de la composición. La solidaridad con el proletariado, la represión política, las injusticias sociales, la lucha por la libertad... son algunos de los temas de la poesía social; pero referidos a un lugar y a un tiempo históricos surge destacadamente el tema de España, con el inevitable recuerdo de la guerra civil. La preocupación por España llena libros enteros como *España, pasión de vida*, de Eugenio de Nora, o *Que trata de España*, de Blas de Otero. Conviene recordar al respecto dos antecedentes próximos: *España, aparta de mí este cáliz*, de César Vallejo, y *España en el corazón*, de Pablo Neruda.

Pasada la época de las polémicas, es preciso reconocer que la poesía social dejó algunos de los poemarios más importantes publicados desde 1939. Aparte los ya citados de Eugenio de Nora y de Blas de Otero, merecen ser destacados *Quinta del 42* (1953) y *Cuanto sé de mí* (1959), de José Hierro; *Pido la paz y la palabra* (1955), de Blas de Otero; *Cantos iberos* (1955), de G. Celaya, y *Nuevos cantos de vida y esperanza* (1952), de Victoriano Crémer.

Mediada la década, hace su aparición un nuevo grupo de poetas que, sin renunciar al compromiso, elevan la calidad artística de la poesía. Se trata de la llamada promoción del 50 por quienes se fijan en la fecha de publicación de sus primeros libros, o promoción del 60, debido a que ésta es la década en la que se consolidan como poetas.

4. La promoción del 60

El nuevo grupo está formado por poetas nacidos entre 1925 (Ángel González) y 1938 (Carlos Sahagún) aproximadamente. Se trata, además de los dos citados, de José Manuel Caballero Bonald, Ángel Crespo, José Agustín Goytisolo, Carlos Barral, José Ángel Valente, Jaime Gil de Biedma, Eladio Cabañero, Antonio Gamoneda, Francisco Brines, Claudio Rodríguez y Félix Grande.

Si de una manera general puede hablarse de un cierto compañerismo, lo cierto es que al principio hubo grupos pequeños de jóvenes que vivían en la misma ciudad, tenían experiencias comunes y eran amigos. Unicamente voy a destacar lo que se ha llamado «la escuela poética de Barcelona», formada por Carlos Barral, J. Gil de Biedma y J. A. Goytisolo, además del crítico José María Castellet y del poeta en lengua catalana Gabriel Ferrater. En la obra de estos poetas, la amistad es un agradable motivo poético. En su conjunto, los poetas todos de la promoción son «los niños de la guerra», pero también los que vivieron —niños o adolescentes— la etapa más dura de la posguerra.

En torno a 1955 aparecen sus primeros libros. En tal fecha se publican *El retorno*, de J. A. Goytisolo, y *A modo de esperanza*, de J. A. Valente. Algunos se habían adelantado, como J. M. Caballero Bonald, con *Las adivinaciones* (1952), y C. Rodríguez, con *Don de la ebriedad* (1953). Vendrán después *Áspero mundo*, de A. González; *Metropolitano*, de C. Barral, y *Compañeros de viaje*, de J. Gil de Biedma, mientras que otros libros primeros aparecerán en el cambio de la década: así sucede con *Las brasas*, de F. Brines, *Sublevación inmóvil*, de A. Gamoneda, o *Las piedras*, de F. Grande. Es, por tanto, en los años sesenta cuando estos poetas llegan a la madurez y se muestran como grupo consolidado.

En fecha oportuna, 1960, J. María Castellet publicó una polémica antología: *Veinte años de poesía española (1939-1959)*, que actuó en la práctica de verdadera presentación y de garantía de calidad de la nueva promoción de poetas, considerada como «segunda generación de posguerra». La primera había plasmado en la *Antología consultada* las dos tendencias poéticas que arrancaban de los años cuarenta y se desarrollaron en los cincuenta. Los poetas de la segunda generación nacen, en general, bajo el magisterio de los grandes poetas sociales —Celaya, Otero, Hierro...—, es decir, se inclinan en un primer momento hacia lo colectivo, para apartarse después de los aspectos más criticados de la poesía social y seguir una trayectoria que, sin renunciar a los principios básicos de aquella poética (realismo, tono narrativo, compromiso moral), prestará más atención a la persona, al individuo, a la intimidad, al tiempo que existirá un mayor cuidado por el lenguaje. Dentro de la propia promoción, los mayores están más cercanos a la estética de los poetas sociales de la primera generación: es el caso de Ángel González, verdadero puente de enlace entre aquéllos y los poetas de su grupo; en cambio, otros más jóvenes e ideológicamente afines a sus compañeros mayores, se hallarán más próximos a las nuevas formas expresivas que surgirán a fines de los sesenta: cabe citar aquí a A. Gamoneda y a F. Grande. Tal es la evolución interna del grupo.

4.1. *El nuevo concepto de la poesía*

Vicente Aleixandre había definido la poesía como comunicación. En tal idea coincidieron los poetas de los años 50. Uno de ellos, Carlos Bousoño, partió de la definición aleixandrina para su análisis de la poesía en un conocidísimo libro que, aparecido en 1952, sufrirá sucesivas reelaboraciones y notables adiciones: *Teoría de la expresión poética*. El concepto de poesía como comunicación sirvió a los primeros poetas sociales para fundamentar la primacía que dieron al tema y al decir sencillo, coloquial y, en los casos peores, prosaico: se trataba de llegar —de comunicar— a la mayoría.

La promoción del sesenta vio pronto los peligros que acechaban tras la definición aleixandrina. Ya en 1953 titulaba Barral un artículo: «Poesía no es comunicación.» Estaba encendida la polémica. Gil de Biedma y Valente verían en la comunicación un elemento más de la poesía, pero no su definición. Para los nuevos poetas la poesía era esencialmente un medio de conocimiento de la realidad, una «revelación de lo encubierto», una «salida hacia la realidad no expresada o incluso ocultada». A esta nueva concepción de la poesía añadían la participación del lector en el acto poético: la poesía —escribirá Gil de Biedma— es «el poema en tanto que asumido en la lectura». El rechazo de la poesía como comunicación y la aceptación de la poesía como conocimiento tenían una consecuencia práctica: evitar el excesivo peso de la temática y enriquecer el lenguaje como instrumento apropiado para acceder a la realidad.

4.2. Caracteres comunes de la promoción del sesenta

A pesar de las marcadas diferencias individuales, es posible referirse a algunos aspectos generales en los que coinciden todos o casi todos los poetas del grupo:

a) En su trayectoria —ya indicada— parten de los presupuestos de la poesía social, pero pronto se inclinarán más hacia la persona: pondrán más énfasis en lo personal que en lo colectivo; puede decirse que parten del yo para poetizar la circunstancia. De ahí la importancia de lo autobiográfico en esta poesía.

b) Aunque las influencias son variadas y dispersas, como rasgo general puede decirse que aceptan el magisterio de los grandes poetas sociales de la generación anterior. Antonio Machado es una referencia común, tanto vital como estética —*Campos de Castilla*— y moral —*Juan de Mairena*—. Entre los del 27, la influencia de Cernuda es innegable. Neruda y Vallejo forman parte también de las devociones del momento.

c) En cuanto a la expresión, intentan una dignificación del lenguaje poético, alejándose del prosaísmo de la poesía social, de los desgarros tremendistas y de las exquisiteces garcilasistas. Quizá su rasgo más llamativo sea la conversión del lenguaje coloquial en artístico; el tono conversacional, antirretórico, no oculta el rigor poético y la cuidada elaboración del poema como un todo. El humor y la ironía les sirven de distanciamiento respecto de las emociones o del mundo poetizado.

d) Los asuntos más frecuentes son: *la evocación de la infancia y de la adolescencia* como paraíso roto —a causa de la guerra— o perdido; unido a tal evocación, *el fluir del tiempo*, la conciencia de la transitoriedad humana, que carga algunos poemas de una vaga tristeza, de nostalgia; *el amor,* que tras los gastados clisés garcilasistas y el repudio de los poetas sociales, reaparece con fuerza, dando cauce a la intimidad e incluso al erotismo; y, en relación con el amor, *la amistad;* *España* fue un tema heredado de los primeros poetas sociales, con fuerte contenido de denuncia, hasta que con la crisis de la poesía social cayó el tema en descrédito; sin embargo, *los asuntos políticos* estarán muy presentes, con visión crítica personal que no excluye lo autobiográfico. Otros asuntos, como *la reflexión sobre la palabra poética* —metapoesía—, por ejemplo, son más ocasionales.

4.3. *Algunos títulos sobresalientes*

Desde el primer momento, la promoción de poetas de que venimos hablando fue vista como un grupo relativamente homogéneo, con rasgos renovadores respecto de la generación precedente, y contó pronto con intentos antologizadores que no es preciso citar aquí. Dentro de la trayectoria del grupo como tal o de cada poeta en particular pueden ser destacados, en cambio, algunos poemarios especialmente valiosos: *Grado elemental* (1962) y *Tratado de urbanismo* (1967), de A. González; *Descrédito del héroe* (1977), de J. M. Caballero Bonald; *Diecinueve figuras de mi historia civil* (1961), de C. Barral; *Salmos al viento* (1958), de J. A. Goytisolo; *Moralidades* (1966), de J. Gil de Biedma; *La memoria y los signos* (1966), de J. A. Valente; *Palabras a la oscuridad* (1966), de F. Brines; *Alianza y condena* (1965), de C. Rodríguez; *Como si hubiera muerto un niño* (1961), de C. Sahagún; *Descripción de la mentira* (1977), de A. Gamoneda, y *Blanco Spirituals* (1967), de F. Grande.

5. La renovación poética: la aparición de los «novísimos»

Con la promoción del 60 termina —según buena parte de la crítica— la poesía de posguerra. Cuando esta promoción está ofreciendo sus mejores frutos —años sesenta—, se da a conocer un nuevo grupo de poetas bien diferenciado de sus predecesores, jóvenes que han nacido pasada la guerra civil y que irrumpen en el mundo literario con una nueva sensibilidad y con una poesía tan absolutamente novedosa que se ha llegado a hablar de «ruptura», palabra grata, por ejemplo, a Luis Antonio de Villena, uno de los componentes de la joven promoción.

Pasada ya la algarabía de los primeros años, tal vez quepa decir que la ruptura consistió en llevar hasta el límite lo que venía sugerido por algunos poetas anteriores. De hecho, la propia promoción del 60 en su conjunto había sufrido una evolución interna que llevaba consigo una mayor atención a la intimidad y al lenguaje. Dentro de ella, algunos miembros se hallan más cercanos a lo que iba a ser la poesía renovadora posterior: es el caso de C. Barral, A. Gamoneda y F. Grande. Tal cercanía a la nueva poesía renovadora puede observarse incluso en la evolución de poetas de la primera generación de posguerra: es el caso del C. Bousoño de *Invasión de la realidad* (1962) y *Oda en la ceniza* (1967) y del José Hierro del *Libro de las alucinaciones* (1964). Hasta Vicente Aleixandre, ya viejo, renueva su creación con un texto ejemplar: *Poemas de la consumación* (1968).

A este clima de renovación poética hay que añadir la recuperación de fenómenos marginales, como el *Postismo* y C. E. de Ory —desde 1970 y debido al interés de F. Grande— o como *Cántico* y sus poetas, estudiados por un «novísimo», Guillermo Carnero.

En tal contexto irrumpe con fuerza y brillantez, hacia la mitad de los sesenta, un grupo juvenil cuyos rasgos más relevantes —exhibicionismo cultural y esteticismo— resultaban, a pesar de todo, extremadamente novedosos. El primer libro importante de estos poetas, *Arde el mar* (1966), de Pere Gimferrer, fue recibido con éxito por la crítica y galardonado con el Premio Nacional de Literatura. Tras él aparecerán: *Dibujo de la muerte* (1967), de Guillermo Carnero; *Teatro de operaciones* (1967), de Antonio Martínez Sarrión; *Una educación sentimental* (1967), de Manuel Vázquez Montalbán; *Cepo para nutria* (1968), de Félix de Azúa; *La muerte en Beverly Hills* (1968), del propio Gimferrer...

5.1. *Nueve novísimos y algunos más*

En 1970 J. María Castellet quiso dar cuenta del nuevo clima poético juvenil con una antología que iba a levantar buen número de polémicas: *Nueve novísimos poetas españoles.* Sus nombres eran: Manuel Vázquez Montalbán, Antonio Martínez Sarrión, José María Álvarez («los seniors», nacidos entre 1939 y 1942), Félix de Azúa, Pere Gimferrer, Vicente Molina-Foix, Guillermo Carnero, Ana María Moix y Leopoldo María Panero («la coqueluche», nacidos entre 1944 y 1948).

En el prólogo, Castellet habla de «ruptura» y de cambio radical, dejando claro que sólo ha seleccionado a un grupo de poetas nacidos después de 1939 y representativos de tal ruptura, dejando fuera a los jóvenes que no se habían propuesto la misma tentativa. Castellet caracteriza a sus novísimos con rasgos que quiero sintetizar aquí:

● Ruptura con el «realismo» típico de la literatura de posguerra; tal ruptura se debe a causas cronológicas, al cambio de gusto literario y, sobre todo, a la formación cultural de los novísimos, de espaldas a sus mayores y basada no en el «humanismo literario», sino en los *mass media:* radio, televisión, prensa, tebeos, comics, canciones, etc.

  ● Aceptación del gusto *camp* por lo que tiene de democratización de la cultura a través de las mitologías creadas por los *mass media* —Vázquez Montalbán— o por lo que representa de innovación —Gimferrer—. En relación con lo *camp* participan de la creación de una mitología popular que incluye el mundo del cine (Yvonne de Carlo, Marilyn Monroe...), el deporte, el comic, la política (Che Guevara...).

● Frente a la lírica «contenutista» de la posguerra, los jóvenes poetas propugnan la autonomía del arte, el valor absoluto de la poesía por sí misma y la autosuficiencia del poema, de forma que éste es antes un signo o un símbolo que un material literario transmisor de ideas o sentimientos.

● La formación literaria de los novísimos es fundamentalmente extranjera: Eliot, Pound, Saint-John Perse, Yeats, Wallace Stevens, los surrealistas franceses, etc. La tradición literaria española la ignoran voluntariamente, con las excepciones de Aleixandre, Cernuda y Gil de Biedma; les interesan más hispanoamericanos como Octavio Paz, Girondo, Lezama...

● Rasgos formales de la poesía novísima: despreocupación hacia las formas tradicionales, evitación del discurso lógico por medio de la escritura automática y técnicas elípticas, de sincopación y de «collage»; introducción de elementos exóticos (temas orientales, exaltación de ciudades desconocidas, mitos clásicos, etc.); experimentación sobre la estructura del lenguaje (Martínez Sarrión, Azúa, Molina-Foix) o desmitificación del lenguaje cotidiano (Vázquez Montalbán, Álvarez, Moix, Panero) o aprovechamiento de los recursos rítmicos y musicales del lenguaje (Gimferrer, Carnero).

A la antología de Castellet se le hicieron rápidos reproches de parcialidad y de montaje editorial. La crítica más chirriante provino del *Equipo «Claraboya»* de León, que en 1971 publicó con tal título el testimonio de lo que fue la revista entre el 63 y el 68, proponiendo, desde la óptica de una poética marxista, una «poesía dialéctica» a la altura de las circunstancias, ética y estéticamente, y tachando a los novísimos de neodecadentes y neocapitalistas. Hoy puede ya decirse que la antología de Castellet apareció en el momento oportuno y que dio a conocer una nueva sensibilidad, si bien no intentó acaparar todas las líneas poéticas que por entonces se estaban fraguando; fue, sí, parcial, en el sentido de ofrecer una línea única, que Castellet consideraba rupturista y en la que coincidieron no sólo los «novísimos» de la polémica antología, sino otros jóvenes poetas, con obras que, en general, participan de algunos o de todos los rasgos analizados por Castellet: Luis Antonio de Villena, con *Sublime solarium* (1971); Antonio Colinas, con *Truenos y flautas en un templo* (1971); Luis Alberto de Cuenca, con *Los retratos* (1971), y *Elsinore* (1972)...

5.2. *Caracteres generales y evolución*

La poesía «novísima» no fue la única tendencia existente entre los jóvenes, pero sí la dominante, la que de forma despectiva se motejó de *estética veneciana* o *venecianismo,* y que, siguiendo a José Luis García Martín, podemos ya caracterizar en su conjunto con tres rasgos esenciales:

1. Culturalismo y esteticismo: a la poesía afluyen lecturas, conocimientos, hechos culturales, etc., que llenan el poema de títulos y nombres propios, en un verdadero alarde de exhibicionismo cultural. «No nos apetecía escribir nada que no tuviera unos orígenes culturales, librescos», ha escrito L. A. de Cuenca. En esta antología pueden leerse poemas muy significativos en este sentido del propio Cuenca y de Gimferrer, Colinas, Carnero y Villena.

El culturalismo —según el citado crítico— desembocó pronto en la «metapoesía», es decir, en la poesía volcada sobre sí misma, en la poesía como tema de la poesía, que se convierte en una reflexión obsesiva en Guillermo Carnero a partir de *El sueño de Escipión* (1971); el lenguaje metapoético puede observarse en poemas incluidos en esta antología de Martínez Sarrión, de Carnero y de L. María Panero.

El culturalismo, unido a un lenguaje rico, «heredero de todos los llamados esteticismos de la Historia» —como ha escrito Carnero—, se traduce en un barroquismo expresivo, bien manifiesto en libros como *Dibujo de la muerte*, del propio Carnero.

2. Incorporación de la sensibilidad *camp*, la característica inicial más llamativa y la que, como moda que era, antes iba a desaparecer; se inicia con *Una educación sentimental* (1967), de Vázquez Montalbán, y afluye a *La muerte en Beverly Hills* (1968), de Gimferrer, y a *Así se fundó Carnaby Street* (1970), de L. María Panero. Tal sensibilidad *camp* la hallamos en poemas de Martínez Sarrión y Gimferrer incluidos en esta antología.

3. Recuperación de la tradición vanguardista de los años veinte. L. A. de Villena entiende la vanguardia como desdén del pasado, actitud de ruptura frente a todos los movimientos de la posguerra y, a cambio, revitalización del Modernismo y de la tradición simbolista, sin que falten los elementos vanguardistas de la escritura. En la presente antología, por ejemplo, los elementos surrealistas y la ausencia de mayúsculas y de puntuación en los poemas de Martínez Sarrión.

Fueron estas las características de la poesía que acaparó la atención crítica a principios de los 70, pero no fue la única poesía joven existente, como ya se ha dicho. Uno de los poetas «venecianos» ha escrito líneas muy sugerentes al respecto. Se trata de Luis Antonio de Villena, que observa como dominante a la estética veneciana entre el 66 y el 73; entre el 73 y el 75 se produciría un giro por el que los poetas novísimos o venecianos buscan sendas más personales que conducen a una depuración estética y al reencuentro por cada poeta de una tradición propia: Colinas reencuentra la tradición romántica más genuina en *Sepulcro en Tarquinia* (1975); Villena reelabora la tradición clásica desde *El viaje a Bizancio* (1978), al igual que L. A. de Cuenca en *Elsinore* (1972); Jaime Siles se inclina hacia la «poesía pura» con obras como *Canon* (1973); Carnero hacia la «metapoesía» con *El sueño de Escipión* (1971), *Variaciones y figuras sobre un tema de La Bruyère* (1974) y *El azar objetivo* (1975)...

Los rasgos más llamativos de la primera hora —venecianismo, lo *camp*, actitud vanguardista...— ceden paso a una poesía de la experiencia, al coloquialismo expresivo, al acercamiento a la promoción del 60, etc. Es en ese momento cuando hacen su aparición otros poetas de la misma generación, pero alejados de la estética novísima dominante, como Fernando Ortiz, Víctor Botas, Ana Rossetti, etc., o cuando comienza el aprecio crítico de otros poetas con obra ya publicada, como Juan Luis Panero. Es, pues, en torno al 75 cuando toda la promoción coincide ya en algunas características que harán hablar de la «generación del 68» —por la influencia del movimiento del mayo francés—, de la «generación del lenguaje» —por la atención prestada al mismo— o de la «generación del 70» —por su papel hegemónico a lo largo de la década.

Con una mayor perspectiva temporal, hoy puede leerse la poesía de muchos de los poetas del 70 en frecuentes recopilaciones de su obra total hasta el momento, llevadas a cabo por colecciones como Visor o Hiperión. En todo caso se trata de una promoción abundantemente antologizada, pudiendo destacar, además de la selección de Castellet, la *Nueva poesía española* (1970), de Enrique Martín Pardo; *Espejo del amor y de la muerte* (1971), de Antonio Prieto; *Joven poesía española* (1979), de C. G. Moral y Rosa María Pereda, y *Poetas de los 70* (1987), de Mari Pepa Palomero.

6. 1975: el fin de una época

En 1975, con la muerte de Franco, terminaba una larga etapa de la vida política española y surgían halagüeñas expectativas que pronto iban a concretarse en el establecimiento de un régimen democrático.

Para muchos, la aparición de los novísimos —o, más ampliamente, de la promoción del 70— significó ya el fin de lo que se venía llamando «poesía de posguerra» y el establecimiento de una nueva sensibilidad acorde con los tiempos nuevos de libertad —libertad política, pero también de expresión y de imaginación— que se avecinaban.

Si puede hablarse de «ruptura» de los novísimos con lo más general de la poesía de posguerra —realismo y eticismo—, lo cierto es que hacia 1975 —adelantándose de nuevo a la evolución política— la poesía entraba por cauces de normalidad, es decir, cesaban las rotundas negaciones de la tradición próxima y cada poeta podía conjugar con fortuna tradición e individualidad. Es manifiesta, a partir de entonces, la estima hacia la poesía de la promoción del 60, de la que algunos poetas de la promoción posterior, como Juan Luis Panero, se sentían muy próximos. Es también a partir de 1975 cuando los poetas del 70, en plena madurez intelectual y con voz personal diferenciada, producen sus mejores obras.

En tal fecha, 1975, la llamada «estética veneciana», en sus rasgos más sorpresivos, puede darse por terminada. Los mismos novísimos han evolucionado, como hemos visto; se dan a conocer algunos poetas de la misma generación ajenos a la estética hasta entonces dominante y, en coincidencia con esta evolución, aparece una nueva promoción de poetas a la que L. A. de Villena ha puesto nombre provisional: «Postnovísimos». En ellos ha observado dos líneas básicas: «el uso personalizado de la tradición clásica» en poetas como José Gutiérrez o Felipe Benítez Reyes —siguiendo la senda que venían trazando Colinas, Cuenca o el propio Villena—; la otra línea es la llamada «poesía del silencio», en la tradición de la «poesía pura», que, cultivada señaladamente por Jaime Siles en la promoción anterior, cuenta con el nombre destacado de Julia Castillo. Pero al lado de estas tendencias, una promoción calificada de abierta y plural muestra muchas otras opciones, entre las que cabe citar el ruralismo simbólico y salmodiante de Julio Llamazares, la herencia surrealista de Blanca Andreu y la apellidada «nueva sentimentalidad» de algunos poetas granadinos seguidores de Gil de Biedma, como Javier Egea y Luis García Montero.

Se trata de poetas que han escrito y publicado sus obras en fechas posteriores a las que enmarcan esta antología. Sin embargo, es posible disponer ya de alguna visión conjunta, provisional por falta de perspectiva temporal; cabe citar antologías como *Las voces y los ecos* (1980), de José Luis García Martín, y *Florilegium* (1982), de Elena de Jongh Rossel, en las que se mezclaban las dos últimas promociones de poetas que —como ya se ha dicho— venían a coincidir por esos años en algunos supuestos básicos. En 1985 Ramón Buenaventura dio a conocer una «antología de la joven poesía española escrita por mujeres» nacidas a partir de 1950, bajo el título de *Las diosas blancas;* más recientemente Julia Barella ha titulado significativamente su selección antológica *Después de la modernidad* (1987), acogiendo, según reza el subtítulo, «poesía española en sus distintas lenguas literarias» que se acomoda a los supuestos de «expresionismo» y «neoclasicismo» que la autora establece en un prólogo repleto de sugerencias tendentes a caracterizar esta poesía, ya no «novísima», que sólo en algún sentido podemos motejar de «postmoderna». Pero, sin duda, el libro que pretendió presentar como tal a la última promoción de poetas fue el ya citado *Postnovísimos* (1986), de Luis Antonio de Villena, que —tras un importante estudio preliminar—

incluye poetas jóvenes nacidos a partir de 1955, al igual que sucede con el núcleo principal de los seleccionados por José Luis García Martín para su antología titulada *La generación de los ochenta* (1988), que muestra —con enorme afán clasificatorio— las vías por donde camina la poesía joven del momento presente.

Bibliografía

Ayuso, José Paulino: *La poesía en el siglo XX: desde 1939*, Madrid, Playor, 1983. Estudio breve y sencillo de las líneas convergentes y divergentes del proceso poético de posguerra, conjugando la visión sincrónica y la diacrónica.

Cano, José Luis: *Poesía española contemporánea. Las generaciones de posguerra*, Madrid, Guadarrama, 1974. Recolección de artículos sobre poemarios de las dos primeras generaciones de posguerra al hilo de su publicación.

García de la Concha, Víctor: *La poesía española de 1935 a 1975*, Madrid, Cátedra, 1987. Dos volúmenes por ahora, que abarcan respectivamente los años 1935-1944 y 1944-1950. Estudio exhaustivo y sistemático del devenir histórico de grupos, poetas y poemarios.

García Martín, José Luis: *La segunda generación poética de posguerra*, Diputación de Badajoz, 1986. Análisis de la generación en su conjunto, de su génesis, poética y tópicos temáticos.

González, José María: *Poesía española de posguerra (Celaya, Otero, Hierro: 1950-1960)*, Madrid, Edi-6, 1982. Análisis original, dentro de las nuevas tendencias críticas, del papel retórico que juega el lector-destinatario en la obra de cada poeta.

Grande, Félix: *Apuntes sobre poesía española de posguerra*, Madrid, Taurus, 1970. Primer estudio panorámico, lleno de juicios atinados, válidos aún en gran parte.

Palomo, María del Pilar: *La poesía en el siglo XX (desde 1939)*, Madrid, Taurus, 1988. Análisis general de las distintas etapas poéticas entre 1939-1980, seguido del estudio de buena parte de los poetas, para terminar con una interesante referencia a la crítica de poesía actual.

Payeras Grau, María: *Poesía española de posguerra,* Madrid, Prensa Universitaria, 1986. Se trata de una síntesis teórica, densa y breve.

Rubio, Fanny: *Revistas poéticas españolas, 1939-1975,* Madrid, Turner, 1976. Indispensable para conocer el papel jugado por las revistas de poesía, además de excelente libro de consulta.

Rubio, Fanny, y Falcó, José Luis: «Estudio preliminar» a *Poesía española contemporánea (1939-1980),* Madrid, Alhambra, 1984, 2.ª ed. Minuciosa reconstrucción del proceso poético desde 1939, a través de sus distintas fases y de la alternancia de escuelas, grupos y escritores aislados.

Sanz Villanueva, Santos: *Literatura actual,* Barcelona, Ariel, 1984. El capítulo cuarto expone la marcha de la poesía desde 1936. Es la guía más clara, sencilla y a la vez profunda con que contamos.

Carlos Bousoño.

Casi el pleno de la "juventud creadora". Dibujo tomado del natural por Suárez del Árbol, en una noche de sábado en el café Gijón.

Dionisio Ridruejo, en sus
últimos tiempos.

Ilustración de José
Caballero para *Sonetos a
la piedra* (1943), de
Dionisio Ridruejo.

Leopoldo Panero.

Luis Rosales.

Luis Felipe Vivanco.

Eugenio de Nora.

Victoriano Crémer.

Jaime Gil de Biedma.

Francisco Brines.

Carlos Barral.

Pere Gimferrer.

Claudio Rodríguez.

Gabriel Celaya.

Cubierta de la segunda edición (1954) de *Los muertos*.

José Luis Hidalgo

LOS MUERTOS

CAMPO DE AMOR

(Canción)

Si me muero, que sepan que he vivido
luchando por la vida y por la paz.
Apenas he podido con la pluma,
apláudanmé al cantar.

Si me muero, será porque he nacido
para pasar el tiempo a los de atrás.
Confío que entre todos dejaremos
al hombre en su lugar.

Si me muero, ya sé que no veré
naranjas de la china, ni el trigal.
He levantado el rastro, esto me basta.
Otros acecharán.

Si me muero, que no me mueran antes
de abriros el balcón de par en par.
Un niño, acaso un niño, está mirándome
el pecho de cristal.

Nota previa

El primer problema que se plantea a la hora de elaborar una antología como la presente es el de la selección, tanto de los poetas como de los poemas. Toda selección es discutible y, por ello, polémica, por lo que esta nota previa quiere ser, antes que nada, una justificación.

1. Los poetas incluidos en esta antología han escrito su obra —o la mayor parte de la misma— a partir de 1939, es decir, han desarrollado su personalidad poética después de la guerra civil. Acoge, pues, esta antología únicamente lo que en un sentido muy lato pueden llamarse generaciones o promociones poéticas de posguerra.

2. No forman parte, por tanto, de esta antología los poetas del 27, ni siquiera aquellos que como Dámaso Alonso y Vicente Aleixandre han tenido una manifiesta incidencia en la poesía que sigue a la guerra civil. Ha de tenerse en cuenta, por otro lado, que los poetas del 27 gozarán de una antología específica en esta misma colección. Duele, sin duda, dejar fuera a Miguel Hernández, pero las circunstancias que rodearon su vida y su muerte hicieron que, desgraciadamente, quedara fuera del proceso evolutivo de la lírica de posguerra; el grueso de su obra, por otra parte, es anterior a la fecha con que se inicia esta antología.

3. Tampoco aparece incluida en la presente selección la poesía del exilio. Por lo ya dicho, muchos de los poetas exiliados —los del 27, por ejemplo— disponen de antologías propias y los jóvenes que iniciaron su obra en el destierro quedaron al margen de la poesía

española del interior y, en buena parte, se incorporaron al quehacer poético del país que los acogió.

4. Los poetas seleccionados responden a los supuestos teóricos de la introducción; se trata, pues, de los más representativos de cada momento y de aquellos que han sido revalorizados en la actualidad. Se echarán en falta, inevitablemente, algunos nombres, pero podrá estarse de acuerdo, al menos, en que los seleccionados son siempre poetas necesarios.

5. Por lo que se refiere a los poemas, he sacrificado en ocasiones el gusto personal en favor de una pretendida objetividad; he tratado, en suma, de que los poemas respondan a las características básicas de cada movimiento. El antólogo es el primero en lamentar la parquedad en el número de poemas de cada autor.

6. Finalmente he de decir que los posibles aciertos se deberán a los propios poetas, cuya obra me ha proporcionado nuevos placeres y conocimientos. Si algún logro cabe pedir a esta antología, el mayor consistirá en que sea capaz de suscitar el interés del alumno —y de cualquier lector— por esta dilatada parcela de nuestra lírica.

ANTOLOGÍA
DE LA POESÍA ESPAÑOLA
(1939-1975)

LUIS ROSALES

CIEGO POR VOLUNTAD Y POR DESTINO

PORQUE TODO ES IGUAL Y TÚ LO SABES,
has llegado a tu casa, y has cerrado la puerta
con ese mismo gesto con que se tira un día,
con que se quita la hoja atrasada al calendario
cuando todo es igual y tú lo sabes.   5
Has llegado a tu casa,
y, al entrar,
has sentido la extrañeza de tus pasos
que estaban ya sonando en el pasillo antes de que
                              [llegaras,
y encendiste la luz, para volver a comprobar   10
que todas las cosas están exactamente colocadas
               [como estarán dentro de un año,
y después,
te has bañado, respetuosa y tristemente, lo mismo
                       [que un suicida,
y has mirado tus libros como miran los árboles sus
                            [hojas,
y te has sentido solo,   15
humanamente solo,
definitivamente solo porque todo es igual y tú lo sabes.

Has llegado a tu casa,
y ahora, querrías saber para qué sirve estar sentado,
para qué sirve estar sentado igual que un náufrago   20
entre tus pobres cosas cotidianas.
Sí, ahora quisiera yo saber
para qué sirven el gabinete nómada y el hogar que
                              [jamás se ha encendido,
y el Belén de Granada[1]
—el Belén que fue niño cuando nosotros todavía
                              [nos dormíamos cantando— 25
y para qué puede servir esta palabra: ahora
esta palabra misma: «ahora»,
cuando empieza la nieve
cuando nace la nieve,
cuando crece la nieve en una vida que quizá está
                              [siendo la mía, 30
en una vida que no tiene memoria perdurable,
que no tiene mañana,
que no conoce apenas si era clavel, si es rosa,
si fue azucenamente[2] hacia la tarde.
                              Sí, ahora
me gustaría saber para qué sirve este silencio que
                              [me rodea, 35
este silencio que es como un luto de hombres solos,
este silencio que yo tengo,
este silencio
que cuando Dios lo quiere se nos cansa en el cuerpo,
se nos lleva,   40
se nos duerme a morir,
porque todo es igual y tú lo sabes.

---

[1] Granada es la ciudad natal de Rosales. [2] *azucenamente:* creación poética
sobre *azucena.*

SÍ, HE LLEGADO A MI CASA, HE LLEGADO, DESDE
                     [LUEGO, A MI CASA,
y ahora es lo de siempre,
lo de nogal diario,   45
los cuadros que aún no he tenido tiempo de colgar y
    [están sobre la mesa que vistió de volantes mi hermana,
la madera que duele,
y la pequeña luz deshabitando la habitación,
y la pequeña luz que es como un hueco en la
                           [penumbra,
y el vaso para nadie   50
y el puñado de sueño,
y las estanterías,
y estar sentado para siempre.
Sí, he vuelto de la calle; estoy sentado;
la nieve de empezar a ser bastante   55
sigue cayendo [1]
sigue cayendo todo, sigue haciéndose igual,
sigue haciéndose *luego,*
sigue cayendo,
sigue cayendo todo lo que era Europa, lo que era mío
    [y había llegado a ser más importante que la vida,   60
lo que nació de todos y era como una grieta de luz
                       [entre mi carne,
sigue cayendo,
sigue cayendo todo lo que era propio,
lo que ya estaba liberado,
lo que ya estaba desdolorido [3] por la vida,   65

---

[3] *desdolorido:* neologismo con el prefijo *des-,* como en v. 140.

(1) La serie que aquí se inicia, bajo el martilleo de «sigue cayendo», expresa el paso del tiempo y la destrucción de las ilusiones.

sigue cayendo,
sigue cayendo todo lo que era humano, cierto y frágil
lo mismo que una niña de seis años que llorara
                                        [durmiendo,
sigue cayendo,
sigue cayendo todo,   70
como una araña a la que tú vieras caer,
a la que vieras tú cayendo siempre,
a la que vieras tú mismo,
tú, tristemente mismo,
a la que vieras tú cayendo hasta arañarte en la
                        [pupila con sus patas velludas   75
y allí la vieras toda,
toda solteramente[4] siendo araña,
y después la sintieras penetrarte en el ojo,
y después la sintieras caminar hacia adentro,
hacia dentro de ti caminando y llenándote,   80
llenándote de araña,
y comprobaras que estabas siendo su camino porque
                                [cegabas de ella,
y todavía después la sintieras igual,
igual que rota
y todavía...

            —¡*Buenas noches, don Luis!*—   85

Sí, ES VERDAD QUE EL SERENO
cuando me abrió esta noche la cancela,
me ha recordado a la palabra «igual»;
me ha recordado
que estaba ya,   90
desde hace muchos años,

---

    [4] *solteramente:* neologismo creado sobre *soltera*.

haciéndose gallego inútilmente
porque ya lo sabía,
porque ya lo sabía,
y casi le zumbaba la boca como un trompo,   95
a fuerza de callar
y de tener la cara expectante y atónita.
Sí, es verdad,
y ahora comprendo por qué me ha recordado
                                [a la palabra «igual»:
era lo mismo que ella,   100
era igual y tenía
las llaves enredadas entre las manos
pero sirviéndole para todo como sus cinco letras,
las cinco llagas de la palabra igual,
las cinco llaves que le sonaban luego,   105
que le sonaban igual que ayer y que mañana,
igual que ahora
                    siento de pronto,
ahogada en la espesura de silencio que me rodea,
como una vibración mínima y persuasiva
de algo que se mueve para nacer,   110
y es un ruido pequeño,
casi como un latido que sufriera,
como un latido en su claustro de musgo,
como un niño de musgo que porque duele tiene
                                [nombre,
tiene ese nombre que únicamente puede escuchar
                                [la madre,   115
ese nombre que ya duele en el vientre,
que ya empieza a decirse a su manera;
y es un sonido de algo interior que vibra,
de algo interior que está subiendo a mi garganta
                                [como el agua en un pozo,
igual que esa palabra que no se piensa todavía
                                [mientras se está diciendo,   120

y después se hace radiante, ávido, irrestañable, [5]
y ahora es ya la memoria que se ilumina como
      [un cabo de vela que se enciende con otra,
y ahora es ya el corazón que se enciende con otro
             [corazón que yo he tenido antes,
y con otro que yo entristezco todavía,
y con otro   125
que yo puedo tener, que estoy teniendo ahora,
un corazón más grande
un corazón para vivirlo, descalzo y necesario,
un corazón reunido,
reunido de otros muchos,   130
igual que un olor único que hacen diversas flores;
y pienso
que quizás estoy ardiendo todo,
que se ha quemado la palabra «igual»,
y que al hacerse transparente y total la memoria,   135
nos vibra el corazón como cristal tañido, [6]
nos vibra,
está vibrando ya con este son que suena,
con este son, con este son que suena enloqueciendo
                   [ya la casa toda,
mientras que se me va desdoloriendo el alma   140
por una grieta dulce. [2]

                            (*La casa encendida*, 1949)

---

[5] *irrestañable:* que no se puede ya detener.   [6] *tañido:* tocado para que suene.

(2) Base anecdótica del poema: una fuerte sensación de monotonía llena el pasado, el presente y el futuro de los gestos cotidianos;
es la desesperanza del «hogar que jamás se ha encendido» porque
la memoria está inactiva y las cosas pierden todo su valor; de
pronto, hay un mínimo anuncio de actividad y, al fin, la memoria

HAY UN DOLOR QUE SE NOS JUNTA EN LAS PALABRAS

Al escultor Carlos Ferreira

SI TÚ SUPIERAS QUE AYER ES VIEJO COMO AMÉRICA,
que ayer es tan escaso que ya no tiene un sol en cada tarde,
que ayer no es como un árbol, sino más bien como un hotel,
y que sus horas no se juntan, no se pueden juntar,
para poder vivirlas económicamente   5
tomando el sol en el pinar de agosto;
si tú supieras que ayer, tal vez, resulta caro,
y que ha vendido en pública subasta
su balneario de sal para las olas,
sus crepúsculos vespertinos   10
y su anestesia cívica,
o si se quiere,
su cerrada y mohosa seguridad de editorial político;
y, finalmente, si tú supieras que un poema
no puede ya volver a ser como un escaparate de joyería; 15
si tú supieras que ahora es preciso que escribamos
desde el solar de la palabra misma,
desde el solar de nuestra propia alma,
porque nada está vivo, sino ella,
porque nada en el mundo tiene ya fuerza para decir
                                                    [que sí, 20
porque nadie puede acordarse de nosotros,

---

se ilumina, enciende pasado, presente y futuro, quema a la palabra
«igual» y el alma se va «desdoloriendo» de dulzura. El verso inicial
es el *leitmotiv* del poema; *igual* es la palabra clave; las reiteraciones
intensifican la sensación de monotonía. Sorprenden los símiles (vv.
20, 68, etc.), los epítetos en contextos infrecuentes (vv. 23, 128, etc.)
y los neologismos (*solteramente...*).

nadie puede regalarnos un traje,
nadie puede saber que hemos tenido un nombre,
sino Dios. [3]

(*Rimas*, 1951)

LA CICATRIZ

A cada hombre le tendríamos que hablar en una
                              [lengua distinta,
a cada amigo le tendríamos que hablar con una voz
                              [distinta
para que nos pudiesen comprender,
pero la lengua personal es tan fiel a sí misma,
tan incomunicable   5
que las palabras son como ataúdes
y sólo llevan de hombre a hombre
su andamio agonizante,
su remanente de silencio
y su estertor.
                Como aquella mañana   10
en que al sentarme en el autobús
vi a mi lado una antigua moneda romana,
una medalla
o una lápida
que hablaba masticando las palabras;   15
era una campesina ya embebida

---

(3) Con técnica surrealista se enfrenta un *ayer* degradado con un *ahora* en el que el poema no puede ser ya objeto de lujo, sino indagación interior que aboca al mismo Dios.

por la intemperie de la noche a tientas
y de la vida a ciegas
que me miraba con un poco de luto en las pupilas
como queriéndome abrigar,   20
y yo no supe contestarle,
y yo callaba junto a ella
porque mi lengua personal es inventada,
enfática,
y como no me sirve para hablar con un obrero
                              [o con un niño,   25
y como no me puede dar la absolución
a veces tengo que ocultarla como se oculta el dinero
                              [en la cartera,
a veces tengo que callar
como hice entonces,
sintiendo de repente   30
la incomunicación
igual que el aletazo de un murciélago,
con su golpe de trapo,
y su asco parcelado sobre el rostro,
donde el labio que calla va convirtiéndose en cicatriz. [4] 35

(*Como el corte hace sangre*, 1974)

(**4**) A través de signos que connotan «muerte» *(ataúdes, agonizan-te*, etc.), se poetiza la insuficiencia del lenguaje, que conduce a la soledad, a la incomunicación, expresada con imágenes degradantes en los versos finales.

LUIS FELIPE VIVANCO [5]

LA CAZA

> *Siento plenamente la dulzura de esta*
> *profesión: ser el sostén de una familia.*
> NOVALIS [1]

Asiduo cazador y padre mío de este mundo:
después de tu visita veraniega,
sé, desde esta cuneta de ortigas y de menta,
que yo también he sido hecho
a imagen y semejanza tuya,   5
que me parezco a ti, que soy un poco

---

[1] *Novalis:* poeta romántico alemán del XVIII.

(5) La poesía de Vivanco —como la de Panero y Rosales—
arraiga en un intimismo que abarca lo familiar («La caza»), la
naturaleza («Qué bien sé lo que quiero») y Dios («El descampado»). Parte de una situación concreta y desgrana detalles realistas a
los que dota de una dimensión trascendente; el aborrecimiento de
la ciudad y la aspiración al campo como lugar de íntima soledad
con Dios son rasgos de un ascetismo espiritual que tiene su correlato
en la austeridad del lenguaje, parco en imágenes o en adjetivacio-
nes sorprendentes.

tu querencia hogareña y tu corteza más agreste,
que tengo tu apetencia de andar, que no me canso
de seguirte —y por eso
voy pisando contigo entre la jara,   10
detrás de ti y tus piernas añosas, [2] tus espaldas,
tu sudor en la siesta,
—tu envejecer remiso por los cerros— que escucho
lo que se mueve apenas dentro de cada mata,
y huelo la sequía del monte bajo, y veo   15
—con mirada que no huye, ciega, hacia el infinito—
cada trozo inspirado del terreno.

Pero he crecido y tengo mi juventud inquieta:
éstas son mis lecturas, mi ambición de estar solo
con Dios, mientras el eco y los espejos me devuelven   20
torpes hechuras mías, sin sustancia
de llanura heredada, sin ese cementerio
—tapiales y bardales, [3] lejos, entre los surcos—,
con muertos de la misma procedencia
que nosotros.

       Yo estoy aborreciendo   25
mis noches de ciudad y mis domingos.
Tú, ya has tomado el tren, vas con sencillos
compañeros. Y duermes en la fonda
de una estación. Madrugas. ¿Son los montes
de Toledo? ¿La sierra del Chorito? [4]   30
¿O el Tajo? ¿Vuela un buitre sobre el agua
primorosa de sol?
       Yo estoy hablando
de cuestiones abstractas, inventándome
la figura ideal de alguna amada,

---

[2] *añosas:* de muchos años. [3] *tapiales y bardales:* paredes de tierra cubiertas con *bardas* de paja o de césped. [4] Pertenece a los Montes de Toledo.

¡perdiéndome ese cielo entre las ramas   35
colgantes de la encina!
Así, engañado, tímido de seriedad, rebelde
de convicciones místicas, he persistido
lejos de ti y tus vastas laderas de montañas.
Pero he crecido más (hacia mi origen)   40
y aquí están, otra vez, tus botas de campo y tu escopeta,
y aquí estoy yo, tocándolas
con manos que no olvidan los soldados de plomo,
a la vuelta del largo paseo, colocando,
desde niño, las dudas —la prisa— de mis pasos   45
sobre tus lentos pasos cazadores.
Aquí estoy, recobrado hijo tuyo, y desde la brumosa
colección de mis sueños, oigo, llamándome
a la indefensa realidad
de la esposa y las hijas, tus disparos...   50

                              (*Continuación de la vida*, 1949)

QUÉ BIEN SÉ LO QUE QUIERO

A Rodrigo Uría

Qué bien sé lo que quiero: sólo un trozo —con rocas,
junto al río Voltoya [1]— de la provincia de Avila.
Sólo un trozo de monte de encinas y berruecos. [2]
Sólo un monte con grandes encinas distanciadas
en sus faldas rocosas, amplias, largas y diáfanas,   5
muchos días seguidos, antes de entrar en Avila
(por las calles prosaicas de las afueras, entre
madrugada y conventos de clarisas, bernardas,
carmelitas descalzas), con el alma descalza.

---

[1] *Voltoya:* afluente del Eresma.   [2] *berruecos:* peñascos.

Sí, ese trozo (con rocas y encinas) me prepara   10
para la entrada en Avila, me instala en su tardanza,
me sujeta a su mucha claridad de horizonte,
me quita de los ojos lo que todos prefieren,
me deja en equilibrio de piedra caballera[3]
y en pujanza absoluta de azul sin importancia.   15

Es un trozo tan alto de fatigas, tan fino
y ocioso de matices, tan activo en suspenso
—a pesar de la sombra creciente del barranco—
que al llegar el crepúsculo no hacen falta campanas.
Es un suelo perpetuo de nieve o sol de agosto   20
y alegres margaritas de primavera escasa.
Es un trozo —y un solo pajarillo que canta—
con vegas del Adaja, y aún del Eresma, [4] lejos,
y cerca una pequeña ciudad amurallada. [5]

¡Qué bien sé lo que quiero!: quedarme entre sus rocas   25
y encinas, oponiéndome a todo lo que sea
merma o deformación política del alma.

EL DESCAMPADO

A Dámaso Alonso

Tú estás en ese taxi parado, sí, eres Tú
—un bulto en el crepúsculo— junto al bordillo blanco
donde se acaba el campo de enfrente o descampado.
Lo sé, aunque no te he visto (y aunque dentro del taxi
no hay nadie). Está lloviendo con fuerza. Está empezando 5
a oler en la ciudad a campo de muy lejos...

---

[3] *piedra caballera:* de gran tamaño y apoyada en una base muy estrecha,
como si estuviera en equilibrio.   [4] *Adaja y Eresma:* afluentes del Duero.   [5] Se
refiere a Ávila.

Y tú estás en el taxi como en una capilla
que fuera entre las hazas[1] ermita solitaria.
(Lo sé, porque esos trigos que se iluminan, lejos...,
y ese río parado, con sus aguas crecidas   10
de pronto...) Llueve fuerte y estás dentro del taxi,
(tal vez junto a ese chófer fatigado al volante.)

Sé que dentro del taxi no hay nadie, pero huele
a lluvia de muy lejos. Suena esa lluvia. Y pienso
sin ganas: ser poeta, suspender en el aire   15
laborioso de un día y otro día unas pocas
palabras necesarias, y quitarse de en medio.
Porque uno —su difícil vivir— ya no hace falta
si quedan las palabras. Ser poeta: orientarse,
como esa luz dudosa cruzando el descampado,   20
y en vez de una existencia brillante, tener alma.
Por eso, algo me quito de en medio: estoy viviendo
como un taxi parado junto al bordillo blanco
(y hay un cerco de alegres sonrisas y de manos
fieles a sus celestes contactos en la sombra).   25
Porque Tú, el más activo —y el más ocioso— estabas
aquí, junto al farol de luz verde en la noche.
Tú, sin libros; Tú, libre, con brazos, con miradas,
estabas sin testigos y medías —ocioso—
mis pasos por mi cuarto (donde caben mis años).   30
Y los trigos en éxtasis de Castilla la Vieja,
los ríos llameantes con sus aguas crecidas,
seguían a lo lejos relevándote (mientras
detrás de mis cristales aparece el retraso
de ese barro, esos charcos del ancho descampado,   35
¡yo también descampado,[2] desterrado del campo!)

                                        (*El descampado*, 1957)

---

[1] *hazas:* tierras de labor.   [2] *descampado:* terreno descubierto; reinterpreta la
palabra como *des-campado:* sin campo, sinónimo de *desterrado.*

LEOPOLDO PANERO

SOLA TÚ

Sola tú junto a mí, junto a mi pecho;
solo tu corazón, tu mano sola
me lleva al caminar; tus ojos solos
traen un poco de luz hasta la sombra
del recuerdo; ¡qué dulce,   5
qué alegre nuestros adiós...! El cielo es rosa,
y es verde el encinar, y estamos muertos,
juntos los dos en mi memoria sola.
Sola tú junto a mí, junto al olvido,
allá donde la nieve, la sonora   10
nieve del Guadarrama, entre los pinos,
de rodillas te nombra;
allá donde el sigilo de mis manos;
allá donde la huella silenciosa
del ángel arrebata la pisada;   15
allá donde la borra...
estamos solos para siempre; estamos
detrás del corazón, de la memoria,

del viento, de la luz, de las palabras,
juntos los dos en mi memoria sola. [6]   20

(*Versos al Guadarrama*, 1949)

ESCRITO A CADA INSTANTE

A Pedro Laín Entralgo

Para inventar a Dios, nuestra palabra
busca, dentro del pecho,
su propia semejanza y no la encuentra,
como las olas de la mar tranquila,
una tras otra, iguales,   5
quieren la exactitud de lo infinito
medir, al par que cantan...
Y Su nombre sin letras,
escrito a cada instante por la espuma,
se borra a cada instante   10
mecido por la música del agua;
y un eco queda solo en las orillas.

¿Qué número infinito
nos cuenta el corazón?
                            Cada latido,
otra vez es más dulce, y otra y otra;   15

(6) Publicado años después, el poema es anterior a 1936, pero en
él se dan muchas de las peculiaridades de la poesía de Panero: la
radical soledad humana (véase v. 17 y la martilleante reiteración
de *sola*, que abre y cierra el poema); el paisaje humanizado (destaca
la *nieve*, reflejo de su contemplación del Teleno, que se alza sobre la
Astorga natal); un tono meditativo y conversacional.

otra vez ciegamente desde dentro
va a pronunciar Su nombre.

Y otra vez se ensombrece el pensamiento,
y la voz no le encuentra.
Dentro del pecho está.
                Tus hijos somos,   20
aunque jamás sepamos
decirte la palabra exacta y Tuya,
que repite en el alma el dulce y fijo
girar de las estrellas. [7]

HASTA MAÑANA

> *...y miedos de la noche veladores.*
> SAN JUAN DE LA CRUZ

Hasta mañana dices, y tu voz
se apaga y se desprende
como la nieve. Lejos, copo a copo,
va cayendo, y se duerme,
tu corazón cansado,   5
donde el mañana está. Como otras veces,
hasta mañana dices, y te pliegas
al mañana en que crees,
como el viento a la lluvia,
como la luz a las movibles mieses.   10

---

(7) Dios es la solución última a la soledad del hombre. A través
de la palabra se camina en su búsqueda, sentida como éxito y
fracaso: nombre escrito y borrado «a cada instante».

Hasta mañana, piensas; y tus ojos
cierras hasta mañana, y ensombreces,
y guardas. Tus dos brazos
cruzas, y el peso leve
levantas, de tu pecho confiado.   15
Tras la penumbra de tu carne crece
la luz intacta de la orilla. Vuela
una paloma sola, y pasa tenue
la luna acariciando las espigas
lejanas. Se oyen trenes   20
hundidos en la noche, entre el silencio
de las encinas y el trigal que vuelve
con la brisa. Te vas hasta mañana
callando. Te vas siempre
hasta mañana, lejos. Tu sonrisa,   25
se va durmiendo mientras Dios la mece
en tus labios, lo mismo
que el tallo de una flor en la corriente;
mientras se queda ciega tu hermosura
como el viento al rodar sobre la nieve;   30
mientras te vas hasta mañana, andando;
andando hasta mañana, dulcemente
por esa senda pura que, algún día,
te llevará dormida hacia la muerte.

HIJO MÍO

A Juan Luis

Desde mi vieja orilla, desde la fe que siento,
hacia la luz primera que torna el alma pura,
voy contigo, hijo mío, por el camino lento
de este amor que me crece como mansa locura.

Voy contigo, hijo mío, frenesí soñoliento   5
de mi carne, palabra de mi callada hondura,
música que alguien pulsa no sé dónde, en el viento,
no sé dónde, hijo mío, desde mi orilla oscura.

Voy, me llevas, se torna crédula mi mirada,
me empujas levemente (ya casi siento el frío);   10
me invitas a la sombra que se hunde a mi pisada,

me arrastras de la mano... Y en tu ignorancia fío,
y a tu amor me abandono sin que me quede nada,
terriblemente sólo, no sé dónde, hijo mío [8]

(Escrito a cada instante, 1949)

---

(8) El arraigo en la familia brota en este poema —el hijo— y en
el anterior —la esposa—: es el amor-costumbre poetizado también
por Rosales y Vivanco; pero ni el remanso hogareño evita la radical
soledad del poeta: alguien tira siempre del hombre y lo lleva, solo,
hacia la muerte (véase vv. 2-3 de «Sola tú»; vv. 33-34 de «Hasta
mañana»); aquí la mano del hijo lo arrastra en un recorrido vital
que acaba con un estremecimiento de soledad ante la incógnita de
la nada.

DIONISIO RIDRUEJO

A UNA RUINA

(Teatro romano)

Fuiste en la tierra creación conclusa, [1]
y libertad del hombre edificada,
distinta y sin futuro; al fin pasada
y desterrada al fin y al fin ilusa.

De un tiempo usó la eternidad tu musa,   5
mas fuiste con el tiempo amortajada
y la materia fue materia y nada
y ni aun recuerdo la razón confusa.

La piedra que fue grada es ya ladera,
la columnata es aluvión y escoria,   10
el arco y el bastión [2] roca y entraña.

---

[1] *conclusa:* acabada.   [2] *bastión:* baluarte, obra de fortificación.

Si algo es forma, es dolor y nada espera.
Sobre tu idea al sol la hierba brota
porque han vuelto la tierra y la montaña.[9]

(*Sonetos a la piedra,* 1943)

España toda aquí, lejana y mía,
habitando, soñada y verdadera,
la duda y fe del alma pasajera,
alba toda y también toda agonía.

Hermosa sí, bajo la luz sin día   5
que me la entrega al mar sola y entera:
campo de la serena primavera
que recata su flor dulce y tardía.

España grave, quieta en la esperanza,
hecha del tiempo y de mi tiempo, España,   10
tierra fiel de mi vida y de mi muerte.

Esta sangre eres tú y esta pujanza
de amor que se impacienta y acompaña
la fe y la duda de volver a verte. [10]

(*Cuadernos de Rusia,* 1944)

(9) Buen ejemplo de la inclinación formalista de Ridruejo: una
dicción y un tema clásicos en la estrofa más clásica de todas, el
soneto, que marcó por su frecuencia buena parte de la poesía de los
años 40.

(10) *Cuadernos de Rusia* es fruto de la experiencia de Ridruejo en
la División Azul. Aquí construye, desde la lejanía, una España
expresada como vivencia personal, íntima y contradictoria: *soñada /
verdadera, duda / fe, alba / agonía, vida / muerte.*

Iban tres azores[1]
debajo del cielo,
tres raudas penumbras
de pasión y duelo.

La paloma blanca   5
se estaba en su alero
arrullando al ave
del amor primero.

Hambre, gloria, vida...
Pero no la vieron.   10
Cerca del ocaso
les nubló lo eterno.

(*En la soledad del tiempo*, 1944)

---

[1] *azores:* aves rapaces diurnas.

JOSÉ GARCÍA NIETO[11]

¿Estoy despierto? Dime. Tú que sabes
cómo hiere la luz, cómo la vida
se abre bajo la rosa estremecida
de la mano de Dios y con qué llaves,

dime si estoy despierto, si las aves   5
que ahora pasan son cifra de tu huida,
si aun en mi corazón, isla perdida,
hay un lugar para acercar tus naves.

Ángel mío, tesón de la cadena,
tibia huella de Dios, reciente arena   10
donde mi cuerpo de hombre se asegura,

---

(11) García Nieto fue la figura más representativa del garcilasismo de posguerra: clasicismo estrófico y formal, técnica refinada,
religiosidad, ingenio...; son rasgos que se observan en los dos
sonetos que siguen. En el poema titulado «1936-1939» se defiende
de las acusaciones de evasión con que se tachó a su obra; trata,
además, de justificar el silencio que extendió su poesía sobre
realidades crueles como la guerra civil; significativamente, abando-
na ahí el clasicismo estrófico en favor del versículo libérrimo.

dime si estoy soñando cuanto veo,
si es la muerte la espalda del deseo,
si es en ti donde empieza la hermosura.

(*Tregua*, 1951)

LA PARTIDA

Contigo, mano a mano. Y no retiro
la postura, [1] Señor. Jugamos fuerte.
Empeñada partida en que la muerte
será baza [2] final. Apuesto. Miro

tus cartas, y me ganas siempre. Tiro   5
las mías. Das de nuevo. Quiero hacerte
trampas. Y no es posible. Clara suerte
tienes, contrario en el que tanto admiro.

Pierdo mucho, Señor. Y apenas queda
tiempo para el desquite. Haz Tú que pueda   10
igualar todavía. Si mi parte

no basta ya por pobre y mal jugada,
si de tanto caudal no queda nada,
ámame más, Señor, para ganarte.

(*La red*, 1955)

---

[1] *postura:* dinero que se juega.   [2] *baza:* cada jugada de naipes.

1936-1939

Como quien desatara ahora un paquete de cartas para
    decir al nuevo amante «quiero que sepas que no
    me importa nada el otro tiempo, que ya no hay
    huella alguna, que ya no reconozco lo que me hizo
    sufrir»,
abro aquella ventana de la cárcel donde ni siquiera «la
    mentira y la envidia» me tuvieron encerrado. [1]
Yo sé lo que es el miedo, y el hambre, y el hambre de
    mi madre y el miedo de mi madre;
yo sé lo que es temer la muerte, porque la muerte era
    cualquier cosa, cualquier equivocación o una sos-
    pecha;
porque la muerte era un accidente en la primavera,
    una pared contra la ternura, un día con boca de
    muerte, y dientes de muerte y esperanza mortuo-
    ria.   5
Yo sé lo que es enfermar en una celda, y defecar entre
    ratas que luego pasaban junto a tu cabeza por la
    noche...
¿Qué me decís ahora los que creíais que sólo me han
    movido a cantar los lirios de un campo imaginario,
    y la rosa de papel, y la novia como Dios manda...?
¿qué me decís los que me visteis pronto limpio y
    peinado, como un niño que quiere llegar con
    puntualidad al colegio sin que nadie adivine el
    estrago de su corazón familiar?
Aunque también os digo que todo era hermoso cerca de
    la muerte menos la muerte misma.

---

[1] «Aquí la envidia y mentira / me tuvieron encerrado» (Fray Luis de
León).

Respirar, y amar de lejos, y morder un pedazo de pan
    era hermoso.   10

Y era hermoso que me prepararan un hato[2] de ropa
    limpia, y que me hiciera llorar el olor que traían
    las sábanas.

Y todo era como nacer cada día, y cada día era más
    bello que la propia esperanza,

y reír tenía un valor más profundo que el profundo
    pozo de la inquietud, que la oscura caverna de la
    impotencia...

Gracias, Señor, por haberme dejado sin heridas en el
    alma, y en el cuerpo, por haberme dado la salida
    sin odio,

por no tener lista de enemigos, ni lugares donde llorar
    por el propio desamparo...   15

Yo sé lo que es el amor; de lo demás no sé.

Quito el balduque[3] porque ahora es tiempo.

He leído en un periódico: «Voici enfin les lettres de
    Victor Hugo a Juliette Drouet». [4]

Se abren ahora porque ya no importa.

Así yo quiero abrir mi corazón, desatando la cuidada
    cinta que le rodeaba sin herirle, y quiero que leáis
    estas cartas antiguas que el mar violento de mi
    patria trajo hasta el arenal de mi juventud absorta
    e inválida.   20

Os juro que no hay una sola gota de sangre que haya
    querido conservar fresca sobre el tiempo;

que quisiera haberme dolido más para ofrecer ahora
    reparación con mi olvido,

o mejor, con mi memoria reclinada

en la triste memoria de mi hermano,

---

[2] *hato:* equipaje.   [3] *balduque:* cinta para atar papeles o cartas.   [4] «He aquí por fin las cartas de Víctor Hugo a Juliette Drouet».

como aquel que en la noche del invierno se junta al
    caminante,   25
y no pregunta,
y une su frío al frío como alivio...
¿No oís cuánto he callado?
¿Qué piedra iba yo a arrojar contra los añicos de
    vuestros cristales?
¿qué cuenta podía pasar a los muertos o a los hijos de
    los muertos?   30
Ahora quito la cinta de las cartas.
Leed; leamos. Son amor vencido.
Tiempo del corazón. Males del hombre.
Golpes de España...
Quemo lo que es mío.   35
Yo, solo, me he quitado «el dolorido sentir».[5]

(*Memorias y compromisos*, 1966)

---

[5] «No me podrán quitar el dolorido / sentir» (Garcilaso de la Vega).

VICTORIANO CRÉMER

FRISO CON OBREROS

Aparecen de pronto.
           ¡No están muertos!
Y si no hablan, es porque las palabras
no dicen sino cosas sin sentido,
por ejemplo: «Hace frío», cuando tienen
pequeñas llamas rojas en la lengua.   5

¿Qué música lejana, qué resuelto
compás impone ritmo a su asombrado
despertar cada día...? ¡No están muertos!
Un corazón les nace con el alba.

Son —desteñido azul— agua profunda,   10
río de frescas márgenes, que busca
su mar de cal y de ladrillo, su hondo
pozo de mineral que hierve y canta.

Cruzan por alamedas con rosales
y les llega un olor de noble tierra.   15
Los mármoles, al sol, recobran brillos
de recóndita rabia o sudor frío.

Pero no se detienen. —¿Están muertos?—.
Indiferentes marchan, escuchando
dentro de sí lejanos ecos. ¿Miran   20
la evidencia total de la mañana?

Los muertos viven sin saber. Pero ellos
viven de su vivir, tan plenamente
que algo que no es la luz ni el aire tiene
concretas resonancias en su sangre.   25

Si quisieran gritar, lo harían, porque
no están muertos, conocen la palabra
que sólo se pronuncia desde el sueño
y es, como un toro, violenta y ácida.

Aparecen de pronto —¿De qué ocultos   30
manantiales de vida?— y permanecen
en la esperanza de los hombres.
                                        ¡Viven
soportando futuro a las espaldas...!(12)

(*Nuevos cantos de vida y esperanza*, 1952)

HOMBRE CONCRETO

El hombre vuelve a lo que sabe. Busca
las raíces de su conocimiento,

(**12**) Poema de contenido obrerista y proletario, con resonancia
«social» al ser publicado en *Laye,* de Barcelona, poco después de
una huelga de transportes que había paralizado la ciudad; de ahí la
inmediatez significativa del primer sintagma —*aparecen de pronto*—,
que, aislado tipográficamente, reclama la atención tan súbitamente
como la irrupción de los obreros en medio del silencio opresor.

las cosas habituales, las palabras
con sustancia, los fieles fundamentos
de sus arquitecturas temporales.   5

El hombre es una música con ecos
que evidencian un ser, que le dan forma
y convierten en sangre el pensamiento
oscuro y misterioso.
           La presencia
concreta de lo humano, el fuego   10
que vivamente alienta, empuja, abrasa
las briznas desnacidas, [1] es lo cierto
de la única certeza: la que duele
y conserva un sabor.
           El hombre entero
se hace de cosas repetidas: días,   15
caminos sin azar, dulces encuentros
en el amor-costumbre, y el trabajo
de vivir, poco a poco y sin remedio.

(A veces, una flor, casi unánime, construye
ante los ojos el asombro; acaso el beso   20
se disfraza de dicha insospechada,
o levantamos la mirada al cielo.)

Pero el hombre regresa a lo que sabe,
a lo que conoce...
           Tiene miedo
de su torpeza de animal errante   25
por los mismos senderos...

Y si Dios le reclama, desde abajo,
metido tristemente en su agujero,

---

[1] *desnacidas:* creación sobre *nacidas.*

rehúye la llamada, porque tiene
miedo de Dios, si no le lleva dentro. [13]   30

(*Tiempo de soledad*, 1962)

TÚ Y YO

(CANTO DE LOS ESPOSOS)

El amor es un templo
hecho a la medida del corazón.
Aquí, a tu lado, siento
el fervor de las cúpulas, el aire
blasonado, el pálpito tranquilo   5
de la piedra.
      Catedral florecida de mis sueños.

¡Cuánta vida en el alma!
Si descorremos juntos el velo del pasado
un golpe de sangre reconstruye
aquel milagro nuestro de querernos.   10
Dulce pan de amor, eucaristía
del beso, comulgado boca a boca,
perdidos en nosotros, confundidos
niños gloriosos en pecado.

(13) Dentro del concepto orteguiano de la vida como quehacer,
el hombre, en la poesía de Crémer, se hace a sí mismo constante y
durativamente, *poco a poco*, lo que conlleva un hacerse de pequeñas
cosas habituales y repetidas que configuran la *costumbre* de vivir. Tales
ideas se enmarcan en la visión unamuniana de la «intrahistoria».

Por el tiempo, venían   15
los agrios heraldos de la guerra,
coronados de mirtos. [1]
             ¿A dónde, a dónde
romperían sus bronces, despojándose
de la pesada carga?
            Les seguíamos
con nuestro amor. A veces,   20
confundido el azorado [2] vuelo
de las palabras, que, urgentes, prometían
tanto amor.
          Sobre el salobre [3] estío,
tú y yo.

Mas el hombre no entiende   25
la extraña conjunción de las estrellas,
y se encuentra, de pronto, desterrado
del torreado [4] paraíso.
           Una mano de viento
arranca las almenas y se pierde
entre las ruinas.
          Nos buscábamos,   30
almas partidas, por sendas paralelas,
pero lejanas.
         (Fueron
días sin cuerpo, noches
tan llenas de silencio,
que el corazón se oía   35
vacilante en el árbol
sin encontrar su eco.)

---

[1] *mirtos:* arrayanes, arbustos de flores blancas y aromáticas.   [2] *azorado:* sobresaltado.   [3] *salobre:* con sabor a sal.   [4] *torreado:* guarnecido con torres.

Gastamos juventud sufridamente,
con paciencia y amor. De nuestra historia,
los hijos en el tiempo,   40
y esta flotante soledad conjunta.

Nos miramos. Te miro. Densa, lenta
pronunciación:
      «¡Esposa mía, esposa!»
digo y el corazón se invade
de resignado azul.
      Sobre el recuerdo,   45
solos tú y yo, inmensamente,
únicos. [14]

(1970)

(Lejos de esta lluvia tan amarga, 1974)

---

[14] Afirmación de amor desde el presente, evocador de un pasado que el poeta llena de contenido autobiográfico: en su realidad vital hay cárceles en pleno noviazgo y un regreso del frente de la guerra civil para casarse.

GABRIEL CELAYA [15]

AVISO

La ciudad es de goma lisa y negra,
pero con boquetes de olor a vaquería,
y a almacenes de grano, y a madera mojada,
y a guarnicionería, [1] y a achicorias, [2] y a esparto.

Hay chirridos que muerden, hay ruidos inhumanos,　　　5
hay bruscos bocinazos que deshinchan
mi absurdo corazón hipertrofiado. [3]

---

[1] *guarnicionería:* taller donde se hacen los correajes para las caballerías.
[2] *achicoria:* planta cuya infusión suele usarse como sucedáneo del café.
[3] *hipertrofiado:* de volumen excesivo.

---

(15) Poeta extenso, variado e inquieto, Celaya recorre una trayectoria que puede etiquetarse sucesivamente de neorromántica, superrealista, social y personal. Es el más representativo de los poetas que cultivaron la poesía social; a esta línea pertenecen los poemas seleccionados, el primero de los cuales manifiesta su solidaridad con el hombre común y la negativa al arte evasivo.

Yo me alquilo por horas; río y lloro con todos;
pero escribiría un poema perfecto
si no fuera indecente hacerlo en estos tiempos.   10

(*Tranquilamente hablando*, 1947)

PASA Y SIGUE

Uno va, viene y vuelve, cansado de su nombre;
va por los bulevares y vuelve por sus versos,
escucha el corazón que, insumiso, golpea
como un puño apretado fieramente llamando,
y se sienta en los bancos de los parques urbanos,   5
y ve pasar la gente que aún trata de ser alguien.

Entonces uno siente qué triste es ser un hombre.
Entonces uno siente qué duro es estar solo.
Se hojean febrilmente los anuarios buscando
la profesión «poeta» —¡ay, nunca registrada!—.   10
Y entonces uno siente cansancio, y más cansancio,
solamente cansancio, tiempo lento y cargado.

Quisiera que escucharais las hojas cuando crecen,
quisiera que supierais lo que es abrirse el aire
creyendo que uno colma de evidencia el instante   15
con su golpe de savia y ascendencia situada,
quisiera que pensarais después de tanto esfuerzo
que esa gloria y sorpresa fueron luz, fueron nada.

Lloraríais conmigo la lágrima o la estrella,
lloraríais verdades de temblor transparente,   20

caeríais como gotas de lo espeso afligido
y en lo pálido y liso diminutos tambores
sonarían al paso de los números neutros
como largos sumandos de implacable cansancio.

Lloraríais, y, ¡ay!, lloro, yo, plural, yo, horadado,   25
desalmándome[1] lento, sintiendo ya los huesos
que, sueltos, se golpean, y al fin, desencajados,
baten, baten, aventan —polvo y paja— mi vida.
Lloraríais si vierais cómo pienso en vosotros.
Lloraríais, y ¡ay!, lloro, lluevo amén mi fatiga.   30

Da miedo ser poeta; da miedo ser un hombre
consciente del lamento que exhala cuanto existe.
Da miedo decir alto lo que el mundo silencia.
Mas ¡ay! es necesario, mas ¡ay! soy responsable
de todo lo que siento y en mí se hace palabra,   35
gemido articulado, temblor que se pronuncia.

Pensadlo: ser poeta no es decirse a sí mismo.
Es asumir la pena de todo lo existente,
es hablar por los otros, es cargar con el peso
mortal de lo no dicho, contar años por siglos,   40
ser cualquiera o ser nadie, ser la voz ambulante
que recorre los limbos procurando poblarlos.

A través de mí pasa: yo irradio transparente,
yo transmito muriendo, yo sin yo doy estado
al hombre que si mira parece que algo exige,   45
y simplemente mira, me está siempre mirando,
y esperando, esperando desde hace mil milenios
que alguien pronuncie un verso donde poder tenderse.

---

[1] *desalmándome:* quedándome sin fuerzas.

Sonámbulos acuden a mí los que no saben
si sufren o si sólo por no muertos del todo   50
aún siguen suspirando sin encontrar su forma,
su expresión absoluta, su descanso y mi olvido.
Y como quien conjura fantasmas yo pronuncio
palabras en que dejo de ser quien soy por ellos.

Cuando grito, no grita mi yo para decirse.   55
Cuando lloro, quien llora dentro de mí es cualquiera,
y es tan sólo en los otros donde vivo de veras.
Mis cantos son los cantos rodados que una mansa
corriente milenaria suaviza y uniforma,
y el murmullo del agua los va deletreando.   60

¡Oh jóvenes poetas!, mirad, estoy llamando,
hundido en ese fondo que aún no ha sido expresado
de los muertos y el muerto que yo sumo al fracaso.
Decid lo que no supe, lo que nadie aún ha dicho.
Yo cumplí lo que pude, pero todo fue en vano,   65
y hoy me siento cansado —perdonadme—, cansado.

No me hagáis más preguntas. Cantad cara al mañana
lo común de la sangre, lo perpetuo y corriente.
No, al solo yo atenidos, penséis que vuestra muerte
es la muerte sin vuelta y el fin de vuestro anhelo.   70
Mientras haya en la tierra un solo hombre que cante,
quedará una esperanza para todos nosotros. [16]

(*Paz y concierto*, 1953)

~~~~~~

(16) Poema dirigido a los jóvenes poetas a los que transmite, a
pesar del cansancio, su mensaje de esperanza en la palabra que siga
cantando «cara al mañana / lo común de la sangre, lo perpetuo y
corriente».

LA POESÍA ES UN ARMA CARGADA DE FUTURO

Cuando ya nada se espera personalmente exaltante,
mas se palpita y se sigue más acá de la conciencia,
fieramente existiendo, ciegamente afirmando,
como un pulso que golpea las tinieblas,

cuando se miran de frente   5
los vertiginosos ojos claros de la muerte,
se dicen las verdades:
las bárbaras, terribles, amorosas crueldades.

Se dicen los poemas
que ensanchan los pulmones de cuantos, asfixiados,   10
piden ser, piden ritmo,
piden ley para aquello que sienten excesivo.

Con la velocidad del instinto,
con el rayo del prodigio,
como mágica evidencia, lo real se nos convierte   15
en lo idéntico a sí mismo.

Poesía para el pobre, poesía necesaria
como el pan de cada día,
como el aire que exigimos trece veces por minuto,
para ser y en tanto somos dar un sí que glorifica.   20

Porque vivimos a golpes, porque apenas si nos dejan
decir que somos quien somos,
nuestros cantares no pueden ser sin pecado un adorno.
Estamos tocando el fondo.

Maldigo la poesía concebida como un lujo   25
cultural por los neutrales
que, lavándose las manos, se desentienden y evaden.
Maldigo la poesía de quien no toma partido hasta
                                        [mancharse.

Hago mías las faltas. Siento en mí a cuantos sufren
y canto respirando.   30
Canto, y canto, y cantando más allá de mis penas
personales, me ensancho.

Quisiera daros vida, provocar nuevos actos,
y calculo por eso con técnica, qué puedo.
Me siento un ingeniero del verso y un obrero   35
que trabaja con otros a España en sus aceros.

Tal es mi poesía: poesía-herramienta
a la vez que latido de lo unánime y ciego.
Tal es, arma cargada de futuro expansivo
con que te apunto al pecho.   40

No es una poesía gota a gota pensada.
No es un bello producto. No es un fruto perfecto.
Es algo como el aire que todos respiramos
y es el canto que espacia cuanto dentro llevamos.

Son palabras que todos repetimos sintiendo   45
como nuestras, y vuelan. Son más que lo mentado.
Son lo más necesario: lo que tiene nombre.
Son gritos en el cielo, y en la tierra, son actos. [17]

(Cantos iberos, 1955)

(17) Poema de gran significación histórica que alcanza «carácter
de manifiesto estético y se convierte en uno de los textos clave de la
poética comprometida de los cincuenta» (Sanz Villanueva). Tiene
carácter programático desde el mismo título, de raíz marxista; la
poesía se concibe como herramienta de redención social; por ello
interesa sobre todo el mensaje («no es un bello producto»), lo que
no evita una cuidada estructura oratoria que ha explicado J. M.
González: introducción (estrofas 1-4), exposición (estrofas 5-9) y
conclusión (tres últimas estrofas).

BLAS DE OTERO[18]

HOMBRE

Luchando, cuerpo a cuerpo, con la muerte,
al borde del abismo, estoy clamando
a Dios. Y su silencio, retumbando,
ahoga mi voz en el vacío inerte.

Oh Dios. Si he de morir, quiero tenerte   5
despierto. Y, noche a noche, no sé cuándo
oirás mi voz. Oh Dios. Estoy hablando
solo. Arañando sombras para verte.

---

(18) *Ángel fieramente humano* y *Redoble de conciencia* son el ejemplo
máximo de poesía desarraigada existencial a través de dos vivencias
predominantes: «sentido opresor de la mano de Dios y protesta por
su obstinado silencio» (V. García de la Concha). Lo observamos en
los sonetos «Hombre» y «Basta». El primero expresa la violencia de
la relación *hombre-Dios*, con lexemas como *luchando, clamando, hablando, arañando* frente a *ahogar, cercenar, sajar*. Tal violencia atañe al
ritmo, dislocado con abruptos encabalgamientos. El verso final
resume la contradictoria condición del hombre. Lo más sorpren-
dente de «Basta», en cambio, es la estremecedora imagen de la
muerte como caída por el hueco sin luz y sin fin de una escalera.

Alzo la mano, y tú me la cercenas. [1]
Abro los ojos: me los sajas [2] vivos.   10
Sed tengo, y sal se vuelven tus arenas.

Esto es ser hombre: horror a manos llenas.
Ser —y no ser— eternos, fugitivos.
¡Ángel con grandes alas de cadenas!

CANTO PRIMERO

Definitivamente, cantaré para el hombre.
Algún día —*después*—, alguna noche,
me oirán. Hoy van —vamos— sin rumbo,
sordos de sed, famélicos [1] de oscuro.

Yo os traigo un alba, hermanos. Surto un agua,   5
eterna no, parada ante la casa.
Salid a ver. Venid, bebed. Dejadme
que os unja [2] de agua y luz, bajo la carne.

De golpe, han muerto veintitrés millones
de cuerpos. [3] Sobre Dios saltan de golpe
—sorda, sola trinchera de la muerte—
con el alma en la mano, entre los dientes

el ansia. Sin saber por qué, mataban;
muerte son, sólo muerte. Entre alambradas
de infinito, sin sangre. Son hermanos   15
nuestros. Vengadlos, sin piedad, vengadlos!

---

[1] *cercenas:* cortas.   [2] *sajas:* cortas, tajas.
[1] *famélicos:* hambrientos.   [2] *unja:* de *ungir* o signar con óleo sagrado, aquí metafóricamente.   [3] Alusión a la Segunda Guerra Mundial.

Solo está el hombre. ¿Es esto lo que os hace
gemir? Oh si supiéseis que es bastante.
Si supiéseis bastaros, ensamblaros.
Si supiérais ser hombres, sólo humanos.   20

¿Os da miedo, verdad? Sé que es más cómodo
esperar que Otro —¿quién?— cualquiera, Otro, [4]
os ayude a ser. Soy. Luego es bastante
ser, si procuro ser quien soy. ¡Quién sabe

si hay más! En cambio, hay menos: sois sentinas [5]   25
de hipocresía. ¡Oh, sed, salid al día!
No sigáis siendo bestias disfrazadas
de ansia de Dios. Con ser hombres os basta. [19]

(*Ángel fieramente humano*, 1950)

BASTA

Imagine mi horror por un momento
que Dios, el solo vivo, no existiera

---

[4] *Otro:* un Dios cualquiera.   [5] *sentinas:* lugares llenos de suciedad.

(**19**) Este poema es puente de unión entre el yo y el nosotros. Se
inicia con una firme resolución de cantar para el hombre. El mensaje
no impide una trama formal llena de contrastes (v. 25), reiteraciones
(vv. 18-19), sinestesias (v. 4), signos con simbolismo mesiánico
(alba, agua, luz, beber, ungir...), apelaciones (vv. 7, 16, 26), interrogaciones retóricas (vv. 17-21), juegos de palabras (vv. 11, 24),
aliteraciones (vv. 3-4, 5-6, 7, etc.), frases hechas alteradas por
sustitución (vv. 12-13: «con el [arma] en la mano, entre los dientes
el [cuchillo]»), rima asonante (AA BB) y ritmo entrecortado.

o que, existiendo, sólo consistiera
en tierra, en agua, en fuego, en sombra, en viento.

Y que la muerte, oh estremecimiento,   5
fuese el hueco sin luz de una escalera,
un colosal vacío que se hundiera
en un silencio desolado, liento. [1]

Entonces ¿para qué vivir, oh hijos
de madre; a qué vidrieras, crucifijos   10
y todo lo demás? Basta la muerte.

Basta. Termina, oh Dios, de malmatarnos.
O si no, déjanos precipitarnos
sobre Ti —ronco río que revierte. [2]

(*Redoble de conciencia*, 1951)

EN EL PRINCIPIO [1] [(20)]

Si he perdido la vida, el tiempo, todo
lo que tiré, como un anillo, al agua,
si he perdido la voz en la maleza,
me queda la palabra.

----

[1] *liento:* húmedo. [2] *revierte:* rebosa (de *reverter*).
[1] «En el principio era el verbo» (Evangelio de San Juan).

(20) «En el principio» y «Fidelidad» son dos actos de fe: en la
palabra y en el hombre, la paz y la patria. En ambos poemas se
observa una cuidada estructura paralelística entre sus tres estrofas.
Puede notarse el distinto aprovechamiento de la asonancia en cada
caso.

Si he sufrido la sed, el hambre, todo   5
lo que era mío y resultó ser nada,
si he segado las sombras en silencio,
me queda la palabra.

Si abrí los labios para ver el rostro
puro y terrible de mi patria,   10
si abrí los labios hasta desgarrármelos,
me queda la palabra.

FIDELIDAD

Creo en el hombre. He visto
espaldas astilladas[1] a trallazos,
almas cegadas avanzando a brincos
(españas a caballo
del dolor y del hambre). Y he creído.   5

Creo en la paz. He visto
altas estrellas, llameantes ámbitos
amanecientes, incendiando ríos
hondos, caudal humano
hacia otra luz: he visto y he creído.   10

Creo en ti, patria. Digo
lo que he visto: relámpagos
de rabia, amor en frío, y un cuchillo

---

[1] *astilladas:* hechas astillas.

Oh no olvidamos, no podrá el olvido
vencer sus ojos contra el cielo abiertos.
Larga es la noche, Tachia.

               ...Escucha el ruido
del alba abriéndose paso —a paso—[3] entre los muertos. 20

                                (*Ancia*, 1958)

NO TE ADUERMAS

    Las dos de la mañana.
    Canta
    un gallo, otro gallo
    contesta.
          El campo
    de mi patria reposa   5
    bajo la media luna.
    Oh derramada España,
    rota guitarra vieja,
    levanta
    los párpados   10
    (canta
    un gallo) que viene,
    llena de vida
    la madrugada.[21]

                     (*Que trata de España*, 1964)

---

[3] *paso -a paso-:* recuerda y reinterpreta la frase hecha *paso a paso*.

(21) Nótese el contenido simbólico de este amanecer.

chillando, haciéndose pedazos
de pan: aunque hoy hay sólo sombra, he visto   15
y he creído.

(*Pido la paz y la palabra*, 1955)

PASO A PASO

Tachia, los hombres sufren. No tenemos
ni un pedazo de paz con que aplacarles;
roto casi el navío[1] y ya sin remos...
¿Qué podemos hacer, qué luz alzarles?

Larga es la noche, Tachia. Oscura y larga   5
como mis brazos hacia el cielo. Lenta
como la luna desde el mar. Amarga
como el amor: yo llevo bien la cuenta.

Tiempo de soledad es éste. Suena
en Europa el tambor de proa a popa.   10
Ponte la muerte por los hombros. Ven. A-[2]
lejémonos de Europa.

Pobre, mi pobre Tachia. No tenemos
una brizna de luz para los hombres.
Brama el odio. Van rotos rumbo y remos...   15
No quedan de los muertos ni sus nombres.

---

[1] *roto casi el navío:* préstamo literario procedente de la oda «A la vida retirada», de Fray Luis de León.   [2] *Ven. A-:* rima con *suena*, v. 9.

LO FATAL

Entre enfermedades y catástrofes
entre torres turbias y sangre entre los labios
así te veo así te encuentro
mi pequeña paloma desguarnecida
entre embarcaciones con los párpados entornados   5
entre nieve y relámpago
con tus brazos de muñeca y tus muslos de maleza
entre diputaciones y farmacias
irradiando besos de la frente
con tu pequeña voz envuelta en un pañuelo   10
con tu vientre de hostia transparente
entre esquinas y anuncios depresivos
entre obispos
con tus rodillas de amapola pálida
así te encuentro y te reconozco   15
entre todas las catástrofes y escuelas
asiéndome el borde del alma con tus dedos de humo
acompañando mis desastres incorruptibles
paloma desguarnecida
juventud cabalgando entre las ramas   20
entre embarcaciones y muelles desolados
última juventud del mundo
telegrama planchado por la aurora
por los siglos de los siglos
así te veo así te encuentro   25
y pierdo cada noche caída entre alambradas
irradiando aviones en el radar de tu corazón
campana azul del cielo
desolación del atardecer
así cedes el paso a las muchedumbres   30
única como una estrella entre cristales
entre enfermedades y catástrofes

así te encuentro en mitad de la muerte
vestida de violeta y pájaro entrevisto
con tu distraído pie   35
descendiendo las gradas de mis versos. [22]

(De *Hojas de Madrid* con *La galerna*.
Publicado en *Verso y prosa*, ed. de 1976)

---

[22] En su última etapa, Otero mostró una renovación que incluía mayor libertad métrica y expresiva, y, en poemas como éste, cierto hermetismo, con elementos oníricos y ausencia de puntuación. Según Alarcos Llorach, el poema alude a la muerte y a lo que la precede, la vida, a través de las experiencias infantiles y juveniles que, bajo la configuración imaginativa de una paloma desguarnecida, acompañan al hombre en todas sus vicisitudes.

JOSÉ HIERRO

CANTO A ESPAÑA

> *... tierras tristes,*
> *tan tristes que tienen alma.*
> ANTONIO MACHADO

Oh España, qué vieja y qué seca te veo.
Aún brilla tu entraña como una moneda de plata
[cubierta de polvo.
Clavel encendido de sueños de fuego.
He visto brillar tus estrellas, quebrarse tu luna en las
[aguas,
andar a tus hombres descalzos, hiriendo sus pies
[con tus piedras ardientes.   5

¿En dónde buscar tu latido: en tus ríos
que se llevan al mar, en sus aguas, murallas y torres
[de muertas ciudades?
¿En tus playas, con nieblas o sol, circundando de luz
[tu cintura?
¿En tus gentes errantes que pudren sus vidas por
[darles dulzor a tus frutos?

Oh, España, qué vieja y qué seca te veo.   10
Quisiera talar con mis manos tus bosques, sembrar
                    [de ceniza tus tierras resecas,
arrojar a una hoguera tus viejas hazañas,
dormir con tu sueño y erguirme después, con la aurora,
ya libre del peso que pone en mi espalda la sombra
                    [fatal de tu ruina.

Oh, España, qué vieja y qué seca te veo.   15
Quisiera asistir a tu sueño completo,
mirarte sin pena, lo mismo que a luna remota,
hachazo de luz que no hiende[1] los troncos ni pone
                    [la llaga en la piedra.

Qué tristes he visto a tus hombres.
Los veo pasar a mi lado, mamar en tu pecho la leche,   20
comer de tus manos el pan, y sentarse después a soñar
                    [bajo un álamo,
dorar con el fuego que abrasa sus vidas tu dura corteza.
Les pides que pongan sus almas de fiesta.
No sabes que visten de duelo, que llevan a cuestas
                    [el peso de tu acabamiento,
que ven impasibles llegar a la muerte tocando
                    [sus graves guitarras.   25

Oh, España, qué triste pareces.
Quisiera asistir a tu muerte total, a tu sueño completo,
saber que te hundías de pronto en las aguas, igual que un
                    [navío maldito.

Y sobre la noche marina, borrada tu estela,
España, ni en ti pensaría. Ni en mí. Ya extranjero
                    [de tierras y días.   30

---

[1] *hiende:* raja.

Ya libre y feliz, como viento que no halla ni rosa,
                              [ni mar, ni molino.
Sin memoria, ni historia, ni edad, ni recuerdos,
                              [ni pena...
...en vez de saberte, oh España, clavel encendido
                         [de sueños de llama,
cofre de dura corteza que guarda en su entraña caliente
la vieja moneda de plata, cubierta de olvido, de polvo
                              [y cansancio... [23]   35

(*Quinta del 42*, 1952)

RÉQUIEM [1]

        Manuel del Río, natural
        de España, ha fallecido el sábado
        11 de mayo, a consecuencia
        de un accidente. Su cadáver
        está tendido en D'Agostino   5
        Funeral Home. Haskell. New Jersey.

---

[1] *Réquiem:* composición musical que se canta en la misa de difuntos y de la que proceden las frases latinas esparcidas por el texto.

---

(23) Tres calificativos testimonian la realidad española: *vieja* (tiempo), *seca* (espacio), *triste* (reacción afectiva); consecuencia: si así es España, mejor verla muerta. Tal es la apariencia retórica. Otros indicios hablan de la España deseada: *aún brilla, clavel encendido de sueños de fuego,* etc. De ahí que el poema ofrezca rasgos noventayochistas: las dos Españas, el unamuniano «me duele España...» Obsérvese el ritmo solemne, que evita encabalgamientos y con predominio de anfíbracos ($\cup - \cup$).

Se dirá una misa cantada
a las 9,30, en St. Francis.

Es una historia que comienza
con sol y piedra, y que termina   10
sobre una mesa, en D'Agostino,
con flores y cirios eléctricos.
Es una historia que comienza
en una orilla del Atlántico.
Continúa en un camarote   15
de tercera, sobre las olas
—sobre las nubes— de las tierras
sumergidas ante Platón. [2]
Halla en América su término
con una grúa y una clínica,   20
con una esquela y una misa
cantada, en la iglesia St. Francis.

Al fin y al cabo, cualquier sitio
da lo mismo para morir:
el que se aroma de romero,   25
el tallado en piedra, o en nieve,
el empapado de petróleo.
Da lo mismo que un cuerpo se haga
piedra, petróleo, nieve, aroma.
Lo doloroso no es morir   30
acá o allá...
                    Requiem aeternam, [3]
Manuel del Río. Sobre el mármol
en D'Agostino, pastan toros

---

[2] Alude a la Atlántida, que, según los griegos, se hallaba frente al estrecho de Gibraltar y se sumergió a causa de un enorme cataclismo.   [3] «Descanso eterno».

de España, Manuel, y las flores
(funeral de segunda, caja   35
que huele a abetos del invierno),
cuarenta dólares. Y han puesto
unas flores artificiales
entre las otras que arrancaron
al jardín... *Liberame Domine*   40
de morte aeterna... [4] Cuando mueran
James o Jacob verán las flores
que pagaron Giulio o Manuel...

Ahora descienden a tus cumbres
garras de águila. *Dies irae.* [5]   45
Lo doloroso no es morir
Dies illa [6] acá o allá,
sino sin gloria...
                    Tus abuelos
fecundaron la tierra toda,
la empapaban de la aventura.   50
Cuando caía un español
se mutilaba el universo.
Los velaban no en D'Agostino
Funeral Home, sino entre hogueras,
entre caballos y armas. Héroes   55
para siempre. Estatuas de rostro
borrado. Vestidos aún
sus colores de papagayo,
de poder y de fantasía. [7]

Él no ha caído así. No ha muerto   60
por ninguna locura hermosa.

---

[4] «Líbrame, Señor, de la muerte eterna». [5] «Día de la ira». [6] «Aquel día».
[7] Se refiere a la época del descubrimiento y conquista de América.

(Hace mucho que el español
muere de anónimo y cordura,
o en locuras desgarradoras
entre hermanos: cuando acuchilla   65
pellejos de vino, derrama
sangre fraterna. [8]) Vino un día
porque su tierra es pobre. El mundo
Liberame Domine es patria.
Y ha muerto. No fundó ciudades.   70
No dio su nombre a un mar. No hizo
más que morir por diecisiete
dólares (él los pensaría
en pesetas). *Requiem aeternam.*
Y en D'Agostino lo visitan   75
los polacos, los irlandeses,
los españoles, los que mueren
en el *week-end.* [9]

                Requiem aeternam.
Definitivamente todo
ha terminado. Su cadáver   80
está tendido en D'Agostino
Funeral Home. Haskell. New Jersey.
Se dirá una misa cantada
por su alma.
                Me he limitado
a reflejar aquí una esquela   85
de un periódico de New York.
Objetivamente, sin vuelo
en el verso. Objetivamente.
Un español como millones

---

[8] Referencias a don Quijote y a la guerra civil.   [9] *week-end:* fin de semana.

de españoles. No he dicho a nadie   90
que estuve a punto de llorar. [24]

(*Cuanto sé de mí,* 1957)

TEORÍA Y ALUCINACIÓN DE DUBLIN [1]

I

TEORÍA

Un instante vacío
de acción puede poblarse solamente
de nostalgia o de vino.
Hay quien lo llena de palabras vivas,
de poesía (acción   5
de espectros; vino con remordimiento).

Cuando la vida se detiene,
se escribe lo pasado o lo imposible

---

[1] *Dublin:* capital de Irlanda; debe leerse sin acento para conservar el ritmo endecasilábico en los versos donde aparece; Dublin tiene significación simbólica.

(24) Hierro clasificó sus poemas en «reportajes» y «alucinaciones». Entre los primeros, con predominio de lo narrativo y lo objetivo, «Réquiem» es de los más característicos: reléanse los versos finales. Destacamos: apariencia de sencillez, debida al uso de un metro poco frecuente (eneasílabos), encabalgamientos continuados, inicio en clave periodística, etc. Tono funeral acentuado por las frases del responso de difuntos. Estructura basada en logrados contrastes o en extensiones semánticas: *Manuel-España, emigrantes-conquistadores, un español-millones de españoles...*

para que los demás vivan aquello
que ya vivió (o que no vivió) el poeta.   10
Él no puede dar vino,
nostalgia a los demás: sólo palabras.
Si les pudiese dar acción...

La poesía es como el viento,
o como el fuego, o como el mar.   15
Hace vibrar árboles, ropas,
abrasa espigas, hojas secas,
acuna en su oleaje los objetos
que duermen en la playa.
La poesía es como el viento,   20
o como el fuego, o como el mar:
da apariencia de vida
a lo inmóvil, a lo paralizado.
Y el leño que arde,
las conchas que las olas traen o llevan,   25
el papel que arrebata el viento,
destellan una vida momentánea
entre dos inmovilidades.

Pero los que están vivos,
los henchidos de acción,   30
los palpitantes de nostalgia o vino,
esos... felices, bienaventurados,
porque no necesitan las palabras,
como el caballo corre, aunque no sople el viento,
y vuela la gaviota, aunque esté seco el mar,   35
y el hombre llora, y canta,
proyecta y edifica, aun sin el fuego.

II

ALUCINACIÓN

Me acuerdo de los árboles de Dublin.

(Imaginar y recordar
se superponen y confunden;   40
pueblan, entrelazados, un instante
vacío con idéntica emoción.
Imaginar y recordar...)

Me acuerdo de los árboles de Dublin...
Alguien los vive y los recuerdo yo.   45
De los árboles caen hojas doradas
sobre el asfalto de Madrid.
Crujen bajo mis pies, sobre mis hombros,
acarician mis manos,
quisieran exprimirme el corazón.   50
No sé si lo consiguen...

Imaginar y recordar...
Hay un momento que no es mío,
no sé si en el pasado, en el futuro,
si en lo imposible... Y lo acaricio, lo hago   55
presente, ardiente, con la poesía.

No sé si lo recuerdo o lo imagino.
(Imaginar y recordar me llenan
el instante vacío.)
Me asomo a la ventana.   60
Fuera no es Dublin lo que veo,
sino Madrid. Y, dentro, un hombre
sin nostalgia, sin vino, sin acción,
golpeando la puerta.

                    Es un espectro
que persigue a otro espectro del pasado: 65
el espectro del viento, de la mar,
del fuego —ya sabéis de qué hablo—, espectro
que pueda hacer que cante, hacer que vibre
su corazón, para sentirse vivo. [25]

(*Libro de las alucinaciones*, 1964)

(25) En las «alucinaciones» todo es más oscuro y vago. «José
Hierro vive totalmente la alucinación en aquel segundo en que
logra la presentización de lo pasado, lo futuro, lo soñado, lo
imposible; cuando el aquí y el allá se superponen, se mezclan, se
confunden...» (A. de Albornoz). Puede analizarse la superposición
espacio-temporal del poema; ejercicio interesante es establecer los
puntos de unión entre I y II.

EUGENIO DE NORA [26]

CARMEN DEL ÁRBOL DORADO

¡El árbol florido,
fugaz primavera,
palacio de trinos!

Pero antes de oírse,
qué lento ha crecido.   5

Abría en la tierra
oscuros caminos;

(26) Al tiempo que en *Cantos al destino, Contemplación del tiempo* y *Siempre* poetizaba motivos como el destino, la muerte o el amor, Nora publicaba anónima y clandestinamente *Pueblo cautivo* (1946), «una de las escasas demostraciones de que la vanguardia política y literaria confluyeron un día» (F. Rubio); con él inauguraba la poesía testimonial en la posguerra, alcanzando la madurez en *España, pasión de vida* (1954); en «Poesía contemporánea» hace una explícita condena de la evasión artística. *Angulares* significará un «reflexivo y estremecido examen de conciencia frente a la realidad total», como muestra «Ser de tiempo», en el que aúna destino personal y colectivo.

pedía en el aire
la vida a suspiros;
al sol, cada día,   10
era oro tupido.

La luz y el silencio,
y un tiempo infinito,
irguieron el tronco
soñando en sí mismo.   15
(Lo adoraba acaso
la estrella en rocío;
en el borde absorto
grabaron su signo
los enamorados...).   20

¿Tiene ahora mil nidos?

¡Corazón del hombre!
(¡Cantos encendidos
del poeta!) ¡Árbol
verde y florecido!   25

(*Siempre*, 53)

PATRIA

La tierra, yo la tengo sobre la sangre escrita.
Un día fue alegre y bella como un cielo encantado
para mi alma de niño. Oh tierra sin pecado,
sobre cuyo silencio sólo la paz gravita.

Pero la tierra es honda. La tierra necesita   5
un bautismo de muertos que la hayan adorado
o maldecido, que hayan en ella descansado
como sólo ellos pueden, haciéndola bendita.

Fui despertado a tiros de la infancia más pura
por hombres que en España se daban a la muerte[1]   10
Aquí y allí, por ella. ¡Mordí la tierra, dura,
y sentí sangre viva, cálida sangre humana!
Hijo fui de una patria. Hombre perdido: fuerte
para luchar, ahora, para morir, mañana.

(1946)

«POESÍA CONTEMPORÁNEA»

Medito a veces
en la triste materia de mi canto.

Bien sé que hay muchos, soñadores,
(como yo rodeados de desgracia y caminos)
pero entre nubes blancas, con sus ángeles   5
abanicando tímidas
alas prerrafaelistas,[1] lejos;
que quizá en el estío
cultivan la nostalgia de la lira imposible,
decoran las palabras, sumisas como rombos   10

---

[1] Nora tenía 13 años al comenzar la guerra civil.
[1] *prerrafaelistas:* propias de un grupo de pintores ingleses del pasado siglo, que llevaron a sus lienzos sensibilidad y lirismo.

de plaza pobre en farolillos
de verbena y papel colorín colorado... [2]

Oh Dios, cómo desamo,
cómo escupo y desprecio
a esos cobardes, envenenadores,   15
vendedores de sueños, mientras ponen
sedas sobre la lepra, ilusión sobre engaño, iris
donde no hay más que secas piedras.
Esclavos, menos
aún, bufones de esclavos.   20

Malditos una y siete veces,
en nombre de la vida, aunque juren que aumentan
la belleza del mundo; en verdad,
la belleza del mundo no precisa
ser aumentada ni disminuida   25
con sus telas. Lo que necesitamos
es una luz, es un desnudo brazo
que señale las cosas. La poesía es eso:
gesto, mirada, abrazo
de amor a la verdad profunda.   30
Ay, ay, lo que yo canto
miradlo en torno y despertad: alerta.

Ahí están, reunidos
en sociedad devoratoria y número.
(Llamar bestia asesina   35
al que, como el pesado
elefante del sátrapa [3]
hunde la pata hasta estrujar el rostro

---

[2] Sugiere que lo anterior, como en los cuentos, se ha acabado; de ahí el desprecio que expresan los versos siguientes. [3] *sátrapa:* tirano, antiguo gobernador de Persia.

que niega; ladrón vil
al emplumado grajo de cadáveres; 40
canalla al miserable...
acaso sepa a música
derrotada, a lamento
débil. A lo que no queremos.)
Pero nombrar no es sueño. 45

No sigáis las palabras. Contra ellos
yo canto hombres que tienen las titánicas caras
talladas como a látigo: sonríen
al dolor, pero miran
al sol, y aprietan 50
los firmes dientes.
       Y ya acabo.
(Esto no es un poema; son palabras
apretadas también, con saña.) Adiós. Es tiempo
de no plantar rosales. [4] ¡Acordaos!

(1947)

(España, pasión de vida, 1954)

SER DE TIEMPO

El canto del gallo, al alba,
los árboles del camino,
la inquietud de cada hora
angustiosa de destino;
la Historia que nos tritura, 5
lo ganado, lo perdido;

---

[4] *rosales:* símbolo de la pura belleza evasiva.

el día de nuestros besos
y el de nuestra muerte, vivos:
cuando al fin hayan pasado
encontrarán su sentido.   10

Con el tiempo.
Con el tiempo en lento giro.

Las sombras de nuestra infancia,
la humildad del musgo herido,
la aspereza de la tierra,   15
la pequeñez del mezquino,
la estupidez del tirano,
la firme verdad del trigo
entre la rosa y la espada
—roto, abrasado y más vivo   20
en el pan—, tendrán su clara
evidencia, su sentido,
con el tiempo.

Con el tiempo repetido.

Nuestro amor, nuestro desprecio,   25
lo que fue azar o es destino,
vino en nuestro vaso, o agua
en su fuente; lo sufrido,
lo gozado; el rojo Octubre
contado, el Julio vivido, [1]   30
sangriento bajo un sol férreo;
la redondez de este siglo...
Todo será claro, cierto,
y completo, y en su sitio,

---

[1] Alusiones al comienzo de la Revolución rusa en octubre de 1917 y de la
guerra civil española en julio de 1936.

más allá, junto y más lejos: 35
a golpes de tiempo vivo.

Del tiempo, latido insomne
que huye también si dormimos
(recuerde el alma), [2] que llega
sonámbulamente vivo   40
mientras soñamos; gastándonos
(ya es tarde) mientras decimos:
Vida, búsqueda, captura
de un tiempo ganado e ido
(no importa mucho) a la muerte.   45
(No somos, y ya hemos sido.)

Pero se oye el mar, el viento
salobre [3] del mar. ¡No hay tiempo!
¡Hay sangre fresca en las rocas!
(¡Vivimos!)   50

(*Angulares*, 1975)

---

[2] «Recuerde el alma dormida» (Jorge Manrique).   [3] *salobre:* con sabor a sal.

RAFAEL MORALES [27]

EL TORO

Es la noble cabeza negra pena,
que en dos furias[1] se encuentra rematada,
donde suena un rumor de sangre airada
y hay un oscuro llanto que no suena.

En su piel poderosa se serena   5
su tormentosa fuerza enamorada
que en los amantes huesos va encerrada
para tronar volando por la arena.

---

[1] *furias:* se refiere a las astas.

~~~~~~

(27) Dentro de la corriente sonetística de los 40, Morales destacó
por su visión neorromántica de la vida y por una retórica neobarro-
ca. El dominio técnico del soneto es evidente en «A un esqueleto de
muchacha»: obsérvese el deíctico anafórico que introduce ordena-
damente los elementos corporales de la muchacha; de igual forma,
en «La acacia cautiva», frente al cerco de la ciudad, la forma
verbal *busca* introduce los tres elementos naturales: *tierra, agua, aire,*
símbolos de la vida libre... «El toro» está construido sobre el
contraste que expresa el sintagma «fuerza represada».

Encerrada en la sorda calavera,
la tempestad se agita enfebrecida,   10
hecha pasión que al músculo no altera:

es un ala tenaz y enardecida,
es un ansia cercada, prisionera,
por las astas buscando la salida.

A UN ESQUELETO DE MUCHACHA

Homenaje a Lope de Vega

En esta frente, Dios, en esta frente
hubo un clamor de sangre rumorosa,
y aquí, en esta oquedad, se abrió la rosa
de una fugaz mejilla adolescente.

Aquí el pecho sutil dio su naciente   5
gracia de flor incierta y venturosa,
y aquí surgió la mano, deliciosa
primicia de este brazo inexistente.

Aquí el cuello de garza sostenía
la alada soledad de la cabeza,   10
y aquí el cabello undoso[1] se vertía.

Y aquí, en redonda y cálida pereza,
el cauce de la pierna se extendía
para hallar por el pie la ligereza.

(El corazón y la tierra, 1946)

---

[1] *undoso:* con ondas.

LA ACACIA[1] CAUTIVA

Cercada por ladrillos y cemento,
por asfalto, carteles y oficinas,
entre discos de luz, entre bocinas
una acacia cautiva busca un viento.

Busca un campo tranquilo, el soñoliento   5
río sonoro que en sus aguas finas
lleva luces que fluyen diamantinas
en sosegado y suave movimiento.

Busca el salto del pez, el raudo brillo
de su escama fugaz y repentina,   10
con rápida sorpresa de cuchillo.

Busca la presurosa golondrina,
no la brutal tristeza del ladrillo
que finge roja sangre en cada esquina.

(*Canción sobre el asfalto*, 1954)

---

[1] *acacia:* árbol que a veces adorna plazas o calles ciudadanas.

VICENTE GAOS [28]

LA NOCHE

Oh, sálvame, Señor, dame la muerte,
no me amenaces más con otra vida;
dame la muerte y cura así esta herida
de mi vida mortal. Haz, Dios, de suerte

que pueda retornar al mundo inerte   5
al que esta ciega noche me convida.
Pon sobre mí tu mano detenida,
tu mano de piedad, tu mano fuerte.

(28) «Serenidad es vehemencia»: son palabras de Gaos que sintetizan su poesía: pasión y lucidez, impulso sometido al rigor formal del soneto. Por su «sentimiento trágico de la vida» es un hondo poeta existencial. La noche, símbolo tradicional, se convierte en el poema «Pájaros» en una nada transitoria y anticipadora de la noche total. Nótese la intensa plasticidad de las «inquietudes» bajo el símil de «aves espectrales».

Dame la muerte, oh Dios, dame tu nada,
anégame[1] en tu noche más sombría,   10
en tu noche sin luz, desestrellada. [2]

Bastante tengo con la luz de un día.
Bastante tengo, oh, muerte deseada.
En ti repose al fin, oh muerte mía.

(Arcángel de mi noche, 1944)

LUZBEL

Arcángel derribado, el más hermoso
de todos tú, el más bello, el que quisiste
ser como Dios, ser Dios, mi arcángel triste,
sueño mío rebelde y ambicioso.

Dios eres en tu cielo tenebroso,   5
Señor de la tiniebla en que te hundiste
y de este corazón en que encendiste
un fuego oscuramente luminoso.

Demonio, Señor mío, haz que en mi entraña
cante siempre su música el deseo   10
y el insaciable amor de la hermosura,

te dije un día a ti, ebrio de saña
mortal. Y, luego a Dios también: No creo.
Pero velaba Dios desde la altura.

(Sobre la tierra, 1945)

---

[1] *anégame:* ahógame.   [2] *desestrellada:* sin estrellas (creación poética sobre *estrellada*).

PÁJAROS

(NOCTURNO)

Como aves espectrales se abalanzan
mis inquietudes en bandada y vienen
a hostigarme en la noche, en la honda noche.
¿Qué puedo hacer yo, solo e indefenso,
para librarme de sus corvos picos,   5
de sus buidas[1] garras, de sus ojos
que implacables reflejan lo más negro
de la vida y la muerte? ¿De sus alas
raudas, pero tenaces, pegajosas,
que me azotan el rostro y huyen, vuelven   10
y huyen de nuevo, helándome la piel?
Dormir, dormir, dormir, cerrar los párpados,
arrebujarme[2] y acogerme al lecho
de blanda soledad. Pedir —¿a quién?—
que el vuelo de esas aves, que su ronda   15
no traspase los límites del sueño,
no me persiga más allá, no cruce
de par en par la noche, la ancha noche,
la alta noche; que cese ya ese ataque
de picos, garras, alas, ojos que   20
implacables reflejan lo más negro
de la vida y la muerte, penetrando
hasta las lindes[3] del sufrir del hombre.

Dormir, dormir, dormir, dormir sin sueños,
sin pesadillas, sin pavor —frontera   25
a ese terror en pie de nuestra vida.

---

[1] *buidas:* afiladas.   [2] *arrebujarme:* taparme, envolverme en la ropa.   [3] *lindes:* límites.

Acogerme a la almohada, hundir en ella
el rostro, y con los párpados cerrados,
solo y tendido anticipar la noche
grande, la noche última, la noche   30
a la que nunca llegarán las aves
que ahora me cercan en su insomne ronda.

Venga esa noche a mí, cese el acoso
de oscuras inquietudes. Que la vida
cese ya. No más sueños. Que la nada   35
—sin pájaros, sin sombras, sin terrores—
me acoja blanda. Y cese yo al fin de
ser hombre: soledad de soledades.

(*Concierto en mí y en vosotros*, 1965)

JOSÉ LUIS HIDALGO [29]

ESPERA SIEMPRE

La muerte espera siempre, entre los años,
como un árbol secreto que ensombrece,
de pronto, la blancura de un sendero,
y vamos caminando y nos sorprende.

Entonces, en la orilla de su sombra,   5
un temblor misterioso nos detiene:
miramos a lo alto, y nuestros ojos
brillan, como la luna, extrañamente.

Y, como luna, entramos en la noche,
sin saber dónde vamos, y la muerte   10
va creciendo en nosotros, sin remedio,
con un dulce terror de fría nieve.

---

(29) Hidalgo tejió en *Los muertos* sus meditaciones sobre la muerte. El interlocutor es un Dios creado como ancla ante la muerte, pero que admite ecos de la duda unamuniana en «Si supiera, Señor...» o una exasperada resignación en «Has bajado.» Hidalgo reitera sus focos imaginativos: «Espera siempre» y «Estoy maduro» coinciden en dos: *árbol* y *luna-noche*. Obsérvese también la reiteración de una misma estructura métrica en tres de los poemas.

La carne se deshace en la tristeza
de la tierra sin luz que la sostiene.
Sólo quedan los ojos que preguntan   15
en la noche total, y nunca mueren.

SI SUPIERA, SEÑOR...

Si supiera, Señor, que Tú me esperas,
en el borde implacable de la muerte,
iría hacia tu luz, como una lanza
que atraviesa la noche y nunca vuelve.

Pero sé que no estás, que el vivir sólo   5
es soñar con tu ser, inútilmente,
y sé que cuando muera es que Tú mismo
será lo que habrá muerto con mi muerte.

HAS BAJADO

Has bajado a la tierra, cuando nadie te oía,
y has mirado a los vivos y contado tus muertos.
Señor, duerme sereno; ya cumpliste tu día.
Puedes cerrar los ojos que tenías abiertos.

ESTOY MADURO

Me ha calentado el sol ya tantos años
que pienso que mi entraña está madura

y has de bajar, Señor, para arrancarme
con tus manos inmensas y desnudas.

Pleno y dorado estoy para tu sueño;   5
por él navegaré como una luna
que irá brillando silenciosamente,
astro frutal sobre tu noche pura.

Una nube vendrá y acaso borre
mi luz para los vivos y, entre lluvia,   10
zumo dulce de Ti, te irá cayendo
la savia de mi ser, como una música.

Será que estaré muerto y entregado,
otra vez, a la tierra de las tumbas.
Pero, sangre inmortal, mi roja entraña   15
de nuevo quemará tu luz futura.

(*Los muertos*, 1947)

CARLOS BOUSOÑO [30]

CRISTO ADOLESCENTE

Oh Jesús, te contemplo aún niño, adolescente.
Niño rubio dorándose en luz de Palestina.
Niño que pone rubia la mañana luciente
cuando busca los campos su mirada divina.

En el misterio a veces hondamente se hundía   5
mirando las estrellas donde su Padre estaba.
Un chorro de luz tenue al cielo se vertía,
al cielo inacabable que en luz se desplegaba.

(30) Según Bousoño, su poesía discurre entre dos polos, resumidos en uno de sus títulos: *Primavera de la muerte*, núcleo cosmovisionario expresado por vez primera en «Cristo adolescente»: «Cristo, de niño, pasa de la mano de su madre por un bosque, donde, *en el instante de la primavera*, está creciendo el árbol de su cruz»; clara superposición temporal, pues, que comunica intensamente la sensación del paso del tiempo. Si la realidad se contempla desde el polo de la muerte, de la nada, aparecerá como vaporosa y fantasmal, como si se disolviera: véase «España en el sueño», con su característico verso final.

Otras veces al mundo mirabas. De la mano
de tu Madre pasabas con gracia y alegría.   10
Pasabas por los bosques como un claror liviano,
por los bosques oscuros donde tu Cruz crecía.

Niño junto a su Madre. Niño junto a su muerte,
creciendo al mismo tiempo que la cruda madera.
Me hace llorar la angustia, oh Cristo niño, al verte 15
pasar por ese bosque junto a la primavera.

(Subida al amor, 1945)

ESPAÑA EN EL SUEÑO

A Carmen Braga

Desde aquí yo contemplo, tendido, sin memoria
el campo. Piedra y campo, y cielo, y lejanía.
Mis ojos miran montes donde sembró la historia
el dulce sueño amargo que sueñan todavía.

Pero el amor fundido en piedra, día a día;   5
pero el amor mezclado con monte, o con escoria,
es duradero y te amo, oh patria, oh serranía
crespa, [1] que te levantas, bajo el cielo, ilusoria.

Campos que yo conozco, cielos donde he existido;
piedras donde he amasado mi corazón pequeño;   10
bosques donde he cantado: sueños que he padecido.

---

[1] *crespa:* áspera, escabrosa.

Os amo, os amo, campos, montañas, terco empeño
de mi vivir, sabiendo que es vano mi latido
de amor. Mas te amo, patria, vapor, fantasma, sueño.

(*Noche del sentido*, 1957)

PRECIO DE LA VERDAD [31]

A Ángel González

En el desván antiguo de raída memoria,
detrás de la cuchara de palo con carcoma,
tras el vestuario viejo ha de encontrarse, o junto al muro
desconchado, en el polvo
de siglos. Ha de encontrarse acaso más allá del pálido
                                    [gesto de una mano   5
vieja de algún mendigo, o en la ruina del alma
cuando ha cesado todo.
Yo me pregunto si es preciso el camino
polvoriento de la duda tenaz, el desaliento súbito

---

(31) En su última etapa Bousoño contempla la realidad desde la seducción que le produce y la expresa con gran complejidad formal, debida, según el propio autor, al análisis racional de lo irreal o al análisis irracional de lo real, lo que lleva consigo el uso de paradojas, símbolos, superposiciones y una mayor expansión del poema en verso libre. En «Precio de la verdad», el propio autor ha observado una tendencia analítica que ve lo general especificado en una larga serie de concreciones y casos particulares. Aspecto llamativo de «La nueva mirada» es el desarrollo independiente del plano B de la metáfora *dolor-orfebre;* de ahí también el aspecto analítico del poema y la plasticidad que adquiere el concepto abstracto.

en la llanura estéril, bajo el sol de justicia,   10
la ruina de toda esperanza, el raído harapo del miedo,
   [la desazón invencible a mitad del sendero que
              [conduce al torreón derruido.
Yo me pregunto si es preciso dejar el camino real
y tomar a la izquierda por el atajo y la trocha, [1]
como si nada hubiera quedado atrás en la casa desierta.
Me pregunto si es preciso ir sin vacilación al horror
                [de la noche   15
penetrar el abismo, la boca de lobo, [2]
caminar hacia atrás, de espaldas hacia la negación,
o invertir la verdad, en el desolado camino.
O si más bien es preciso el sollozo de polvo en la
             [confusión de un verano
terrible, o en el trastornado amanecer del alcohol
             [con trompetas de sueño   20
saberse de pronto absolutamente desiertos, o mejor,
es quizá necesario haberse perdido en el sucio trato
                 [del amor,
haber contratado en la sombra un ensueño,
comprado por precio una reminiscencia de luz,
                  [un encanto
de amanecer tras la colina, hacia el río.   25
Admito la posibilidad de que sea absolutamente preciso
haber descendido, al menos alguna vez, hasta el fondo
             [del edificio oscuro,
haber bajado a tientas el peligro de la desvencijada
   [escalera, que amenaza ceder a cada paso nuestro,
y haber penetrado al fin con valentía en la indignidad,
              [en el sótano oscuro.
Haber visitado el lugar de la sombra,   30
el territorio de la ceniza, donde toda vileza reposa

---

[1] *trocha:* vereda estrecha que sirve de atajo. [2] *boca de lobo:* oscuridad absoluta.

junto a la telaraña paciente. Haberse avecindado
                                        [en el polvo,
haberlo masticado con tenacidad en largas horas de sed
o de sueño. Haber respondido con valor o temeridad
al silencio   35
o la pregunta postrera y haberse allí percatado
                                        [y rehecho.
Es necesario haberse entendido con la malhechora
                                        [verdad
que nos asalta en plena noche y nos desvela de pronto
                                        [y nos roba
hasta el último céntimo. Haber mendigado después
                                        [largos días
por los barrios más bajos de uno mismo, sin esperanza
                                        [de recuperar lo perdido,   40
y al fin, desposeídos, haber continuado el camino sincero
   [y entrado en la noche absoluta con valor todavía.

                                        (*Oda en la ceniza,* 1967)

LA NUEVA MIRADA

Dame la mano, sufrimiento, dolor, mi viejo amigo.
Dame la mano una vez más y sé otra vez mi compañero,
como lo fuiste tantas veces en el oscuro atardecer.
Cruzaban las gaviotas sobre el cielo,
se ennegrecía el mar con la tormenta próxima.   5
Dame la mano una vez más, pues ahora sé
lo que entonces no supe. Sé recibirte sin rencor
ni reproche. Acepto tu visita oscura.

Es en mis ojos, sufrimiento, dolor,
donde laboras tu más fino quehacer,   10

donde ejercitas tu destreza, tu habilidad
de orfebre
sin par. Allí
depositas al fin tu redención, pones como sobre un altar
con delicadeza extremada,   15
tu hechura exquisita, y alzas, en medio de la noche,
                                        [el milagro
lentamente a los cielos, la joya finísima,
el espectáculo de oro,
trabajado sin prisa, acumulada realidad que acomodas
                                              [después
a mi nueva mirada.   20
Y es así como ahora, tras tu trabajo en la honda cueva,
en la recóndita guarida donde yo padecí tu febril
                                        [creación,
es así como ahora
puedo mirar,
tras el mundo habitual, un mundo ardiente.   25
Arden las llamas del color tras el gris habitual,
tras de la oscuridad se encarniza la luz, se redondea
            [el rosa, esplende [1] el animado carmín,
y todavía más allá, tras la trascendida apariencia, se ve
de otro modo, transparentándose hacia una eternidad,
un país nuevo.   30

Un país nuevo, inmóvil en la luz,
tras de la oscuridad de mi agitada noche.

                                        (*Las monedas contra la losa*, 1973)

---

[1] *esplende:* resplandece.

JOSÉ MARÍA VALVERDE [32]

ORACIÓN POR NOSOTROS LOS POETAS

Señor, ¿qué nos darás en premio a los poetas?
Mira, nada tenemos, ni aun nuestra propia vida;
somo los mensajeros de algo que no entendemos.
Nuestro cuerpo lo quema una llama celeste;
si miramos, es sólo para verterlo en voz.   5

No podemos coger ni la flor de un vallado
para que sea nuestra y nada más que nuestra,
ni tendernos tranquilos en medio de las cosas,
sin pensar, a gozarlas en su presencia sólo.
Nunca sabremos cómo son de verdad las tardes,   10
libre de nuestra angustia su desnuda belleza;
jamás conoceremos lo que es una mujer
en sus profundos bosques donde hay que entrar callado.

---

(32) Los dos poemas iniciales muestran la poesía arraigada en la fe católica de Valverde. «Vida es esperanza» —en hexámetros, a la manera de Darío, de quien toma una serie de préstamos literarios— lanza un enérgico «basta» contra viejos mitos, aprovechados por los ricos para «cerrar el mañana» a los pobres.

Tú no nos das el mundo para que lo gocemos,
Tú nos lo entregas para que lo hagamos palabra.   15
Y después que la tierra tiene voz por nosotros
nos quedamos sin ella, con sólo el alma grande...

Ya ves que por nosotros es sonora la vida,
igual que por las piedras lo es el cristal del río.
Tú no has hecho tu obra para hundirla en silencio,   20
en el silencio huyente de la gente afanosa;
para vivirla sólo, sin pararse a mirarla...
Por eso nos has puesto a un lado del camino
con el único oficio de gritar asombrados.
En nosotros descansa la prisa de los hombres.   25
Porque, si no existiéramos, ¿para qué tantas cosas
inútiles y bellas como Dios ha creado,
tantos ocasos rojos, y tanto árbol sin fruta,
y tanta flor, y tanto pájaro vagabundo?
Solamente nosotros sentimos tu regalo   30
y te lo agradecemos en éxtasis de gritos.
Tú sonríes, Señor, sintiéndote pagado
con nuestro aplastamiento de asombro y maravilla.

Esto que nos exalta sólo puede ser tuyo.
Sólo quien nos ha hecho puede así destruirnos   35
en brazos de una llama tan cruel y magnífica.

... Tú que cuidas los pájaros que dicen tu mensaje,
guarda en la muerte nuestros cansados corazones;
dales paz, esa paz que en vida les negaste,
bórrales el doliente pensamiento sin tregua.   40
Tú nos darás en Ti el Todo que buscamos;
nos darás a nosotros mismos, pues te tendremos
para nosotros solos, y no para cantarte.

(*Hombre de Dios,* 1945)

LA MAÑANA

En la mañana, en su fino y mojado
aire, subes y vuelves a la casa,
con el latir de gente, y los trabajos;
te corona el rumor del mercadillo,
y el carpintero habrá sacado el pote   5
pegajoso a la puerta, y dará golpes,
y el triciclo de carga va llevando
la buena nueva, porque tú me llegas
con tu cesto, cargada de milagros;
te acompaña la leche, como un niño   10
que anda mal, que se tiende y que se mancha,
el queso, denso espacio de pureza
concretada y punzante, y el fulgor
antiguo del aceite, la verdura
aún viva, sorprendida mientras duerme,   15
las patatas mineras[1] y pesadas
de querencia[2] de suelo, los tomates
con fresco escalofrío; los pedazos
crueles de la carne, y un aroma
noble de pan por todo, y su contacto   20
rugoso de herramienta. Ya se inunda
mi faro pensativo[3] de riquezas,
de materias preciosas; considero
la textura[4] del vino y de la fruta,
estudio mi lección de olores: noto   25
que todo se hace yo porque lo traes
a entrar en mí, y estamos en la mesa
elevados, las cosas y nosotros,

---

[1] *mineras:* por criarse bajo la tierra.   [2] *querencia:* tendencia hacia algo.
[3] *faro pensativo:* la frente, el pensamiento.   [4] *textura:* disposición que presentan
las partículas de un cuerpo o un objeto.

en el nombre del mundo, como pobre
desayuno de Dios, a que nos coma.   30

(Versos del domingo, 1954)

VIDA ES ESPERANZA[1]

Basta de *razas ubérrimas,*[2] *sangre de Hispania fecunda,*
nada de *marcha triunfal,* ni *cortejo,* ni *viejas espadas;*
en espíritu unidos, en miseria y *en ansias y lengua,*
siervos dispersos, rumiando, lo más, un pasado de mito,
bajo los ojos de Dios, los de lengua española, ¿qué somos? 5
¿Qué hemos dejado en su libro, qué cuentas, qué penas?
Si algo supimos cantar de su gloria en el mundo,
mucho pecamos alzando la cruz como espada (gritaba
el obispo del Cid, al galope: *Ferid, caballeros,*
por amor de... el Criador, dice el texto Pidal,[3] *caridad,*   10
Per Abbat,[4] ¿qué es peor?), y hasta hoy día retumban
                                                    [Cruzadas.
Pague, Señor, cada cual su pecado, y el pueblo,
víctima siempre, se libre de deuda y castigo.
¿De qué sirve el destello del Siglo de Oro al cansado?
¿Y don Quijote y el buen gobernador Sancho Panza,   15
de qué, al que no sabe leer ni esperar en un sueño?
Nuestra gente habla y dice: «trabajo», «mañana»,
                                              [«pues claro»,

---

[1] Un poemario de Rubén Darío se titula *Cantos de vida y esperanza;* de dos poemas de este libro —«Salutación del optimista» y «Marcha triunfal»— proceden las palabras en bastardilla de los vv. 1-3. [2] *ubérrimas:* muy fértiles. [3] Se refiere a D. Ramón Menéndez Pidal, editor del *Cantar de Mio Cid.* [4] *Per Abbat:* aún se discute si se trata del autor o de un copista del *Cantar de Mio Cid.*

«los chicos», «es tarde», «el jornal», «un café»,
                                        [«no se puede»;
no hay ni cultura europea ni estirpe latina en sus bocas,
sólo el escueto ademán del que afianza la carga
                                        [en los hombros.   20
El que es siervo no habla español, ni habla inglés,
                                        [ni habla nada;
su palabra es la mano de un náufrago que se agarra
                                        [a las olas,
y las cosas le pesan y embisten sin volverse lenguaje.
Nadie cree ya en pueblos-Mesías, [5] «destinos», «valores»;
la tierra es un solo clamor, y el niñito en Vietnam
                                        [o en el Congo   25
llora lo mismo que el niño en Jaén o en los Andes.
Pero el rico es más fuerte que nunca, y su miedo le hace
más hábil y duro, y pretende cerrar el mañana;
se arman los créditos, vuelan alarmas por radio, y,
                                        [en tanto,
se amontona la cólera sacra de pueblos y pueblos.   30
Y algo se mueve también, con palabra española,
y suena a menudo: «esto no puede seguir así», o algún
                                        [viejo
proverbio con nuevo sabor como: «no hay mal que cien
                                        [años dure».
Y hasta si fuera a valer para un poco de paz y justicia,
más valdría borrar nuestra lengua, nuestro ser,
                                        [nuestra historia.   35
La esperanza nos llama a poner nuestra voz en el coro
que para todos exige la escasa ración que nos debe
                                        [la vida,
en la historia del hombre, en su ambiguo avanzar,
                                        [malo y bueno,

---

[5] *pueblos-Mesías:* pueblos salvadores, predestinados.

trabajando y cayendo, pero acaso ayudando a los
[pobres,
hasta entrar bajo el juicio secreto, el amor enigmático, 40
la memoria de Dios donde un día las lenguas se
[fundan...

(*Años inciertos*, 1971)

CARLOS EDMUNDO DE ORY [33]

LA CASA MUERTA

Paso a paso llegué a la verja un día
no habiendo nadie y con mi poca altura
abrí la puerta y penetré en la oscura
casa que estaba en su interior vacía.

Como la lluvia allí no me podía   5
dormité con un sueño que aún me dura;
pues bien, nunca saldré de esta aventura
la que yo llamo la ventura mía.

---

(33) Ory construyó en las dos composiciones iniciales poemas
intensamente visionarios que ofrecen la expresión del yo «ruinoso»
a través de procedimientos característicos del postismo: metros
clásicos descoyuntados por reiteraciones excesivas (vv. 12-13 de «El
rey de las ruinas»), juegos de palabras *(aventura-ventura, espesa
esperanza)*, verbos a fin de frase, palabras disonantes en el contexto
(monocromo, fotocopia), coloquialismos *(pues bien)*, ausencia de puntuación, etc. En el tercer poema destacan los contrastes *(vida /
muerte, despiertan / duermen, sollozos / gozos...)* y la unión de amor y
muerte.

Yo soy aquella la lejana casa
y aquel el hombre triste que la habita   10
empeñado en no abrir jamás la puerta.

No el viento pasa. No la lluvia pasa.
Ni aún nadie se le acerca porque evita
el miedo que le da la casa muerta.

(*Madrid*, 1947)

EL REY DE LAS RUINAS

Estoy en la miseria Dios mío qué te importa
Ya mi casa es un dulce terraplén de locura
Un vuelo de lechuzas un río con el fondo
lacrado[1] en mi semblante... ¡Dios mío qué te importa
Mi casa es un relincho de muerto monocromo[2]   5
cuna de remembranza[3] gran rincón de dolor
Allí ya no se duerme si no es para gritar
con una boca hambrienta de espesas esperanzas
Flores ayer y hoy sus faldas son escombros
Mi rostro de color negro aguanta la puerta   10
y al fin no sé qué hacer con tanta fotocopia
¡Estoy en la miseria! Se dice la miseria
y nada es la miseria... ¡Dios mío qué miseria!
Por el resuelto abismo subo las escaleras
del torreón oculto para pedir limosna   15
Entro llamo ay ay ¡Señorito! ¡Ay! ¡Ay!
No puede ser así usted no se parece
¡Aparición! ¿Quién soy? Te pido yo una cama

---

[1] *lacrado:* sellado [2] *monocromo:* de un solo color. [3] *remembranza:* recuerdo.

para abrigar mis labios con un sueño anticuado
No te pongas así no te asustes de mí   20
¡Ayaymiseñoritoustedyanoeselmismo![4]
Parece usted de veras un cansado harapiento
Me da pena su ombligo lleno de soledad
Ropa y candela[5] diome y cené con la vieja
con la comadre atónita que mientras como reza   25
Riendo yo le explico: «Soy el rey de las ruinas»
Y ella plasma un quejido: «¿Qué es eso señorito?»

(*Madrid, 1947*)

SERENATA

Verdad que la mujer tiene siempre deseos
¡Oh rito infranqueable la mujer tiene brazos!
Con frecuencia la miro deseando comprenderla
cuando zumba el ataúd diurno del amor.

La corriente de sed se aplaca en sus dos pechos   5
La mujer con su costra de silencio se embarca
en una triste y lenta marejada de olvido
La noche es otra tumba que en su ser se coloca.

Con frecuencia la miro con frecuencia la toco
y sus ropas de llanto me despiertan la muerte   10
Y sus ropas de tela y sus telas de almíbar
me despiertan la vida me despiertan y duermen.

---

[4] Todo junto con el fin de imitar el lenguaje hablado.   [5] *candela:* vela, lumbre.

¡Oh cortina furiosa constante y enemiga!
No puedes ya volar sin un temblor debajo
Quiero apretar tus dedos melosos y algo turbios   15
Quiero besar sus besos y quiero estar tus noches.

Nos separa una vida de color del desierto
Nos espera una historia de sollozos y gozos
Ya me ves ya me oyes nos estamos amando
Nunca están separados los lejanos lejanos.   20

Los lejanos se encuentran y tus grandes suspiros
lloverán como ampos[1] azules sobre el polvo
Odio los besos dados odio el ancla en los cuerpos
Porque espero la boca repitiendo tus labios.

Pero te veo plena de lujos misteriosos   25
Te cubre a ti una negra y transparente nube
No miras a esta clase de seres mas que lejos
Mientras sola debates tu pálida locura.

Verdad que la mujer tiene siempre deseos
Mentira que me quieres oh reina de la dicha   30
Oh reina de la dicha oh misérrima madre
Oh misérrima dicha oh desolado imperio.

(*Madrid, abril* 1949)

(*Poesía, 1945-1969*)

---

[1] *ampos:* copos de nieve.

MIGUEL LABORDETA [34]

SEVERA CONMINACIÓN[1] DE UN CIUDADANO DEL MUNDO

Mataos
pero dejad tranquilo a ese niño que duerme en una cuna.
Si vuestra rabia es fuego que devora tal cielo
y en vuestras almohadas crecen las pistolas:
destruíos aniquilaos ensangrentad   5
con ojos desgarrados los acumulados cementerios
que bajo la luna de tantas cosas callan
pero dejad tranquilo al campesino
que cante en la mañana
el azul nutritivo de los soles.   10

---

[1] *conminación:* exigencia severísima, bajo amenaza.

(34) «Autobiografía espiritual, atroz y tierna a la vez, de una alma solitaria» (R. Senabre) es la poesía de Labordeta, ligada a la corriente surrealista. En sus primeros libros dominan los matices existenciales; después se constituye en testimonio histórico. A esta etapa pertenecen los dos poemas seleccionados, donde lo «atroz» y lo «tierno» caminan juntos: véanse los imperativos contundentes de «Severa conminación» frente a los seres para los que se solicita piedad. Nótese, además, la cuidada correlación diseminativo-recolectiva.

Invadid con vuestro traquetreo
los talleres los navíos las universidades
las oficinas espectrales donde tanta gente languidece
triturad toda rosa hallad al noble pensativo
preparad las bombas de fósforo y las nupcias del agua
[con la muerte   15
que han de aplastar a las dulces muchachas paseantes
en esta misma hora que sonríe
por una desconocida ciudad de provincias
pero dejad tranquilo al joven estudiante
que lleva en su corazón un estío secreto.   20

Inundad los periódicos las radios los cines las tribunas
de entelequias [2] estructuras incompatibilidades
pero dejad tranquilo al obrero que fumando un pitillo
ríe con los amigos en aquel bar de la esquina.

Asesinaos si así lo deseáis   25
exterminaos vosotros: los teorizantes de ambas cercas
que jamás asiríais un fusil de bravura
pero dejad tranquilo a ese hombre tan bueno y tan
[vulgar
que con su mujer pasea en los económicos atardeceres.

Aplastaos pero vosotros   30
los inquisitoriales azuzadores de la matanza
los implacables dogmáticos de estrechez mentecata
los monstruosos depositarios de la enorme Gran Estafa
los opulentos energúmenos que en alza favorable
[de cotizaciones
preparáis la trituración de los sueños modestos   35
bajo un hacha de martirios inútiles.

---

[2] *entelequias:* productos de la imaginación, cosas irreales.

Pisotead mi sepulcro también
os lo permito si así lo deseáis inclusive y todo
aventad mis cenizas gratuitamente
si consideráis que mi voz de la calle no se acomoda
                              [a vuestros fines suculentos   40
pero dejad tranquilo a ese niño que duerme en una
                                                    [cuna
al campesino que nos suda la harina y el aceite
al joven estudiante con su llave de oro
al obrero en su ocio ganado fumándose un pitillo
y al hombre gris que coge los tranvías   45
con su gabán roído a las seis de la tarde.

Esperan otra cosa.
Los parieron sus madres para vivir con todos
y entre todos aspiran a vivir tan sólo esto
y de ellos ha de crecer   50
si surje
una raza de hombres con puñales de amor inverosímil
hacia otras aventuras más hermosas.

                                          (*Epilírica*, 1961)

1936

fue en la edad de nuestro primer amor
cuando los mensajes son propicios al precoz embelesamiento
y los suaves atardeceres toman un perfume dulcísimo
en forma de muchacha azul o de mayo que desaparece
cuando   5
unos hombres duros como el sol del verano
ensangrentaban la tierra blasfemando

de otros hombres tan duros como ellos
tenían prisa por matar para no ser matados
y vimos asombrados con inocente pupila   10
el terror de los fusilados amaneceres
las largas caravanas de camiones desvencijados
en cuyo fondo los acurrucados individuos
eran llevados a la muerte como acosada manada
era la guerra el terror los incendios era la patria suicidada 15
eran los siglos podridos reventando
vimos las gentes despavoridas en un espanto de
                                        [consignas atroces
iban y venían insultaban denunciaban mataban
eran los héroes decían golpeando
las ventanillas de los trenes repletos de carne de cañón[1] 20
nosotros no entendíamos apenas el suplicio
y la hora dulce de un jardín con alegría y besos
fueron noches salvajes de bombardeo noticias lúgubres
la muerte banderín de enganche[2] cada macilenta[3]
                                        [aurora
y héteme aquí solo ante mi vejez más próxima   25
preguntar en silencio
qué fue de nuestro vuelo de remanso
por qué pagamos las culpas colectivas
de nuestro viejo pueblo sanguinario
quién nos resarcirá[4] de nuestra adolescencia destruida 30
aunque no fuese a las trincheras?

vanas son las preguntas a la piedra
y mudo el destino insaciable por el viento
mas quiero hablarte aquí de mi generación perdida

---

[1] *carne de cañón:* gente expuesta sin consideración al riesgo de ser matada.
[2] *banderín de enganche:* puesto para enganchar reclutas. [3] *macilenta:* descolorida, pálida. [4] *resarcirá:* compensará.

de su cólera paloma en una sala de espera con un reloj
[parado para siempre   35
de sus besos nunca recobrados
de su alegría asesinada
por la historia siniestra
de un huracán terrible de locura

(*Los soliloquios*, 1969)

RICARDO MOLINA [35]

ELEGÍA VII

A Ginés Liébana

En Sandua[1] aúlla el viento por los viejos tejados,
por los muros ruinosos y la negra veleta.
El avellano esfuma su contorno en la niebla
y el torrente ensordece los valles desolados.

Los nogales sacuden sus mil hojas de agua   5
anunciando el otoño en los campos aún verdes.

---

[1] *Sandua:* nombre de una mansión arruinada y de su entorno, escenario
amoroso de las *Elegías.*

(35) Molina parte de hechos reales y vincula Amor y Naturaleza. La «Elegía VII» es una «visión alegórica de una Sandua en
ruinas que para el poeta es símbolo de su propia historia y de su
presente» (G. Carnero), en un paisaje otoñal. En la «Elegía XI» la
naturaleza sirve de referencia al impulso amoroso, destacando la
correlación diseminativo-recolectiva de la última estrofa. Como
todos los poemas de la *Elegía de Medina Azahara,* «Vida callada»,
en tono sereno, es «una meditación sobre la fugacidad del amor, de la
felicidad, de la belleza» (G. Carnero).

Las nubes se derrumban como un trono solemne
sobre la silenciosa calma de las montañas.

Los violentos despojos de la oscura tormenta
en las aguas salvajes se destiñen y flotan.   10
En los rosales queda todavía una rosa
y al aspirarla mi alma se inunda de tristeza.

Y no sé si esa rosa solitaria y tardía
es acaso la pena que quedó aquí una tarde
y que luego en silencio dio un aroma suave   15
y ahora me pone triste después de tantos días.

No lo sé... Sin embargo, me detengo en la puerta
de la casa en ruinas perdida entre los montes
y la sombra angustiosa de los próximos bosques
cae sobre mi vida cada vez más espesa.   20

He cruzado el umbral... La soledad recorre
el patio oscurecido con sus plantas de musgo.
El suelo está mojado. Los muros están húmedos.
En las ventanas fulge[2] un instante la tarde.

Oh abrir esa ventana al viento y a la lluvia,   25
a los fuegos del cielo y a las hojas marchitas
y sentir al pasar las largas galerías
seguirme mis pisadas pavorosas[3] y oscuras.

Oh llegar al lejano dormitorio que abre
al campo dos balcones con cortinas de nubes   30
y besar en la sombra los recuerdos más dulces,
los recuerdos aquellos que no sospecha nadie.

---

[2] *fulge:* brilla. [3] *pavorosas:* que causan pavor, espanto.

Oh Sandua en ruinas al borde del torrente
que en los avellanares se despeña estruendoso,
¿qué busca en tus tejados y en tu veleta el viento?,   35
¿por qué la lluvia azota tus rotas cristaleras
y se sienta en tus bancos, fatigado, el otoño?

Oh Sandua de muros negros y amarillentos
que un solo rosal tienes y una rosa tan solo,
¿por qué mi corazón lo mismo que un arroyo   40
quiere besar tus pobres paredes derruidas
como cuando la sierra se desborda en otoño?

Oh Sandua a la sombra del nogal milenario
que da calma y frescura por las tardes al pozo,
¿por qué está siempre el cielo nublado sobre ti?,   45
¿por qué la soledad pasea por tu patio
y en tu torre suspira desolado el otoño?

¿Qué frases de otro tiempo se extinguen en tus salas,
qué recuerdos pesados y dulces como lágrimas,
qué dicha temblorosa, qué apagados sollozos,   50
qué risas como flores en los labios cansados,
qué esperanza amarilla como un cielo de otoño?

Oh Sandua que mueres un poco cada día,
conserva tus fantasmas: yo no he de despertarlos.
Conserva ese misterio que alienta en tus ruinas,   55
que no he de profanar tampoco tu misterio
ni turbar tu silencio con mi melancolía.

No he de abrir a la vida tus ventanas cerradas,
no he de evocar tu historia junto a la chimenea
y no he de recorrer tus largas galerías,   60
pues algo que se siente y que nunca se explica
me detiene en el patio igual que en una tumba.

Y cuando vuelvo a Córdoba, que brilla en la llanura
entre los encinares, al fin de la cañada,
me digo que la vida es tan indiferente   65
como el valle desierto donde mueres, oh Sandua,
y me digo también que en un valle tan dulce
y sombrío, mi vida sería semejante
a tus grises ruinas ahogadas por las nubes.

Y al volver la cabeza para ver por vez última   70
tu torreón lejano bañado por la luna
me parece que mi alma es ese triste arcángel
que gira en la veleta al impulso del viento,
y mi vida una casa que ya no habita nadie,
que invaden las malezas y las brumas de otoño;   75
una casa en ruinas perdida entre los montes,
olvidada en un valle salvaje y melancólico...

ELEGÍA XI

Cuando derrite el cielo el sol de julio
buscan los bueyes las espesas sombras,
los segadores de color cobrizo
las frescas jarras y los pozos húmedos;
las cabras, los retoños del olivo,   5
y yo —lento y errante por el día—
la terrestre dulzura de tu cuerpo.

Pues la verbena[1] en flor, la verde prímula[2]
y las vides silvestres cuyos pámpanos
sombrean la roja frente de los sátiros,[3]   10

---

[1] *verbena:* planta.   [2] *prímula:* planta.   [3] *sátiros:* semidioses de la Mitología, mitad hombre y mitad cabra.

y el soto umbrío que un arroyo baña
y que al pasar el viento vibra todo
como lira de hojas plateadas,
y las colgantes driadas[4] que enroscan
sus guirnaldas de azules campanillas   15
en el tronco del álamo sonante,
y la zarza espinosa donde tiembla
—sombra y rocío— un dios enamorado,
no tienen para mi alma la dulzura
ni la dorada gracia de tu cuerpo.   20

Como la rosa móvil y redonda
del girasol sigue el curso del astro,
como el agua en la fuente campesina
se arquea y luego cae en claro chorro,
como el fruto maduro comba grávido   25
la rama que sustenta su opulencia,
como el águila gira por el cielo
y se cierne, voraz, sobre el rebaño,
así mi alma gravita, gira y cae
—fruto, flor, agua y águila— en tu cuerpo.   30

(*Elegías de Sandua*, 1948)

VIDA CALLADA

De la vida callada de las plantas
aprendo olvido. Al cielo
alza el almezo[1] sus ramas gimientes
de ruiseñores.

---

[4] *driadas:* ninfas de los bosques.
[1] *almezo:* árbol de copa ancha y flores solitarias.

Me detengo un instante. La memoria   5
se adormece a su sombra. De mi vida
pasada nada quiero, vana imagen
que huye como el agua.

En la tarde otras tardes profundizan
esta hora. El sosiego que me invade   10
no altera mi tristeza.
Acaso la eterniza. ¿Todo muere?
¿Morirá mi dolor? Toda mi vida
se me aparece ahora como un ansia
frustrada de hermosura.

                Claro almezo   15
eleva entre tus ramas plañideras[2]
mi corazón callado hasta la luna.

                (*Elegía de Medina Azahara*, 1957)

---

[2] *plañideras:* gimientes.

PABLO GARCÍA BAENA [36]

SÓLO TU AMOR Y EL AGUA

Sólo tu amor y el agua... Octubre junto al río
bañaba los racimos dorados de la tarde,
y aquella luna odiosa iba subiendo, clara,
ahuyentando las negras violetas de la sombra.
Yo iba perdido, náufrago por mares de deseo,   5
cegado por la bruma suave de tu pelo.
De tu pelo que ahogaba la voz en mi garganta
cuando perdía mi boca en sus olas de niebla.
Sólo tu amor y el agua... El río, dulcemente,
callaba sus rumores al pasar por nosotros,   10
y el aire estremecido apenas se atrevía
a mover en la orilla las hojas de los álamos.
Sólo se oía, dulce como el vuelo de un ángel
al rozar con sus alas una estrella dormida,

(36) Muy apreciado por los poetas de los 70, uno de ellos lo ha
calificado de «poeta barroco, sensualista, personalista, esteticista y
decadente». Algunos de estos adjetivos convienen ya a la etapa
inicial de *Rumor oculto,* cobrarán todo su esplendor en *Antiguo
muchacho* y decrecerán en *Óleo.* Véanse los poemas, uno de cada
libro.

el choque fugitivo que quiere hacerse ⌐terno,   15
de mis labios bebiendo en los tuyos la vida.
Lo puro de tus senos me mordía en el pecho
con la fragancia tímida de dos lirios silvestres,
de dos lirios mecidos por la inocente brisa
cuando el verano extiende su ardor por las colinas.   20
La noche se llenaba de olores de membrillo,
y mientras en mis manos tu corazón dormía,
perdido, acariciante, como un beso lejano,
el río suspiraba...
      Sólo tu amor y el agua...

                          (*Rumor oculto*, 1946)

EL CORPUS[1]

Primavera es, acaso, ese niño que ríe por el jardín.
Acaso, esa mano que dice adiós en el balcón del atardecer,
o sólo rosas rojas como el fuego de Pentecostés[2]
en un seto sombrío.
La Primavera pone su lirio en las ruinas   5
y la genciana[3] azul en la alquería,[4]
y en la selva, desnuda, destrenza su cabello negro como
                                [un torrente;
y cuando las ciudades duermen entre las torres de
                                [su orgullo,
la Primavera abre el prodigio de sus cuatro jardines,
y el primer jardín se llama Marzo,   10

---

[1] *Corpus*: festividad de la Eucaristía.   [2] *el fuego de Pentecostés:* en tal fiesta
judía, el Espíritu Santo se posó en lenguas de fuego sobre los Apóstoles.
[3] *genciana*: planta.   [4] *alquería*: casa de labor, lejos de poblado.

y es verde como una túnica de vino y esmeraldas
que ciñera como labios, como manos, nuestro cuerpo.
El segundo jardín es amargo y su noche se llama
[Getsemaní. [5]
El tercero es semejante a un príncipe que cantara
[bajo los cedros
con el jirón último de la tarde en sus manos,   15
y su nombre es Mayo.
El cuarto jardín se llama Junio,
y sus flores, abrumadas de escarlata y de oro,
son como bengalas ardiendo entre los peces de un
[estanque,
y un Árbol de frutos purísimos, gigante, se levanta   20
amparando con su sombra la palidez obispal de las
[hortensias
y el relámpago sangriento de la clavia [6]
y su nombre, Corpus,
es fresco como la palabra fuente oída entre sueños en
[una noche de calentura.

Recuerda aquel aroma de las hierbas pisadas...   25
Las carretas lentas que bajan del monte al arroyo frío
[de los mastrantos. [7]
Los juncos perfumando las varas de los lábaros. [8]
El altar, con las velas ardiendo al sol,
donde los Santos Mártires destiñen la sangre lívida [9]
[de su cuello
bajo la espada cálida de la tarde.   30
Un viento entre las calles perdido
apaga en silencio los cirios de los fieles.

---

[5] *Getsemaní:* lugar donde fue apresado Jesucristo. [6] *clavia:* planta.
[7] *mastrantos:* planta muy común en las orillas de los ríos (también *mastranzos*). [8] *lábaros:* estandartes con la Cruz y el monograma de Cristo. [9] *lívida:* amoratada.

El armiño[10] y la grana[11] ostentan su opulencia en
                             [balcones cerrados
al crecer como fronda que subiera hasta un cielo de
                             [calor y de pétalos
la azucena bermeja de las limpias trompetas.   35
Los niños con cestillos de mimbre derramando las
                          [flores sobre el sol y la arena.
Las sandalias bordadas de las vírgenes pisan las
                         [blancas clavellinas
que levantan su olor como una tentación,
y en la seda grosella, celeste, color fresa, de angélicas
                         [dalmáticas,[12]
bordonea[13] la siesta igual que una moscarda de
                         [berilos[14] azules. 40
Se adormecen los ojos de la cal y del oro...
Un éxtasis de incienso flota al compás de la música.
Las navetas[15] doradas guardan los sofocantes perfumes
                         [del Oriente
que escapan, como pájaros de plumas fastuosas, desde
                         [los braserillos,
en busca de los árboles de nombres aromáticos: benjuí
                         [y cinamomo. 45
La tarde abre su cofre de rubíes y silencio.
Los ciriales[16] se inclinan gráciles como mieses.
¡O salutaris hostia!,[17] cantan las colegialas bajo los
                         [blancos velos,
y desde la campiña que Junio hace vibrar con vihuelas[18]
                         [de insectos,
llega el rumor de una campana,   50

---

[10] *armiño:* piel suave del animal así llamado. [11] *grana:* paño fino. [12] *dalmáticas:* vestiduras sagradas. [13] *bordonea:* suena roncamente. [14] *berilos:* esmeraldas. [15] *navetas:* cajas para incienso u otros perfumes. [16] *ciriales:* candeleros para cirios. [17] *¡O salutaris hostia!:* ¡Oh, hostia de salvación! [18] *vihuelas:* guitarras.

anhelante como un seno desnudo después de haber
                              [corrido
que bañara sus venas azuladas de ecos en el frescor
                                    [del aire.
En el vidrio angustioso de los fanales[19]
brilla la rubia abeja ardiente de la llama.
Trémulas campanillas anuncian la Custodia   55
en suave temblor de cristal y de trigo.
Racimos palpitantes entrelazan sus pámpanos por la
                              [plata desnuda de los ángeles.
La cera goteando marchita los bordados
y la piedad vuelca sus bandejas de flores
ante la enhiesta espiga que guarda entre sus oros,   60
como un pétalo blanco de virginal harina, el limpio
                              [corazón del Sacramento.[37]

(*Antiguo muchacho*, 1950)

CUANDO LOS MENSAJEROS...

Cuando los mensajeros golpeen los postigos
y su voz, a través de la vieja madera,
penetre como un viento de música y de plata,
oh corazón, no temas, no tiembles, amor mío.

---

[19] *fanales:* campanas de cristal que protegen la llama.

(37) «El Corpus» es ejemplo paradigmático de las peculiaridades del grupo cordobés de *Cántico*. El tema se centra en la evocación infantil del Corpus y en la celebración pagana de la primavera; léxico lujoso y ornamental, destacando el decorado vegetal y los objetos litúrgicos; apela a todos los sentidos (colores, aromas, etc.). Barroquismo, suntuosidad y plasticidad.

Un soplo de destino apagará la llama entre los labios   5
y en las barcas de estío los floridos remeros callarán
                              [para siempre.
La mano, entre las cuerdas de nobles instrumentos,
quedará y la canción, pájaro inacabado,
buscará nido en las brillantes gemas[1] solitarias
de los desnudos cuerpos pulidos al aliento del mar y de
                              [los astros,   10
quietos y deslumbrantes como árboles de mármol
donde una fruta dulce y venenosa se pudre lentamente.
Yacerán sepultados en bancales[2] de olvido
la balanza sutil del orfebre y la brújula
que guía por el sueño la flota misteriosa   15
y el atril[3] y los báculos,[4] la tralla[5] y los arneses,[6]
silenciosos testigos de unas sombras extintas[7].
Y el rubí como un diente de sangre clavado en la garganta
y el vaso que derrama el hechizo del vino
y el azul brazalete como pámpano áureo enroscado
                              [a la carne,   20
el punzón y los búcaros.[8]
Lo que un día tuvo el fuego de un instante,
eternidad proclama.
Oh corazón, oh amor, amor mío que tiemblas
solitario al rumor del bosque que respira,   25
no temas.
Las puertas con su triple candado están cerradas
y aún hay vida en mis manos. Duerme dulce
hasta que un alba púrpura selle de polvo el labio
y nos lleve flotando a los altos sitiales.[9]   30

                                        (*Óleo*, 1958)

---

[1] *gemas:* piedras preciosas. [2] *bancales:* tierras cultivadas. [3] *atril:* mueble
para sostener libros abiertos. [4] *báculos:* bastones. [5] *tralla:* látigo. [6] *arneses:*
armaduras. [7] *extintas:* muertas. [8] *búcaros:* vasijas de barro. [9] *sitiales:* asientos de ceremonia.

Para que yo me llame Ángel González,
para que mi ser pese sobre el suelo,
fue necesario un ancho espacio
y un largo tiempo:
hombres de todo mar y toda tierra,   5
fértiles vientres de mujer, y cuerpos
y más cuerpos fundiéndose incesantes
en otro cuerpo nuevo.
Solsticios[1] y equinoccios[2] alumbraron
con su cambiante luz, su vario cielo,   10
el viaje milenario de mi carne
trepando por los siglos y los huesos.
De su pasaje lento y doloroso,
de su huida hasta el fin, sobreviviendo
naufragios, aferrándose   15

---

[1] *solsticios:* épocas en las que la diferencia de duración entre el día y la noche es máxima. [2] *equinoccios:* épocas en que la duración del día y la noche son iguales.

(38) Los motivos de A. González, analizados por Alarcos Llorach, pueden resumirse así: el hombre está solo en el mundo y sólo caben dos consuelos: sentirse eslabón («Para que yo me llame...») y testigo («El campo de batalla») de la historia humana, o bien refugiarse en el amor o en lo marginal (prostitutas, desvalidos...).

al último suspiro de los muertos,
yo no soy más que el resultado, el fruto,
lo que queda, podrido, entre los restos;
esto que veis aquí,
tan sólo esto: 20
un escombro tenaz, que se resiste
a su ruina, que lucha contra el viento,
que avanza por caminos que no llevan
a ningún sitio. El éxito
de todos los fracasos. La enloquecida   25
fuerza del desaliento...

                                    (*Áspero mundo*, 1956)

EL CAMPO DE BATALLA

Hoy voy a describir el campo
de batalla
tal como yo lo vi, una vez decidida
la suerte de los hombres que lucharon,
muchos hasta morir,   5
otros
hasta seguir viviendo todavía.

No hubo elección:
murió quien pudo,
quien no pudo morir continuó andando,   10
los árboles nevaban lentos frutos,
era verano, invierno, todo un año
o más quizá: era la vida
entera
aquel enorme día de combate.   15

Por el oeste el viento traía sangre,
por el este la tierra era ceniza,
el norte entero estaba
bloqueado
por alambradas secas y por gritos,   20
y únicamente el sur,
tan sólo
el sur,
se ofrecía ancho y libre a nuestros ojos.

Pero el sur no existía: 25
ni agua, ni luz, ni sombra, ni ceniza
llenaban su oquedad, su hondo vacío:
el sur era un enorme precipicio,
un abismo sin fin de donde,
lentos,   30
los poderosos buitres ascendían.

Nadie escuchó la voz del capitán
porque tampoco el capitán hablaba.
Nadie enterró a los muertos.
Nadie dijo: 35
«Dale a mi novia esto si la encuentras
un día.»

Tan sólo alguien remató a un caballo
que, con el vientre abierto,
agonizante,   40
llenaba con su espanto el aire en sombra:
el aire que la noche amenazaba.

Quietos, pegados a la dura
tierra,
cogidos entre el pánico y la nada,   45
los hombres esperaban el momento

último,
sin oponerse ya,
sin rebeldía.

Algunos se murieron,   50
como dije,
y los demás, tendidos, derribados,
pegados a la tierra en paz al fin,
esperan
ya no sé qué   55
—quizá que alguien les diga:
«Amigos, podéis iros, el combate...»

Entre tanto,
es verano otra vez,
y crece el trigo   60
en el que fue ancho campo de batalla.

(*Sin esperanza, con convencimiento*, 1961)

CAMPOSANTO EN COLLIURE[1]

Aquí paz,
y después gloria.

Aquí,
a orillas de Francia,
en donde Cataluña no muere todavía   5

---

[1] *Colliure:* pueblo del Mediterráneo francés —Collioure—, escrito aquí en catalán, donde está enterrado Antonio Machado (véanse vv. 10 y 35).

y prolonga en carteles de «Toros à Ceret»[2]
y de «Flamenco's Show»[3]
esa curiosa España de las ganaderías
de reses bravas y de juergas sórdidas,
reposa un español bajo una losa:

paz

10

y después gloria.

Dramático destino,
triste suerte
morir aquí
      —paz
y después...—

perdido,

15

abandonado
y liberado a un tiempo
(ya sin tiempo)
de una patria sombría e inclemente.

Sí; después gloria.

20

Al final del verano,
por las proximidades
pasan trenes nocturnos, subrepticios,[4]
rebosantes de humana mercancía:
mano de obra barata, ejército

25

vencido por el hambre
      —paz...—,
otra vez desbandada de españoles[5]
cruzando la frontera, derrotados
—...sin gloria.

---

[2] *Toros à Ceret:* toros en Ceret (población francesa muy cercana a la frontera española). [3] *Flamenco's Show:* espectáculo de flamenco. [4] *subrepticios:* ocultos. [5] Alusión a los republicanos que pasaron la frontera al fin de la guerra civil y a la ola de emigrantes en los años 60.

Se paga con la muerte   30
o con la vida,
pero se paga siempre una derrota.

¿Qué precio es el peor?
                            Me lo pregunto
y no sé qué pensar
ante esta tumba,   35
ante esta paz
                —«Casino
de Canet: spanish gipsy dancers», [6]
rumor de trenes, hojas...—,
ante la gloria ésta
—...de reseco laurel—   40
que yace aquí, abatida
bajo el ciprés erguido,
igual que una bandera al pie de un mástil.

Quisiera,
a veces,   45
que borrase el tiempo
los nombres y los hechos de esta historia
como borrará un día mis palabras
que la repiten siempre tercas, roncas. [39]

(*Grado elemental*, 1962)

---

[6] *spanish gipsy dancers:* bailarines españoles de flamenco.

[39] Tema: el éxodo de los derrotados por la guerra civil (como
A. Machado, a quien se homenajea) o por el hambre (los emigrantes). Comienza con una frase hecha que reitera y reinterpreta;
utiliza el «collage»: inclusión de letras de carteles que anuncian una

PRIMERA EVOCACIÓN

Recuerdo
bien
a mi madre.
Tenía miedo del viento,
era pequeña   5
de estatura,
la asustaban los truenos,
y las guerras
siempre estaba temiéndolas
de lejos,   10
desde antes
de la última ruptura
del Tratado suscrito
por todos los ministros de asuntos exteriores.

Recuerdo   15
que yo no comprendía.
El viento se llevaba
silbando
las hojas de los árboles,
y era como un alegre barrendero   20
que dejaba las niñas
despeinadas y enteras,
con las piernas desnudas e inocentes.

Por otra parte, el trueno
tronaba demasiado, era imposible   25
soportar sin horror esa estridencia,

España de «charanga y pandereta»; tono reflexivo que origina
numerosos paréntesis que, a su vez, dan lugar a un ritmo entrecortado.

aunque jamás ocurría nada luego:
la lluvia se encargaba de borrar
el dibujo violento del relámpago
y el arco iris ponía   30
un bucólico fin a tanto estrépito.

Llegó también la guerra un mal verano.
Llegó después la paz, tras un invierno
todavía peor. Esa vez, sin embargo,
no devolvió lo arrebatado el viento.   35
Ni la lluvia
pudo borrar las huellas de la sangre.
Perdido para siempre lo perdido,
atrás quedó definitivamente
muerto lo que fue muerto.   40

Por eso (y por más cosas)
recuerdo muchas veces a mi madre:

cuando el viento
se adueña de las calles de la noche,
y golpea las puertas, y huye, y deja   45
un rastro de cristales y de ramas
rotas, que al alba
la ciudad muestra desolada y lívida;
cuando el rayo
hiende [1] el aire, y crepita, [2]   50
y cae en tierra,
trazando surcos de carbón y fuego,
erizando los lomos de los gatos
y trastocando el norte de las brújulas;

---

[1] *hiende:* rasga.   [2] *crepita:* ruge como la leña que arde.

y, sobre todo, cuando   55
la guerra ha comenzado,
lejos —nos dicen— y pequeña
—no hay por qué preocuparse—, cubriendo
de cadáveres mínimos distantes territorios,
de crímenes lejanos, de huérfanos pequeños... [40]   60

(*Tratado de urbanismo*, 1967)

---

(40) Poema estructurado en tres partes y en torno a tres fenómenos: el *viento,* los *truenos,* la *guerra.* La primera parte (vv. 1-14)
presenta las reacciones de la madre *(tenía miedo, la asustaban, estaba
temiéndola);* en la segunda parte (vv. 15-40), la reacción del niño:
sólo hay temor ante la *guerra,* cuyas consecuencias no evitarán ni el
viento, ni la *lluvia;* de ahí que en la parte tercera (vv. 41-60) los tres
fenómenos originen temor y susciten la «primera evocación» por
antonomasia, la madre.

JOSÉ MANUEL CABALLERO BONALD [41]

MI PROPIA PROFECÍA ES MI MEMORIA

Vuelvo a la habitación donde estoy solo
cada noche, almacén de los días
caídos ya en su espejo naufragable.
Allí, entre testimonios maniatados,
yace inmóvil mi vida: sus papeles   5
de tornadizo[1] empeño.
                                    La madera,
el temblor de la lámpara, el cristal
visionario, los frágiles
oficios de los muebles, guardan
bajo sus apariencias el continuo   10
regresar de mis años, la espesura
tenaz de mi memoria, toda

---

[1] *tornadizo:* fácilmente variable.

(41) Caballero Bonald es poeta de expresión cuidada y actitud reflexiva, con frecuente recurrencia a la memoria, como sucede en el primer poema, en el cual la experiencia temporal se expresa por la identificación de *memoria* y *esperanza,* lo que da lugar a contrastes del tipo *memoria-profecía, historia-porvenir, oscuras-diáfanas, noche-luz, denegadas-ofrecidas.* Obsérvese, en este sentido, la semejanza con «Suplantaciones» (v. 18), último poema seleccionado.

la confluencia simultánea
de torrenciales sueños que me inundan.

Mundo recuperable, lo vivido   15
se congrega impregnando las paredes
donde de nuevo nace lo caduco.
Reconstruidas ráfagas de historia
juntan el porvenir que soy. (Oh habitación
a oscuras, súbitamente diáfana   20
bajo el fanal del tiempo repetible.)

Suenan rastros de luz allá en la noche.
Estoy solo y mis manos
ya denegadas, ya ofrecidas,
tocan papeles (este amor, aquel   25
sueño), olvidadas siluetas, vaticinios[2]
perdidos. Allí mi vida a golpes
la memoria me horada[3] cada día.

Imagen ya de mi exterminio,
se realiza de nuevo cuanto ha muerto.   30
Mi propia profecía es mi memoria:
mi esperanza de ser lo que ya he sido.

(*Memorias de poco tiempo*, 1954)

BLANCO DE ESPAÑA[1]

Escribo la palabra libertad,
la extiendo
sobre la piel dormida de mi patria.

---

[2] *vaticinios:* predicciones.   [3] *horada:* taladra, traspasa de parte a parte.
[1] *Blanco de España:* combina, al menos, dos significados: el de *blanco de España* como 'pintura usada para blanquear', y color blanco —luz, sol...— propio de España.

Cuántas salpicaduras, ateridas
entre sus letras indefensas, mojan   5
de fe mis manos, las consagran
de olvido.

                ¿Quién se sacrificó
por quién?

                Tarde llegué a las puertas
que me abrieron, tarde llegué
desde el refugio maternal   10
hasta el lugar del crimen,
con la paz aprendida
de memoria y una palabra pura
yerta sobre el papel atribulado.

Blanco de España, ensombrecido   15
de púrpura, [2] madre y madera
de odio, olvídate
del número mortal, bruñe [3] y colora
los hierros sanguinarios
con las ciegas tinturas del amor,   20
para que nadie pueda recordar
las divididas grietas de tu cuerpo,
para escribir tu nombre sobre el mío,
para encender con mi esperanza
la piel naciente de tu libertad. [(42)]   25

(*Las horas muertas*, 1959)

---

[2] *púrpura:* rojo; aquí, metafóricamente, sangre.   [3] *bruñe:* abrillanta.

[(42)] Este poema y el que sigue vierten la experiencia personal
del poeta en relación con la patria.

NO TERMINARÍA NUNCA

Ahora podría decir todo
lo que pienso,
lo que nunca
me dejaron saber: fui niño
entre alambradas,   5
crecí despacio y solo, iba
aprendiendo a callar,
me asomaba a la vida, puse
mi libertad encima
                de mis años.

Tiempo y distancia, ahora   10
todo está junto, se interpone
como un cristal de sangre
en medio de mi infancia.
Regreso al territorio
que no pude vivir,   15
remonto la tiniebla de los días
que ya me señalaron para siempre
con el contrario signo
de la paz, pongo
lo que me queda de alegría   20
en la ultrajada casa de mi hermano.

Podría hablar
y no terminaría nunca. No
terminaría nunca.

(*Pliegos de cordel*, 1963)

SUPLANTACIONES

Unas palabras son inútiles y otras
acabarán por serlo mientras
elijo para amarte más metódicamente
aquellas zonas de tu cuerpo aisladas
por algún obstinado depósito   5
de abulia, [1] los recodos
quizá donde mejor se expande
ese rastro de tedio
que circula de pronto por tu vientre,

y allí pongo mi boca y hasta   10
la intempestiva cama acuden
las sombras venideras, se interponen
entre nosotros, dejan
un barrunto [2] de fiebre y como un vaho
de exudación de sueño   15
y otras cavernas vespertinas,

y ya en lo ambiguo de la noche escucho
la predicción de la memoria:
dentro de ti me aferro
igual que recordándote, subsisto   20
como la espuma al borde de la espuma
mientras se activa entre los cuerpos
la carcoma voraz de estar a solas.

(*Descrédito del héroe*, 1965-74) (1977)

---

[1] *abulia:* falta de voluntad.   [2] *barrunto:* presentimiento.

CARLOS BARRAL [43]

LE ASOCIO A MIS PREOCUPACIONES

> *Y hase de notar, que estas cosas son aora muy*
> *a la postre, después de todas las visiones, y*
> *revelaciones que escriviré, y del tiempo que*
> *solía tener oración, a donde el Señor me dava*
> *muy grandes gustos y regalos.* [1]

Preferiría ahora imaginar
que te soñaba como un robot
metálico o como un antiguo caminante
hecho de humanidades o de audacia.
Pero a la primera juventud es propia   5
una ternura sin reservas,
y luego... la tradición más inmediata...

---

[1] Cita del *Libro de la vida*, de Santa Teresa.

(43) Barral ofrece en sus versos la propia experiencia, como muestran los dos poemas iniciales. El primero indaga en la experiencia religiosa a través de la evolución psicológica del adolescente, desde el fervor ingenuo, pasando por la duda y la rutina hasta la exclusión de Dios, a quien no se nombra en el poema.

Te invocaba según un largo rito,
torturándome hacia los pormenores de tu imagen.
Tocaba los objetos, te buscaba   10
revolviendo memoria.
Después, con los brazos en cruz, sobre la cama,
pasaba tiempo y tiempo.
             Conocía
que estabas por un dulce cansancio
y entonces me tendía sin mirarte,   15
sabiéndote allí cerca,
y te contaba mis deseos:

—Haz que el año que viene... Que otro día...
Haz que la chica que encontré el domingo
(o si prefieres aunque sea otra)...   20
Haz que yo pueda ser... Y, sobre todo...

Tu presencia asentía a cada cosa,
tu blanco estar allí, tu inabordable
reino, transfigurando el sueño en lejanías:
el suave chasquido con que hiende   25
el tajamar[2] las ondas
o unas ramas de abeto iluminadas,
flotando como un astro en el azul inmóvil...

Cada cita nocturna, cada encuentro
rescataba una parte del vivir diario: 30
los muros del colegio, los siniestros pasillos o las voces
de la mesa familiar cuando se hablaba de dinero
y además los pecados,
la vergonzosa marca del sexo
y el duermevela[3] de las imaginaciones.   35

---

   [2] *tajamar:* tablón curvado en la proa de los barcos, que sirve para cortar el agua.   [3] *duermevela:* sueño ligero.

En las horas vacías, por el día,
a veces te ofrecías como un premio
fugaz, pasabas un instante
rozándome, en medio del silencio cargado del estudio,
como un soplo de aire que se dibuja sobre el agua   40
quieta,
o en las veladas tristes, en familia,
junto a la radio tonante, [4]
o cuando la humillación me acaloraba.

Mas luego nuestro amor, según el tiempo   45
pasaba por la boca de los que te adulan,
se fue haciendo difícil, nuestras noches
de vez en vez más raras.
Comenzó a incomodarme
la sociedad de tus amigos, la dudosa   50
verdad de tus quehaceres...

Lo sé. No fue tan simple.
Sé que un día
mutilé la costumbre, sentí un poco
de rubor (la redujimos,   55
a lo más perentorio)... [5]

¡Qué rápidas visitas en los últimos meses!
Y aprendía
a ver el mundo sin ti,
a llenar tu vacío con las cosas.   60

No recuerdo
exactamente cómo terminó.
Más tarde
me parecía un sueño nuestra historia.

---

[4] *tonante:* tronante.   [5] *perentorio:* urgente.

HOMBRE EN LA MAR

II

Y tú, amor mío, ¿agradeces conmigo
las generosas ocasiones que la mar
nos deparaba de estar juntos? ¿Tú te acuerdas,
casi en el tacto, como yo,
de la caricia intranquila entre dos maniobras,   5
del temblor de tus pechos
en la camisa abierta cara al viento?

Y de las tardes sosegadas,
cuando la vela débil como un moribundo
nos devolvía a casa muy despacio...   10
Éramos como huéspedes de la libertad,
tal vez demasiado hermosa.

El azul de la tarde,
los húmedos violetas que oscurecían el aire
se abrían   15
y volvían a cerrarse tras nosotros
como la puerta de una habitación
por la que no nos hubiéramos
atrevido a preguntar.
          Y casi
nos bastaba un ligero contacto,   20
un distraído cogerte por los hombros
y sentir tu cabeza abandonada,
mientras alrededor se hacía triste
y allá en tierra, en la penumbra
parpadeaban las primeras luces.   25

(*Diecinueve figuras de mi historia civil*, 1961)

MÁS SOBRE LA INSOLENCIA DEL ALBA

Sí, es como un sucio animal que recorre el mundo
escapando a las redes del huso meridiano
detrás de los correos del aire en que dormitan
o velan sobre el vientre los hombres de negocios,
las modelos de tapa [1] o los habituales del congreso.   5
O merodea sin prisa y por encima
de los buques obscuros que parecen sin nadie.
Que es como una rata enorme
y asustadiza en el cielo borroso de los trópicos
o como un pez alargado e inmóvil   10
en los condados áridos del frío.

Que en todas partes suscita la sirena o el látigo
o el timbre modesto y lúgubre de los despertadores.
Que en la alcoba introduce los húmedos hocicos
y lame el flanco de la muchacha dormida y lo destiñe   15
y que fija un instante sobre el que parpadea
un ojo muerto y gris, sanguinolento.
Y que huye y huye provocando catástrofes,
descarrilando trenes pálidos y desorientados.

Que hurga en los hospitales y husmea cementerios   20
y va dejando un rastro de baba violeta
por entre los escombros de las fiestas tribales.
La aurora es un martillo,
es como una bandada de sordos bombarderos,
un vuelo de rapaces sobre gentes   25
de precaria existencia, que no saben,

---

[1] Alude a las señoritas que posan para las tapas de las revistas y a las que
se parecen a ellas.

que no han pensado aún si la detestan
y ya la reconocen y la temen;
es como una amenaza.
Es blanca sobre el lecho pringoso del insomne, [2]   30
como una vaga niebla, una falsa distancia.

(Tan lejos el relieve del desnudo inmediato,
extraño y arrogante.)

La aurora tiene trompa y huecos los carrillos,
bolsas de piel vacía y bolsas llenas de agua,   35
porque la aurora es fláccida, [3] o a veces
ajena y envarada [4] inútilmente
y habrá que levantarse y orinarla. [(44)]

(*Informe personal sobre el alba*, 1970)

---

[2] *insomne:* desvelado, sin sueño. [3] *fláccida:* fofa. [4] *envarada:* estirada y rígida.

---

(44) Frente al tradicional canto de alabanza, el alba es denostada porque separa la noche —reino de la libertad— del problemático día. Obsérvese la animalización como procedimiento degradante: *sucio animal, rata enorme, húmedos hocicos, lame, hurga, husmea*, etc.

JOSÉ AGUSTÍN GOYTISOLO [45]

LOS CELESTIALES

No todo el que dice: Señor, Señor, entrará en el reino...

(MAT., 7, 21)

Después y por encima de la pared caída,
de los vidrios caídos, de la puerta arrasada,
cuando se alejó el eco de las detonaciones
y el humo y sus olores abandonaron la ciudad,
después, cuando el orgullo se refugió en las cuevas,   5
mordiéndose los puños para no decir nada,
arriba, en los paseos, en las calles con ruina
que el sol acariciaba con sus manos de amigo,
asomaron los poetas, gente de orden, por supuesto.

---

(45) En Goytisolo aparece «una nítida conciencia generacional», escribe Sanz Villanueva en relación con «Los celestiales» («historia lírica de la posguerra») y con el entronque machadiano del «Homenaje en Colliure». En idéntico sentido pueden leerse los dos últimos poemas. Nótese el lenguaje claro y directo en todos los casos.

Es la hora, dijeron, de cantar los asuntos   10
maravillosamente insustanciales, es decir,
el momento de olvidarnos de todo lo ocurrido
y componer hermosos versos, vacíos, sí, pero sonoros,
melodiosos como el laúd,
que adormezcan, que transfiguren,   15
que apacigüen los ánimos, ¡qué barbaridad!

Ante tan sabia solución
se reunieron, pues, los poetas, y en la asamblea
de un café, [1] la votación, sin más preámbulo,
fue Garcilaso desenterrado, llevado en andas, paseado   20
como reliquia, por las aldeas y revistas,
y entronizado en la capital. El verso melodioso,
la palabra feliz, todos los restos,
fueron comida suculenta, festín de la comunidad.

Y el viento fue condecorado, y se habló   25
de marineros, de lluvia, de azahares, [2]
y una vez más, la soledad y el campo, como antaño,
y el cauce tembloroso de los ríos,
y todas las grandes maravillas,
fueron, en suma, convocadas.   30

Esto duró algún tiempo, hasta que, poco
a poco, las reservas se fueron agotando.
Los poetas, rendidos de cansancio, se dedicaron
a lanzarse sonetos, mutuamente,
de mesa a mesa, en el café. Y un día,   35
entre el fragor [3] de los poemas, alguien dijo: Escuchad,
fuera las cosas no han cambiado, nosotros
hemos hecho una meritoria labor, pero no basta.

---

[1] Alude al café Gijón de Madrid, lugar de tertulias literarias en la posguerra. [2] *azahares:* flores del naranjo y del limonero. [3] *fragor:* estrépito.

Los trinos y el aroma de nuestras elegías,
no han calmado las iras, el azote de Dios.   40

De las mesas creció un murmullo
rumoroso como el océano, y los poetas exclamaron:
Es cierto, es cierto, olvidamos a Dios, somos
ciegos mortales, perros heridos por su fuerza,
por su justicia, cantémosle ya.   45

Y así el buen Dios sustituyó
al viejo padre Garcilaso, y fue llamado
dulce tirano, amigo, mesías
lejanísimo, sátrapa⁴ fiel, amante guerrillero
gran parido, asidero de mi sangre, y los Oh, Tú,   50
y los Señor, Señor, se elevaron altísimos, empujados
por los golpes de pecho en el papel,
por el dolor de tantos corazones valientes.

Y así perduran en la actualidad.

Ésta es la historia, caballeros,   55
de los poetas celestiales, historia clara
y verdadera, y cuyo ejemplo no han seguido
los poetas locos, que, perdidos
en el tumulto callejero, cantan al hombre,
satirizan o aman el reino de los hombres,   60
tan pasajero, tan falaz,⁵ y en su locura
lanzan gritos, pidiendo paz, pidiendo patria,
pidiendo aire verdadero.

                                        (*Salmos al viento*, 1958)

---

⁴ *sátrapa:* tirano. ⁵ *falaz:* engañoso.

HOMENAJE EN COLLIURE[1]

Aquí, junto a la línea
divisoria, este día
veintidós de febrero,
yo no he venido para
llorar sobre tu muerte,　　　　　5
sino que alzo mi vaso
y brindo por tu claro
camino, y por que siga
tu palabra encendida,
como una estrella, sobre　　　　　10
nosotros ¿nos recuerdas?
Aquellos niños flacos,
tiznados, que jugaban
también a guerras, cuando,
grave y lúcido,[2] ibas,　　　　　15
don Antonio, al encuentro
de esta tierra en que yaces.

LA GUERRA

De pronto, el aire
se abatió, encendido,
cayó como una espada,
sobre la tierra. ¡Oh, sí,
recuerdo los clamores!　　　　　5

---

[1] *Colliure:* pueblo francés donde murió Antonio Machado un 22 de febrero de 1939, y en cuyo cementerio está enterrado.　[2] *lúcido:* clarividente.

Entre el humo y la sangre,
miré los muros
de la patria mía, [1]
como ciego miré
por todas partes,   10
buscando un pecho,
una palabra, algo
donde esconder el llanto.

Y encontré sólo muerte,
ruina y muerte   15
bajo el cielo vacío.

(*Claridad*, 1961)

EL OFICIO DEL POETA

Contemplar las palabras
sobre el papel escritas,
medirlas, sopesar
su cuerpo en el conjunto
del poema, y después,   5
igual que un artesano,
separarse a mirar
cómo la luz emerge
de la sutil textura.

Así es el viejo oficio   10
del poeta, que comienza

---

[1] Los vv. 7 y 8 son el comienzo de un conocido soneto de Quevedo que
deja también huellas en los versos finales.

en la idea, en el soplo
sobre el polvo infinito
de la memoria, sobre
la experiencia vivida,   15
la historia los deseos,
las pasiones del hombre.

La materia del canto
nos la ha ofrecido el pueblo
con su voz. Devolvamos   20
las palabras reunidas
a su auténtico dueño.

(*Algo sucede*, 1968)

JAIME GIL DE BIEDMA

INFANCIA Y CONFESIONES

A Juan Goytisolo

Cuando yo era más joven
(bueno, en realidad, será mejor decir
muy joven)
         algunos años antes
de conoceros y
recién llegado a la ciudad,   5
a menudo pensaba en la vida.
                  Mi familia
era bastante rica y yo estudiante.

Mi infancia eran recuerdos de una casa
con escuela y despensa y llave en el ropero, [1]
de cuando las familias   10
acomodadas,
             como su nombre indica,
veraneaban infinitamente

---

[1] Reminiscencia del «Retrato» machadiano que encabeza *Campos de Castilla*, con alusión a la célebre máxima de Joaquín Costa: «despensa y escuela».

en *Villa Estefanía* o en *La Torre
del Mirador* [2]
        y más allá continuaba el mundo
con senderos de grava y cenadores   15
rústicos, decorado de hortensias pomposas,
todo ligeramente egoísta y caduco.
Yo nací (perdonadme)
en la edad de la pérgola [3] y el tenis. [4]

La vida, sin embargo, tenía extraños límites   20
y lo que es más extraño: una cierta tendencia
retráctil. [5]
        Se contaban historias penosas,
inexplicables sucedidos
donde no se sabía, caras tristes,
sótanos fríos como templos.
               Algo sordo   25
perduraba a lo lejos
y era posible, lo decían en casa,
quedarse ciego de un escalofrío.

De mi pequeño reino afortunado
me quedó esta costumbre de calor   30
y una imposible propensión [6] al mito. [(46)]

(*Compañeros de viaje,* 1959)

---

   [2] Lugares del veraneo barcelonés de la clase alta.   [3] *pérgola:* armazón de plantas situado en un jardín.   [4] Recuerda unos versos de Alberti en *Cal y canto:* «Yo nací —¡respetadme!— con el cine».   [5] *retráctil:* que tiene capacidad de retirarse o encogerse, ocultándose.   [6] *propensión:* inclinación, tendencia.

(46) Muchas de las características de Gil de Biedma las hallamos en este poema: inicio anecdótico en primera persona, tono confesional y narrativo, lenguaje conversacional que no evita clisés de la

BARCELONA JA NO ÉS BONA, O MI PASEO
SOLITARIO EN PRIMAVERA[1]

A Fabián Estapé

Este despedazado anfiteatro,
impío honor de los dioses, cuya afrenta
publica el amarillo jaramago,
ya reducido a trágico teatro,
¡oh fábula del tiempo! representa
cuánta fue su grandeza y es su estrago.

RODRIGO CARO[2]

En los meses de aquella primavera
pasaron por aquí seguramente
más de una vez.
Entonces, los dos eran muy jóvenes
y tenían el Chrysler[3] amarillo y negro.   5
Los imagino al mediodía, por la avenida de los tilos,
la capota del coche salpicada de sol,
o quizá en Miramar, [4] llegando a los jardines,
mientras que sobre el fondo del puerto y la ciudad
se mecen las sombrillas del restaurante al aire libre,   10

---

[1] Combina un dicho popular catalán con el título de un poema de Nicasio Álvarez de Cienfuegos. [2] Rodrigo Caro es el autor de la «Canción a las ruinas de Itálica», de donde proceden estos versos (véase v. 75). [3] *Chrysler:* una marca de coche. [4] *Miramar:* zona alta barcelonesa, frente al mar.

lengua ordinaria, ritmo apropiado, con el uso del verso libre muy encabalgado, referencias a la propia clase social (la alta burguesía), etc. Debicki analizó este poema como una sucesión de realidades e ilusiones que van modificándose entre sí. Sugestivamente, J. Olivio Jiménez ha estudiado la poesía de Gil de Biedma como una dialéctica entre lo real y lo irreal.

y las conversaciones, y la música,
fundiéndose al rumor de los neumáticos
sobre la grava del paseo.
                          Sólo por un instante
se destacan los dos a pleno sol
con los trajes que he visto en las fotografías: 15
él examina un coche muchísimo más caro
—un Duesemberg *sport* con doble parabrisas,
bello como una máquina de guerra—
y ella se vuelve a mí, quizá esperándome,
y el vaivén de las rosas de la pérgola   20
parpadea en la sombra
de sus pacientes ojos de embarazada.
Era en el año de la Exposición. [5]

Así yo estuve aquí
dentro del vientre de mi madre,   25
y es verdad que algo oscuro, que algo anterior me trae
por estos sitios destartalados.
Más aún que los árboles y la naturaleza
o que el susurro del agua corriente
furtiva, reflejándose en las hojas   30
—y eso que ya a mis años
se empieza a agradecer la primavera—,
yo busco en mis paseos los tristes edificios,
las estatuas manchadas con lápiz de labios,
los rincones del parque pasados de moda   35
en donde, por la noche, se hacen el amor...
Y a la nostalgia de una edad feliz
y de dinero fácil, tal como la contaban,
se mezcla un sentimiento bien distinto
que aprendí de mayor,

_____

[5] Se refiere a la Exposición Universal de Barcelona en 1929.

este resentimiento   40

contra la clase en que nací,
y que se complace también al ver mordida,
ensuciada la feria de sus vanidades
por el tiempo y las manos del resto de los hombres.

¡Oh mundo de mi infancia, cuya mitología   45
se asocia —bien lo veo—
con el capitalismo de empresa familiar!
Era ya un poco tarde
incluso en Cataluña, pero la *pax* burguesa [6]
reinaba en los hogares y en las fábricas,   50
sobre todo en las fábricas —Rusia estaba muy lejos
y muy lejos Detroit. [7]
Algo de aquel momento queda en estos palacios
y en estas perspectivas desiertas bajo el sol,
cuyo destino ya nadie recuerda.   55
Todo fue una ilusión, envejecida
como la maquinaria de sus fábricas,
o como la casa en Sitges, o en Caldetas, [8]
heredada también por el hijo mayor.

Sólo montaña arriba, cerca ya del castillo,   60
de sus fosos quemados por los fusilamientos,
dan señales de vida los murcianos.
Y yo subo despacio por las escalinatas
sintiéndome observado, tropezando en las piedras
en donde las higueras agarran sus raíces,   65
mientras oigo a estos chavas [9] nacidos en el Sur

---

[6] *pax burguesa:* irónicamente, por relación con la *pax romana,* caracterizada por la tranquilidad de que gozaron los pueblos sometidos por Roma. [7] Ciudad industrial de Estados Unidos. [8] Sitges, Caldetas: poblaciones costeras de veraneo. [9] *chavas:* término propio del catalán barcelonés, con connotaciones étnicas, geográficas y de clase.

hablarse en catalán, y pienso, a un mismo tiempo,
en mi pasado y en su porvenir.

Sean ellos sin más preparación
que su instinto de vida   70
más fuertes al final que el patrón que les paga
y que el *salta-taulells*[10] que les desprecia:
que la ciudad les pertenezca un día.
Como les pertenece esta montaña,
este despedazado anfiteatro   75
de las nostalgias de una burguesía. [(47)]

(*Moralidades,* 1966)

CONTRA JAIME GIL DE BIEDMA

¿De qué sirve, quisiera yo saber, cambiar de piso,
dejar atrás un sótano más negro
que mi reputación —y ya es decir—,
poner visillos blancos
y tomar criada,   5
renunciar a la vida de bohemio,
si vienes luego tú, pelmazo,
embarazoso huésped, memo vestido con mis trajes,

---

[10] *salta-taulells:* dependiente de comercio; familiarmente, hortera (término propio del catalán barcelonés de anteguerra).

(47) Poema de fuerte denuncia social. Sobresale el arrepentimiento de clase, la «conciencia de la personalidad partida» (González Muela), en ricas perspectivas temporales.

zángano de colmena, inútil, cacaseno, [1]
con tus manos lavadas,   10
a comer en mi plato y a ensuciar la casa?

Te acompañan las barras de los bares
últimos de la noche, los chulos, las floristas,
las calles muertas de la madrugada
y los ascensores de luz amarilla   15
cuando llegas, borracho,
y te paras a verte en el espejo
la cara destruida,
con ojos todavía violentos
que no quieres cerrar. Y si te increpo,   20
te ríes, me recuerdas el pasado
y dices que envejezco.

Podría recordarte que ya no tienes gracia.
Que tu estilo casual y que tu desenfado
resultan truculentos   25
cuando se tienen más de treinta años,
y que tu encantadora
sonrisa de muchacho soñoliento
—seguro de gustar— es un resto penoso,
un intento patético.   30
Mientras que tú me miras con tus ojos
de verdadero huérfano, y me lloras
y me prometes ya no hacerlo.

Si no fueses tan puta!
Y si yo no supiese, hace ya tiempo,   35
que tú eres fuerte cuando yo soy débil
y que eres débil cuando me enfurezco...

---

[1] *cacaseno:* necio, grosero y sucio; también, bobo, simplón.

De tus regresos guardo una impresión confusa
de pánico, de pena y descontento,
y la desesperanza   40
y la impaciencia y el resentimiento
de volver a sufrir, otra vez más,
la humillación imperdonable
de la excesiva intimidad.

A duras penas te llevaré a la cama,   45
como quien va al infierno
para dormir contigo.
Muriendo a cada paso de impotencia,
tropezando con muebles
a tientas, cruzaremos el piso   50
torpemente abrazados, vacilando
de alcohol y de sollozos reprimidos.
Oh innoble servidumbre de amar seres humanos,
y la más innoble
que es amarse a sí mismo! [48]   55

(*Poemas póstumos*, 1968)

---

[48] Desdoblamiento: el yo moralista se dirige con violentos
reproches al yo bohemio. El drama acaba en una fusión de amor y
odio. Los tres versos finales, a modo de conclusión reflexiva,
intentan universalizar el drama personal.

JOSÉ ÁNGEL VALENTE[49]

«SERÁN CENIZA...»[1]

Cruzo un desierto y su secreta
desolación sin nombre.
El corazón
tiene la sequedad de la piedra
y los estallidos nocturnos   5
de su materia o de su nada.

Hay una luz remota, sin embargo,
y sé que no estoy solo;
aunque después de tanto y tanto no haya
ni un solo pensamiento   10
capaz contra la muerte,[2]
no estoy solo.

---

[1] Cita del soneto de Quevedo «Amor constante más allá de la muerte».
[2] Alusión a un verso de Vallejo en el poema «Masa»: «¡Tanto amor y no poder nada contra la muerte!».

(49) Valente ha sido calificado de realista por su sobriedad expresiva y por su alusión a episodios concretos. Una segunda lectura llevará a significados más amplios; de ahí el valor simbólico del poema «Serán ceniza...»: el curso de la vida, con afirmación final de la misma.

Toco esta mano al fin que comparte mi vida
y en ella me confirmo
y tiento cuanto amo, 15
lo levanto hacia el cielo
y aunque sea ceniza lo proclamo: ceniza.
Aunque sea ceniza cuanto tengo hasta ahora,
cuanto se me ha tendido a modo de esperanza.

(*A modo de esperanza*, 1955)

A DON FRANCISCO DE QUEVEDO, EN PIEDRA

cavan en mi vivir mi monumento[1]

Yo no sé quién te puso aquí, tan cerca
—alto entre los tranvías y los pájaros—
Francisco de Quevedo, de mi casa.

Tampoco sé qué mano
organizó en la piedra tu figura 5
o sufragó los gastos,
los discursos, la lápida,
la ceremonia, en fin, de tu alzamiento.

Porque arriba te han puesto y allí estás
y allí, sin duda alguna, permaneces, 10
imperturbable y quieto,
igual a cada día,
como tú nunca fuiste.

---

[1] Verso final del soneto de Quevedo que comienza: «¡Fue sueño ayer; mañana será tierra.»

Bajo cada mañana
al café de la esquina,   15
resonante de vida,
y sorbo cuanto puedo
el día que comienza.

Desde allí te contemplo en pie y en piedra,
convidado de tal piedra[2] que nunca   20
bajarás cojeando
de tu propia cojera[3]
a sentarte en la mesa que te ofrezco.

Arriba te dejaron
como una teoría de ti mismo,   25
a ti, incansable autor de teorías
que nunca te sirvieron
más que para marchar como un cangrejo
en contra de tu propio pensamiento.

Yo me pregunto qué haces   30
allá arriba, Francisco
de Quevedo, maestro,
amigo, padre
con quien es grato hablar,
difícil entenderse,   35
fácil sentir lo mismo:
cómo en el aire rompen
un sí y un no sus poderosas armas,
y nosotros estamos
para siempre esperando   40
la victoria que debe
decidir nuestra suerte.

---

[2] Alusión al título de la obra de Tirso de Molina, *El burlador de Sevilla y convidado de piedra*.   [3] Quevedo padecía cojera.

Yo me pregunto si en la noche lenta,
cuando el alma desciende a ras de suelo,
caemos en la especie y reina   45
el sueño, te descuelgas
de tanta altura, dejas
tu máscara de piedra,
corres por la ciudad,
tientas las puertas   50
con que el hombre defiende como puede
su secreta miseria
y vas diciendo a voces:
—Fue el soy un será, pero en el polvo
un ápice hay de amor que nunca muere. [4]   55

¿O acaso has de callar
en tu piedra solemne,
enmudecer también,
caer de tus palabras,
porque el gran dedo un día   60
te avisara silencio? [5]

Dime qué ves desde tu altura.
Pero tal vez lo mismo. Muros, campos,
solar de insolaciones. Patria. [6] Falta
su patria a Osuna, [7] a ti y a mí y a quien   65
la necesita.
       Estamos
todos igual y en idéntico amor
podría comprenderte.

---

[4] Recuérdense estos versos de Quevedo: «Soy un fue, y un será, y un es cansado»; «polvo serán, mas polvo enamorado». [5] Recuérdese el comienzo de la «Epístola satírica y censoria»: «No he de callar, por más que con el dedo, / [...], silencio avises...». [6] Un soneto de Quevedo comienza: «Miré los muros de la patria mía». [7] «Faltar pudo su patria al grande Osuna» (Quevedo).

                    Hablamos
mucho de ti aquí abajo, y día a día
te miro como ahora, te saludo   70
en tu torre de piedra,
tan cerca de mi casa,
Francisco de Quevedo, que si grito
me oirás en seguida.

Ven entonces si puedes,   75
si estás vivo y me oyes
acude a tiempo, corre
con tu agrio amor y tu esperanza —cojo,
mas no del lado de la vida— si eres
el mismo de otras veces. [50]   80

                              (*Poemas a Lázaro*, 1960)

                    NO INÚTILMENTE

Contemplo yo a mi vez la diferencia
entre el hombre y su sueño de más vida,
la solidez gremial de la injusticia,
la candidez azul de las palabras.

No hemos llegado lejos, pues con razón me dices   5
que no son suficientes las palabras
para hacernos más libres.

---

   (50) Con el poema anterior tiene éste en común los préstamos
literarios; con los siguientes, la presencia de un interlocutor, que da
al poema un tono conversacional. Obsérvense en el poema siguiente distintas fórmulas coloquiales.

Te respondo
que todavía no sabemos
hasta cuándo o hasta dónde
puede llegar una palabra,   10
quién la recogerá ni de qué boca
con suficiente fe
para darle su forma verdadera.

Haber llevado el fuego un solo instante
razón nos da de la esperanza.   15

Pues más allá de nuestro sueño
las palabras, que no nos pertenecen,
se asocian como nubes
que un día el viento precipita
sobre la tierra   20
para cambiar, no inútilmente, el mundo.

(_La memoria y los signos_, 1966)

HOMBRE A CABALLO

Venías a caballo.

La infancia se llenaba de rebeldes metales.

Erguido y solo,
joven abuelo mío, en una estampa
que ya era entonces de otro tiempo.   5

Tú venías vestido de ti mismo
y trajeado de tu propia hombría.

Nunca hablabas de ti.
Eras firme y secreto.
Y sin saber por qué   10
ocupaba más sitio tu persona
que muchos hombres juntos.

Había nieblas bajas en la tierra
y vidas subrepticias.
(Hablo del tiempo de mi infancia.)   15

Venías a caballo.

Jamás me hablaste
                        (tú entre todos)
de dios.
                Esta omisión recuerdo.
Gracias.
                Luego
te vi ya muerto,   20
vestido igual de tu secreta hombría.

La noche de tu vela
lloré aterrado entre vertiginosas
sombras.

Recuerdo la mañana,   25
el despacioso paso de tu cuerpo
y el llanto ritual
bajo la tenue luz de la tierra nativa
que hoy se cierne, contigo, en la memoria. [51]

(*El inocente*, 1970)

(51) Evocación de la figura del abuelo y, con ella, de la infancia
y de la guerra civil (véanse vv. 2,13-15).

FRANCISCO BRINES [52]

El balcón da al jardín. Las tapias bajas
y gratas. Entornada la gran verja.
Entra un hombre sin luz y va pisando
los matorrales de jazmín, le gimen
los pies, no mira nada. Qué septiembre   5
cubre la tierra, lentos nardos suben,
y suben las palomas con las alas
el aire, el sol, y el mar descansa cerca.
El viento ya no quema. Riegan lentos
los pasos que da el agua, las celindas[1]   10
todas se entregan. Los insectos se alzan
a vivir por las hojas. En el pecho
le descansan las barbas, sigue andando

---

[1] *celindas:* plantas.

(52) Características de la poesía de Brines: actitud reflexiva,
tendencia a lo personal, escenas anecdóticas, uso artístico del
lenguaje corriente y un tema central: el paso destructor del tiempo,
camino de la muerte. Consigue una intensa emoción temporal con
determinados procedimientos: *a)* símbolos disémicos, como en el
poema inicial, donde la anécdota de apariencia realista conlleva un
significado más hondo; *b)* yuxtaposiciones temporales de gran
complejidad, como en «Mere road».

sin luz. Todo lo deja muerto, negras
aves del cielo, caedizas hojas,   15
y cortada en el hielo queda el agua.
El jardín está mísero, y habita
ya la ausencia como si se tratase
de un corazón, y era una tierra verde.
Cruza la diminuta puerta. Llegan   20
del campo aullidos, y una sombra fría
penetra en el balcón y es un aliento
de muerte poderoso. Es la casa
que se empieza a caer, húmeda y sola. (53)

(*Las brasas*, 1960)

MERE ROAD [1]

Todos los días pasan,
y yo los reconozco. Cuando la tarde se hace oscura,
con su calzado y ropa deportivos,
yo ya conozco a cada uno de ellos, mientras suben en
                                              [grupos
o aislados,   5
en el ligero esfuerzo de la bicicleta.
Y yo los reconozco, detrás de los cristales de mi cuarto.
Y nunca han vuelto su mirada a mí,
y soy como algún hombre que viviera perdido en una
                              [casa de una extraña ciudad,
una ciudad lejana que nunca han conocido,   10

---

[1] Nombre de una calle de Oxford en la que vivió el poeta.

(53) Obsérvese la objetivación de la experiencia a través de un
sujeto poemático, a cuyo paso se muestran los efectos destructores
del tiempo sobre el jardín y la casa, sobre la vida.

o alguien que, de existir, ya hubiera muerto
o todavía ha de nacer;
quiero decir, alguien que en realidad no existe.
Y ellos llenan mis ojos con su fugacidad,
y un día y otro día cavan en mi memoria este recuerdo 15
de ver cómo ellos llegan con esfuerzos, voces, risas
               [o pensamientos silenciosos,
o amor acaso.
Y los miro cruzar delante de la casa que ahora
                      enfrente construyen
y hacia allí miran ellos,
comprobando cómo los muros crecen,   20
y adivinan la forma, y alzan sus comentarios
cada vez,
y se les llena la mirada, por un solo momento,
       [de la fugacidad de la madera y de la piedra.

Cuando la vida, un día, derribe en el olvido sus
                    [jóvenes edades,
podrá alguno volver a recordar, con emoción, este
                 [suceso mínimo   25
de pasar por la calle montado en bicicleta, con
                  [esfuerzo ligero
y fresca voz.
Y de nuevo la casa se estará construyendo, y
      [esperará el jardín a que se acaben estos muros
para poder ser flor, aroma, primavera,
(y es posible que sienta ese misterio del peso de mis ojos, 30
de un ser que no existió,
que le mira, con el cansancio ardiente de quien vive,
pasar hacia los muros del colegio),
y al recordar el cuerpo que ahora sube
solo bajo la tarde,   35
feliz porque la brisa le mueve los cabellos,
ha cerrado los ojos

para verse pasar, con el cansancio ardiente de quien
           [sabe
que aquella juventud
fue vida suya.   40
Y ahora lo mira, ajeno, cómo sube
feliz, encendiendo la brisa,
y ha sentido tan fría soledad
que ha llevado la mano hasta su pecho,
hacia el hueco profundo de una sombra.   45

(Palabras a la oscuridad, 1966)

CUANDO YO AÚN SOY LA VIDA

A Justo Jorge Padrón

La vida me rodea, como en aquellos años
ya perdidos, con el mismo esplendor
de un mundo eterno. La rosa cuchillada
de la mar, las derribadas luces
de los huertos, fragor de las palomas   5
en el aire, la vida en torno a mí,
cuando yo aún soy la vida.
Con el mismo esplendor, y envejecidos ojos,
y un amor fatigado.

¿Cuál será la esperanza? Vivir aún;   10
y amar, mientras se agota el corazón,
un mundo fiel, aunque perecedero.
Amar el sueño roto de la vida

y, aunque no pudo ser, no maldecir
aquel antiguo engaño de lo eterno.   15
Y el pecho se consuela, porque sabe
que el mundo pudo ser una bella verdad. [54]

(*Aún no*, 1971)

(54) Es este poema un buen ejemplo del vivir como «un ejercicio
sucesivo de despojamiento y dejación», que llevó a Brines a un
idéntico y «progresivo desnudamiento del estilo» (Bousoño).

CLAUDIO RODRÍGUEZ

Como si nunca hubiera sido mía,
dad al aire mi voz y que en el aire
sea de todos y la sepan todos
igual que una mañana o una tarde.
Ni a la rama tan sólo abril acude   5
ni el agua espera sólo el estiaje. [1]
¿Quién podría decir que es suyo el viento,
suya la luz, el canto de las aves
en el que esplende [2] la estación, más cuando
llega la noche y en los chopos arde   10
tan peligrosamente retenida?
¡Que todo acabe aquí, que todo acabe
de una vez para siempre! La flor vive
tan bella porque vive poco tiempo
y, sin embargo, cómo se da, unánime,   15
dejando de ser flor y convirtiéndose
en ímpetu de entrega. Invierno, aunque
no esté detrás la primavera, saca
fuera de mí lo mío y hazme parte,
inútil polen que se pierde en tierra   20
pero ha sido de todos y de nadie.

---

[1] *estiaje:* época de disminución del agua de un río o un lago a causa de la
sequía. [2] *esplende:* resplandece.

Sobre el abierto páramo, el relente[3]
es pinar en el pino, aire en el aire,
relente sólo para mi sequía.
Sobre la voz que va excavando un cauce   25
qué sacrilegio este del cuerpo, este
de no poder ser hostia para darse. [(55)]

(*Don de la ebriedad*, 1953)

CON MEDIA AZUMBRE[1] DE VINO

¡Nunca serenos! ¡Siempre
con vino encima! ¿Quién va a aguarlo ahora
que estamos en el pueblo y lo bebemos
en paz? Y sin especias,
no en el sabor la fuerza, media azumbre   5
de vino peleón, doncel o albillo,
tinto de Toro.[2] Cuánto necesita
mi juventud; mi corazón, qué poco.
¡Meted hoy en los ojos el aliento
del mundo, el resplandor del día! Cuándo   10
por una sola vez y aquí, enfilando
cielo y tierra, estaremos ciegos. ¡Tardes,

---

[3] *relente:* humedad atmosférica en las noches serenas.
[1] *azumbre:* medida de poco más de dos litros. [2] *peleón, doncel, albillo, tinto de Toro:* tipos de vino; Toro es una población zamorana.

[(55)] «Poesía [...] como un don, y ebriedad como un estado de entusiasmo», explica el poeta; pero, como otro oficio cualquiera, sólo cobra valor en la entrega, en la solidaridad. Adviértase cómo la naturaleza sirve de referencia. Métricamente coincide con «Alto jornal» y «Un suceso» en el uso de endecasílabos asonantados.

mañanas, noches, todo, árboles, senderos,
cegadme! El sol no importa, las lejanas
estrellas... ¡Quiero ver, oh, quiero veros! 15
Y corre el vino y cuánta,
entre pecho y espalda cuánta madre
de amistad fiel nos riega y nos desbroza.
Voy recordando aquellos días. ¡Todos,
pisad todos la sola uva del mundo: 20
el corazón del hombre! ¡Con su sangre
marcad las puertas![3] Ved: ya los sentidos
son una luz hacia lo verdadero.
Tan de repente ha sido.
Cuánta esperanza, cuánta cuba hermosa 25
sin fondo, con olor a tierra, a humo.
Hoy he querido celebrar aquello
mientras las nubes van hacia la puesta.
Y antes de que las lluvias del otoño
caigan, oíd: vendimiad todo lo vuestro, 30
contad conmigo. Ebrios de sequía,
sea la claridad zaguán[4] del alma.
¿Dónde quedaron mis borracherías?
Ante esta media azumbre, gracias, gracias
una vez más, y adiós, adiós por siempre. 35
No volverá el amigo fiel de entonces.[56]

---

[3] Se trata de una reminiscencia bíblica. [4] *zaguán:* vestíbulo.

(56) Canto a la amistad en un ambiente típico de la promoción del 60. Pero se trasciende lo concreto hacia un sentido universal (véase vv. 7-15); es lo que Bousoño llamó «realismo metafórico», que permite expresiones como las de los vv. 17-18 y 20-21. Lo mismo puede decirse de «Alto jornal» (el salario del obrero es, al mismo tiempo, signo del sentido de la vida) y de «Un suceso». Ejemplifican lo que la poesía tiene de conocimiento: «ver la realidad desenmascarada de su falsa apariencia» (González Muela).

ALTO JORNAL

Dichoso el que un buen día sale humilde
y se va por la calle, como tantos
días más de su vida, y no lo espera
y, de pronto, ¿qué es esto?, mira a lo alto
y ve, pone el oído al mundo y oye,   5
anda, y siente subirle entre los pasos
el amor de la tierra, y sigue, y abre
su taller verdadero, y en sus manos
brilla limpio su oficio, y nos lo entrega
de corazón porque ama, y va al trabajo   10
temblando como un niño que comulga
mas sin caber en el pellejo, [1] y cuando
se ha dado cuenta al fin de lo sencillo
que ha sido todo, ya el jornal ganado,
vuelve a su casa alegre y siente que alguien   15
empuña su aldabón, [2] y no es en vano.

(Conjuros, 1958)

UN SUCESO

> *Bien est verté que j'ai amé*
> *et ameroie voulentiers...*
> FRANÇOIS VILLON[1]

Tal vez, valiendo lo que vale un día,
sea mejor que el de hoy acabe pronto.

---

[1] *sin caber en el pellejo:* se dice cuando uno está muy contento. [2] *aldabón:* aldaba, llamador metálico.

[1] Villon es el más notable poeta medieval francés: «Bien es verdad que he amado / y amaría de buen grado...»

La novedad de este suceso, de esta
muchacha, casi niña pero de ojos
bien sazonados[2] ya y de carne a punto   5
de miel, de andar menudo, con su moño
castaño claro, tu tobillo hendido
tan armoniosamente, con su airoso
pecho que me deslumbra más que nada
la lengua... Y no hay remedio, y le hablo ronco   10
como la gaviota, a flor de labio
(de mi boca gastada), y me emociono
disimulando ciencia e inocencia
como quien no distingue un abalorio[3]
de un diamante, y le hablo de detalles   15
de mi vida, y la voz se me va, y me oigo
y me persigo, muy desconfiado
de mi estudiada habilidad, y pongo
cuidado en el aliento, en la mirada
y en las manos, y casi me perdono   20
al sentir tan preciosa libertad
cerca de mí. Bien sé que esto no es sólo
tentación. Cómo renuncio a mi deseo
ahora. Me lastimo y me sonrojo
junto a esta muchacha a la que hoy amo,   25
a la que hoy pierdo, a la que muy pronto
voy a besar muy castamente sin que
sepa que en ese beso va un sollozo.

(*Alianza y condena*, 1965)

---

[2] *sazonados:* maduros.   [3] *abalorio:* adorno de poco valor.

CARLOS SAHAGÚN

EN EL PRINCIPIO

En el principio, el agua
abrió todas las puertas, echó las campanas al vuelo,
subió a las torres de la paz —eran tiempos de paz—,
bajó a los hombros de mi profesor
—aquellos hombros suyos tan metafísicos,   5
tan doctrinales, tan
florecidos de libros de Aristóteles—,
bajó a sus hombros, no os engaño,
y saltó por su pecho como un pájaro vivo.

Ah, no te olvido,   10
a ojos cerrados te recuerdo tapiando las ventanas,
sobre el papel en blanco de la vida
dejando caer tinteros y palabras de piedra.
Y era lo mismo: yo seguía puro;
los últimos de clase, los expulsados por llevar ternura
[en los bolsillos,   15
seguíamos puros como el viento.
Antes de Thales de Mileto, [1]

---

[1] *Thales de Mileto,* matemático y filósofo griego, del siglo VI antes de Cristo.

mucho antes aún de que los filósofos fueran canonizados,
cuando el diluvio universal,
el llanto universal,   20
y un cielo todavía universal,
el agua contraía matrimonio con el agua,
y los hijos del agua eran pájaros, flores, peces, árboles,
eran caminos, piedras, montañas, humo, estrellas.
Los hombres se abrazaban, uno a uno,   25
como corderos, las mujeres
dormían sin temor, los niños todos
se proclamaban hijos de la alegría, hermanos
de la yerba más verde,
los animales se dejaban   30
llevar, no estaban solos —nadie estaba solo—,
y era feliz el aire aun sin ponerse en movimiento,
y en el espejo de unas manos llenas de agua
iba a mirarse la esperanza, y estaba limpia, y sonreía.

(Aquí quisiera hablar, abrir un libro —aquí,   35
en este instante sólo—
de aquel poeta puro que sin cesar cantaba:
«El mundo está bien hecho, el mundo está
bien hecho, el mundo
está bien hecho...»[2] —aquí, en este instante sólo—).   40

¡Y cómo no iba a estar bien hecho,
si en aquel tiempo las palomas altas
se derretían como copos,
si era inocente amarse desesperadamente,
si las mañanas claras, recién lavadas, daban   45
su generoso corazón al hombre!

---

[2] Estas palabras proceden de un poema de Jorge Guillén.

Aquello era la vida,
era la vida y empujaba,

               pero,
cuando entraron los lobos, después, despacio,

                      [devorando,
el agua se hizo amiga de la sangre,   50
y en cascadas de sangre cayó, como una herida,
cayó sobre los hombres
desde el pecho de Dios, azul, eterno. [57]

                    (*Profecías del agua*, 1958)

COSAS INOLVIDABLES

Pero ante todo piensa en esta patria,
en estos hijos que serán un día
nuestros: el niño labrador, el niño
estudiante, los niños ciegos. Dime
qué será de ellos cuando crezcan, cuando   5
sean altos como yo y desamparados.
Por mí, por nuestro amor de cada día
nunca olvides, te pido que no olvides.
Los dos nacimos con la guerra. Piensa
lo mal que estuvo aquella guerra para   10
los pobres. Nuestro amor pudo haber sido
bombardeado, pero no lo fue.

---

(57) *Profecías del agua* es un «anecdotario de infancia y adolescencia» (A. Hernández), como se observa en este poema: el contraste *agua-sangre* evoca la pureza de la infancia (con referencia intertextual a la «poesía pura») frente a las tragedias posteriores.

Nuestros padres pudieron haber muerto
y no murieron. ¡Alegría! Todo
se olvida. Es el amor. Pero no. Existen   15
cosas inolvidables: esos ojos
tuyos, aquella guerra triste, el tiempo
en que vendrán los pájaros, los niños.
Sucederá en España, en esta mala
tierra que tanto amé, que tanto quiero   20
que ames tú hasta llegar a odiarla. Te amo,
quisiera no acordarme de la patria,
dejar a un lado todo aquello. Pero
no podemos insolidariamente
vivir sin más, amarnos, donde un día   25
murieron tantos justos, tantos pobres.
Aun a pesar de nuestro amor, recuerda. [58]

(*Como si hubiera muerto un niño*, 1959)

UN LARGO ADIÓS

Ese tren que cruza Castilla
de madrugada, ese tren largo y perezoso
que se detiene acá y allá, en lugares previstos pero
                                        [desconocidos,
que se mueve en la noche
como si se incendiara un bosque entero y amplio,   5
no puede ser el del olvido.

(58) «La infancia irrecuperable, la aparición del primer amor»
(J. L. Cano) son temas de su promoción que se entrecruzan en *Como
si hubiera muerto un niño,* especialmente en este poema en el que hay
también ecos noventayochistas referidos a España.

A través de lo oscuro, de las obligaciones
deprimentes,
tú puedes comprobarlo. Estamos lejos
uno de otro y todo sirve   10
para marcar bien las distancias;
y sin embargo, el aire de la noche,
el sueño, el despertar de tanta ausencia,
me traen recuerdos vivos, restos puros
de todos los naufragios: 15
el mar mediterráneo en calma (en mi ciudad o en
                                              [Nápoles),
un pinar castellano, o bien
un día de junio a pleno sol entre mis brazos.

¡Tanta dicha no puede ser
irrepetible!   20

Yo busco tu silencio de otros días,
tus palabras de entonces, la belleza
de un gesto tuyo, el resplandor seguro
de aquellos instantes.
Busco las cosas ciertas,   25
las que me salvan de no estar contigo
día a día, por siempre.
Y te pregunto desde esta hora triste:
los momentos felices
¿han de partir con ese tren   30
que ahora cruza Castilla, han de perderse oscuramente,
sin piedad, en la noche? [(59)]

                                        (*Estar contigo*, 1973)

---

(59) Obsérvese la imagen central: *olvido = tren*. Pueden notarse
los abundantes conceptos espacio-temporales a que da lugar el
tema.

ANTONIO GAMONEDA [60]

SUBLEVACIÓN

Juro que la belleza
no proporciona dulces
sueños, sino el insomnio
purísimo del hielo,
la dura, indeclinable   5
materia del relámpago.

Hay que ser muy hombre para
soportar la belleza:
¿quién, invertido, separa,
hace tumbas distintas   10
para el pan común y la
música extremada?

(**60**) Al margen de los grupos poéticos, Gamoneda pertenece cronológica e ideológicamente a la promoción del 60; pero su investigación formal lo acerca a la generación siguiente. *Sublevación inmóvil* fue un libro cercano a la estética de su promoción. El poema «Sublevación» conjuga lo estético y lo social (belleza y libertad); la tensión interior se vierte en heptasílabos de ritmo vivo a base de interrogaciones, exclamaciones, aseveraciones y paradojas («sublevación de paz», «tormenta inmóvil»).

Ay de los fugitivos,
de los que tienen miedo
de sus propias entrañas.   15
Si una vez el silencio
les hablase, ¿sabrían
respirar la angustiosa
bruma de los espíritus?
¿Cantarían su propia   20
conversación al espectro?

Y aquellos otros, estos
miserables amados,
justificados por el dolor:
advertid que tan sólo   25
a los perros conviene
crecimiento de alarido.

Algo más puro aún
que el amor, debe
aquí ser cantado;   30
en cales vivas, en
materias atormentadas,
algo reclama curvas
de armonía. No es
la muerte. Este orden   35
invisible
                es
                        la libertad.

La belleza no es
un lugar donde van
a parar los cobardes.
Toda belleza es   40
un derecho común
de los más hombres. La

evasión no concede
libertad. Sólo tiene
libertad quien la gana.   45

Solicito
una sublevación
de paz, una tormenta
inmóvil. Quiero, pido
que la belleza sea   50
fuerza y pan, alimento
y residencia del dolor.

Un mismo canto pide
la justicia y la
belleza.
    Sea la luz   55
un acto humano.
      Se puede
morir
   por esta
libertad.

(*Sublevación inmóvil*, 1960)

BLUES[1] DEL CEMENTERIO

Conozco un pueblo —no lo olvidaré—
que tiene un cementerio demasiado grande.
Hay en mi tierra un pueblo sin ventura
porque el cementerio es demasiado grande.

---

[1] *Blues:* canción del folclore negro-americano que influyó en el origen y desarrollo del jazz, y cuyo texto suele tener elevado valor poético.

Sólo hay cuarenta almas en el pueblo.   5
No sé para qué tanto cementerio.

Cierto año la gente empezó a irse
y en muchas casas no quedaba nadie.
El año que la gente empezó a irse
en muchas casas no quedaba nadie.   10
Se llevaban los hijos y las camas.
Tenían que matar los animales.

El cementerio ya no tiene puertas
y allí entran y salen las gallinas.
El cementerio ya no tiene puertas   15
y salen al camino las ortigas.
Parece que saliera el cementerio
a los huertos y a las calles vacías.

Conozco un pueblo. No lo olvidaré.
Ay, en mi tierra sin ventura,   20
no olvidaré a mi pueblo.

¡Qué mala cosa es haber hecho
un cementerio demasiado grande! [61]

(*Blues castellano* (1961-66), 1982)

---

(61) Publicado muy tarde, *Blues castellano* sigue en escritura a
Sublevación inmóvil. Es, sobre todo, la búsqueda de un ritmo. «Blues
del cementerio» parte de una breve anécdota que retorna obsesiva-
mente a través de paralelismos con variaciones y de reiteraciones
que originan un rimado irregular, con «autorrimas», y una sensación de agobio que roza con el absurdo y con el quejido.

DESCRIPCIÓN DE LA MENTIRA

El óxido se posó en mi lengua como el sabor de
                          [una desaparición.

El olvido entró en mi lengua y no tuve otra conducta
                          [que el olvido,

y no acepté otro valor que la imposibilidad.

Como un barco calcificado[1] en un país del que
                          [se ha retirado el mar,

escuché la rendición de mis huesos depositándose
                          [en el descanso;   5

escuché la huida de los insectos y la retracción[2]
        [de la sombra al ingresar en lo que quedaba de mí;

escuché hasta que la verdad dejó de existir en el espacio
                          [y en mi espíritu,

y no pude resistir la perfección del silencio.

. . . .

La yerba como un silencio. La yerba atravesada
                  [por los insectos tercos en la felicidad.

Este descanso que no cesa bajo las páginas soleadas...
                          [Vigilad esa yerba   10

---

[1] *calcificado:* hecho cal.   [2] *retracción:* retroceso.

Esta es la luz acumulada por difuntos y códices atribuidos
     [al incesto, ³ a las historias con animales fugitivos.

Todo es mortal en la serenidad; hay un país para el
                                        [desengañado,

y su visión es tan blanca como la droga de la eternidad.

Tú, en la despensa de los híbridos, ⁴ abres el libro
     [de la envidia, lees cantos eléctricos aprendidos
     [de tus hermanos, eres azul en la indignidad.

Mi porvenir se aloja en el arrepentimiento. Ante tus
     [jícaras ⁵ vacías mi porvenir es partidario de los insectos. 15

Y el corazón pesa en obras agotadas.

¿Qué sabes tú de la mentira? Bajo la costra del hastío,
                              [en la urticaria ⁶ del cobarde,

un metal distinguido, un racimo de uñas abrasadas

profundiza en la muerte. Es la pasión de la inutilidad;

es la alegría de las máscaras reunidas en el estudio
     [de la yerba, verdes y codiciables en los estuarios ⁷ de
                                              [la sombra,   20

---

     ³ *incesto:* relación sexual entre parientes próximos.   ⁴ *híbridos:* productos de
individuos de distinta especie, o de elementos de distinta naturaleza.   ⁵ *jíca-
ras:* tazas.   ⁶ *urticaria:* erupción en la piel, con picazón.   ⁷ *estuarios:* terrenos
inmediatos a una ría, invadidos por el mar.

única especie conciliada, única y resistente a la pericia
    [del recuerdo, a la censura de los hombres cansados;
    [fresca como un grito de alondra bajo las aguas.

Ah, la mentira en el corazón vaciado por un
                          [cuchillo invisible.

Ah, la mentira, ciencia del silencio.

             * *   * * *   * * *

El olvido es mi patria vigilada y aún tuve un país
                [más grande y desconocido.

He retornado entre un silencio de párpados a aquellos
    [bosques en que fui perseguido por presentimientos
        [y proposiciones de hombres enfermos. 25

Es aquí donde el miedo ve la fuerza de tu rostro: tu
             [realidad en la desaparición

(que se extendía como la lluvia en el fondo de la noche;
    [más lenta que la tristeza, más húmeda que labios
          .   [sobre mi cuerpo.)

Eran los grandes días de la traición.

Me alimentaba la fosforescencia. Tú creaste la mentira
    [entre las piernas de mi madre; no existía el dolor
         [y tú creaste la compasión.

Tú volvías a las hortensias.   30

Y sollozaste bajo la lente de los comisarios.

Y vi la luz de la inutilidad.

Mi boca es fría en las plegarias. Este relato
[incomprensible es lo que queda de nosotros. La
[traición prospera en corazones inviolables.

Profundidad de la mentira: todos mis actos en el espejo
[de la muerte. Y los carbones resplandecen sobre la
[piel de héroes aún despiertos en el umbral
[de la imbecilidad.

Y ese alarido entre cristales, esas heridas que no son
[visibles más que en el instante del amor...   35

¿Qué hora es ésta, qué yerba crece en nuestra juventud? [62]

(*Descripción de la mentira,* (1975-76), 1977)

~~~~~~

(62) Tres fragmentos de un único texto. En el inicial destacan
una serie de lexemas *(desaparición, olvido,* etc.) que desembocan en
una palabra clave, *silencio.* Dentro del mismo clima el fragmento
intermedio introduce un *tú* de múltiples referencias; el fragmento
final —último del libro— recoge conceptos anteriores (obsérvense
las reiteraciones léxicas) y ofrece llaves de interpretación: *a)* el v. 33
alude al hermetismo del texto, a su proyecto narrativo y a su
temática residual; *b)* el v. 34 alude a la perspectiva desde la que se
ha escrito el texto: la muerte. Nótese, además, el esquema métrico y
rítmico (versículos, reiteraciones léxicas, sintácticas y conceptua-
les), la imaginería de tipo irracionalista y el lenguaje creativo, lejos
del usual.

FÉLIX GRANDE

MADRIGAL

Soledad, tú no eres un sereno vacío;
tú eres esta distancia, tú eres esta inclemencia,
tú eres mi sentimiento inútil, sin destino,
tú eres mi pequeñez desnuda y sin soberbia.

Soledad, tú no eres la nada, tú no eres   5
la sombra pura; tú eres, soledad, imperfecta;
tú eres un montoncito de escombros míos pasados
y futuros, y un poco de vana inteligencia.

Tú eres tan desvalida, tan pobre y confinada
como yo mismo; tú eres como yo de harapienta: 10
tu vida está a jirones como la vida mía;
yo te quiero, pequeña soledad sin grandeza.

Tú eres casi una hermana, casi una novia eres,
me eres casi una esposa, casi una compañera;
tú eres algo que un día se quedará conmigo   15
para siempre, y entonces no nos daremos cuenta.

Soledad, tú no eres la soledad del mundo
—el mundo es una cosa vaga que no me encuentra—;
sirves a un solo amo y por un breve plazo:
vales poco. Te quiero, soledad sin grandeza[63]   20

(Las piedras, 1964)

Donde fuiste feliz alguna vez
no debieras volver jamás: el tiempo
habrá hecho sus destrozos, levantado
su muro fronterizo
contra el que la ilusión chocará estupefacta.[1]   5
El tiempo habrá labrado,
paciente, tu fracaso
mientras faltabas, mientras ibas
ingenuamente por el mundo
conservando como recuerdo   10
lo que era destrucción subterránea, ruina.

Si la felicidad te la dio una mujer
ahora habrá envejecido u olvidado
y sólo sentirás asombro
—el anticipo de las maldiciones.
Si una taberna fue, habrá cambiado
de dueño o de clientes
y tu rincón se habrá ocupado
con intrusos fantasmagóricos

---

[1] *estupefacta:* atónita.

(63) Una sintaxis simple intensifica progresivamente la emoción
estética. Tras dos estrofas iniciales paralelas («tú no eres»-«tú
eres»), la tercera introduce un símil personificador («como yo»),
que permite los términos de parentesco de la estrofa siguiente; la
final reitera ideas y formas anteriores. Nótese la desmitificación del
concepto de «soledad».

que con su ajeneidad[2] te empujan a la calle, al vacío.   20
Si fue un barrio, hallarás
entre los cambios del urbano progreso
tu cadáver diseminado.

No debieras volver jamás a nada, a nadie,
pues toda historia interrumpida   25
tan sólo sobrevive
para vengarse en la ilusión, clavarle
su cuchillo desesperado,
morir asesinando.

Mas sabes que la dicha es como un criminal   30
que seduce a su víctima,
que la reclama con atroz dulzura
mientras esconde la mano homicida.
Sabes que volverás, que te hallas condenado
a regresar, humilde, donde fuiste feliz.   35

Sabes que volverás
porque la dicha consistió en marcarte
con la nostalgia, convertirte
la vida en cicatriz;
y si has de ser leal, girarás errabundo[3]   40
alrededor del desastre entrañable
como girase un perro ante la tumba
de su dueño... su dueño... su dueño...[64]

(*Música amenazada*, 1966)

---

[2] *ajeneidad:* condición de ajeno.   [3] *errabundo:* errante, que anda de aquí
para allá.

(64) Intensa vivencia del tiempo expresada por el contraste: *no
debieras volver jamás* (tres estrofas primeras) / *volverás* (las dos últimas).

TELAS GRACIOSAS DE COLORES ALEGRES

Según *ABC* [1] de hoy Johnson [2] ha motivado
un nuevo agonizante en la capital de Malasia [3]
(se ve un caído junto a la bota de un policía
y la bandera norteamericana en un ángulo de la derecha) *.

Caminando por la acera de Alenza [4] en busca del kiosko 5
recordé moderadamente a una amante que tuve en Málaga.
Aquel soldado castellano que se llamó Jorge Manrique
escribió sobre esto palabras permanentes. Cuán presto
se va el placer, cómo se pasa la vida, aquellos días
de Málaga o del medioevo qué fueron sino verduras
                                    [de las eras [5]   10

Vuelvo a casa silbando una melodía de Fats Willer. [6]
También aquella época de jazz comienza a ser prehistoria:
algunos artistas negros de nuestros días atomizados
desprecian en Louis Armstrong sus reverencias a los
                                    [altos yanquis
y soplan sobre sus trompetas con la furia de un
                                    [juramento.   15
Y mientras, Charlie Parker sigue muriendo ay sigue
                                    [muriendo
y Vallejo [7] se extiende en la conciencia de los jóvenes

---

[1] *ABC:* diario madrileño. [2] *Lyndon B. Johnson:* presidente de Estados
Unidos entre 1963 y 1968. [3] La capital de Malasia es Singapur. [4] *Alenza:*
calle madrileña. [5] Distintas citas de las *Coplas a la muerte de su padre,* de J.
Manrique (véase también vv. 37-38). [6] *Fats Willer* y, más abajo, *Louis
Armstrong* y *Charlie Parker:* músicos de jazz. [7] *Vallejo:* poeta peruano, autor
de *España, aparta de mí este cáliz,* libro del que procede el v. 16.

~~~~~~

* *ABC*, 1-11-66.

que leen poesía y que esperan el veredicto de lord
[Russell
y Sartre[8] y muchos más contra los importantes del país
más poderoso de la tierra (de esto hay señales
[inequívocas). 20

Paca, viste a la niña con colores alegres:
tal vez vengan hoy los abuelos, esa pareja de casi
[ancianos
que han sufrido bastante y trabajado como bestias
[de carga.
Ella tuvo ocho hijos, enterró tres, atendió enfermedades
y zurció ropa de los otros cinco; él, ah cómo lo amo,   25
hombre de precisas palabras, nos educó con su conducta,
perdió una guerra, enterró a sus padres, soportó
desesperación económica y separación de los suyos
y hambre y frío y calor y fatiga e insomnio,
todo cuanto nuestro país reserva a los matrimonios
[miserables. 30
Pon a Lupe los pendientes de oro y repite conmigo:
si alguna vez exiliamos a esos dos viejos de nuestro
[corazón
seremos unos hijos de perra, unos bastardos. Paca,
viste a la niña con colores alegres. Señores:
agoniza un manifestante en la capital de Malasia.   35

Y va desfalleciendo la mañana debajo de un sol casi
[baldío
mientras pasa mi juventud, las justas y los torneos,
paramentos, bordaduras, qué fueron sino rocío de los
[prados.

---

[8] *Russell* y *Sartre*: filósofos británico y francés respectivamente; el primero organizó en 1967 el «Tribunal Internacional contra los crímenes de guerra en Vietnam», presidido por Jean-Paul Sartre (véase v. 39).

Y mientras caen bombas y muertos sobre las junglas
                              [del Vietnam.

Ahora recuerdo una travesía solitaria y paciente   40
por calles de París. Era una madrugada de septiembre,
venía de amar a una mujer, iba a dormir a casa de un
                              [amigo
en la calle Maurice Ripoche; y caminaba y caminaba
rememorando al mismo tiempo mis insustituibles
                    [y pequeños sucesos de hombre
y la Revolución Francesa, y calculaba de memoria
                              [mis francos   45
bajo una amable lluvia que mojaba
mis sucios cabellos, mis manos; que resbalaba
sobre mi fervor de vivir y la calamidad del mundo.

Escribo para vosotros, testarudos, calamitosos seres
que deambuláis en este laberinto agrietado de nuestro
                              [siglo.   50
Os mando estas cartas porque creo en el fenómeno
                              [poético,
lenguaje enloquecido y apesadumbrado que se derrite
                              [de calor
ante un malasio que agoniza entre el plomo y la rabia.
Escribo porque amo atrozmente lo que aún no ha
                              [sido todavía,
como lo amáis vosotros, gente, que vais por las ciudades 55
recordando y deseando, con un periódico arrugado
y un corazón que se hincha como un aullido en un
                              [barranco.
Escribo esta carta mientras oigo los ruidos de la cocina
y veo pasar el tiempo como un megaterio[9] por la
                              [dulce ventana.

---

[9] *megaterio:* mamífero fósil americano del período cuaternario.

Escribo porque no soy un degenerado, porque estoy muy
                                                [en deuda 60
con dos viejos que languidecen en la edad al borde
                                               [de su nieta,
con una persona pequeña vestida con telas graciosas,
con seres que me dieron o me dan, con gentes que
                                               [pasan,
con años que transcurren camino de los siglos,
con un sueño de amistad popular que cruza
                                           [solitario 65
como un viejo vehículo del mar por el mar de la historia. [65]

(*Blanco spirituals*, 1967)

---

(65) En una especie de monólogo interior se entreveran tres
motivos: una noticia periodística, un paseo durante el que el sujeto
poemático recuerda y reflexiona y una visita familiar. Lo caótico
del mundo poetizado atrae nombres y ecos de áreas diversas:
periodismo, política, jazz, etc. Todo ello dentro de un dolor
existencial y colectivo que da lugar a imprecaciones y denuncias.

ANTONIO MARTÍNEZ SARRIÓN [66]

el cine de los sábados

maravillas del cine galerías
de luz parpadeante entre silbidos
niños con sus mamás que iban abajo
entre panteras un indio se esfuerza
por alcanzar los frutos más dorados   5
ivonne de carlo[1] baila en scherazade
no sé si danza musulmana o tango
amor de mis quince años marilyn[2]
ríos de la memoria tan amargos

---

[1] *Ivonne de Carlo:* actriz de cine que interpretó la danza de *Sherazade.*
[2] *Marilyn Monroe:* célebre actriz norteamericana.

~~~~~~

(66) Martínez Sarrión patentiza muchos de los rasgos que Castellet atribuyó a los novísimos. En los dos poemas primeros hallamos
una temática novedosa (el cine y sus mitos), una sintaxis basada en
la yuxtaposición (eliminación de nexos), ausencia de puntuación y
de mayúsculas, acumulación de imágenes cercanas al surrealismo,
sensibilidad *camp*... Compárese, sin embargo, la visión del mismo
personaje —Marilyn— en ambos poemas.

luego la cena desabrida y fría   10
y los ojos ardiendo como faros

(*Teatro de operaciones*, 1960)

REQUISITORIA GENERAL POR LA MUERTE
DE UNA RUBIA[1]

acodados en las irreales barandas
acodados resistiendo la marea de aromas
azaleas tamarindos
luna de california en el lento week-end
errantes aves marinas
                              también   5
los barcos también
los barcos hacia lejanas islas madrepóricas[2]
también los marineros empañados
                              también
los bidones vacíos las botellas vacías
las boyas arrancadas al pacífico   10
cuando acabó la victoriosa empresa
también los habitantes abisales[3]
estaban al acecho marilyn

recuento de jugadas medias azules
prendas floridas en los hondos rincones   15
el incinerador a toda la presión

---

[1] Se refiere a Marilyn Monroe, que se suicidó en 1962.   [2] *islas madrepóricas:* en el océano Pacífico.   [3] *abisales:* propio de las profundidades marinas; aquí, metafóricamente.

la inminente llegada del lechero
y
tú
con la muñeca fea la estantería con freud[4]   20
las últimas camelias del jugador de béisbol
la cintura tronchada
                         sirenas
impasibles en las rocas ella
fitzgerald[5] canta luces de pasadena[6]
tobogán de la angustia blanca luz sideral   25
también ellos
fumaban incansables y distantes
en los horrendos bungalows la luna aparatosa
en el lento week-end de california
laberinto de gatos vidrios en el asfalto   30
sombras inmemoriales casas de té llamadas
al vacío también
ellos
con pelucas postizas reventando de alcohol
suicidio de john gilbert[7]   35
farsas de paula strasberg[8] hediondez
del dramaturgo norteamericano[9]

mil barcos de basora[10] cargados con especias
techos de muérdago[11] *happy*
christmas[12] vigilias   40
esperando los besos imposibles

---

[4] *Sigmund Freud:* médico austríaco, creador del psicoanálisis.   [5] *Ella Fitzge-rald:* cantante norteamericana de jazz.   [6] *Pasadena:* ciudad de California (véanse vv. 4 y 29).   [7] *John Gilbert:* galán de cine que se suicidó en 1935.   [8] *Paula Strasberg:* mujer de Lee Strasberg, dirigía con él el Actor's Studio.   [9] *el dramaturgo norteamericano:* alude a Arthur Miller, que estuvo casado con Marilyn.   [10] *Basora:* ciudad de Iraq.   [11] *muérdago:* plan-ta.   [12] *happy christmas:* feliz Navidad.

también

ellos los hornos crematorios
los pájaros nocturnos rebosantes de herrumbre
la sofocada baja amenazante noche
boulevard   45
del crepúsculo
                    ráfagas
de terror en los ojos enormes de mi amor
aferrada a su sucio frasco de nembutal[13]

(Pautas para conjurados, 1970)

LUZ DE LÁMPARA

> *sur le vide papier que la blancheur défend.*
> S. M.[1]

Esta necesidad de trazar cordenadas
en primera persona del singular presente:
no distancia, no tecla
lista para la *fuga per canonem:*[2] *grilletes.*[3]

                    Y la ilusión-dejadme   5
                    de desaparecer

labrando un tenue rastro en la tierra baldía
—camino de babosa para ser más exactos—

---

[13] *nembutal:* barbitúrico de acción rápida con el que se suicidó Marilyn.
[1] S. M.: Stéphane Mallarmé: «Sobre el papel vacío que la blancura defiende». [2] *fuga per canonem:* término musical. [3] *grilletes:* mecanismos para asegurar una cadena.

que por lo mismo pierde desolación. Oído
finísimo: *Un batir de alas*[4]   10
y he ahí ya el milagro: los sentidos
si incompletos, bastantes. Ya construir es fácil
o mentir:
la adusta proporción de la cuartilla en blanco,
su centro por completo inaccesible: puñados de papel   15
en la cinta sin fin del deterioro. Túmulo
del lenguaje, pajaritas
de tinta piadoras en los tubos del órgano,
sindetikón[5] que mutila la página. Porque ya está resuelto
el gran enigma: no hay cuerpo de memoria   20
que acompañe al monarca a la imperiosa tumba
y conectar la música no empañó en absoluto
el odioso esplendor de los bustos reales
agrupados sin orden en las logias[6] sin tiempo. [(67)]

(Una tromba mortal para los balleneros, 1975)

---

[4] *Un batir de alas:* de la Rima X de Bécquer: «rumor de besos y batir de alas.»   [5] *sindetikón:* marca de un pegamento.   [6] *logias:* reuniones de la franc-masonería.

(67) La poesía volcada sobre sí misma: «metapoesía». Se instala en una tradición (Mallarmé) y el poema atrae ecos intertextuales (Bécquer, Eliot en v. 7), tecnicismos (v. 4)... Todo dentro de un llamativo «culturalismo» de época. El poema es un reducto: él es su propio tema; de ahí su hermetismo.

PERE GIMFERRER

ODA A VENECIA ANTE EL MAR DE LOS TEATROS

*Las copas falsas, el veneno y la calavera
de los teatros.*

GARCÍA LORCA

Tiene el mar su mecánica como el amor sus símbolos.
Con qué trajín se alza una cortina roja
o en esta embocadura de escenario vacío
suena un rumor de estatuas, hojas de lirio, alfanjes, [1]
palomas que descienden y suavemente pósanse.   5
Componer con chalinas[2] un ajedrez verdoso.
El moho en mi mejilla recuerda el tiempo ido
y una gota de plomo hierve en mi corazón.
Llevé la mano al pecho, y el reloj corrobora
la razón de las nubes y su velamen[3] yerto.   10
Asciende una marea, rosas equilibristas
sobre el arco voltaico[4] de la noche en Venecia
aquel año de mi adolescencia perdida,

---

[1] *alfanjes:* sables cortos y corvos.   [2] *chalinas:* corbatas anchas que se atan
con una lazada grande.   [3] *velamen:* velas de una embarcación.   [4] *arco voltaico:*
descarga eléctrica luminosa.

mármol en la Dogana[5] como observaba Pound[6]
y la masa de un féretro en los densos canales.   15
Id más allá, muy lejos aún, hondo en la noche,
sobre el tapiz del Dux,[7] sombras entretejidas,
príncipes o nereidas[8] que el tiempo destruyó.
Qué pureza un desnudo o adolescente muerto
en las inmensas salas del recuerdo en penumbra.   20
¿Estuve aquí? ¿Habré de creer que éste he sido
y éste fue el sufrimiento que punzaba mi piel?
Qué frágil era entonces y por qué. ¿Es más verdad,
copos que os diferís en el parque nevado,
el que hoy así acoge vuestro amor en el rostro   25
o aquél que allá en Venecia de belleza murió?
Las piedras vivas hablan de un recuerdo presente.
Como la vena insiste sus conductos de sangre,
va, viene y se remonta nuevamente al planeta
y así la vida expande en batán[9] silencioso,   30
el pasado se afirma en mí a esta hora incierta.
Tanto he escrito, y entonces tanto escribí. No sé
si valía la pena o la vale. Tú, por quien
es más cierta mi vida, y vosotros que oís
en mi verso otra esfera, sabréis su signo o arte.   35
Dilo, pues, o decidlo, y dulcemente acaso
mintáis a mi tristeza. Noche, noche en Venecia
va para cinco años, ¿cómo tan lejos? Soy
el que fui entonces, sé tensarme y ser herido
por la pura belleza como entonces, violín   40
que parte en dos el aire de una noche de estío
cuando el mundo no puede soportar su ansiedad
de ser bello. Lloraba yo, acodado al balcón
como en un mal poema romántico, y el aire

---

[5] *la Dogana:* la Aduana de Venecia. [6] *Ezra Pound:* (1885-1972), gran
poeta norteamericano que pasó en Venecia parte de su existencia. [7] *Dux:*
jefe electivo de la república de Venecia. [8] *nereidas:* ninfas marinas. [9] *batán:*
máquina de gruesos mazos usada en fábricas de paños.

promovía disturbios de humo azul y alcanfor.   45
Bogaba en las alcobas, bajo el granito húmedo,
un arcángel o sauce o cisne o corcel de llama
que las potencias últimas enviaban a mi sueño.
                    Lloré, lloré, lloré.
¿Y cómo pudo ser tan hermoso y tan triste?
Agua y frío rubí, transparencia diabólica   50
grababan en mi carne un tatuaje de luz.
Helada noche, ardiente noche, noche mía
como si hoy la viviera! Es doloroso y dulce
haber dejado atrás la Venecia en que todos
para nuestro castigo fuimos adolescentes   55
y perseguirnos hoy por las salas vacías
en ronda de jinetes que disuelve un espejo
negando, con su doble, la realidad de este poema. [68]

                                   (Arde el mar, 1966)

LA MUERTE EN BEVERLY HILLS [1]

IV

Llevan una rosa en el pecho los enamorados
[y suelen besarse entre un rumor de girasoles y hélices.

---

[1] *Beverly Hills:* lugar de Los Angeles que sucedió a Hollywood en la preferencia de las estrellas de cine.

(68) *Arde el mar* es «una elegía de la adolescencia no vivida» (García Martín) o perdida (v. 13), y la «Oda a Venecia», «pura escenografía imaginaria, donde el inexperto muchacho llora por no alcanzar más que con palabras aquella vivencia imposible» (González Muela). Poema clásico de la poesía «novísima»: sensibilidad, cultura, barroquismo, «venecianismo»... Frente a la poesía realista, paraísos soñados; frente a lo coloquial, lenguaje muy «poetizado», léxico culto y ritmo marcado (alejandrinos).

Hay pétalos de rosa abandonados por el viento en
[los pasillos de las clínicas.

Los escolares hunden sus plumillas entre uña y carne
[y oprimen suavemente hasta que la sangre empieza
[a brotar. Algunos aparecen muertos bajo los
[últimos pupitres.

Estaré enamorado hasta la muerte y temblarán mis
[manos al coger tus manos y temblará mi voz cuando
[te acerques y te miraré a los ojos como si llorara.

Los camareros conocen a estos clientes que piden una
[ficha en la madrugada y hacen llamadas inútiles,
[cuelgan luego, piden una ginebra, procuran sonreír,
[están pensando en su vida. A estas horas la noche
[es un pájaro azul.   5

Empieza a hacer frío y las muchachas rubias se
[miran temblando en los escaparates. Un chorrear
[de estrellas silencioso se extingue.

Luces en un cristal espejeante[2] copian el esplendor
lóbrego de la primavera, sus sombrías llamaradas
azules, sus flores de azufre y de cal viva, el grito
[de los ánades[3] llamando desde el país de los muertos.[(69)]

(*La muerte en Beverly Hills*, 1968)

----

   [2] *espejeante:* que refleja las imágenes.   [3] *ánades:* patos.

(69) El tema de *La muerte en Beverly Hills* es «la nostalgia y la
indefensa necesidad de amor» (Gimferrer). Su marco de referencia
es el cine americano, aquí, en concreto, películas policíacas de H.
Bogart. Cada versículo es como un «flash»: breves escenas sin

BY LOVE POSSESSED [1]

Me dio un beso y era suave como la bruma
dulce como una descarga eléctrica
como un beso en los ojos cerrados
como los veleros al atardecer
pálida señorita del paraguas   5
por dos veces he creído verla su vestido estampado el
    [bolso el pelo corto y aquella forma de andar muy
                          [en el borde de la acera.
En los crepúsculos exangües [2] la ciudad es un torneo
    [de paladines [3] a cámara lenta sobre una pantalla
                          [plateada
como una pantalla de televisión son las imágenes de mi
                       [vida los anuncios
y dan el mismo miedo que los objetos volantes venidos
    [de no se sabe dónde fúlgidos [4] en el espacio.
Como las banderolas caídas en los yates de lujo   10
las ampollas de morfina [5] en los cuartos cerrados de
                      [los hoteles
estar enamorado es una música una droga es como
                    [escribir un poema
por ti los dulces dogos [6] del amor y su herida carmesí. [7]
Los uniformes grises de los policías los cascos las cargas
    [los camiones los jeeps los gases lacrimógenos

---

[1] *By love possessed:* poseídos por el amor, título de una novela —posteriormente pasada al cine— del norteamericano James Cozzens. [2] *exangües:* literalmente, sin sangre. [3] *paladines:* caballeros. [4] *fúlgidos:* brillantes. [5] *morfina:* producto analgésico y soporífero. [6] *dogos:* perros. [7] *carmesí:* color de grana.

conexión aparente. También en el poema siguiente el cine proporciona términos metafóricos y sugiere imágenes en buena parte yuxtapuestas.

aquel año te amé como nunca llevabas un vestido
                  [verde y por las mañanas sonreías   15
Violines oscuros violines del agua
todo el mundo que cabe en el zumbido de una línea
                  [telefónica
los silfos[8] en el aire la seda y sus relámpagos
las alucinaciones en pleno día como viendo fantasmas
                  [luminosos
como palpando un cuerpo astral   20
desde las ventanas de mi cuarto de estudiante
y muy despacio los visillos
con antifaz un rostro me miraba
el jardín un rubí bajo la lluvia

                          (*Extraña fruta y otros poemas*, 1969)

---

[8] *silfos:* espíritus elementales del aire.

ANTONIO COLINAS [70]

INVOCACIÓN A HÖLDERLIN [1]

El levitón [2] gastado, el sombrero caído
hacia atrás, las guedejas [3] de trapo y una llama
en las cuencas profundas de sus dos ojos bellos.
No sé si esta figura maltrecha, al caminar,
escapa de un castigo o busca un paraíso   5
De vez en cuando palpa su pecho traspasado
y toma la honda queja para el labio sin beso.

---

[1] *Hölderlin:* poeta romántico alemán, de la Suabia (v. 17), precursor de la
sensibilidad contemporánea. Cursó estudios eclesiásticos (v. 20) y vivió
largos años en la locura (vv. 10 y 22). [2] *levitón:* levita larga, prenda
masculina. [3] *guedejas:* cabellera larga.

(70) Al esteticismo culturalista de su generación añade Colinas
un lirismo esencial enraizado en el romanticismo alemán de Hölderlin y Novalis (véanse títulos): búsqueda de la belleza absoluta e
indagación en el misterio que oculta la realidad; la noche es el
momento propicio para la revelación. A este mundo poético de
densa belleza lo amenaza, sin embargo, la muerte (obsérvese en los
tres primeros poemas). Si, por lo dicho, Colinas fue llamado
«neorromántico», la métrica usada (alejandrinos blancos en estas
composiciones) y el sereno discurrir del verso dotan a sus poemas de
un cierto «clasicismo».

Oh Hölderlin, a un tiempo andrajo y vara en flor,
nido pleno de trinos, muñeco maltratado.
A tu locura se abren los bosques más sombríos.   10
No ves cómo las fuentes se quiebran de abandono
cada vez que te acercas con tu paso cansado,
cada vez que desatas tu carcajada rota,
cada vez que sollozas tirado entre la yerba.
¡Qué claro estaba escrito tu sino bajo el cielo...!   15
Antes de que pusieras tu mano en el papel
fríos soles de invierno cruzaban la Suabia,
dejaban por las nubes agrios trazos verdosos.
Cuando tú, silencioso y enlutado, leías
latín en una celda ya hubo duendes extraños   20
sembrando por tus venas no sé qué fuego noble.
Y antes de que acabaras hablando a las estatuas
aves negras picaban tus dos ojos azules.
Hölderlin vagabundo, Hölderlin ruiseñor
de estremecido canto sin ojos y sin rama,   25
ahora que cae espesa la noche del otoño
contempla a nuestro lado la enfebrecida luna,
deja fluir tu queja, tus parloteos mágicos,
deja un silbo tan sólo de tu canto en el aire.
Detén por un momento tu caminar y espanta   30
la muerte que en tus hombros encorvada te acecha.
Rasga los polvorientos velos de tu memoria
y que discurra el sueño, y que sepamos todos
de dónde brota el agua que sacia nuestra sed.

(*Preludios a una noche total*, 1969)

ESCALINATA DEL PALACIO

Hace ya mucho tiempo que habito este palacio.
Duermo en la escalinata, al pie de los cipreses.

Dicen que baña el sol de oro las columnas,
las corazas color de tortuga, las flores.
Soy dueño de un violín y de algunos harapos.   5
Cuento historias de muerte y todos me abandonan.
Iglesias y palacios, los bosques, los poblados,
son míos, los vacía mi música que inflama.
Salí del mar. Un hombre me ahogó cuando era niño.
Mis ojos los comió un bello pez azul   10
y en mis cuencas vacías habitan escorpiones.
Un día quise ahorcarme de un espeso manzano.
Otro día me até una víbora al cuello.
Pero siempre termino dormido entre las flores,
beodo[1] entre las flores, ahogado por la música   15
que desgrana el violín que tengo entre mis brazos.
Soy como un ave extraña que aletea entre rosas.
Mi amigo es el rocío. Me gusta echar al lago
diamantes, topacios, las cosas de los hombres.
A veces, mientras lloro, algún niño se acerca   20
y me besa en las llagas, me roba el corazón.

(*Truenos y flautas en un templo,* 1972)

GIACOMO CASANOVA ACEPTA EL CARGO DE BIBLIOTECARIO QUE LE OFRECE, EN BOHEMIA, EL CONDE DE WALDSTEIN[1]

Escuchadme, Señor, tengo los miembros tristes.
Con la Revolución Francesa van muriendo
mis escasos amigos. Miradme, he recorrido

---

[1] *beodo:* borracho.
[1] *Giacomo Casanova:* famoso aventurero veneciano del XVIII al que persiguió la Inquisición (vv. 13 y 14) y que acabó de bibliotecario del conde de Waldstein en el castillo de Dux, como indica el título.

los países del mundo, las cárceles del mundo,
los lechos, los jardines, los mares, los conventos,   5
y he visto que no aceptan mi buena voluntad.
Fui abad entre los muros de Roma y era hermoso
ser soldado en las noches ardientes de Corfú. [2]
A veces he sonado un poco el violín
y vos sabéis, Señor, cómo trema [3] Venecia   10
con la música y arden las islas y las cúpulas.
Escuchadme, Señor, de Madrid a Moscú
he viajado en vano, me persiguen los lobos
del Santo Oficio, llevo un huracán de lenguas
detrás de mi persona, de lenguas venenosas.   15
Y yo sólo deseo salvar mi claridad,
sonreír a la luz de cada nuevo día,
mostrar mi firme horror a todo lo que muere.
Señor, aquí me quedo en vuestra biblioteca,
traduzco a Homero, escribo de mis días de entonces,   20
sueño con los serrallos [4] azules de Estambul [(71)].

NOVALIS [1]

Oh, Noche, cuánto tiempo sin verte tan copiosa
en astros y en luciérnagas, [2] tan ebria de perfumes.

---

[2] Ciudad griega, en la isla de igual nombre, que perteneció a Venecia en tiempos antiguos.   [3] *trema:* tiembla.   [4] *serrallos:* lugares donde tienen sus mujeres los mahometanos.
[1] Poeta romántico alemán, autor de los *Himnos a la noche*, en los que combina simbolismo y misticismo.   [2] *luciérnagas:* insectos cuyas hembras emiten luz fosforescente.

(71) El sesgo narrativo no aminora el lirismo. Tras la anécdota, el sentido moral: «el tema central es el de la vejez y la caducidad humana» (Colinas).

Después de muchos años te conozco en tus fuegos
azules, en tus bosques de castaños y pinos.
Te conozco en la furia de los perros que ladran   5
y en las húmedas fresas que brotan de lo oscuro.
Te sospecho repleta de cascadas y parras.

Cuánto tiempo he callado, cuánto tiempo he perdido,
cuánto tiempo he soñado mirando con los ojos
arrasados de lágrimas, como ahora, tu hermosura.   10
Noche mía, no cruces en vano este planeta.

Deteneos esferas y que arrecie la música.
Noche, Noche dulcísima, pues que aún he de volver
al mundo de los hombres, deja caer un astro,
clava un arpón[3] ardiente entre mis ojos tristes   15
o déjame reinar en ti como una luna.[(72)]

(*Sepulcro en Tarquinia,* 1975)

---

[3] *arpón:* especie de lanza para pescar.

(72) Ejemplo de exultante sensorialidad —aromas, luces, colores, sonidos—, según J. Olivio Jiménez. Ansia de belleza absoluta,
cósmica: sueño y realidad, en tenue contraste, están presentes
también en todos los poemas anteriores.

GUILLERMO CARNERO [73]

CAPRICHO EN ARANJUEZ [1]

Raso amarillo a cambio de mi vida.
Los bordados doseles, [2] la nevada
palidez de las sedas. Amarillos
y azules y rosados terciopelos y tules [3]
y ocultos por las telas recamadas [4]   5
plata, jade [5] y sutil marquetería. [6]

---

[1] *Aranjuez:* villa al sur de Madrid, residencia de los Reyes desde Felipe II
y célebre por su palacio y sus jardines.   [2] *doseles:* techos o alas sobre un lecho
o sobre un altar.   [3] *tules:* tejidos que forman malla.   [4] *recamadas:* bordadas.
[5] *jade:* piedra preciosa.   [6] *marquetería:* ebanistería, trabajo con maderas
finas.

---

(73) Los dos poemas iniciales pertenecen a *Dibujo de la muerte,*
poemario de agudo esteticismo. Obsérvese —siguiendo a Bousoño— el mundo seleccionado: lugares y épocas refinados
(Aranjuez, siglo XVIII), telas suntuosas (terciopelos, tules...), pre-
ciosidades (jade, caoba...), decorados (doseles, columnas...), abun-
dante colorido, inspiración en el arte (arquitectura, cuadro de
Watteau)... Nótese, además, la riqueza de epítetos en el primer
poema, las reiteraciones (principio y final) y contrastes significativos (vv. 7 y 13), los ricos juegos verbales... Dentro del mencionado
esteticismo, compárense tema y tono de uno y otro poema.

Fuera breve vivir. Fuera una sombra
o una fugaz constelación alada.
Geométricos jardines. Aletea
el hondo transminar[7] de las magnolias.   10
Difumine el balcón, ocúlteme
la bóveda de umbría enredadera.
Fuera hermoso morir. Inflorescencias[8]
de mármol en la reja encadenada:
perpetua floración en las columnas   15
y un niño ciego juega con la muerte.
Fresquísimo silencio gorgotea
de las corolas de la balaustrada. [9]
Cielo de plata gris. Frío granito
y un oculto arcaduz[10] iluminado.   20
Deserten los bruñidos candelabros
entre calientes pétalos y plumas.
Trípodes de caoba, pebeteros[11]
o delgado cristal. Doce relojes
tintinean las horas al unísono.   25
Juego de piedra y agua. Desenlacen
sus cendales[12] los faunos. [13] En la caja
de fragante peral están brotando
punzantes y argentinas[14] pinceladas.
Músicas en la tarde. Crucería,[15]   30
polícromo[16] cristal. Dejad, dejadme
en la luz de esta cúpula que riegan
las trasparentes brasas de la tarde.
Poblada soledad, raso amarillo
a cambio de mi vida.   35

---

[7] *transminar:* penetrar el olor.   [8] *inflorescencias:* formas de agruparse las flores de una misma rama.   [9] *balaustrada:* barandilla.   [10] *arcaduz:* caño de agua.   [11] *pebeteros:* vasos para quemar perfumes.   [12] *cendales:* telas finas transparentes.   [13] *faunos:* semidioses con cabeza y tronco de hombre y patas de cabra.   [14] *argentinas:* plateadas.   [15] *crucería:* adorno gótico de molduras entrecruzadas en las bóvedas.   [16] *polícromo:* de varios colores.

EL EMBARCO PARA CYTEREA[1]

Sicut dii eritis[2]
Gen. III, 4—

Hoy que la triste nave está al partir,
con su espectacular monotonía,
quiero quedarme en la ribera, ver
confluir los colores en un mar de ceniza
y mientras tenuemente tañe[3] el viento   5
las jarcias[4] y las crines[5] de los grifos[6] dorados
oír lejanos en la oscuridad
los remos, los fanales,[7] y estar solo.
Muchas veces la vi partir de lejos,
sus bronces y brocados[8] y sus juegos de música: 10
el brillante clamor
de un ritual de gracias escondidas
y una sabiduría tan vieja como el mundo.
La vi tomar el largo
ligera bajo un dulce cargamento de sueños,   15
sueños que no envilecen y que el poder rescata
del laberinto de la fantasía,
y las pintadas muecas de las máscaras
un lujo alegre y sabio,
no atributos del miedo y el olvido.   20
También alguna vez hice el viaje
intentando creer y ser dichoso

---

[1] Es el título del cuadro más famoso de Watteau: los amantes se embarcan alegres hacia la isla de los placeres. [2] *Sicut dii eritis:* seréis como dioses (Génesis). [3] *tañe:* toca. [4] *jarcias:* aparejos de un buque. [5] *crines:* cerdas del cuello de algunos animales. [6] *grifos:* animales fabulosos, mitad águila y mitad león. [7] *fanales:* faroles grandes de los barcos o de los puertos. [8] *brocados:* telas entretejidas con oro y plata.

y repitiendo al golpe de los remos:
aquí termina el reino de la muerte.
Y no guardo rencor   25
sino un deseo inhábil que no colman
las acrobacias de la voluntad,
y cierta ingratitud no muy profunda.

(*Dibujo de la muerte*, 1967)

ELOGIO DE LINNEO[1]

El poder de una ciencia
no es conocer el mundo: dar orden al espíritu.
Formular con tersura[2]
el arte magna de su léxico
en orden de combate: el repertorio mágico   5
de la nomenclatura y las categorías,
su tribunal preciso, inapelable prosa
bella como una máquina de guerra.
Y recorrer con método
los desvaríos de su lógica; si de pájaros hablo,   10
prestar más atención a las aves zancudas. [74]

(*El sueño de Escipión*, 1971)

---

[1] *Linneo:* naturalista sueco del siglo XVIII, autor de una famosa clasificación de las plantas. [2] *tersura:* pureza, propiedad.

[74] Este poema y el que sigue son reflexiones «metapoéticas».
Al arte de Carnero, en su segunda etapa, puede aplicársele lo que
dice de Linneo, cambiando «ciencia» por «poema», según Bousoño,
que resume el tema: «lo que parece racional [...] no lo es»:

PUISQUE RÉALISME IL Y A[1]

Vuelve la vista atrás y busca esa evidencia
con que un objeto atrae a la palabra propia
y el uno al otro se revelan; en el mutuo contacto
experiencia y palabra cobran vida,
no existen de por sí, sino una en otra;   5
presentido, el poema que aún no es
vuela a clavarse firme en un punto preciso
del tiempo; y el que entonces fuimos ofrece
en las manos de entonces, alzadas, esa palabra justa.
No así; gravitan las palabras y su rotunda hipótesis   10
ensambla su arquitectura; más allá es el desierto
donde la palabra alucina hasta crear su doble:
creemos haber vivido porque el poema existe;
lo que parece origen es una nada, un eco.

(*Variaciones y figuras sobre un tema de La Bruyère*, 1974)

---

[1] *Puisque réalisme il y a:* puesto que existe el realismo (Baudelaire).

desvaríos de la naturaleza (aves zancudas) y de la razón racionalis-
ta («desvaríos de su lógica»); el arte debe admitir «las motivaciones
irracionales de la creación junto a las conscientes».

LEOPOLDO MARÍA PANERO [75]

LA METAMORFOSIS

La tierra le dio su cálido abrazo. Por sus venas la sangre
ya no fluía, no tenía alma, pero sí más fuerza que nunca.
Quién sabe lo que sería. Un árbol o una roca. De vez en
cuando el graznido de un cuervo en el bosque o un
ruiseñor que se posaba silencioso sobre sus ramas. Cada   5
dos o tres años el calor de una mano.

LAS BRUJAS

Bastó un gesto, una palabra vuestra para que todo se
hiciese aire, o menos que aire... Brujas que hablábais el

---

(75) De Leopoldo María Panero suelen subrayarse las divergen-
cias con su generación: tendencia autodestructiva, lucidez suicida,
obsesiones paranoicas, etc. Los mitos infantiles sirven no a la
añoranza, sino a la ruptura. El poema último apunta a una
necesidad destructiva para crear la poesía autosuficiente (metapoesía). El ritmo se rompe en continuos paréntesis y en saltos concep-
tuales que dificultan el acceso (coordinaciones anómalas —versos
iniciales—, yuxtaposiciones, «fragmentos», citas cultas —v. 9— o
populares —v. 19—, etc.).

lenguaje del viento, a medianoche, el lenguaje del
viento golpeando las ventanas, el lenguaje del viento
crujiendo en los desvanes, el lenguaje olvidado del   5
viento. El lenguaje de la noche, qué hizo de vosotras el
sol, su torpe claridad, su exactitud brutal, qué fue de
vosotras cuando el sol secó para siempre nuestras
almas... Qué fácil entonces el miedo, brujas, brujas
aventadas por el soplo de un demonio más terrible que   10
el mismo demonio...
Qué extraño maleficio no deja llegar la noche, oh
deshacer, deshacer con un gesto el mundo...

20.000 LEGUAS DE VIAJE SUBMARINO [1]

Como un hilo o aguja que casi no se siente
como un débil cristal herido por el fuego
como un lago en que ahora es dulce sumergirse
oh esta paz que de pronto cruza mis dientes
este abrazo de las profundidades   5
luz lejana que me llega a través de la inmensa lonja
                                   [de la catedral desierta
quién pudiera quebrar estos barrotes como espigas
dejadme descansar en este silencioso rostro que nada
                                                    [exige
dejadme esperar el iceberg que cruza callado el mar
                                                 [sin luna
dejad que mi beso resbale sobre su cuerpo helado   10

---

[1] Título de una famosa novela de Julio Verne.

cuando alcance la orilla en que sólo la espera es posible
oh dejadme besar este humo que se deshace
este mundo que me acoge sin preguntarme nada este
              [mundo de titíes[2] disecados
morir en brazos de la niebla
morir sí, aquí, donde todo es nieve o silencio   15
que mi pecho ardiente expire tras de un beso a lo que
                    [es sólo aire
más allá el viento es una guitarra poderosa pero él
                        no nos llama
y tampoco la luz de la luna es capaz de ofrecer
                    [una respuesta
dejadme entonces besar este astro apagado
traspasar el espejo y llegar así adonde ni siquiera el
                [suspiro es posible 20
donde sólo unos labios inmóviles
    ya no dicen o sueñan
y recorrer así este inmenso Museo de Cera
deteniéndome por ejemplo en las plumas recién nacidas
o en el instante en que la luz deslumbra a la crisálida
y algo más tarde la luna y los susurros   25
y examinar después los labios que fulgen
cuando dos cuerpos se unen formando una estrella
y cerrar por fin los ojos cuando la mariposa
próxima a caer sobre la tierra sorda
quiere en vano volver sus alas hacia lo verde que ahora
                [la desconoce 30

                (*Así se fundó Carnaby Street*, 1970)

---

[2] *titíes:* monos pequeños sudamericanos.

EL CANTO DEL LLANERO SOLITARIO

3

Dormir en un algodón y el canto de las sirenas
y el león en invierno y los pájaros (volando en círculo)
que no existen
          y las flores del ártico
y Urana
perfectamente desmayándose
                  sin manos   5
      (Verf)
minimización del ritmo en favor de una escritura
de la profundidad en favor de la superficie
del símbolo en favor de la imagen
y Santo Tomás (o era Aderman?) lloraba
rey difunto conquista el cielo   10
las estrellas ya no serán ojos
sino luminosa opacidad
         SEÑOR DE LAS FORMAS
fragmentos de una conversación con el crepúsculo
dormir en un algodón
una vez muerto, o cielo   15
las estrellas no serán ojos
sino tinieblas clarificadas, o clavos
en los ojos
        y las ostras
no esperaban a nadie en el fondo del mar (las llaves)
como un muñeco sin brazos cuando oscurece   20
(asesinaba por medio
de una cámara fotográfica) la palabra
está devaluada, flota en el vacío
y son torpes sus pasos, perezosa
como si fuera agua, así es preciso   25

acrisolar su destrucción
en una nueva extensión lingüística
negadora del agua, de las formas babosas
de lo informe, de lo vago o disuelto
en una nueva extensión no acústica (que será el mar)   30
en que no habrá Prose (y será entonces una prosa
              [aparente, purificada de todo lirismo)
ni poema, sino piedra (y será entonces una poeticidad
   [no enemiga, pero al menos sí ignorante de la prosa
rebasando fronteras de hielo
en una superficie única
no dependiente de lo designado, ni de ninguna otra ley 35
(asesinaba)
construyendo (a
sesinaba) sus propias leyes
como un castillo en el vacío,

                              (*Teoría*, 1973)

LUIS ALBERTO DE CUENCA [76]

PASIÓN, MUERTE Y RESURRECCIÓN
DE PROPERCIO DE ASÍS [1]

Lo que passó ya falta; lo futuro
Aún no se vive; lo que está presente,
No está, porque es su esencia el movimiento.
                                GABRIEL BOCÁNGEL [2]

Sombras, Propercio, sombras, gavilanes
oscuros, imprecisos, niebla pura,
cincha, brida y espuela. No profanes
el mástil del amor, la arboladura

---

[1] Poeta latino del siglo I antes de Cristo; buena parte de su obra canta las
dulzuras y tormentos de su amor por Cintia (v. 13). [2] Poeta barroco, autor
de *La lira de las musas,* muy admirado por los «novísimos» por su brillante
imaginería y sus aciertos expresivos.

[76] Se trata del poeta de mayor carga cultural, como se ve en
los poemas que siguen, todos ellos inspirados en motivos librescos.
Fijémonos especialmente en el último de los poemas seleccionados:
clásicos griegos y occidentales, cineastas y novelistas americanos...
Hay un refinado exhibicionismo: usa una edición *princeps,* advierte
que «melancolía» es un cultismo, etc. Cae, además, en la voluntaria
erudición (vv. 12-14); sin embargo, este poema ha sido visto como
punto de inflexión hacia la interiorización del culturalismo, que se
convierte en confesión personal (vv. 11, 15, 44 y 45).

del deseo, la ofrenda de los manes[3],   5
con la triste verdad de tu locura,
cosmética, veneno, miel, divanes,
y el perfume letal de la lectura.

Conocerás un puente de cuchillos,
la brisa del instante, el terciopelo   10
remoto como el torso de una diosa.

Sudor frío de muerte, tenues brillos
de Cintia envuelta en luminoso velo,
y, al fin, la permanencia de la rosa.

EL CABALLERO, LA MUERTE Y EL DIABLO[1]

ALBRECHT DÜRER

He aquí el antiguo caballero de la rosa y el triunfo
príncipe de los labios que sugieren la duda o la sonrisa
he aquí el irreprochable señor de las victorias
caudillo en las batallas más azules
portador del emblema sagrado de la raza   5
en el palor[2] de brumas conductor de los pueblos
en la brasa del odio y la conquista

He aquí los laberintos de carcoma
la sed de los atletas derrotados

---

[3] *manes:* las almas de los muertos en la mitología romana. Los poetas latinos llamaban también *manes* a los dioses infernales y en ocasiones a los *lares* o dioses del hogar.

[1] Famoso grabado en cobre del pintor germano Albrecht Dürer —Durero— (1471-1528), natural de Nuremberg (v. 26). [2] *palor:* palidez.

el cuervo de las simas inferiores   10
la Discordia sangrienta
los *carmina*[3] volubles que doblegan las alas del Misterio
y conducen su pecho adolescente hacia una esclavitud
                                     [de polvo y sombra
la enfebrecida sierpe del Imperio en el árbol maldito
                                     [de la Sabiduría
nunca más para siempre mañana tal vez desde sí
                                     [hacia dónde   15
los ángeles de Pacher Konrad Witz[4] el recuerdo como
                                     [un hacha de fuego
ilumina la estancia débilmente del trono fugazmente
                                     [oscurece
el tránsito del viento por los patios helados
detener con escudos nobiliarios los pasos enjoyados
                                     [de la Muerte
con poderosas lanzas abatir el Infierno sepultarlo en el
                                     [mar   20
Mas he aquí la tiniebla de las enredaderas y los magos
el sepulcro tu espada las mujeres que amaran la seda de
                                     [tus ojos
la furia incontenible de tus noches la cruel impostura de
                                     [tus besos
las doncellas germánicas de nombres infinitos
todo lo que conjura o desvanece la dorada zozobra
                                     [de tu cuerpo desnudo   25
y asevera —distiende las palomas de Nürnberg—
ser la palabra si el dolor existe
como yugo dulcísimo veneno en la copa esmaltada
                                     [de los dioses.

                                                 (*Elsinore*, 1972)

---

    [3] *carmina:* poemas. [4] *Michael Pacher:* pintor y escultor austríaco del si-
glo XV; *Konrad Witz:* pintor germano del mismo siglo; ambos preludian el
arte de Durero.

DE Y POR MANUEL MACHADO [1]

La felicidad no es, evidentemente, sólo un cuerpo,
ni el destello casi apagado de unos ojos sobre la cama.
Si fuera así, no habría sido necesario encontrar en
                                        [Alberto Magno [2]
cierta referencia a los bueyes atribuida a Heráclito. [3]
Todo esto se me ocurre porque acabo de recibir un
                                        [precioso ramo de serpientes   5
y tengo un libro de Manuel Machado abierto sobre la
                                        [mesa.
El libro es una *princeps* [4] de *Alma,* [5] como era de esperar,
y está abierto por un poema llamado «Oriente».
En el poema se nos habla de Marco Antonio y de
[Cleopatra, y de un siervo que muere al beber una
                                        [copa.
Ello me ha conducido, sin poderlo evitar, a Plutarco,
[escritor griego de cierta fama durante el período
                                        [de entreguerras,   10
y debo reconocer que he releído su *Antonio* con el
                                        [mismo entusiasmo de aquellos días. [6]
(Luego descubriría que había olvidado por enésima vez
que Shakespeare lo conoció en la versión inglesa de
                                        [North,
y que sir Thomas North [7] conocía el griego

---

[1] *Manuel Machado:* hermano de Antonio Machado, vivió entre 1874 y
1947; su poesía se mantiene en la órbita del Modernismo.   [2] *Alberto Magno:*
filósofo y teólogo alemán del siglo XIII, maestro de Santo Tomás de
Aquino.   [3] *Heráclito,* filósofo griego del siglo V antes de Cristo, que concibe
el mundo como un continuo devenir a través de una lucha de contrarios.
[4] *princeps:* primera edición.   [5] *Alma:* primer libro de M. Machado en 1900.
[6] *Plutarco:* escritor griego del siglo I después de Cristo, autor de *Vidas
paralelas,* obra en la que se incluye la biografía de Marco Antonio.   [7] *Sir
.Thomas North:* su traducción al inglés de la *Vida de los varones ilustres,* de
Plutarco, fue utilizada por Shakespeare para *Antonio y Cleopatra.*

[aproximadamente igual que Unamuno. [8])

Mientras me asaltan todos estos fantasmas eruditos,
 [los automóviles siguen murmurando a mi alrededor.   15
El hecho de que la gran ciudad se vaya poniendo
     [inhabitable es algo que no me disgusta,
como no me disgustan las chicas figuradas en las
              [*pinball machines*, [9]
ni las películas de Hawks con Cary Grant o Wayne,
     [ni los guiones de Hammett para el pincel heroico
                  [de Raymond. [10]
El poeta —recuerdo un *topos* [11] de Petrarca— va
 [caminando casi siempre por campos muy desiertos,
y no negaré que estoy pensando en ciertos desiertos
                  [americanos   20
(me los recuerdan esos crótalos [12] que acabo de alojar
                  [en un jarrón
para que nadie, nadie, ni siquiera mi perro, los vaya
                  [a confundir
con el *bouquet* [13] de rosas que alguien dejó olvidado sobre
                 el lecho, en el dormitorio).

A veces —vuelvo a Shakespeare— una nube se parece
                  [a un dragón,
el viento a un oso o a una ciudadela relativamente
                  [expugnable. [14]   25
Son imágenes, imágenes que se ciernen sobre nuestras
                  [cabezas,

---

[8] *Unamuno* se interesó más por la filosofía y la literatura que por el griego, materia de la que era catedrático.   [9] *pinball machines:* máquinas de juego.   [10] Toda esta serie de personajes americanos son conocidos por su relación con el cine, como actores, directores o guionistas.   [11] *topos:* lugar común, tema o procedimiento estilístico reiterado.   [12] *crótalos:* serpientes venenosas americanas (recuérdese el v. 5).   [13] *bouquet:* ramo.   [14] *expugnable:* conquistable.

posibles máscaras del invierno o velos del atardecer.
Lo que hoy es un caballo —sigue Shakespeare— puede
    [ser luego un pensamiento o un anillo de compromiso:
hasta los compromisos son, en el fondo, agua en el agua.

Si del poema «Oriente», una perfecta gema [15]
                        [modernista,   30
he pasado a Plutarco por lo de la perdida adolescencia
y he llegado a fijar mis reales por una tarde en cinco
    [actos de una tragedia que no había sabido leer, [16]
no ha sido —lo prometo— para empañar el brillo de la
                           [joya primera, [17]
ni para convertirla en simple piedra, estampa o rata
                           [de laboratorio;
permanece en mí todo su impacto argumental, la
             [difícil tersura de sus palabras.   35
Y detrás del respeto que me ofrece lo inútil —amistad,
                         [gesto, gema—
puedo ver hoy al hombre que ha partido su mentira
                         [conmigo,
puedo ver a Manuel Machado, sonriente en su *princeps*
                     [sobre la mesa,
a Manuel el prodigioso, a Manuel el funámbulo, [18]
a quien debo querer hasta el final, porque así lo
    [quisieron mis abuelos, y yo los obedezco en todo,   40
y, al cabo, sólo Marco Antonio será capaz de
                   [derrotar a Marco Antonio,
y todo esto no deja —no puede dejar— de ser bello
    [en este momento en el que sigo propagando por
    [los desiertos del mundo, tal vez americanos,

---

[15] *gema:* piedra preciosa. [16] Se refiere a la tragedia de Shakespeare, *Antonio y Cleopatra* (véase v. 13). [17] Alude al poema «Oriente» (véase v. 8). [18] *funámbulo:* equilibrista sobre un alambre (aquí, metafóricamente).

las ondas de unos pasos tan tardos y tan lentos al
                           [menos como los de Petrarca,
por este camino clausurado por donde voy, aunque
                           [los áspides[19] me conhorten,[20]
solo y recluso en esa bilis negra que vierte al castellano
                           [el cultismo[21] melancolía.[22]   45

(Homenaje a los Machado, *Cuadernos Hispanoamericanos*, 304-307,
octubre-diciembre, 1975; enero, 1976.)

---

[19] *áspides:* serpientes venenosas.   [20] *conhorten:* consuelen.   [21] *cultismo:* palabra latina que no ha sufrido transformaciones fonéticas al incorporarse al castellano.   [22] *melancolía:* además de su significado hoy común, esta voz designaba uno de los humores del cuerpo humano, la «bilis negra».

JAIMES SILES [77]

GÉNESIS DE LA LUZ

La luz es un ave que se quema,
    que se inflama encendida, que se nace
del carcaj[1] de la noche, saeta en la distancia
traspasando los anquilosados[2] nervios de lo oscuro.
Sin humos, sin diabólicos embrujos ni fármacos,
    tan sólo
resplandor, titileante[3] brillo, filo de daga[4]   5
en busca de algún cuerpo donde abrir
                                de la sangre
las vetas minerales, el manantial enrojecido
del lamento, las compuertas de la rabia retenida
que en los dientes encuentra su muralla.

---

[1] *carcaj:* aljaba, caja para llevar las flechas.   [2] *anquilosados:* paralizados.
[3] *titileante:* centelleante.   [4] *daga:* arma blanca, más corta que la espada.

(77) Siles tiende a la abstracción intelectual y a la concentración: es la suya una «poética de la intensidad», según se ha dicho. El último de los poemas seleccionados es un buen ejemplo. En el primero, «Génesis de la luz», destacan las imágenes, con toques de surrealismo a veces (vv. 12-13).

Qué alaridos de júbilo! ¡Qué embriaguez de belleza!   10
¡Qué rojos siderales![5] ¡Qué carnívoramente ha parido
                                            [este alba!
Y un corazón seccionado
llueve sangre entre copas de pinos. Un pájaro se
                                            [engendra
de plumaje de fuego y pico de bengala[6]
que va ardiendo los aires, que deja tras de sí   15
un tumulto de lava, de bella, pura, ancestral[7]
lava, lava, lava.

TRAGEDIA DE LOS CABALLOS LOCOS

A Marcos Granell

Dentro de los oídos,
                    ametralladamente,
escucho los tendidos galopes de caballos,
        de almifores[1] perdidos
                            en la noche.
Levantan polvo y viento,
                    al golpear el suelo
sus patas encendidas,
                    al herir el aire
sus crines despeinadas,
                            al tender como sábanas   5
sus alientos de fuego.
Lejanos, muy lejanos,
                    ni la muerte los cubre,

---

[5] *siderales:* estelares, propios de las estrellas o astros.   [6] *bengala:* fuego de artificio.   [7] *ancestral:* antigua.

[1] *almifores:* caballos.

desesperan de furia
                hundiéndose en el mar
y atravesándolo como delfines vulnerados[2] de tristeza.
Van manchados de espuma
                con sudores de sal
                      [enamorada,   10
ganando las distancias
                y llegan a otra playa
y al punto ya la dejan,
                luego de revolcarse, gimientes,
después de desnudarse las espumas
                y vestirse con arena.
De pronto se detienen. Otra pasión los cerca,
el paso es sosegado
                y no obstante inquieto,   15
los ojos coruscantes,[3], previniendo emboscadas.
El líquido sudor que los cubría
                se ha vuelto de
                [repente escarcha gélida.[4]
Arpegian[5] sus cascos al frenar
                el suelo que a su pie
                [se desintegra.
Ahora han encontrado de siempre, sí, esperándoles
                [las yeguas que los miran.
Ya no existe más furia, ni llama que el amor, la dicha
                [de la sangre,   20
las burbujas amorosas que resoplan
                al tiempo que
                [montan a las hembras.
Y es entonces el trepidar[6] de pífanos,[7] el ruido de
                [cornamusas,[8] el musical estrépito

---

[2] *vulnerados:* heridos. [3] *coruscantes:* brillantes. [4] *gélida:* helada. [5] *arpegian:* suenan como arpegios. [6] *trepidar:* vibrar. [7] *pífanos:* flautines. [8] *cornamusas:* instrumento de viento, semejante a la trompeta.

que anuncia de la muerte la llegada.
Todos callan. Los dientes se golpean quedándose
soldados.
      Oscurece. La muerte los empaña, ellos
          [se entregan y súbito   25
como en una caracola fenecida,[9] en los oídos escucho
un desplomarse patas rabiosas, una nube de polvo
          [levantado por crines,
un cataclismo de huesos que la noche se encarga
          [de enviar hacia el olvido. [78]

                   (*Génesis de la luz*, 1969)

LUDWIG VAN BEETHOVEN PIENSA ANTES DE
INTERPRETAR POR ÚLTIMA VEZ

                      A Ángel García López

¡Qué insistencia habrá de ti, en mí mismo,
en los pliegues que ocultan mi entusiasmo,
si poseí tu ser y por ti he sido
transparente sonido de una Forma,

---

[9] *fenecida:* muerta.

[78] Formalmente, Siles tiende al ritmo marcado, combinando
metros con base en la acentuación endecasilábica (nótese la frecuencia de versos que suman 7 + 7, por ejemplo). Conviene su-
brayar la abundancia de contrastes (vv. 15, 17, *día / noche, vida /
muerte*, etc.) y algunas imágenes (vv. 9, 13...), que han hecho hablar
de «tensión barroca». Sin embargo, lo grandioso del poema reside
en la «visión» de la «tragedia» a la que abocan los «caballos locos»
(vv. 1-2: «Dentro de los oídos... escucho...»; v. 26: «en los oídos
escucho...»).

de una Mente en zig-zag vuelta a sí misma,   5
de una Forma que en formas se consume!

¡Ah, música, detente!
Contempla mi estupor[1] y muda queda,
pues sólo el eco sonará despacio
una vez que de ti seas la sombra,   10
la transparencia aquella que de nadie
fue nada, sólo sino[2] de sí misma.

Ciñe y horada[3] para ti el espacio,
ninguna bóveda soportará tu impulso,
rompe mis dedos, corta mis sentidos,   15
nada dejes atrás que te sujete.

Pero vuelves a mí, que soy tú misma,
y el silencio termina, se va abriendo.
De dos en dos su cuerpo ignoto[4] crea
y nos hizo ya ser: ser ambos juntos,   20
uno en el otro prisionero. Todo
ha vuelto a sí, la música,
yo mismo...

(*Canon,* 1973)

---

[1] *estupor:* asombro. [2] *sino:* destino. [3] *horada:* perfora. [4] *ignoto:* desconocido.

LUIS ANTONIO DE VILLENA [79]

INICIO DE ELEGÍA

No es fácil disponer en materia de afectos.
Ni librarse al momento del recurso torpe
de interjección o enigma, ni es fácil, por supuesto,
eludir el vegetal sagrado de la loa[1] o el
alcázar fugaz del panegírico. [2]
Es gris la tarde. Y semeja que pesa. Géricault,
la barca de la Medusa, esté donde esté, siempre

---

[1] *loa:* alabanza, poema en alabanza de una persona. [2] *panegírico:* elogio, escrito laudatorio.

~~~~~~

(79) Esteticismo, decadentismo, culturalismo... son palabras aplicadas al Villena de *El viaje a Bizancio,* que asocia «la experiencia (el placer) del cuerpo y la experiencia (el placer) de la palabra» (J. Olivio Jiménez). En los poemas seleccionados destaca: la celebración de la belleza del cuerpo joven, con rasgos de sensualidad y voluptuosidad, en un lenguaje también bello, de rica sensorialidad (rubios, dorados, aromas, tacto suave sobre la piel), enmarcado en una naturaleza armoniosa y estival que sugiere esplendentes imágenes (vv. 11-17 de «Inicio de elegía» y 8-11 de «Dominio de la noche»): tal vitalismo es también cultura en forma de citas, de nombres propios y hasta de «collage» en el primer poema.

quisiera estar en otra parte. [3] La belleza
en el viento y todos los árboles desnudos.
Amor, amor, ¿qué cuerpo me sugieres desde lejos?   10
¿Qué sol de llama y piel me vuelves a traer
en el recuerdo? El agua está en sus labios
y el absynto [4] en sus ojos. No es fácil rezagarse
del recuerdo. Una palabra apenas. Pero el mar
está unido ya a tu cabello rubio, el aire   15
a tu desnudo, y el estío a tus besos, a tu
forma de andar y de decir. A cuanto la
imagen constituye aunque el día lo niegue.
Amor, ¿qué dulzura de entrega y púber [5] maravilla
me insinúas fugaz desde el largo recuerdo?   20
Todos los autores agregan que la melancolía
no va acompañada de fiebre, lo que la distingue
del frenesí o delirio y de la melancolía especial
relacionada con la fiebre pestilente. Los caracteres
que la distinguen de la demencia son el temor   25
y la tristeza, y lo que la diferencia de otras
afecciones comunes en que también existen el miedo
y la aflicción es que éstos aparecen sin causa. [6]
No es fácil, pues, como decía, disponer en materia
                                     [de afectos.

LABIOS BELLOS, ÁMBAR SUAVE

Con sólo verte una vez te otorgué un nombre,
para ti levanté una bella historia humana.

---

[3] *Théodore Géricault:* pintor francés (1791-1824); su lienzo *La barca de la Medusa* es considerado como el manifiesto de la pintura romántica. [4] *absynto:* bebida hecha con ajenjo. [5] *púber:* adolescente. [6] Larga cita de la *Anatomía de la melancolía,* de Robert Burton, médico humanista inglés del siglo XVII.

Una casa entre árboles y amor a medianoche,
un deseo y un libro, las rosas del placer
y la desidia. Imaginé tu cuerpo   5
tan dulce en el estío, bañado entre las
viñas, un beso fugitivo y aquel espera
no te vayas aún, aún es temprano.
Te llegué a ver totalmente a mi lado.
El aire oreaba [1] tu cabello, y fue sólo   10
pasar, apenas un minuto y ya dejarte.
Todo un amor, jazmín de un solo instante.
Mas es grato saber que nos tuvo un deseo,
y que no hubo futuro ni presente ni pasado.

DOMINIO DE LA NOCHE

Tu regardais dormir ma belle negligeance
P. VALERY [1]

El cabello se esparce suavemente en el lino,
como un mar que es el oro si despacio amanece.
Suavemente se pliegan las pestañas, y los
besos se duermen en los labios y respiran flores.
Ignora la cintura que es sagrada la mano   5
que sorprende un leve ardor, la mano abandonada
sobre la piel, la distante luz blanca
que recorre las piernas y sus bahías dulces,
la extensión marina del lino que se tuerce,
las playas invisibles de la espalda. Todo ignora.   10

---

[1] *oreaba:* ventilaba.
[1] «Tú mirabas dormir mi hermosa negligencia» (Paul Valéry).

Y otra mano se expande así, muy quedamente,
y al moverse, el impulso descubre más ocultas
dulzuras. Besos. Deseos. Amor. Ignoradas bahías.
Duermes. Y yo miro dormir tu joven negligencia.

(*El viaje a Bizancio* (1972-74), 1978)

Documentos y juicios críticos

I. Sobre la posguerra inmediata: años 40

1. *En un texto muy citado, Alarcos Llorach explica las causas que motivaron la poesía «garcilasista» y «divinista» en los años iniciales de la posguerra.*

La labor poética de la posguerra se abre bajo el signo de Garcilaso, cuyo centenario se había celebrado o comenzado a celebrar en 1936. Era natural que la primera etapa poética después de las hostilidades, como reacción ante una realidad hosca, buscara la tranquilidad de ánimo, el beleño que adormeciera pasiones o rencores. Para ello, nada mejor que el cultivo de una poesía con primacía de lo musical externo, el uso de melodías en que lo de menos fuese la carne de las palabras y lo más el canturreo que pudiera dar sopor a los ojos fatigados por tres años de lucha y reblandecidos por la luz hiriente de una realidad cruda. Tampoco habría que desechar el posible temor de muchos poetas a ser sinceros: para acallar los gritos interiores lo más adecuado era distraerse con minucias primorosas y abalorios formalistas.

Después, junto con la tendencia formalista, renace la poesía de tono religioso. La vuelta a Dios, sincera o no —que de todo habría—, era un portillo de escape por donde podían salir vivencias del poeta inexpresables sin la envoltura religiosa. Rara era la invocación a Dios en la poesía de la generación de 1927; ahora —años cuarenta—, en cambio, su mención se hace frecuente, insistente: Dios —creído o creado por el poeta— es el interlocutor a quien se dirigen poemas y poemas. Se explica: mientras el poeta de

1927 vive —tal Guillén— en un mundo que «está bien hecho», el poeta nuevo de la década de los cuarenta habita un planeta desquiciado; en casa, huellas de una guerra fraterna; en torno, las fuerzas universales desenfrenadas; decididamente, el mundo ya no está bien hecho, no hay posible asiento, faltan apoyos en lo visible, y el poeta busca realidades más altas e intemporales que le sostengan y le guíen. Si es creyente, posee ya estos seguros cables y se recoge al amparo de lo celeste; si la creencia le falta, la añora o la inventa o la sueña, y viviendo de este sueño hace de la necesidad virtud, y al Señor —si inventado no importa— se dirige pidiendo refugio y repaire de los vientos alborotados del mundo.

> Emilio Alarcos Llorach: *La poesía de Blas de Otero*, Salamanca, Anaya, 1966, pp. 19-20.

2. *Dentro de las distintas tendencias poéticas de la «primera generación de posguerra», Carlos Barral observa una cierta homogeneidad en la pobreza del estilo.*

Seguramente, la causa profunda de la regresión de la poesía española de la inmediata posguerra a fórmulas estilísticas puramente imitativas de los clásicos del Renacimiento y del Barroco fue la más o menos consciente voluntad de mantenerse en la inocuidad temática, causa a la que seguramente ayudaría la exaltación del nacionalismo y de los polvorientos valores tradicionales.

[...]

De la primera poesía de posguerra, cuajada en pétreos sonetos y en vacuas volutas verbales, poco hay que decir, y por otra parte, ya casi nadie la recuerda sino por intercesión de algún poema satírico más moderno. Además, el estilo, tan directamente tomado de las antologías escolares, no le pertenecía. No tenía estilo alguno. La historia de los estilos poéticos nace más bien mediados los 40 y al margen de libros momentáneamente tan solitarios y a la larga tan definitivamente fecundos como *Hijos de la ira* y *Sombra del paraíso*. Me refiero a aquella poesía que muchas veces tuvo calidad, pero que tan igual a sí misma fue mientras estuvo vigente, dominada por la manía confesional, aquella poesía religiosa algunas veces deísta a lo Rilke y otras valientemente devota, pero que no me interesa ahora citar desde el punto de vista de las emociones de que partía y que tampoco citaré con nombres y apellidos. Todos los lectores de entonces recuerdan aquel período de poesía tirando a mística, de voces que pretendían ser bondadosas y puras de intención y en que, como ha dicho Jaime Gil de Biedma, «la palabra Dios, uno de los pocos monosílabos prestigiosos de la lengua, recorrió en todas las posiciones sintácticas, las cumbres acentuales del endecasílabo castellano». No quiero que pueda parecer que esa fase de la poesía española me parece en bloque digna de olvido. En los poetas de la escuela santanderina se pueden exhumar todavía espléndidos poemas, y en casi todos los poetas que entonces estuvieron en vanguardia se encuentran buenos textos; por otra parte, subrayan el período libros extraordinarios, como *La casa encendida,* de Rosales, pero era una poesía en conjunto aburridísima y estilísticamente gris. Estaba llena de palabras prestigiosas no rebuscadas, sino comunes, como esa de Dios que antes citaba, y como edificada sobre la idea de que existían palabras más poéticas que otras, y objetos y motivos primordiales para la poesía. Por la misma razón que separaba esa poesía de la experiencia cotidiana y concreta del poeta ciudadano, miembro de una comunidad, de una clase y de un grupo, el estilo literario no tenía relación con la experiencia cotidiana del lenguaje, quiero decir simultáneamente del habla y del lenguaje de la vida intelectual.

[...]

Pero poco a poco esa moda mística fue virando hacia una estética neorromántica y subió el tono expresivo en una cierta tradición de Aleixandre. Esa poética de los años 50 solía resumirse en la frase «poesía como comunicación» y se instrumentalizó en un libro de Carlos Bousoño, *Teoría de la expresión poética,* cuya segunda parte consistía en un inteligente análisis, en lenguaje saussuriano, de procedimientos y figuras de estilo, pero cuya parte filosófica estaba llena de esas limitaciones favorables a una poesía emotiva y trémula. Una poesía que no podía dejar de crear sus contrarios, que se agruparon en una línea de poesía polémica, cuyo origen se remonta a los primeros libros de Eugenio de Nora, y en la que confluyeron los inmediatos antecesores de los poetas sociales, Crémer, Celaya y Blas de Otero en su segunda etapa. Pero si contraria y diferente en las actitudes básicas, esa poesía era, en aquellos años, escasamente creativa al nivel del estilo y del lenguaje; en unos casos tendió a la epigonía nerudiana; en otros, al prosaísmo más directo, así es que los poetas que se situaron entre ambas corrientes acumularon a un léxico escogido un recitativo gris y monótono, parco en metáforas o con recurso a un sistema metafórico con mucha tradición literaria. En uno y otro caso, y en las zonas intermedias, se trataba de una poesía con escaso paisaje o de paisaje convencional y con escasa presencia de cosas materiales. La textura estilística de la poesía religiosa o de tema «noble» y de la poesía de religión política era bastante uniforme. Nadie esperaba de cada libro recién aparecido, como en cambio parece que se espera hoy, sorpresas y novedades.

> Carlos Barral: «Reflexiones acerca de las aventuras del estilo en la penúltima literatura española», *Cuadernos para el Diálogo*, XIV extraordinario, mayo, 1969, pp. 40-41.

II.   Sobre la poesía social: años 50

El más representativo de los «poetas sociales», Gabriel Celaya, planteó en 1952 su «poética», que fue, al mismo tiempo, una defensa apasionada de la poesía comprometida.

La Poesía no es un fin en sí. La Poesía es un instrumento, entre nosotros, para transformar el mundo. No busca una posteridad de admiradores. Busca un porvenir en el que, consumada, dejará de ser lo que hoy es.

* * *

Nada de lo que es humano debe quedar fuera de nuestra obra. En el poema debe haber barro, con perdón de los poetas poetísimos. Debe haber ideas, aunque otra cosa crean los cantores acéfalos. Debe haber calor animal. Y debe haber retórica, descripciones y argumento, y hasta política. Un poema es una integración y no ese residuo que queda cuando en nombre de «lo puro», «lo eterno» o «lo bello», se practica un sistema de exclusiones.

La Poesía no es neutral. Ningún hombre puede ser hoy neutral. Y un poeta es por de pronto un hombre.

* * *

La Poesía es «un modo de hablar». Pero expresar no es dejar ahí, proyectada en un objeto fijo —poema o libro—, la propia intimidad. No es convertir en «cosa» una interioridad, sino dirigirse a otro a través de la cosa-poema o la cosa-libro.

La Poesía no está encerrada y enjaulada en los poemas. Pasa a través de éstos como una corriente y consiste precisamente en ese pasar transindividual, en ese ser del creador y el receptor uno para el otro y en el otro, en ese contacto y casi cortocircuito de dos hombres que, más allá de cuanto puede explicitarse, vibran a una.

El cortocircuito quema y deja en nada la materia verbal.

* * *

Nuestra Poesía no es nuestra. La hacen a través nuestro mil asistencias, unas veces agradecidas, otras, inadvertidas. Nuestra deuda —la deuda de todos y de cada uno— es tan inmensa que mueve a rubor. Aunque nuestro señor yo tienda a olvidarlo, trabajamos en equipo con cuantos nos precedieron y nos acompañan.

Estamos «obligados» a los otros. Y no sólo porque hemos recibido en depósito un legado que nos trasciende, sino también porque el poeta siente como suya la palpitación de cuanto calla, y la hace ser —debe hacerla ser— diciéndola. Esta es precisamente su misión. No expresarse a sí mismo, sino mantenerse fiel a esas voces más vastas que buscan en él la articulación y el verso, la expresión que les dé a luz.

* * *

Nuestros hermanos mayores escribían para «la inmensa minoría». Pero hoy estamos ante un nuevo tipo de receptores espectantes. Y nada me parece tan importante en la lírica reciente como ese desentenderse de las minorías y, siempre de espaldas a la pequeña burguesía semiculta, ese buscar contacto con unas desatendidas capas sociales que golpean urgentemente nuestra conciencia llamando a vida. Los poetas deben prestar voz a esa sorda demanda. En la medida en que lo hagan «crearán» su público, y algo más que un público.

> Gabriel Celaya: «Poesía eres tú», en *Antología consultada de la joven poesía española*, Valencia, 1952, pp. 44-46.

2.   *Desde una posición más serena que la de panegiristas y detractores de la «poesía social», Félix Grande intenta definirla y legitimar su existencia.*

Entiendo por poesía social aquella que toma la decisión de constituirse en testimonio; testimonio, fundamentalmente, sobre realidades colectivas. La legitimidad de esta corriente de nuestra lírica de posguerra (que no es un invento, sino la reactualización del sentimiento, siempre vivo en la cultura, de las injusticias que erosionan o irritan la convivencia social) está convalidada en una frase del escritor argentino Abelardo Castillo: «El hombre crea cosas porque las necesita.» Una necesidad puede ser el resultado de una situación insatisfactoria. Puede decirse entonces que la poesía social es una necesidad de la cultura motivada por la presión de las hostilidades de la realidad. La fraternidad, la denuncia de lo real hostil, el coraje —acaso sean actitudes equivalentes— han constituido su principal proyecto. Su principal obstáculo, en nuestro país, ha sido su propia exasperación. La poesía social nació apresuradamente, de manera en cierto modo fugitiva. Fue mirada con adhesión pasional, o de reojo, o por encima del hombro. Se desarrolló como un hombre público: con amigos agobiantes y enemigos demoledores: asfixiándose entre aplausos, indiferencia y anatemas. Todo eso, si no justifica sus desfallecimientos, al menos explica su exasperación. Bajo el ruido de los aullidos de entusiasmo, las repulsas y los aristocráticos gestos de repugnancia, tenía que respirar como un buceador: a bocanadas y de modo poco elegante; luego se sumergía de nuevo para continuar su trabajo. Con esa exasperación a la espalda, debe señalarse que la poesía social ha soportado en sí misma una tensión subsidiaria: el combate entre la urgencia que la originaba y la serenidad que le reclamaba la ambición de una eficacia duradera. Hay que indicar que, en nombre de la poesía social, se han escrito algunos de los peores poemas del mundo: acaso mil, dos mil, cinco mil. Pero esto no invalida la existencia y la oportunidad del punto de vista sobre la realidad que fue motivo del desarrollo de la poesía social, ni invalida muchos poemas sociales que han nacido con la suficiente grandeza como para convalidar a la vez aquel punto de vista y este, correlativo, género de poesía. Hubo un tiempo en que algún crítico en ejercicio, sin duda sumamente amante del riesgo (al menos del riesgo semántico), llegó a la estremecedora conclusión de que la poesía social no existe. Consideraciones sesudas de ese género merecen un comentarista mejor dispuesto que yo. Continuemos: ni aun el impresionante número de libros mediocres que dentro de esta corriente se han escrito dejó de cumplir un servicio, aunque sólo fuese por colaborar —aun con poca voz y desafinada— en la convalidación de la corriente como tal. Tomada la poesía social como expresión de los conflictos colectivos, en nuestro país, cuantitativamente, y salvadas muchas excepciones, se la podría llamar algo así como un inconmensurable bodrio. Pero ese bodrio también señala la existencia de los conflictos (aparte de que también pueden reunirse voluminosos bodrios de poesía amorosa, de poesía religiosa, de poesía cotidiana, de poesía paisajística, de poesía urbana, etcétera: ¿los detractores de la poesía social no habían pensado en eso?). Ha habido contra esta corriente lírica algún ataque más taimado, casi diría más inteligente: se ha repetido hasta el hartazgo que *toda* poesía es social, pretendiendo hacernos olvidar que no se trata únicamente del *resultado* de un poema (resultado no siempre social), sino también de su *propósito* (no siempre cumplido). Sería esclarecedor, en función de una correcta comprensión de este fenómeno cultural, investigar, además de su resultado, el propósito del poema. Después podríamos argumentar en cada caso si ese propósito fue o no alcanzado. Pero, a mi modo de ver, para aproximarnos a la gran cantidad de libros sociales escritos en nuestro país (casi todos malos, desde luego) es incorrecto avanzar aseverando que toda poesía es social: eso es una trampa. Es poesía social, buena o mala, aquella que nace *con voluntad de serlo*. La restante puede también resultar social en ocasiones. Pero lo que define a un poema social no es únicamente su alcance, sino la posición en que el autor se sitúa. Resumo estas líneas en tres apartados: *a)* la poesía surgida con voluntad de ser social no nació por generación espontánea; tuvo causas: la situación nacional y europea al término de la segunda guerra mundial, las tensiones internas y el desarrollo de la guerra fría internacional, y el propósito de colaborar en la transformación de aquella situación (propósito, por otra parte, siempre presente en cualquier cultura que se desarrolle dentro de realidades demasiado contradictorias); *b)* las propias contradicciones de la poesía social española (ingenuidad al establecer un fantasmagórico predominio del tema sobre la forma, deliberado encarcelamiento en la «sencillez» —léase «pobreza»— expresiva, y en las formas más monótonas de estructura, hasta el punto de que se ha llegado a decir, con razón, que gran parte de la poesía social era reaccionaria o al menos regresiva en su estética) le hicieron desmoronarse muchas veces como obra estética y como obra social, pero también motivaron el deseo de investigación nacido de todo fracaso; y *c)* este haber adquirido «la experiencia de sus equivocaciones» (cito una frase de Julia Uceda) le permitió después investigar con mayor lucidez —y con la mayor serenidad que le consiente la lenta modificación de la realidad total del país— sobre las formas estructurales y expresivas que pueden hacerla más eficaz, más artística y, por lo mismo, más social.

Félix Grande: *Apuntes sobre poesía española de posguerra*, Madrid, Taurus, 1970, pp. 54-57.

III.　Sobre la promoción del 60

1.　*Frente a la poesía como comunicación, que fundamentó los modos de ser de la poesía en los años 50, Valente expone una idea de la poesía en la que coincidieron la mayor parte de los poetas de su promoción: la poesía como medio de conocimiento de la realidad.*

En los últimos años, cuanto se ha escrito entre nosotros sobre poesía ha girado de modo concorde sobre la idea de la poesía como comunicación. Entiendo, por mi parte, que cuando se afirma que la poesía es comunicación no se hace más que mencionar un efecto que acompaña al acto de la creación poética, pero en ningún caso se alude a la naturaleza del proceso creador. La poesía es para mí, antes que cualquier otra cosa, un medio de conocimiento de la realidad. Es posible que incluso desde un punto de vista práctico y con miras a una *defensa* contemporánea de la poesía, la idea de ésta como *conocimiento* ofrezca interés mucho más radical que la teoría de la *comunicación*.

[...]

En el momento de la creación poética, lo único *dado* es la experiencia en su particular unicidad (objeto específico del poeta). El poeta no opera sobre un conocimiento previo del material de la experiencia, sino que ese conocimiento se produce en el mismo proceso creador y es, a mi modo de ver, el elemento en que consiste primariamente lo que llamamos creación poética. El instrumento a través del cual el conocimiento de un determinado material de experiencia se produce en el proceso de la creación es el poema mismo. Quiero decir que el poeta conoce la zona de realidad sobre la que el poema se erige al darle forma poética: el acto de su expresión es el acto de su conocimiento. Sólo en ese sentido me parece adquirir una auténtica dimensión de profundidad la afirmación de Goethe: «La suprema, la única operación del arte consiste en dar forma.»

Por eso todo momento creador es en principio un sondeo en lo oscuro. El material sobre el que el poeta se dispone a trabajar no está clarificado por el conocimiento previo que el poeta tenga de él, sino que espera precisamente esa clarificación. El único medio que el poeta tiene para sondear ese material informe es el lenguaje: una palabra, una frase, quizá un verso entero (ese verso que según se ha dicho nos regalan los dioses y que, a veces, debemos devolverles intacto). Ese es el precario comienzo. Nunca es otro.

Todo poema es, pues, una exploración del material de experiencia no previamente conocido que constituye su objeto. El conocimiento más o menos pleno del objeto del poema supone la existencia más o menos plena (en la poesía hay grados) del poema en cuestión. De ahí que el proceso de la creación poética sea un movimiento de indagación y tanteo en el que la identificación de cada nuevo elemento modifica a los demás o los elimina, porque todo poema es un conocimiento «haciéndose».

[...]

La poesía aparece así, de modo primario, como revelación de un aspecto de la realidad para el cual no hay más vía de acceso que el conocimiento poético. Ese conocimiento se produce a través del lenguaje poético y tiene su realización en el poema. Porque es éste la sola unidad de conocimiento poético posible: no un verso, por excelente o bello que pueda parecer, ni un procedimiento expresivo, por eficaz o caracterizador que resulte, sino el poema como estructura donde esos elementos coexisten en fluida dependencia, corrigiéndose y ajustándose para formar un tipo de unidad superior.

Por existir sólo a través de su expresión y residir sustancialmente en ella, el conocimiento poético conlleva, no ya la posibilidad, sino el hecho de su comunicación. El poeta no escribe en principio para nadie, y escribe de hecho para una inmensa mayoría, de la cual es el primero en formar parte. Porque a quien en primer lugar tal *conocimiento* se *comunica* es al poeta, en el acto mismo de la creación.

> José Ángel Valente: «Conocimiento y comunicación», en *Poesía última*, Madrid, Taurus, 1975, 3.ª edición, pp. 155-161.

2. *En el siguiente texto, Santos Sanz Villanueva observa en los poetas de la promoción del sesenta una superación formal y temática de los planteamientos sociales de la generación anterior.*

Frente a la negación en términos bastante absolutos de los *maiores* del «realismo social» que se ha practicado en la última década, estos poetas del 60 no los rehusan sino que, por decirlo de alguna manera, los superan. Entiéndaseme bien que no estoy haciendo un juicio de valor. Afirmo que superan los planteamientos sociales por los dos frentes por los que habían hecho agua. Por el de la forma, mediante una mayor atención a la palabra, lejos de la aparente sencillez neorrealista. Por el del contenido, iniciando una exploración más profunda del hombre; si se quiere, una ampliación del campo de la realidad (¡qué tremenda palabra!) que había quedado bastante constreñida a lo aparencial.

Por muy importantes que sean estas dos diferencias, podrían inducir a error si de ellas se desprende una tajante negación de los principios crítico-sociales. Porque lo que permanece es nada menos que lo más válido, lo menos perecedero de éstos, el sentido de compromiso moral con el mundo, la irrenunciable instalación del poeta en un grupo social y, más allá, en una comunidad nacional e incluso superior. Y todavía añadiría algo. El trasfondo de la poesía social hay que buscarlo en una reacción del artista frente a particulares problemas sociopolíticos. Esta reacción es indisoluble de un par de preguntas que ocupan, incluso, la rotulación de algunos importantes libros de la crítica occidental de nuestro siglo: ¿qué es la literatura? ¿para qué sirve la literatura? Durante una época se pensó que servía para transformar el mundo (a algunos hasta les pareció que la literatura no tenía ninguna utilidad y que era mejor empuñar el fusil que escribir versos). Hoy nos parece algo ingenua esta afirmación, pero fue una respuesta histórica —equivocada o no— que requiere un profundo respeto. Yo soy de los que piensan que ninguna época se equivoca estéticamente. Juzgo que algo de inocencia sí que hubo en lo que se entendía que era el alcance del hecho artístico (y no sólo literario). Estos poetas del sesenta, lo que más transformaron fue la fe en el alcance de esa eficacia. Como consecuencia, se acomodaron en el mundo en busca de una respuesta para la persona sumergida en un contexto social. Esto lleva a la indagación, si se quiere, de las «señas de identidad» (por decirlo con el paradigmático título de Juan Goytisolo) de la persona y del poeta. Estas señas de identidad son oscuras, duras, amargas y producen una crispación que claramente se ve en un Gil de Biedma o en un Grande. Por ahí la motivación crítica se ha mantenido y, unida a la mayor eficacia formal, han conseguido una poesía más auténtica, menos pendiente de condicionamientos extraliterarios.

Santos Sanz Villanueva: «Los inciertos caminos de la poesía de postguerra», en *Nueve poetas del resurgimiento*, Barcelona, Ámbito, 1976, pp. 268-270.

294 Documentos y juicios críticos

IV. Sobre los «novísimos» y afines

1. *José Olivio Jiménez, tratando de encuadrar a Antonio Colinas dentro de las coordenadas estéticas de su generación, enumera «las primeras tensiones que, en un primer acercamiento, en ella se descubren».*

De entrada: un extremado apurar la belleza autónoma de la palabra, en una suerte de preciosismo verbal que, sin desmedro de la hondura de intuiciones y visiones a cuyo servicio ese preciosismo se pone siempre en los aquí nombrados, iría continuamente desde *Arde el mar* (1966), de Pere Gimferrer; *Dibujo de la muerte* (1967), de Guillermo Carnero, y *Tigres en el jardín* (1968), de Antonio Carvajal, hasta *Himnica* (1979), de Luis Antonio de Villena. Impregnación creciente en el lenguaje de las posibilidades expresivas del irracionalismo poético (Antonio Martínez Sarrión, Leopoldo María Panero), que en algún momento puede llegar a un asumido y personal modo de neosurrealismo. Entramado del discurso poético sobre frecuentes apoyaturas culturales (Gimferrer, Carnero, Marcos-Ricardo Barnatán, Villena), no exento, en los miméticos, de la hora de quedarse en un aire de erudición libresca excesiva, pegadiza y exterior. Ardua vigilancia intelectual sobre una palabra que se quiere esencial y tensa, en un modo superficialmente asimilable al de la poesía pura de entreguerras, vuelta por lo general al escrutinio de las verdades últimas del ser y la realidad (Jaime Siles, Andrés Sánchez Robayna). Un cierto hermetismo crítico, no ejercido desde las libertades y «solturas» del irracionalismo, a partir de un peculiar y en ocasiones críptico manejo del lenguaje (Félix de Azúa, Barnatán). Una afanosa voluntad de experimentación radical sobre la materia lingüística, que lleva a sus últimas consecuencias las aspiraciones neovanguardistas de estos años, la cual puede conducir a implacables puestas en cuestión de la lógica interna y las formas de esa materia (Jenaro Taléns, José Miguel Ullán), y que desde esa misma estimulación precipitará en algunos la desconfianza y destrucción total de la propia palabra: letrismo, poesía visual gráfica, antirrepresentativa (Ullán, Fernando Millán, Jesús García Sánchez). Y por fin, pero ocupando un lugar clave en el diagnóstico de la época, la indagación (más o menos) teórica sobre la poesía dentro del texto poemático; esto es, la poesía cumplida como crítica de la poesía, la reflexión metapoética (sostenidamente en Carnero y Taléns, pero también en Gimferrer, Azúa, Panero) —tendencia esta última de larga tradición en la poesía moderna occidental y que ha sido estudiada por Carlos Bousoño en su prólogo al libro *Ensayo de una teoría de la visión* (1979), de Guillermo Carnero. Si en algún nivel vienen a coincidir todos estos variadísimos impulsos será en la voluntad común de rescatar los más libérrimos derechos de la imaginación en el juego de la poesía y la más definida concienciación lingüística en el trabajo del poema—, el designio de renovar totalmente el lenguaje y de liberarlo de enajenantes premisas extrapoéticas, aun a riesgo y práctica, en los casos de mayor violencia, de su propia abolición.

No es hora de incluir ya en la anterior enumeración el aprovechamiento poético de la mitología *camp*, tan ostensible en los inicios de esta hornada generacional, por haber delimitado sólo un episodio incidental y superado de la misma. Ni tampoco sobrará advertir que las catalogaciones de poetas en cada una de las direcciones someramente enunciadas tienen sólo una finalidad ilustrativa general y no cubren, en todos los casos, más que *un* aspecto de los respectivos poetas.

> José Olivio Jiménez: «La poesía de Antonio Colinas», prólogo a *Poesía, 1967-1981*, de A. Colinas, Madrid, Visor, 1984, pp. 12-14.

2. *Al cabo de diez años de la publicación de la antología titulada* Nueve novísimos poetas españoles *(1970), de J. M.ª Castellet, pudo establecerse ya la significación de los «novísimos» y afines en su conjunto, tal como hizo Julia Barella en el siguiente artículo.*

Hoy, desde la perspectiva limitada de diez años, atendiendo exclusivamente a los textos poéticos publicados, podríamos afirmar que nos encontramos con una poesía que se debate entre el deseo y la negación del objeto deseado. Una poesía que busca la forma de incorporarse a una realidad cuya percepción le es falseada por la palabra; de incorporarse a esa realidad «ficticia», pues en ella va a residir la posibilidad de encontrar la constante y la seguridad de

ser: la identidad. Y esta búsqueda de la identidad se convierte en
uno de los temas subyacentes más frecuente en los versos de todos
los poetas citados.

El lenguaje parece ser el único sustento de esa realidad, la única
posibilidad de ordenación (al tiempo que pone de manifiesto la
relación azarosa entre el significado y el referente). De ahí la
fascinación por el lenguaje al que todos acaban por rendir culto.
Vemos cómo cuidan la elección de palabras, su posición en el texto,
seleccionan la terminología, el vocabulario... El tema del lenguaje
se llega a enfocar de tal manera que acaba por conducir, en
algunos casos, irremediablemente a la monótona contemplación o
al narcisismo. Y es que hay un deseo de vivir en las palabras... El
lenguaje se mitifica y así ejerce su autoridad sobre el propio poeta
que se convierte en siervo de la ficción o del artificio en el que él
mismo ha participado. Hoy día esta «fascinación» se resuelve en un
nihilismo demagógico o en un lirismo de mero artificio que acaban
por aprisionar al poeta. Poesía retoricista que se aproxima a los
bizantinismos propios de un momento de crisis y decadencia.

A pesar de parte de la crítica que no ve o vio más que artificio, y
por encima de los errores más o menos juveniles que el tiempo
parece subsanar, hoy día no se puede dudar de la calidad de los
poemas de Gimferrer, Carnero, Villena, Colinas o Azúa. Vemos en
los libros publicados en los cinco últimos años una mayor pretensión a despojar el poema de florituras, citas culturales y artificios;
caminan hacia la desnudez y claridad (Colinas, Gimferrer), y/o
hacia la abstracción (Carnero); mientras que en otros casos se
embarcan en composiciones desde la intelectualidad filológica,
psicoanalítica o retórica. Pero tanto en unos como en otros parece
que lo contemplado linda con la nada, con el vacío o con la
muerte...

La revelación del vacío y del azar —el anticausalismo— hace
inaprehensible o fútil lo existente. Vacío real, vacío verbal o
imagen que resulta de dos espejos enfocados. Esta revelación niega
la creencia en ese «algo» que, detrás de las ilusiones subjetivas o del
artificio, facilita la explicación de las cosas y otorga, de alguna
manera, cierto orden y propósito al Universo.

Los últimos poemas de Gimferrer, por ejemplo, ejemplifican esta
idea situándose en la inanidad del ser, vaciándose de ese «algo» que

hace a las cosas pensables y explicables. Vaciamiento que si la sabiduría no templa desemboca —algunos casos podríamos citar— en una situación de hundimiento continuo, o de éxtasis de negativas —permítaseme esta posibilidad— revelaciones en torno a un eje circular, cerrado y sin aparente salida.

En estos últimos cinco años se han ido configurando posturas y estilos poéticos más personales. Mientras los que podríamos llamar *snobs* se jactan de una superficial familiaridad con el mundo de lo incomprensible, otros, apremiados por sentir y vivir plenamente el momento, buscan esos instantes únicos de visión lúcida donde el paso del tiempo parece detenerse. Todos ellos tal vez son conscientes de que lo buscado en el fondo no es otra cosa que sentido a la vida y un nuevo orden racional.

Cada poeta comienza a configurar su mundo de resonancias tradicionales y su «deseada» individualidad. Pero si en escasos momentos se arriesgan al «yo» en el discurso no es por otra razón que por saber que aceptar la limitación de un sujeto significa incluirse en la dualidad nacimiento muerte. De ahí que los poemas se acojan, desde esta perspectiva de sujeto, a una serie azarosa de emociones potencialmente posibles: aquéllas que el sujeto siente como propias sufren un proceso de despersonalización —más o menos riguroso según los casos— que las convierte en «posibles» y así se incluyen en el poema. Los sentimientos llegan a contenerse con acotaciones de cierta luminosidad que los despersonalizan y distancian. Hay casos donde la vivencia es un mero trámite que facilita el montaje del poema, y no por esta razón deja éste de contener indudable tensión lírica y poder evocador.

Después de diez años esta «generación» de poetas ha encontrado la respetabilidad deseada. Ahora ya no sienten la necesidad de negar a sus antepasados (frecuentes fueron las declaraciones en poéticas, entrevistas, artículos, etc., en contra de las generaciones precedentes), sino que admiten y advierten sobre la estrecha relación que con ellos mantienen; desean incluirse en la tradición española y por encima de este loable deseo, incluirse, de la misma manera, en la tradición europea, para lo cual saben elegir a aquellos escritores que den estilo y prestigio a sus poemas: Pierre Jean Jouve, Stevenson, Eliot, Pound, W. Stevens, W. Carlos Williams, etc.

Hay que tener en cuenta que todos los poetas citados tienen una formación predominantemente literaria —algunos son profesores de Universidad (Carnero, Talens, Siles, Azúa); si bien hubo un momento en el que se exhibían esos conocimientos culturales atropelladamente parece ser que hoy, pasados los años de la rebeldía juvenil, de la «pose» de frío distanciamiento, de elitismos *demodé,* ven la necesidad de buscar vías más personales, de centrarse en sí mismos y en el acto de creación poética.

Por muy distintos caminos, desde la lógica de lo irracional, desde la lucidez de la locura, desde la geometría del caos, o la tensión equilibradora del cosmos, sus poemas parecen intentar construir un idioma poético que, como proyección del logos, rescate al poeta del vacío, de la nada, del caos... La poesía no versa sólo sobre sí misma, sino que debe mantener un discurso paralelo que ejemplifique su inclusión en la categoría de lo misterioso, que advierta sobre la existencia de la otra realidad. Instalada en este campo las posibilidades son múltiples.

Julia Barella: «Poesía en la década de los 70: en torno a los Novísimos», *Ínsula,* núm. 410, enero, 1981.

Orientaciones para el estudio de la *Poesía española* (1939-1975)

Puesto que se trata de una antología, estas orientaciones serán estrictamente una guía para el estudio de los poemas seleccionados, que, por otra parte, pretenden ser una muestra representativa de los diferentes caminos que siguió la poesía en lengua española entre dos fechas concretas de especial relevancia histórica. No puede olvidarse el carácter didáctico de la colección en que aparece esta antología, lo que justifica, a mi modo de ver, la delimitación del campo poético en parcelas concretas.

1. Aspectos temáticos

1.1. *Tendencia al intimismo*

La vuelta al intimismo se atribuye a un grupo de poetas amigos que buscaron en la interioridad lo esencial del hombre: Rosales, Panero, Vivanco y Ridruejo. Pasado el naufragio de la guerra civil, estos poetas necesitan raíces a las que agarrarse: es lo que Dámaso Alonso llamó «poesía arraigada». El arraigo lo hallaron en la *familia*, la *tierra* y *Dios*. Tal temática ha hecho hablar de una «poética de lo cotidiano», que tiene siempre, en último término, un trasfondo religioso. Se trata también de la primera contribución importante a la «rehumanización» poética de la posguerra.

— Obsérvese esa concepción de la poesía intimista en el poema titulado «Hay un dolor que se nos junta en las palabras», de Rosales.

— Adviértase cómo la palabra «alma» ejemplifica el mundo íntimo personal en los poemas de Rosales.

— Anota los elementos cotidianos que aparecen en «Ciego por voluntad y por destino», de Rosales. El propio poeta habla de «cosas cotidianas» (v. 21).

El *amor* es tema frecuente del grupo. Su peculiaridad es la dimensión familiar (amor a los padres, a la esposa, a los hijos) y religiosa. Por ello suele tratarse de un amor vivido en un ambiente diario, acostumbrado, sin manifestaciones de carácter extraordinario.

— Anota los seres familiares presentes en los poemas de Vivanco y Panero.

— Señala palabras y locuciones que indican el ambiente del amor-costumbre en uno y otro poeta.

— Explica algunas referencias últimas a Dios al tratar el tema del amor.

De igual manera, el paisaje adquiere dimensiones trascendentes.

— Enumera los elementos paisajísticos que aparecen en «La caza», de Vivanco, y en «Sola tú», de Panero.

— Compáralos significativamente con «A una ruina», de Ridruejo.

— ¿Por qué puede hablarse de ascetismo espiritual en «Qué bien sé lo que quiero», de Vivanco? Puede también decirse que se trata de un paisaje voluntariamente pobre: ¿por qué?

Dios es la referencia última de todo. Dios, por ejemplo, cierra el poema de Rosales, «Hay un dolor...». De ahí que la poesía del grupo sea, en sentido estricto, religiosa.

— Obsérvese el afán religioso en «La caza», de Vivanco.

— En «El descampado», del mismo poeta, todo queda envuelto por la presencia de Dios. Señálense las palabras más significativas al respecto.

En esa mirada al ser íntimo, estos poetas chocaron con problemas humanos de carácter existencial, veta esta común a poetas más jóvenes de los años cuarenta.

— Estúdiese el tema de la «soledad» y sus connotaciones en «Ciego por voluntad...», de Rosales, y en «Sola tú» e «Hijo mío», de Panero.

— ¿Qué características presenta el Dios de «Escrito a cada instante», de Panero?

1.2.   *El hombre: problemática existencial*

En la Introducción indicábamos que en los años cuarenta la poesía trazó un camino desde el *yo* al *nosotros*. En el primer estadio hablábamos de «poesía existencial»; en el segundo, de «poesía social». En el epígrafe titulado «Las nuevas voces de la poesía existencial» distinguíamos una corriente realista y otra de carácter metafísico, pero en uno y otro caso el hombre como ser en el mundo da lugar a toda una problemática «existencial». Su aparición se debió a un complejo de causas que van desde lo literario (reacción contra el garcilasismo) y lo filosófico (antecedentes españoles, como Unamuno, la filosofía existencial francesa, etc.) hasta lo histórico-social (guerra civil, guerra mundial, etc.). Todo este conjunto de causas origina la manifestación poética de sentimientos humanos como la soledad, el vacío, la incertidumbre, el miedo, el dolor, la angustia del vivir y del morir y la búsqueda de un refugio sereno o atormentado en Dios, como posible remedio o como simple invocación agónica.

Fue Blas de Otero quien expresó con mayor intensidad poética la angustia existencial del yo; de ahí que centremos de momento el interés en algunos de los poemas suyos de esta antología, singularmente en «Hombre» y «Basta».

— «Hombre» expresa la violenta relación del hombre con Dios, que puede observarse anotando las acciones humanas enfrentadas con las respuestas también activas de Dios en el primer terceto.

— ¿Qué palabras indican que el silencio de Dios no es pasivo?

— Descifra el significado del último verso.

— El ritmo dislocado colabora a la sensación angustiosa que transmite el soneto, pero también el léxico. Señala los sustantivos especialmente indicativos.

— Señala algunos aspectos del soneto «Basta» que inciden en motivos poetizados en «Hombre».

— La angustia vital en ambos sonetos tiene una causa última: la eternidad depende de la existencia de Dios. La duda asoma en las dos composiciones. Explíquese este aspecto con referencia también a «Canto primero».

Muchas de las preocupaciones que expresó con fortuna Blas de Otero tuvieron en otros poetas manifestaciones peculiares. Es el caso de Vicente Gaos, de José Luis Hidalgo o de un poeta formalmente distinto: Carlos Edmundo de Ory.

— La dureza de Dios está presente también en Gaos e Hidalgo. Analiza este aspecto.

— De igual manera puedes examinar el temor a la nada en ambos poetas.

— Señala cómo se manifiesta en Gaos e Hidalgo el simbolismo tradicional de la «noche».

— Anota las palabras y expresiones que en «El rey de las ruinas», de Ory, ofrecen la visión del *yo* degradado.

Frente a las expresiones de angustia religiosa observadas hasta ahora, José María Valverde «presenta la poesía arraigada en los cimientos de la fe», según ha escrito García de la Concha.

— Relee «Oración por nosotros los poetas» y resume su contenido significativo.

— ¿No hay, a pesar de todo, alguna expresión de queja?

1.3. *El hombre: problemática social*

La problemática social nace de la interacción entre los hombres que conviven en sociedad. La poesía que da cuenta de esta problemática se convierte en la expresión del *nosotros*. El mentado camino del *yo* al *nosotros* se percibe con claridad en «Canto primero», de Otero, que es un punto central en la reorientación de su poesía. Cuando la poesía se detuvo fundamentalmente en el *nosotros* se habló de «poesía social», predominante en la década del 50. Para entender su desarrollo remito a las páginas correspondientes de la Introducción. Véanse también los documentos 2.1 y 2.2

La poesía social hizo del tema el eje compositivo; de ahí el interés en examinar los temas preferentes.

Inicialmente conviene tener en cuenta que los poetas sociales se plantearon en sus propios textos las funciones de la poesía. No se trata de decir qué es la poesía, sino de saber cómo y para qué sirve. Es en la obra de Celaya donde mejor encontramos explicitados estos aspectos.

— En «Pasa y sigue» hallamos la negación de la poesía intimista; ¿en qué verso?

— Al mismo tiempo niega Celaya el concepto romántico del poeta como ser singular. Explica este aspecto releyendo «Pasa y sigue».

— Fíjate en este título: «La poesía es un arma cargada de futuro.» Intenta ligarlo con la definición de poeta en «Pasa y sigue».

— Señala las características que debe tener la poesía social, según se deduce de la lectura de los poemas de Celaya.

— Compara las ideas presentes en «La poesía es un arma...» con las que el mismo Celaya expone en el documento 2.1.

La afirmación tajante de un tipo de poesía y de sus funciones trajo como consecuencia el ataque a poéticas opuestas, en concreto a la poesía evasiva, esteticista o formalista.

— Analiza este aspecto en «Aviso» y «La poesía es un arma...», de Celaya, y en «Poesía contemporánea», de Nora.

Un hecho que la poesía social tuvo muy en cuenta fue el destinatario: la mayoría, el hombre de la calle.

— Obsérvese el decidido comienzo de «Canto primero», de Otero.
— Enumera las formas verbales que indican un destinatario plural en los poemas de Celaya.

La poesía social quiso ser testimonio de su tiempo histórico y colaborar a la redención de los humildes y a la transformación de la sociedad. Por ello, el indigente social y el trabajador —seres en los que se manifiestan con mayor claridad las injusticias sociales— pasan a ser tema de la poesía. Es lo que alguno llamó «obrerismo». Vamos a fijarnos en dos poemas: «Friso con obreros», de V. Crémer, y «Réquiem», de J. Hierro.

— ¿Qué significado puede tener en el poema de Crémer la insistencia en «No están muertos»?
— Selecciona los elementos «realistas» de «Réquiem».
— ¿Cómo se destaca el funeral pobre del trabajador emigrante en el mismo poema?
— Hay una cierta solidaridad obrera en «Réquiem»; ¿en qué versos?

La poesía social se alza como testimonio; decíamos de un tiempo histórico, pero también de un espacio, de un aquí y un ahora: la España del momento. Se enmarca dentro de una tradición secular que ve a *España como preocupación,* título de un libro de Dolores Franco, y que tuvo en los hombres del 98 (Unamuno, Azorín, etc.) sus más característicos representantes; algunos de sus rasgos reaparecen en los jóvenes de la posguerra: en ambos casos, la protesta, el dolor, la interrogación sobre España, sucedieron a una situación conflictiva que puso ´de relieve la dramática o trágica realidad. Se trata de un «sentimiento angustiado y doloroso de la patria, cargado de furias y penas, como el de un amante abrasado en el fuego de su amor. Es toda una generación, o mejor dicho dos, puesto que la siguiente, más joven, hereda el tema, compartiendo ese sentimiento exasperado de la patria y reflejándolo desnudamente en su poesía» (J. L. Cano).

— El sentimiento de la patria se mueve entre la exasperación y la esperanza. Señala ambos aspectos en «Canto a España», de Hierro.

— Recoge las expresiones de esperanza presentes en «España toda aquí...», de Ridruejo, y «Fidelidad» y «No te aduermas», de Otero.

— Enumera los mitos sobre España contra los que Valverde lucha en «Vida es esperanza».

— ¿Sabrías interpretar, dentro de su contexto, el último verso de «España en el sueño», de Bousoño?

— Compara brevemente la visión de España que aparece en los poemas de Bousoño y de Hierro.

La visión de España no puede separarse del hecho histórico de la guerra civil, vivido en la propia carne por los poetas llamados del 36 y por la primera generación de posguerra. La guerra misma puede ser tema del poema, acompañada de otras connotaciones: dolor, sangre, muerte, cárcel, miedo... Frecuentemente el poeta ve la tierra de su patria empapada en sangre o sembrada de muertos, como se observa en «Patria», de Eugenio de Nora.

— Un poema de García Nieto y otro de Labordeta tienen parecido título; sin embargo, son muy distintos temáticamente, ¿por qué?

— Señala algunos rasgos temáticos comunes al poema de Labordeta y a «Patria», de Nora.

España y la guerra civil continúan presentes en la poesía de la promoción del 60, pero enmarcados, generalmente, en otro más amplio: el paso del tiempo.

1.4. *La vivencia del tiempo en la promoción del 60*

Es el rasgo temático más llamativo de la promoción. Su poesía se tiñe de evocaciones de infancia y de adolescencia, de figuras desaparecidas, o bien, el propio fluir temporal del hombre hacia la muerte llena de contenido los poemas. Fijémonos de momento en la poetización de la guerra civil: es algo muy presente en el poeta de mayor edad, Ángel González («El campo de batalla», «Homenaje en Colliure»), pero significativamente el último de sus poemas en esta antología se titula «Primera evocación». Es lo típico de la promoción: se evoca la infancia o la adolescencia perdidas o destruidas por la guerra.

— Señala las diferencias entre la *guerra,* por un lado, y el *trueno* y el *viento,* por el otro, en «Primera evocación».

— Estudia y compara cómo aparece la experiencia infantil de la guerra en «Homenaje en Colliure», de Goytisolo, «No terminaría nunca», de Caballero Bonald, y «Cosas inolvidables», de Sahagún.

— De qué modo expresa Sahagún la ruptura que supuso la guerra en su poema «En el principio».

Examinemos ahora otros motivos que aparecen en la poesía a través de la evocación.

— Selecciona las referencias al tiempo recuperable en «Mi propia profecía es mi memoria», de Caballero Bonald.

— «Le asocio a mis preocupaciones», de Barral, expone un proceso psicológico temporal: señala las partes de ese proceso en el poema.

— ¿Qué aspecto temático de «Hombre a caballo», de Valente, puede relacionarse con el mencionado poema de Barral?

— El contraste pasado / presente, en los poemas de Gil de Biedma, tiene fuertes connotaciones ideológicas. Explica este aspecto.

— Analiza la intensa temporalidad que expresa «Para que yo me llame Ángel González...»

Quizá nadie ha expresado el efecto destructor del tiempo con tanta fortuna, emoción e intensidad como Francisco Brines.

— Obsérvese en «El balcón da al jardín...» el súbito deterioro causado por el tiempo.

— Indica qué palabras dan cuenta del deterioro en el resto de los poemas.

— Establézcanse semejanzas y diferencias temáticas entre los poemas de Brines y «Donde fuiste feliz alguna vez...», de Félix Grande.

— La idea del tiempo como retorno cíclico está presente en «Mere Road», de Brines; ¿por qué?

1.5. *Renovación temática*

Con los poetas que irrumpen a fines de los sesenta —«novísimos»— afluyen una serie de temas poco o nada frecuentados por la poesía anterior, lo que no implica ausencia de preocupaciones comunes a la lírica de todos los tiempos (amor, muerte, etc.). Como especialmente llamativos interesa destacar: la creación de una mitología popular extraída del cine, como indicó Castellet, o del comic, de lecturas, etc.; el tema de la belleza y, en relación con él, el de la reflexión metapoética.

— Señálense las abundantes referencias cinematográficas en los poemas de Martínez Sarrión.

— ¿Cómo personaliza el poeta tales mitos?

— ¿Por qué puede decirse que «La muerte en Beverly Hills» guarda un parecido con escenas cinematográficas?

— ¿Qué sentido tienen las imágenes cinematográficas en «By love possessed», de Gimferrer?

Fijémonos ahora en la belleza como tema poético. No suele ser un canto a la belleza en abstracto, sino encarnada en algo concreto: objetos artísticos en Carnero, cuerpos jóvenes en Villena... La belleza puede ser un recuerdo, un sueño o una añoranza en Gimferrer, un deseo absoluto en Colinas, etc.

— Enumera las referencias concretas a la belleza en «Oda a Venecia...».

— ¿Qué elementos del cuerpo selecciona Villena? ¿Qué sentimientos despiertan?

— Con una reproducción a la vista de «El embarco para Cyterea», de Watteau, relee el poema de igual título de Carnero y explica la interiorización que se produce en los versos finales.

— ¿Qué elementos de «Novalis», poema de Colinas, llevan a interpretarlo como un deseo de belleza absoluta?

— Establézcanse las diferencias entre el concepto de belleza presente en los poemas citados y el que Gamoneda poetiza en «Sublevación».

La poesía de los setenta venía cuajada de nombres propios y citas: era una exhibición de culturalismo que tiene su muestra más característica en el poema «De y por Manuel Machado», de L. A. Cuenca. Tal culturalismo abocó a la reflexión sobre la poesía misma o «metapoesía». La preocupación por la poesía y sus funciones se dio en los «poetas sociales», como ya vimos; en esta antología pueden además verse poemas de Rosales, Vivanco, Hierro, Goytisolo, Valente..., en los que se reflexiona sobre la palabra o el oficio del poeta; pero los poetas de los setenta inciden sobre el tema de manera más obsesiva, al tiempo que la poesía se vuelca sobre sí misma, exenta de otras posibles referencias, como mundo autónomo, autosuficiente, dentro de una tradición que tuvo en Mallarmé su punto culminante; tal abstracción crea no pocas dificultades de comprensión.

> — Intenta desentrañar el hermetismo de «Luz de lámpara», de Martínez Sarrión, o de «El canto del llanero solitario», de L. M.ª Panero.
> — «Puisque réalisme il y a», de Carnero, presenta el proceso de creación como mutua revelación de experiencia y palabra; ¿cómo se explica dentro del contexto el verso último?

2. El lenguaje poético

2.1. *Selección léxica*

El léxico responde necesariamente a los contenidos poemáticos, por lo que, estudiados éstos, sólo caben breves reflexiones en torno a las palabras que un poeta o un grupo de poetas suele elegir con frecuencia mayor y que caracterizan su mundo poético; se trata especialmente de fijar cuáles son las palabras-clave en cada momento. Si leemos el primer poema de la antología, parece claro que la reiteración de la palabra *igual* la convierte en clave léxica de la que derivan símiles, sinónimos (mismo, exactamente...), juegos verbales (estaban, están, estarán...), etc.

> — ¿Qué otras palabras se reiteran significativamente a lo largo del poema?
> — Leyendo «La cicatriz», ¿se observa en el léxico de Rosales alguna evolución respecto a los poemas anteriores?

Fijémonos ahora en los poemas de Vivanco, Panero, Ridruejo y García Nieto. Se ha subrayado la preferencia por el léxico relativo a la naturaleza; pero ésta suele ser escenario amoroso —bucolismo— o estar dotado de trascendencia religiosa.

> — Comprueba la austeridad del lenguaje y su trascendencia religiosa en el léxico escogido por Vivanco.

Hijos de la ira, de Dámaso Alonso, supuso una ruptura en la utilización del léxico por la introducción de términos infrecuentes en la poesía. La que vendría después, aprovecharía la lección, al menos en lo que suponía de violencia frente al vocabulario idílico del garcilasismo. La poesía de tono existencial usa términos que indican *lucha, vacío, muerte;* sustantivos como *sombra, niebla, ceniza, sueño, soledad, nada, silencio, dolor, miedo, llanto,* etc., reaparecen con frecuencia al lado de *Dios* como destinatario de las súplicas. Es en Blas de Otero donde hallamos mayores logros en cuanto a la selección léxica de carácter existencial.

> — Traza una lista de sustantivos del soneto «Hombre» y agrúpalos por afinidad semántica (por semas comunes).
> — Haz lo mismo con las formas verbales.
> — Compáralos con los sustantivos y verbos del soneto «Basta».
> — Contrasta la selección léxica de Otero con el soneto «¿Estoy despierto...?», de García Nieto.

Uno de los objetivos prioritarios de la poesía social era llegar a la mayoría. Unido a una actitud realista y a una pretensión de objetividad, dio lugar a un vocabulario sencillo, coloquial, directo, sin alardes retóricos; de ahí también el uso de nombres propios, al referirse a un aquí y un ahora históricos (España y sus pueblos) y a los personajes humildes que dan cuenta del destinatario natural de esa poesía. Paremos la atención inicialmente sobre «Réquiem», de Hierro.

— Relee los últimos ocho versos y observa la afirmación de objetividad y de sencillez. ¿Qué datos concretos (fechas, horas, precios...) aparecen en el poema?

— El tono narrativo convencional se debe, en parte, al léxico. Examina este aspecto.

— ¿Qué función tienen los nombres propios empleados?

— No siempre se mantiene «sin vuelo en el verso»: observa los vv. 25-29 y 48-59.

— Relee «Poesía contemporánea», de Nora, y confronta el léxico que en el poema quiere caracterizar a una poesía evasiva con el de la poesía comprometida.

— Anota los imperativos que aparecen en «Severa conminación...», de Labordeta; ¿qué tonalidad de sentimiento producen?

Al llegar a la promoción del sesenta, un crítico literario ha hablado, a propósito de léxico, de *prosaísmo*, entendiendo por tal «la utilización frecuente y caracterización de palabras con escasa o nula tradición poética, con referentes muy comunes, vulgares» (J. P. Ayuso). Dentro de la variedad individual, el mismo crítico señala que esta promoción tiene preferencia en su conjunto por el léxico político, con perspectiva crítica, el léxico urbano como marco de la acción, el léxico amoroso referente a la intimidad no convencional o a la relación sexual; a ello hay que añadir el léxico con riquísimas matizaciones temporales.

— Rasgo llamativo es el uso de frases coloquiales muy lexicalizadas («Bueno, en realidad...», «por otra parte...», etc.). Anota las locuciones de este tipo que halles en los poemas de Gil de Biedma y de A. González.

— Enumera el léxico urbano de «Barcelona ja no és bona...», de Gil de Biedma.

— Estudia el léxico amoroso en «Hombre en la mar», de Barral, y «Suplantaciones», de Caballero Bonald, indicando las distintas connotaciones afectivas en cada caso.

— Rasgo diferenciador de C. Rodríguez es el uso del léxico referente al mundo natural y rural, castellano en concreto. Compruébalo en el primero de sus poemas.

— La cohesión textual de «Descripción de la mentira», de Gamoneda, se observa en el léxico: haz una lista de las palabras que tienen como sema común «muerte», y señala cuántas se repiten y cuántas veces.

Dos aspectos léxicos llamaron la atención en la poesía «novísima» de los setenta: su riqueza y su carácter culto y refinado: *légamo, brocado, núbil, ópalos*, etc. Ello unido a la profusión de nombres propios de distintas áreas de la actividad humana, dificultaba el acceso al poema. Nos fijaremos en un poema ejemplar en este sentido: «Capricho en Aranjuez», de G. Carnero.

— Relee la llamada de atención **73** y completa la selección léxica en cada uno de los apartados que allí se hacen.

— Fíjate en la adjetivación: ¿qué connotaciones presenta?

— Esta «estética del lujo» tuvo en los poetas cordobeses de *Cántico* su antecedente próximo; demuéstralo estudiando el léxico de «El Corpus», de García Baena.

2.2. *Recursos estilísticos*

Por afán didáctico y con el fin de facilitar la comprensión, examinaremos cada tendencia lírica dentro de tres aspectos bien delimitados: fónico (onomatopeyas, aliteraciones...), morfosintáctico (anáforas, reiteraciones, paralelismos...) y semántico (contrastes, gradaciones, metáforas, símbolos...). El campo es tan amplio que únicamente caben algunas orientaciones generales para referirse después a casos muy concretos.

Hasta llegar a la poesía de contenido netamente existencial, la poesía intimista del grupo de Rosales y la de los garcilasistas prefirió limar aristas fónicas y evitar una fuerte expresividad fónica. En cambio, la reiteración se convierte en un procedimiento básico en la estructura del poema, como puede observarse en el primer poema de la antología. Semánticamente suelen evitar estos poetas fuertes contrastes, mientras que en el uso de los procedimientos imaginarios muestran mucha variedad.

— Indica las palabras y frases que se repiten en «Hay un dolor...», de Rosales.

— Estudia la reiteración y sus valores poéticos en «Sola tú», de Panero.

— Anota los símiles más sorprendentes de «Ciego por voluntad y por destino», de Rosales, y explica cuál es la base de comparación.

> — ¿Qué razones explican el parco uso de la imagen en
> «Qué bien sé lo que quiero», de Vivanco?
> — Indica el simbolismo del poemita «Iban tres azo-
> res...», de Ridruejo.

Nadie muestra mejor que Blas de Otero el aprovechamiento de los recursos lingüísticos en la obra artística. De
ahí que la crítica le haya prestado tanta atención. Lo más
llamativo, a primera vista, es la utilización de los sonidos
con valor expresivo, en forma de juegos de palabras o
atracciones fónicas (una palabra atrae a otra de gran
parecido fónico, pero dispar semánticamente: *ojos-sajas, hom-
bre-hambre*, etc.) y de aliteraciones. Nos limitamos al poema
«Paso a paso».

> — Señala algunas atracciones fónicas.
> — Se trata de una composición muy aliterada; ¿qué
> sonidos se reiteran en los vv. 2 y 4?
> — Compara estas aliteraciones con las de los vv. 14-15
> de «Fidelidad».
> — ¿Qué otras aliteraciones encuentras?
> — La aliteración tiene valor expresivo si el poder
> sugestivo de los sonidos es acorde con el contenido del
> poema; ¿sucede tal acuerdo en este poema? Razona la
> respuesta.

Blas de Otero, en su creciente preocupación social, tendió
a una mayor sencillez, pero en los casos mejores supo
mantener la tensión creativa.

> — Analiza el paralelismo entre las tres estrofas de
> «Fidelidad».

De igual modo, en los demás poetas sociales podemos hallar cuidadas estructuras, incluso en los poemas aparentemente más sencillos.

— Explica la correlación reiterativa presente en los vv. 23-29 de «Réquiem», de Hierro.

Uno de los recursos a los que Otero sacó mayor partido fue al *encabalgamiento*.

— En relación con el encabalgamiento, señala la distinta estructura de cuartetos frente a tercetos en el poema «Hombre».
— Explica algunos valores del encabalgamiento en «Fidelidad» y en «Paso a paso».

Semánticamente, Otero hace uso de la antítesis fuerte en su etapa primera con el fin de intensificar significativamente los dos planos contrastados; son índice también de violencia interior.

— Compruébese lo dicho en el soneto «Hombre».

Alarcos Llorach subrayó la originalidad imaginativa de Otero; una de sus características es la imagen en movimiento, en permanente tensión.

— Analiza en tal sentido la estremecedora imagen de «Basta» en el segundo cuarteto.

Los poemas de Otero presentes en esta antología suelen concluir con una especie de *epifonema* o afirmación resumidora. Lo curioso es que tal conclusión final se deja a una imagen condensadora, como se comprueba en «Hombre» y «Basta». En otras ocasiones, acude al simbolismo tradicional para finalizar el poema.

— Explica el simbolismo tradicional en «Paso a paso» y «No te aduermas».

Con la promoción del sesenta se generalizaron usos no relevantes en los campos fónicos y morfosintáctico. Uno de los más sugerentes en el último aspecto es la construcción del poema con una sintaxis conversacional. Para lograrla se crea en ocasiones un interlocutor, que puede ser Dios, la amada, una figura histórica o literaria o el propio yo desdoblado.

— Indica en qué poemas se da alguno de estos interlocutores.

— En «Infancia y confesiones», de Gil de Biedma, el tono conversacional asoma en expresiones comunes, lexicalizadas, fraseología voluntariamente prosaica, citas intertextuales desfiguradas... Explica este aspecto.

— Indica el tipo de sintaxis conversacional a que da lugar la presencia de un interlocutor en «Contra Jaime Gil de Biedma», y en «No inútilmente», de Valente.

— Una de las singularidades de C. Rodríguez reside en la marcha sintáctica del verso y del poema; analízala en «Alto jornal».

Con la irrupción de los «novísimos» entraban en la poesía técnicas neovanguardistas que Castellet resumía con este título: «Escritura automática, técnicas elípticas, de sincopación y de *collage*.» Se evitaba el desarrollo lógico del discurso y en no pocas ocasiones se eliminaba la puntuación ortográfica. El mismo Gimferrer escribió por entonces: «Suelo proceder por elipsis; es decir, que de una primera redacción más extensa de mis poemas elimino los nexos de asociación de ideas.»

— Intenta reponer los nexos en «By love possessed», de Gimferrer.

Sin embargo, en otros poetas de la promoción lo característico es la construcción sintáctica lógica, pero muy literaturizada en otros aspectos (exclamaciones, invocaciones, vocativos prestigiosos, recurrencias, etc.).

— Analiza alguno de estos aspectos en «Novalis», de A. Colinas.

La generación novísima dio un nuevo auge a la imagen, que usó con profusión y en rica variedad. Fue —con otros recursos ya vistos: culturalismo, léxico culto y refinado, etc.— lo que le dio carácter sumamente esteticista.

— Observa la profusión de imágenes (símiles y metáforas) en «By love possessed», de Gimferrer.
— «Génesis de la luz», de Siles, se construye a partir de una metáfora inicial. Analiza la estructura metafórica de todo el poema.

3. Aspectos métricos

Sólo de forma breve y general podemos acercarnos a la métrica de la poesía española desde 1939.

Acabada la guerra civil, la poesía tendió en España a una métrica tradicional que tuvo en la preguerra magníficos representantes (Guillén, Miguel Hernández, etc.). Tercetos, décimas y sonetos cobraron auge. De hecho, ya Rosales, Ridruejo y Bleiberg habían compuesto libros enteros antes de la guerra con métrica clasicista, tal como se señala en la Introducción. El garcilasismo, por su parte, hizo del soneto su estrofa más representativa. A pesar de la relevancia que cobró el verso libre tras *Hijos de la ira* y *Sombra del Paraíso,* la mayor parte de los poetas existenciales y sociales compusieron buen número de sonetos, como puede observarse en esta antología. Algunos de ellos se movieron dentro de cauces más clásicos (Morales); otros, como Blas de Otero, logran romper el ritmo tradicional a través, fundamentalmente, de una cadena de encabalgamientos abruptos. Como consecuencia de todo ello, el endecasílabo y la rima consonante resultaron privilegiados.

No fue el soneto, sin embargo, la única forma estrófica utilizada. Ciñéndonos a la antología, en una cala ni profunda ni exhaustiva, hallamos silvas asonantadas (Panero), romances endecasilábicos (Crémer, Hidalgo), serventesios endecasilábicos (Otero) o en alejandrinos (Bousoño), etc. Puede afirmarse que la poesía social se movió entre el verso libre y la tendencia al estrofismo, muchas veces con rima cero, como puede observarse en poemas de Crémer y Celaya en esta antología.

— Analiza la métrica de «Sola tú», de Panero, y de «Iban tres azores...», de Ridruejo.

— Explica la forma métrica de «En el principio» y «Fidelidad», de Blas de Otero.

— Indica el tipo de rima y su distribución estrófica en el «Canto primero», de Otero, y la «Elegía VII», de Molina.

Respecto al verso libre, los ejemplos de D. Alonso y de V. Aleixandre fueron fecundos. En algunos de los poetas de esta antología puede notarse la evolución: el caso más claro es, sin duda, el de Luis Rosales, que con *La casa encendida* aborda el poema largo, en versículos, sin distribución estrófica. Cuando los poetas de la primera generación de posguerra utilizan el verso libre suelen usar el ritmo endecasilábico, es decir, versos combinables con el endecasílabo (pentasílabos, heptasílabos, alejandrinos o versos de mayor número de sílabas, construidos por la suma de algunos de los versos citados). De hecho, el esquema acentual del endecasílabo (en 6.ª y 10.ª sílabas o en 4.ª, 8.ª y 10.ª) se convierte en el eje de la composición.

— Analiza la métrica de «Poesía contemporánea», de Nora, y de «Cuando los mensajeros...», de García Baena.

Los poetas de la promoción del sesenta continúan este uso del verso libre fundado sobre combinaciones con el endecasílabo, verso este escondido muchas veces en fragmentos menores o en escalonamientos sobre la página; el poema se concibe como un todo, como una unidad de composición que suele distribuirse en estrofas irregulares o paraestrofas. No es infrecuente el poema construido con versos blancos regulares. Varias de estas posibilidades las hallamos en los poemas de Brines.

— «El balcón da al jardín...» tiene regularidad silábica. Analiza su métrica.

— «Mere Road», en cambio, está compuesto en verso libre, aunque de ritmo endecasilábico. Explica este hecho.

La poesía «novísima» supuso en el campo de la métrica una atención mayor al ritmo del poema que, generalmente, va sujeto a medidas precisas, con tendencia a algunos metros, entre los que cabe citar la predilección por el alejandrino.

— Analiza la métrica de «Oda a Venecia...», de Gimferrer, y de «Novalis», de Colinas.

— Estudia la «Tragedia de los caballos locos», de Siles, desde el punto de vista rítmico.

Índice de poemas

A don Francisco de Quevedo, en piedra (JOSÉ A. VA-
LENTE) 204
A un esqueleto de muchacha (R. MORALES) 127
A una ruina (D. RIDRUEJO) 80
Alto jornal (C. RODRÍGUEZ) 218
Aviso (G. CELAYA) 94

Barcelona ja no és bona, o mi paseo solitario en primavera
(J. GIL DE BIEDMA) 197
Basta (B. DE OTERO) 102
Blanco de España (J. M. CABALLERO BONALD) 179
Blues del cementerio (A. GAMONEDA) 227
By love possessed (P. GIMFERRER) 249

Camposanto en Colliure (A. GONZÁLEZ) 172
Canto a España (J. HIERRO) 109
Canto primero (B. DE OTERO) 101
Capricho en Aranjuez (G. CARNERO) 256
Carmen del árbol dorado (E. DE NORA) 119
Ciego por voluntad y por destino (L. ROSALES) 61
Como si nunca hubiera sido mía (C. RODRÍGUEZ) 215
Con media azumbre de vino (C. RODRÍGUEZ) 216
Contra Jaime Gil de Biedma (J. GIL DE BIEDMA) 200
Cosas inolvidables (C. SAHAGÚN) 222
Cristo adolescente (C. BOUSOÑO) 136

Cuando los mensajeros... (P. GARCÍA BAENA) 164
Cuando yo aún soy la vida (F. BRINES) 213

De y por Manuel Machado (L. A. DE CUENCA) 269
Descripción de la mentira (A. GAMONEDA) 229
Dominio de la noche (L. A. DE VILLENA) 280
Donde fuiste feliz alguna vez (F. GRANDE) 234

El balcón da al jardín. Las tapias bajas (F. BRINES) 210
El caballero, la muerte y el diablo (L. A. DE CUENCA) . . 267
El campo de batalla (A. GONZÁLEZ) 170
El canto del llanero solitario (L. M. PANERO) 264
El cine de los sábados (A. MARTÍNEZ SARRIÓN) 240
El corpus (P. GARCÍA BAENA) 164
El descampado (L. F. VIVANCO) 73
El embarco para Cyterea (G. CARNERO) 258
El oficio de poeta (J. A. GOYTISOLO) 193
El rey de las ruinas (C. E. DE ORY) 149
El toro (R. MORALES) 126
Elegía VII (R. MOLINA) 157
Elegía XI (R. MOLINA) 160
Elogio de Linneo (G. CARNERO) 259
En el principio (B. DE OTERO) 103
En el principio (C. SAHAGÚN) 220
Escalinata del palacio (A. COLINAS) 252
Escrito a cada instante (L. PANERO) 76
España en el sueño (C. BOUSOÑO) 137
España toda aquí, lejana y mía (D. RIDRUEJO) 81
Espera siempre (J. L. HIDALGO) 133
Estoy maduro (J. L. HIDALGO) 134
¿Estoy despierto? Dime. Tú que sabes (J. GARCÍA NIETO) . . 83

Fidelidad (B. DE OTERO) 104
Friso con obreros (V. CRÉMER) 88

Génesis de la luz (J. SILES) 273
Giacomo Casanova acepta el cargo de bibliotecario que le
ofrece, en Bohemia, el conde de Waldstein (A. COLINAS) 253

Has bajado (J. L. HIDALGO)   134
Hasta mañana (L. PANERO)   77
Hay un dolor que se nos junta en las palabras (L. ROSALES)   67
Hijo mío (L. PANERO)   78
Hombre (B. DE OTERO)   100
Hombre a caballo (J. A. VALENTE)   208
Hombre concreto (V. CRÉMER)   89
Hombre en la mar (C. BARRAL)   186
Homenaje en Colliure (J. A. GOYTISOLO)   192

Iban tres azores (D. RIDRUEJO)   82
Infancia y confesiones (J. GIL DE BIEDMA)   195
Inicio de elegía (L. A. DE VILLENA)   278
Invocación a Hölderlin (A. COLINAS)   251

La acacia cautiva (R. MORALES)   128
La casa muerta (C. E. DE ORY)   148
La caza (L. F. VIVANCO)   70
La cicatriz (L. ROSALES)   68
La guerra (J. A. GOYTISOLO)   192
La mañana (J. M. VALVERDE)   144
La metamorfosis (L. M. PANERO)   261
La muerte en Beverly Hills (P. GIMFERRER)   247
La noche (V. GAOS)   129
La nueva mirada (C. BOUSOÑO)   140
La partida (J. GARCÍA NIETO)   84
La poesía es un arma cargada de futuro (G. CELAYA) . .   98
Labios bellos, ámbar suave (L. A. DE VILLENA)   279
Las brujas (L. M. PANERO)   261
Le asocio a mis preocupaciones (C. BARRAL)   183
Lo fatal (B. DE OTERO)   107
Los celestiales (J. A. GOYTISOLO)   180
Ludwig van Beethoven piensa antes de interpretar por
    última vez (J. SILES)   276
Luz de lámpara (A. MARTÍNEZ SARRIÓN)   243
Luzbel (V. GAOS)   130

Madrigal (F. GRANDE)   233
Más sobre la insolencia del alba (C. BARRAL)   187

Mere Road (F. BRINES) 211

Mi propia profecía es mi memoria (J. M. CABALLERO
BONALD) 178

[Mil novecientos treinta y seis] 1936 (M. LABORDETA) . 154

[Mil novecientos treinta y seis - Mil novecientos treinta y
nueve] 1936-1939 (J. GARCÍA NIETO) 85

No inútilmente (J. A. VALENTE) 207

No te aduermas (B. DE OTERO) 106

No terminaría nunca (J. M. CABALLERO BONALD) . . . 181

Novalis (A. COLINAS) 254

Oda a Venecia ante el mar de los teatros (P. GIMFERRER) 245

Oración por nosotros los poetas (J. M. VALVERDE) 142

Pájaros (V. GAOS) 131

Para que yo me llame Ángel González (A. GONZÁLEZ) 175

Pasa y sigue (G. CELAYA) 95

Pasión, muerte y resurrección de Propercio de Asís (L. A. DE
CUENCA) 266

Paso a paso (B. DE OTERO) 105

Patria (E. DE NORA) 120

«Poesía contemporánea» (E. DE NORA) 121

Precio de la verdad (C. BOUSOÑO) 138

Primera evocación (A. GONZÁLEZ) 175

Puisque réalisme il y a (G. CARNERO) 260

Réquiem (J. HIERRO) 111

Requisitoria general por la muerte de una rubia (A. MARTÍ-
NEZ SARRIÓN) 241

Ser de tiempo (E. DE NORA) 123

«Serán ceniza...» (J. A. VALENTE) 203

Serenata (C. E. DE ORY) 150

Severa conminación de un ciudadano del mundo (M. LA-
BORDETA) 152

Si supiera, Señor... (J. L. HIDALGO) 134

Sola tú (L. PANERO) 75

Sólo tu amor y el agua (P. GARCÍA BAENA) 163
Sublevación (A. GAMONEDA) . . . . . : 225
Suplantaciones (J. M. CABALLERO BONALD) 182

Telas graciosas de colores alegres (F. GRANDE) 236
Teoría y alucinación de Dublin (J. HIERRO) 115
Tragedia de los caballos locos (J. SILES) 274
Tú y yo (V. CRÉMER) 91

Un largo adiós (C. SAHAGÚN) 223
Un suceso (C. RODRÍGUEZ) 218

Vida callada (R. MOLINA) 161
Vida es esperanza (J. M. VALVERDE) 145
[Veinte mil] 20.000 leguas de viaje submarino (L. M. PA-
NERO) 262

SE TERMINÓ DE IMPRIMIR ESTA EDICIÓN
EL DÍA 2 DE SEPTIEMBRE DE 1991

LAUS  DEO